GOVERNING JAPAN

MODERN GOVERNMENTS

General Editor
Gillian Peele
Fellow and Tutor in Politics, Lady Margaret Hall, Oxford

Consulting Editor
Max Beloff
Former Gladstone Professor of Government and Public Administration at the
University of Oxford

Titles include:

Governing Germany
William E. Paterson and David Southern

Governing the UK
Third Edition
Gillian Peele

Governing Japan
Third Edition
J. A. A. Stockwin

Forthcoming:

Governing the USA
Gillian Peele

GOVERNING JAPAN
Divided Politics in a Major Economy

Third Edition

J. A. A. Stockwin

BLACKWELL
Publishers

Copyright © J. A. A Stockwin 1975, 1982, 1999

The right of J. A. A. Stockwin to be identified as author of this work has been asserted in accordance with the Copyright, Designs and Patents Act 1988.

First published by Weidenfeld and Nicholson in 1975
Second edition published 1982

Third edition first published 1999

2 4 6 8 10 9 7 5 3 1

Blackwell Publishers Ltd
108 Cowley Road
Oxford OX4 1JF
UK

Blackwell Publishers Inc.
350 Main Street
Malden, Massachusetts 02148
USA

British Library Cataloguing in Publication Data
A CIP catalogue record for this book is available from the British Library.

Library of Congress Cataloging-in-Publication Data

Stockwin, J. A. A. (James Arthur Ainscow)
    Governing Japan: divided politics in a major economy/J.A.A.
Stockwin.
        p. cm. — (Modern governments)
    Includes bibliographical references and index.
        ISBN 0-631-21212-4 (alk. paper). — ISBN 0-631-21213-2 (pbk. : alk. paper)
        1. Japan—Politics and government—1945–   2. Japan—Economic policy—1945–   I. Title.   II. Series.
JQ1631.S76 1998
320.952—dc21   98-28670
                                                                                              CIP

Typeset in 10¹/₂ on 12 pt Sabon
by Newgen Imaging Systems (P) Ltd, Chennai, India
Printed in Great Britain by MPG Books Ltd, Bodmin, Cornwall.

This book is printed on acid-free paper.

To my daughter Jane
with love

Contents

General Editor's Introduction   ix

List of Tables   xi

Maps   xii

Acknowledgements   xv

Conventions   xvii

1 Introduction: Why Study the Politics of Japan?   1

2 The Legacy of History   10

3 The Influence of Social Norms and Behaviour   23

4 Post-war Reforms and the 'Time of Troubles', 1945–1960   36

5 Politics of Economic Growth and
   Political Survival, 1960–1989   54

6 Demise of the Old System, Groping Towards the New:
   The Politics of the 1990s   70

7 The Structure and Process of Central Government:
   Is Japan a Bureaucratic Polity?   93

8 Parliament and Parliamentary Elections   113

9 The Politics of Party: The Liberal Democrats and
   their Rivals   132

10 Some Problems of the Constitution   162

11 Domestic Political Issues   180

12 Issues of Foreign Policy and Defence   202

13 Conclusions: The Analytical Challenge of
    Japanese Politics   218

Notes   223

Further Reading   255

Index   261

General Editor's Introduction

The series, of which this volume forms a part, is intended as a contribution to the study of comparative government. It aims to provide clear and comprehensive analyses of a number of major countries which have been selected either because of their intrinsic importance or because their pattern of government is of special interest to students of political science. Although the series is primarily aimed at students and teachers in higher education, it is hoped that the style and presentation will make them attractive and accessible to a general readership as well.

Arthur Stockwin's eagerly awaited reinterpretation of Japanese politics meets the goals of the series precisely. It is a book which fully satisfies the needs of political scientists interested in the changing character of Japanese government while at the same time offering the general reader insight into the cultural, institutional and economic character of the country. Much has changed in Japanese politics and in her role in the world economy since 1982 when Professor Stockwin, an internationally recognized authority on Japan, published the second edition of his study *Japan: Divided Politics in a Growth Economy* in this series. The current work is a wholly new examination of the Japanese political system which takes into account the extensive transformation of Japan's party structure and the fluctuations in her economic and political stability. The analytical quality and clarity of exposition will make it essential reading for everyone concerned with Japanese policy and politics. I am delighted to have this new volume in the series and I am sure it will command as extensive an international readership as its predecessor.

Gillian Peele
Series Editor

List of Tables

6.1	*Asahi* telephone poll, 3 and 4 November 1990	74
6.2	Composition of the Hosokawa Government	81
8.1	Standing committees of the House of Representatives and House of Councillors (January 1995)	119
8.2	House of Representatives election 1986: Chiba No. 1 constituency	124
8.3	House of Representatives election 1990: Chiba No. 1 constituency	125
8.4	House of Representatives Election 1993: Chiba No. 1 constituency	125
8.5	House of Representatives election 1996 (new system): single-member constituencies	129
8.6	House of Representatives election 1996 (new system): proportional representation constituency: Shikoku block (total seats = 7)	130
9.1	Patterns of dominance and cohesion within the party system, 1946–1997	134
9.2	Members of the House of Representatives, by party, October 1996 general elections	136
9.3	The subsequent success rate of LDP parliamentarians newly elected in the 1980, 1983, 1987, 1990, and 1993 lower house general elections	138
9.4	Local or non-local origin of parliamentarians elected in October 1996 lower house general elections	139
9.5	Educational background of parliamentarians, October 1996 lower house general elections	142
9.6	Career background of parliamentarians, October 1996 lower house general elections	144
9.7	Percentage of the total vote, and seat total, of the various parties in the regional blocs, October 1996 lower house general elections	146
9.8	House of Representatives election results, 1946–1996	158

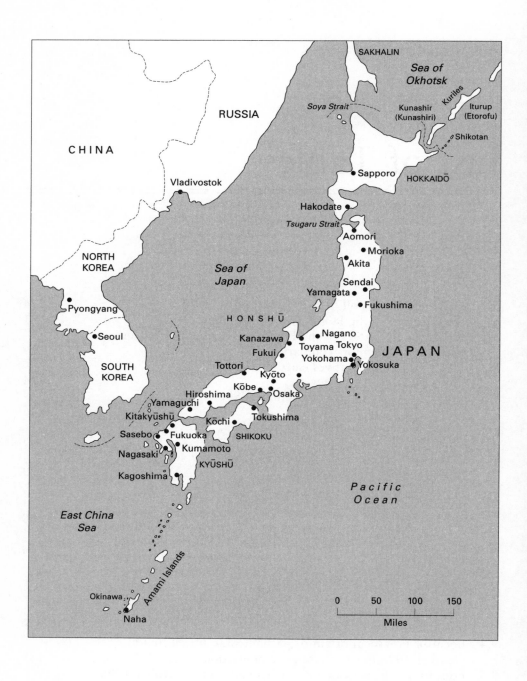

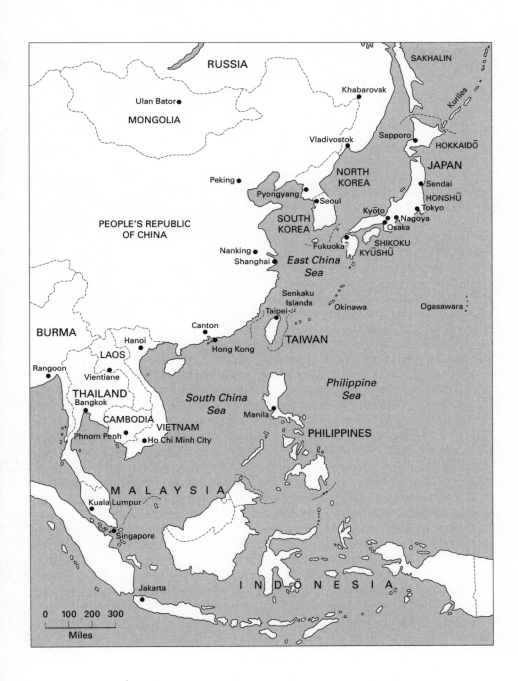

Acknowledgements

This book is the product of an interest in Japanese politics going back many years, including several periods of research in Japan. I should like to thank the British Council for funding a period at the Faculty of Law, Hokkaidō University, in 1990, and the Japan Foundation for enabling me to stay at the Institute of Social Science, University of Tokyo, in 1990–1. A substantial part of this book was written during four months as Visiting Professor at the same Institute between January and April 1997. I am most grateful to Professor Wada Haruki, Director of the Institute, and Professor Banno Junji, former Director, for making my stay both possible and enormously interesting.

Directly or indirectly (in some cases just through inspiration), the book owes much to colleagues and friends in several countries. Indeed, they are so numerous that I can only pick out a few names from a far longer list. In Japan I am particularly grateful to Abe Shirō, Aiuchi Toshikazu, the late Araki Toshio, Banno Junji, Fukui Haruhiro, the late Hayashi Shigeru, Inoguchi Takashi and Kuniko, Ishida Takeshi and his son Hiroshi, Ishikawa Masumi, Itō Daiichi, Mito Takamichi, David Morris, Muramatsu Michio, Nakamura Kenichi, Nishida Yoshiaki, Nishihira Shigeki, the late Okamoto Tomotaka, Watanabe Akio, Watanabe Osamu, John Welfield and Yamaguchi Jirō; in Australia to Sydney Crawcour, Peter Drysdale, James Horne, Rikki Kersten, Hayden Lesbirel, Gavan McCormack, Richard Mason, Aurelia George Mulgan, Purnendra Jain, Alan Rix, David Sissons and Sandra Wilson; in the UK (Oxford) to Jenny Corbett, Roger Goodman, Joy Hendry, James McMullen, Brian Powell, Mark Rebick, Dorothie Storry and Ann Waswo, and (elsewhere) to Kweku Ampiah, Lesley Connors, Ronald Dore, Reinhard Drifte, Glenn Hook, Stephen Johnson, Stephen Large, Ian Neary and David Williams; in the United States to Lawrence Beer, Kent Calder, John Campbell, Gerald Curtis, Chalmers Johnson, Ellis Krauss, Daniel Okimoto, T. J. Pempel, Susan Pharr, Bradley Richardson and Leonard Schoppa; in Canada to Frank Langdon; in Israel to Ehud Harari and Ben-Ami Shillony; in Italy to Peter Dale and in Germany to Park Sung-Jo.

Over the years I have received enormous stimulation and insight from my graduate students, not forgetting also undergraduates. Students are in the business of looking at phenomena with fresh eyes. To the two universities in which I have been privileged to spend my academic career – the Australian National University and the University of Oxford (in particular, the Nissan Institute of Japanese Studies and St Antony's College) – I give unreserved thanks. Finally, to my wife Audrey and to the rest of my family, I thank you for helping me to see that there are also worlds of surprising interest beyond the mesmeric arena of Japanese politics.

Conventions

Throughout this book, Japanese names are given in their proper order, with the surname first and the personal name second. When, however, works written in English by Japanese writers are cited in footnotes, the order more natural to English is preserved. Macrons are used over vowels which are lengthened in Japanese pronunciation, in order to distinguish them from short vowels; thus *fukoku* but *kyōhei*. For the names of Tokyo, Osaka and Kyoto, however, macrons are omitted. It should be noted that a 'long' vowel is given in pronunciation approximately twice the length of a 'short' vowel. Another useful pronunciation hint is that a double consonant is doubled in length when spoken, as in Italian. Thus *Nikkei* is spoken roughly as 'Nick Kaye', not 'Nick eh' (BBC newsreaders please note!). While on the subject of pronunciation, it is worth emphasizing that Japanese single vowels are not diphthongs, as so often in English. Thus *rōdō* (labour) is spoken as 'raw door', not 'roe doe'.

It has long seemed to this writer that the accepted English translations for several Japanese political terms are unsatisfactory, and therefore the convention has been adopted in this book of either retaining the Japanese word or employing a more normal English word, in the following cases: *tennō* (not 'emperor'); *habatsu* (not 'faction'); Parliament, not 'Diet'; *han* (not 'clan', 'fief' or 'domain'); *Meiji ishin* (not Meiji Restoration). Where the English-language title of a Japanese organization has been changed from one accurately representing the meaning of the Japanese to an inaccurate or distorted translation, we continue with the original translation. For instance, the party *Nihon shakaitō* was correctly rendered as 'Japan Socialist Party' in the years before 1991, when it was changed in English to 'Social Democratic Party of Japan'. It was not until 1996, however, that the *Japanese* title was changed to *Shakai minshutō* (Social Democratic Party). For the years between 1991 and 1996, therefore, we continue to use 'Japan Socialist Party' (JSP), but use SDP from 1996. In the case of the *Shinshintō*, we prefer to give the Japanese title, rather than what in this case is an inaccurate, albeit official, translation 'New Frontier Party' (NFP). We have also kept to the Japanese titles for most of the newer parties, and also for the

Kōmeitō, where there were different usages in respect of its English title. *Jichishō* is correctly translated as 'Ministry of Local Autonomy', not 'Ministry of Home Affairs', which is its official title in English, being a reversion to pre-war usage in English, but not in Japanese.

1

Introduction: Why Study the Politics of Japan?

On 20 October 1996 Japan experienced a general election which was supposed to 'break the mould' of the political system and usher in a new, more open and more competitive form of politics. Real and tangible deregulation of the economy would follow as would a swathe of other reforms which would ultimately turn Japan from an international enigma into a 'normal state'. The elections would mark a crucial milestone in a process of reform initiated on 9 August 1993, when the 37-year near-monopoly of power by the Liberal Democratic Party (LDP) came to an end and a multiparty coalition excluding the LDP took over. The scene was set for a steady process of beneficent reform, consolidating Japan as a healthy, Western-style, democratic state, acting unreservedly as a key participant – as befitted her enormous economic capacity – in the management of a stable international environment.

The results of the general election, however, turn out to be far more ambiguous, and for reformers, unsatisfactory. Despite a new electoral system that was supposed to open the way to the politics of potential alternation between two major parties competing on the basis of alternative electoral programmes, the LDP came within 12 seats of restoring its absolute majority, while the party which had most loudly proclaimed the need to reform the whole political system (the *Shinshintō* or New Frontier Party – NFP) actually lost seats. Moreover, the newly constituted single-member constituencies (300 out of a total of 500), introduced ostensibly as a means of ensuring that party and programme should prevail over personality and the parish pump, if anything increased the parochialism of politics because the size of these electorates was considerably smaller than that of the multimember electorates which had preceded them under the old system.[1]

There were two further, much remarked and potentially worrying aspects of the election results. The first was that the party which, ever since the 1940s, had mounted the most trenchant critique of LDP single-party rule, the *Shakai minshutō* (Social Democratic Party), which for most of the period of its existence had been known as the *Nihon Shakaitō* (Japan Socialist Party), was reduced to a rump of 15 seats in the House of Representatives.[2] This no doubt related to the fact that it had entered into an unlikely coalition government with the LDP in 1994, and more immediately that it had split, with many of its members joining the *Minshutō* (Democratic Party) formed in September 1996.

The second was that a high degree of political apathy, manifesting itself in low voting turnout rates, was increasingly apparent in the 1990s. The turnout in the elections to the House of Representatives elections of 1990, 1993 and 1996 had been 65.5, 60.3 and 59.6 per cent respectively. No doubt many electors were expressing their unhappiness with the political games that their politicians had been playing over the previous several years, though unfamiliarity with the new electoral system may also have played a part.

The present book is written in an attempt to make at least partly comprehensible what to the outside observer (and indeed to many Japanese themselves) often appears to be the great muddle of Japanese politics. A member of the BBC *Newsnight* team – makers of a high-quality television series on international issues and events – recently told the author that whenever an item relating to the politics of Japan needs to be dealt with, the immediate reaction is one of panic: 'how can we interpret what is happening in a system so impossible to understand?'[3]

If this book manages to provide some guidelines towards such understanding, it will have succeeded in its aim. The fundamental premise on which the book is based is that Japanese politics – much like other aspects of Japanese life – are susceptible to the same kinds of analysis as are regularly applied to the politics of other countries, which may be more familiar, for geographical and cultural reasons, to the reader. Obvious as this proposition may appear to some, it is subject to attack from two diametrically opposite positions. Adherents of the first position argue that for manifold reasons of history, geography and culture, there is simply no realistic possibility of understanding Japan using 'Western' categories and techniques of analysis. Japan, to all intents and purposes, is *sui generis*. Japan is *unique*. The nation, its people, institutions and practices can only be understood in their own terms.[4] The opposite position, expressed once to the author by a hardline political scientist, is that the idea of any sort of cultural difference or uniqueness on the part of Japan is irrelevant to the study of its politics and should not even enter into the discussion.[5] In my view, however, this position is much too purist. The very fact that much of Japanese history until the modern period, occurred outside the influence of Judaeo-Christian civilization [6] ought to put us on our guard in relation to the view that comparisons can or should be made without any concern for cultural differences. On the other hand, to regard such differences as an unbridgeable gap between Japan and the rest of the world (especially the Western world), as do the more extreme of the *nihonjinron*[7] writers, seems equally unacceptable. Japan is indeed unique, as is Germany, or Bulgaria or Brazil, but there is assuredly no reason for believing that it is *uniquely* unique.

This book is a very substantially updated and revised version of the author's *Japan: Divided Politics in a Growth Economy*, which first appeared in 1975, and then in a second, revised edition in 1982.[8] It may be useful to recall the basis of the approach taken in the two editions of the original book in order better to appreciate the underlying philosophy underlying the present volume. The original book (like the present one) was one of a series on modern governments, the series having a definite institutional bias. In the words of the introduction to the first and second editions by the series editor, Lord Beloff: '... our authors have kept in mind that while the nature of a country's formal institutions may be explained as the product of its political culture, the informal aspects of politics can only be understood if the legal and institutional framework is kept in mind.'[9] The author paid due regard to this intention of the series in writing the first edition. At the same time, an attempt to understand the dynamics of Japanese politics in the early 1970s (the first edition was substantially completed by the end of 1973) led to the ideas embodied in the title: *Japan: Divided Politics in a Growth Economy*. It may be helpful to explain what lay behind the original title.

'Divided Politics' was intended to reflect the political turbulence of the late 1960s and early 1970s. Even though the tensions of the early 1970s were probably not as intense as those experienced during the 1950s (and especially during the Kishi administration, 1957–60), they were still very substantial, and there were a number of highly divisive issues on the political agenda, in the spheres of foreign and defence policy, industrial relations, education policy, and, most importantly, the Constitution. The seven-and-a-half year cautious prime ministership of Satō Eisaku had recently come to an end, and he had been succeeded by a man forged in a different mould, Tanaka Kakuei, a self-made man pursuing bold and provocative solutions to political problems. By the end of 1973, however, the Tanaka regime was already in trouble, with inflationary trends about to be greatly exacerbated by the impact of the OPEC oil shock. The LDP had lost votes at every Lower House general election between 1958 and 1972 (though the Opposition had fragmented over the same period) so that the ending of the LDP monopoly on power could be plausibly predicted in the foreseeable future. In retrospect, we know that the political 'shocks' of the early 1970s were to lead to a notably more conservative period, as the electorate took stock and voted for continuity and for the consolidation of material gains. But the signs of that did not emerge until the middle of the decade.

In 1970, the American futurologist Herman Kahn had published *The Emerging Japanese Superstate*,[10] a rather early (but not the first[11]) attempt to extrapolate from the spectacular growth of the Japanese economy during the 1960s on to a future where Japan would be exercising impressive political as well as economic power. Kahn's book combined a realist approach to international relations with heavy reliance on Ruth Benedict's wartime anthropological study of Japanese society, with its emphasis on mutual obligations having to be 'repaid ten thousand times'[12] Kahn believed that before too long constitutional and other constraints on the projection of military power by Japan would largely disappear and she would become a formidable force to be reckoned with on the world stage.[13]

This was a period also in which the notion of 'consensus' as a key understanding the way the economy, society and polity worked in practice became fairly widespread. It was in part in an endeavour to throw doubt on the 'consensus' model that the notion of 'divided politics' was incorporated into the title by the present author. Whereas consensus implied the relative absence of adversarial politics, as known in many Western countries, divided politics implied not only that political outcomes resulted from the working out of clashes of interests and opinions, but that divisions, in some areas of policy at least, ran deep.

The second edition was published in 1982, under the same title. In the interim, the decline in the fortunes of the LDP had been spectacularly reversed by its victory in the June 1980 general elections for the House of Representatives. Moreover government policies of high spending on social welfare, agricultural subsidies and other purposes, were in the process of being replaced by far more conservative policies based on fiscal rectitude. The political system appeared to have settled down into a conservative mould, the LDP was firmly in the saddle, a combination of conservative politicians, government bureaucrats and representatives of the corporate sector was effectively running the country, and the Opposition parties seemed chronically demoralized. The idea that divisive political issues were exhausted and that politics, in Bernard Crick's sense of political conflict,[14] no longer existed was being widely canvassed, at least as a broad organizing principle for the understanding of Japanese politics.[15]

In preparing the second edition, the author still maintained his opposition to this kind of approach. Even though it had to be conceded that the steam had gone out of a number of political issues that had stirred political controversy and fuelled some serious clashes a decade earlier, even though the LDP had bounced back into a position of political dominance, and although parties and interest groups which were traditionally seen as part of the Opposition to the LDP now seemed either confrontational and weak or, more commonly, all too willing to put themselves in the position of LDP clients, this did not seem to add up to a situation devoid of conflict and division. The decade up to 1980 had seen a gladiatorial faction fight *within* the ranks of the LDP between the supporters of Fukuda Takeo on the one hand and a combination of Tanaka Kakuei and Ōhira Masayoshi on the other, for control of the party. This had led to a major political crisis in the latter half of 1979 and the first half of 1980, which came close to splitting the LDP. Indeed, had it not been for the sad but fortuitous event of Prime Minister Ōhira's sudden death in the middle of the election campaign of June 1980, the party might well have failed to hold itself together.[16] In a sense, it is true, this was a political crisis that failed to materialize, but it was a close call for the party, which chastened by the events of 1979–80 succeeded, for a few years at least, in putting its affairs in order. Moreover, it could safely be predicted that a new set of political issues was emerging (and not all of the old ones had been satisfactorily resolved), which would continue to divide the polity.

The item 'growth economy' seemed uncontroversial in 1973, even though the first oil crisis was about to stop the economy in its tracks. Japan had just experienced a decade and a half of economic growth running at an average of around 10 per cent per annum. In global terms this was unprecedented, and arguably effected the most profound social and economic transformation of Japan in her history. Even though some have argued that the benefits of economic growth did not sufficiently percolate through to the well-being of the people as a whole,[17] it is impossible to deny the profound changes that occurred in Japanese society, for good or ill, between the mid-1950s and the mid-1970s. By the early 1980s the economy had assimilated the effects of the two oil crises and, although growth rates of 10 per cent per annum were a thing of the past, the economy was growing by 4 or 5 per cent most years, which by contemporary international standards was more than respectable.

The combination of 'divided politics' with 'growth economy' in the first edition of the book had itself a certain rationale. In 1972 Zbigniew Brzezinski had published a book entitled *The Fragile Blossom: Crisis and Change in Japan*.[18] In very large part this was a riposte to Kahn's expansive vision of the future for Japan. Brzezinski was concerned to emphasize potential or actual weaknesses and instabilities in the broad structure of the Japanese politico-economic system. This was a time when the notion of external 'shocks', capable of effecting serious harm upon Japan, was much in vogue among Japanese commentators, as evidenced in the notion of a 'flexible frame society', propounded by Professor Nagai Yōnosuke.[19] According to this idea, Japan, like a 'flexible frame' high-rise building, designed to bend but not collapse in severe earthquakes, could withstand some sorts of shock, but might be fatally damaged by others, particularly those emanating from external sources. In retrospect it is obvious that the politico-economic system of Japan was endowed with a great deal more resilience than such theories allowed for, but at the same time they administered a salutary dose of scepticism to the over-simplified and over-sanguine views about the prospects for Japan that were a perhaps inevitable legacy of the high-growth period. What the present author sought to do under the rubric of his chosen title for the first and second editions of the book was to strike a balance between a positive appraisal of the extraordinary phenom-enon of Japanese economic growth, and a cautious – to some extent sceptical – analysis of the capacities of the political system itself. Indeed, such caution and scepticism may be regarded as prescient, to some extent at least, of the politics of the 1990s.

What then of Japan's political experience during the 1980s and 1990s, which will be a principal focus of the present volume? The first point to be made is that with Japan clearly established as the world's second largest economy by the 1980s, both the volume and quality of writing about Japan in her many aspects has enormously increased by comparison with the 1960s and 1970s. So far as politics is concerned, there is now a most respectable corpus of good quality research and analysis on nearly all aspects of the system. The bulk of this research has been carried out by Japanese and American scholars, but much worthwhile research is also being produced by scholars resident in (or origin-ating from) Australia, Britain, Canada, Germany, India, Israel, the Republic of Korea, New Zealand and elsewhere. The tendency evident in the past for Japanese and non-Japanese scholars to operate in separate spheres and virtually to talk past each other has now largely broken down, and collaborative projects involving Japanese and non-Japanese political scientists have become common-place. Indeed, one may be pardoned for thinking that it is more often theoretical or ideological orientation irrespective of nationality, rather than nationality itself, that is likely to be the most accurate predictor of the conclusions to a particular piece of writing. It should hardly be surprising, however, that there are still differences of perspective and assumption between scholars for whom Japan is their own nation, and those for whom it is not.

Secondly, the political experience of Japan since 1982 shows patterns of greater complexity and variety than in the period between the early 1950s and the early 1980s. In the earlier period, the transformation of the nation from the post-war shambles to economic modernity absorbed the energies of much of the population and nearly all the energies of the ruling elite. Japan was relatively insulated from international pressures, both through a highly regulated economic regime tolerated, until late in the period, by the United States, and by having been incorporated into a quasi-alliance system of security under the Japan–United States Mutual Security Treaty. The latter did, it is true, create substantial difficulties in domestic politics, which tested the ingenuity of governments to sort out, but it made it possible for military spending to be kept at reasonably low levels and for any military threat from neighbouring states (to what extent such threats existed was a matter of controversy) to be deterred. The fact that no Japanese servicemen were killed in combat over the 40 years from 1952 is the symbol of how easy it was for the government to concentrate on matters other than military.

From the early 1980s, however (possibly slightly earlier), the sand began to shift a little underfoot. The Japanese economy was already so large and powerful that the US (and other states to a lesser extent) were no longer willing to tolerate what they saw as highly protectionist economic policies by Japan. Insistent pressure was placed upon the Japanese authorities to reduce or preferably remove not only overt, but also what were seen as the more insidious covert, measures of industrial and commercial protection with which the economy was assumed to be blanketed, and to deregulate the highly controlled financial system.[20] Moreover, the breakneck pace of economic growth had granted to large corporate firms (and to not a few firms in the medium-sized sector) the means wherewith to raise capital on international money markets in such a way that they were no longer able so readily to be brought into line by government as they were (though there is controversy about the extent of government control over them even in the 1960s) during the era of comprehensive government regulation.

The 1980s also saw important initiatives (particularly under the prime ministership of Nakasone Yasuhiro, 1982–7) in the direction of government financial retrenchment and privatization of enterprises in the public sector (most significantly the national railways). A tighter line on agricultural subsidies began to be implemented and the lifting of agricultural protection on certain items (especially beef and citrus) foreshadowed the fateful lifting of the 100 per cent protection of the rice market in 1993.

The labour union movement was drastically reorganized at the end of the decade and labour became increasingly incorporated into the decision-making structure of government. In one sense this may be regarded as an important stage in the incorporation of ever wider interest circles into the government decision-making structure.[21] From another perspective, however, this very process of further incorporation has tended to create increasing complexity in decision making because of the greater number of interests whose concerns need to be taken into account in the making of decisions. Indeed, while it is in one sense advantageous for government to have the large majority of interests on its side, on the other hand it flies in the face of the principle of the 'minimum winning coalition', which says that the smallest size of winning coalition capable of winning will optimize the amount of spoils of office accruing to each of its constituent members. If nearly everybody is part of government, the spoils of office are spread too thin and the members of the coalition of interests represented in government may voice their discontent, with destabilizing consequences.

If the 1980s were a period in which political decision making took a gradually increasing complexity, the 1990s (more precisely, the period from 1989 with a crucial watershed in 1993) began the unravelling of the existing political system based on an LDP monopoly of power. This process has proved extremely confused and messy, and there is uncertainty about whether at any deep level real reform has taken, or is taking, place at all. The re-election of the LDP to a near-majority of lower house seats in October 1996 may appear to reinforce the view of the sceptics that reform of the system has been still born. Nevertheless, I wish to argue that moves towards political change in the 1990s reflect a rather deep malaise in politics, economy and society. So much transformation, at so many levels, has taken place in Japan since her defeat in 1945 that the institutional structure and practice of politics has failed sufficiently to adapt. Seen in the light of history, this should not unduly surprise us. Trite as the remark may appear, the 1990s are for Japan a transitional period between one system of managing her affairs and another that has not yet fully emerged. From a very early stage in this process it seemed likely that this process of transition would be a long process, and would not simply be accomplished by juggling with political alliances, changing the electoral system and effecting marginal measures of deregulation and decentralization. The problem for analysis is, however, that nobody can yet predict *what* kind of new system is going to emerge. And this leads us on to a conceptual problem of great importance.

It is extremely tempting to base one's predictions on existing models elsewhere, and to take refuge in assumptions of convergence. In the case of predictions about Japan the model so often implicitly or explicitly employed is one combining the 'small state', highly deregulated and market-oriented, with that of the 'normal state', fully integrated into the international system in a political and military, as well as economic, sense.[22] We shall in this book, however, be arguing vigorously that both from an empirical and a normative point of view, notions of convergence towards a set of norms based on current international orthodoxies are likely to be a poor and inadequate guide to the paths along which Japan will – or even ought to – tread. Here we need briefly to return to our earlier discussion about the relevance or irrelevance of culture to political analysis in the Japanese case. While entirely rejecting *nihonjinron*-type special pleading, we maintain that the sum of Japan's historical, cultural and social experiences in recent centuries amounts to a body of considerations needing to be taken with the utmost seriousness in understanding current developments. This is not to deny the so-called 'globalization' of the world economy, nor to underestimate the external pressures upon Japan. But Japan is not simply a *taker* of pressures from the outside world. Even despite the economic difficulties of the 1990s, which took a turn for the worse in 1997, we should not forget that Japan is second only to the United States as a major global economic power house, and the Japanese, even despite current discontents widely aired in the media, have a sense of the singularity of their own nation which greatly reduces national permeability to *fundamental* change imposed from the outside.

An interesting comparison may be made between the process of political change in Japan in the 1990s and the processes of political change in the ex-Communist world over essentially the same period. In both cases hardly anybody, even among the most renowned and fashionable analysts, predicted the collapse of the old system, but in both cases, once the system had 'collapsed' (the quotation marks are deliberate), the prevailing assumption among outside observers was that what had occurred amounted to 'End of History', to use Francis Fukuyama's felicitous but surely misleading phrase.[23] In this context the critique of Fukuyama by David Williams, who dares to suggest that the example of Japan shows that history is still very much alive and kicking, deserves to be taken seriously.[24]

Japan, as the twentieth century draws to its close, faces a set of difficult and challenging problems, the solution or non-solution (or half-solution) to which seems likely to determine the health of the Japanese polity for a long time to come. It may be slightly overstating the matter to speak in terms of 'crises', but in concluding this chapter it is possible to identify six such crises which seem certain to remain central to the political agenda over a number of years.

1. A crisis of political power   The monopoly position of the LDP is no longer assured as it was for so many years, even though it remains the largest party and in government. But a stable and flexible party *system* to replace the old LDP-dominant system has yet to be found. As will become evident later in the book, the obstacles to the emergence of an effective and generally acceptable system are serious.

2. A crisis of bureaucracy   Much ink has been spilled in recent years on the question of whether the government bureaucracy really runs Japan. This debate will be referred to at some length in the course of the book, but what concerns us here is that in the 1990s the bureaucracy is under attack to an unprecedented extent for allegedly mishandling important economic issues over the period of the so-called economic 'bubble' of the late 1980s and since the collapse of the bubble early in the 1990s. The authority of the bureaucracy is threatened as seldom in its past history, as parts of it are mired in corruption scandals previously thought to be the province of politicians and businessmen, but it would be foolish to underestimate its capacity to reinvent itself in such a way as to regain its authority and prestige. A most important set of issues is involved here, given that there are predominant (though not universally held) elements in the Japanese bureaucratic ethos which have been at variance with market-oriented philosophies of deregulation.

3. A crisis of political apathy and lack of confidence in government   It is difficult to separate out how far the declining rates of voting turnout in the

1990s result from contingent circumstances of political transition, and how far from more deep-seated causes. Much hinges on the nature of the voting process in Japan, and in particular on the kinds of motivation activating voters when they cast their votes. Do voters vote on the basis of a rational appraisal of a party and its policies, on the basis of image as presented through the media, on the basis of national considerations or local considerations, or (as so often in Japan) on the basis of personal obligation to an individual candidate, however indirect? A number of complex issues are involved, and the direction of change is not entirely clear.

4. A crisis of economic management and maintenance of economic dynamism The economy is no longer that of a 'developing nation', nor has it been since the 1970s. Its maturation, however, has led to a number of problems that need to be discussed. One of these is the so-called 'hollowing out' of the economy occasioned by the fact that much industry is being located overseas (most notably in Southeast Asia) to take advantage of costs that are much lower than those obtaining in Japan. Another is the astonishing level of indebtedness, which led to the collapse of a number of financial institutions (including banks) in 1997–8. Unemployment rates were also rising sharply from previously low levels. Widespread corruption and 'special relationships' were seen as threatening economic efficiency.

5. A crisis of popular satisfaction with life chances It is obvious to many ordinary people in Japan that even though Japan has a huge economy, second only to that of the United States, this has not delivered a standard of living to match. This is partly a question of what comparisons are made. Plainly, the average standard of living in Japan is far in excess of what it was a generation ago. But when comparisons are made with some other countries, certain components of the standard of living – most notably housing, but also more intangible things like personal freedom in relation to employers – are often seen to lag behind.

6. A crisis of the Constitution and of world role This is an old issue (more accurately, set of issues) which seems likely to become an even more important part of the political agenda in years to come. Constitutional inhibitions on the projection of military force have been a matter of controversy for practically the whole period since the Occupation, and the issue has been handled over the years through a series of subtle and often ingenious compromises. The time may be approaching, however, when rather more innovative approaches to the questions involved may emerge. The whole question of revision of the 1946 Constitution (not only article nine, the 'peace clause') but also parts of it relating to government, citizens' rights etc., are currently the subject of widespread discussion. If the Constitution is to be revised, however, it would be unwise to assume that the old conservative agenda across a range of constitutional issues will simply be followed. Some quite surprising (and remarkably 'Japanese') outcomes are eminently possible.

These six items do not exhaust the problematic issues facing Japan in the late 1990s but, as we shall see, they are at the core of debate.

2

The Legacy of History

The idea that you cannot understand the contemporary politics of a nation without a good understanding of its history is today hardly controversial, even though much contemporary political science appears to take history for granted. This may be reasonable enough where the general historical context is familiar, for instance in analysing the politics of a European country where analyst and target audience are firmly embedded in the Judaeo-Christian tradition.

With Japan, on the other hand, there is a case for saying that the need to come to grips with the historical background of the nation assumes a rather special significance. It is important here not to go too far and imply that Japanese politics is simply and solely the inevitable product of Japanese history. There is nothing inevitable about political outcomes, in Japan or elsewhere, since human beings have the quality of free will, and politicians calculate advantage without necessarily referring to precedent.

Nevertheless, the course of Japanese history is sufficiently distinct from that of western Europe or North America that political analysts carrying with them the unconscious intellectual assumptions derived from life in those areas have an acute need to be sensitive to the historical experiences of the Japanese people. Over the past century and a half we may find many instances of distorted analysis stemming from a failure to understand that the Japanese historical legacy includes certain features that are greatly at variance from those of Western countries.[1]

The understanding of history is important for the comprehension of politics essentially for two reasons, whether we are talking of Japan or elsewhere.

Firstly, it is reasonable to expect that history will have determined the boundaries of the state and nation, moulded the fundamental shape of the polity, shaped attitudes – positive or negative – to government, created or inhibited a sense on the part of citizens that they may be capable of affecting policy, created certain assumptions about the economy, including the role of government in economic matters, shaped attitudes to war, attitudes to neighbouring states and to many other matters. Moreover, the legacy of catastrophic events, such as defeat in war, may stay in the national consciousness and affect political outcomes over very long periods of time.

Secondly, history is not merely an objective set of data to which the citizens all have equal access. The interpretation, and at times the manipulation, of a nation's historical legacy should be taken into account. The interpretation of history is constantly being revised, not only by professional historians, but by more superficial interpreters in the mass media[2] and in some cases by governments or politicians with particular political programmes to pursue.[3]

In the case of Japan, the historical legacy is, not surprisingly, cumulative. Crucially formative periods include the impact of China from the seventh century, the influence of Spanish and Portuguese missionaries in the sixteenth century, leading to the Christianizing of a portion of the Japanese population, more than two and a half centuries of self-imposed national isolation under the Tokugawa Shogunate (early seventeenth century to the mid-nineteenth century), the modernizing and expansionist impetus of the Meiji regime (established 1868), a semi-liberal period after the First World War, and the rampant militarism that emerged during the years 1931–45 (We shall leave the legacy of events after 1945 to later chapters.) Although it is possible to discover rough parallels between certain historical developments in Japan and developments in Europe (for instance, between medieval European feudalism and somewhat parallel relationships in Japan during the Tokugawa period, or between Weber's 'puritan ethic' and aspects of the 'samurai ethic'), it is best to treat Japanese history as sufficiently distinct from that of Europe (or, indeed, from that of China) to merit analysis in terms which pay rigorous attention to the singularities of the Japanese case. It hardly needs emphasizing that this in no way rules out sensible historical comparison between Japan and elsewhere, but the mechanical application of inappropriate external models should be carefully guarded against.

The impact of China upon Japan over several centuries can hardly be over-estimated. Not only did Japan assimilate the main elements of the Chinese writing system to her own, very different, language, but China exerted an inestimable impact upon Japanese religious concepts, political organization, literary creation and even city planning.[4] Not only did Confucianism come to Japan from China, but Buddhism arrived via China (and Korea), contributing to the complex mixture of religious beliefs and practices (including the native *Shintō*) with which the nation came to be endowed. The view is common in the Chinese-speaking world that Japanese culture is unoriginal, because it derived from China. Though not without a grain of truth, this view is much exaggerated, since in the area of political values, for instance, at least one crucial departure from Chinese Confucianism emerged after that set of doctrines entered Japan. Whereas the Chinese version held that an unjust or tyrannous sovereign could morally be overthrown, this element largely dropped out of sight in Japanese Confucianism.[5] Again, during the Tokugawa period, at a time when intense leader–follower relations prevailed between local lords and their retainers, much argument took place about whether in the case of a clash of loyalties, it was loyalty to one's lord, or loyalty to one's family, that ought to prevail. In Japan, the predominant answer was that one's lord had a prior claim on one's loyalty, and one's family was secondary. Generally speaking, in China the reverse was the case.[6] Nevertheless, the legacy of Chinese Confucianism enshrined the values of an ordered society, the importance of form, hierarchy, deference to superiors and paternalistic government – values which remain politically relevant even at the end of the twentieth century.

The sixteenth century – known, in a famous phrase, as 'Japan's Christian Century'[7] – may be regarded as a period of warlordism, which was gradually moving towards the national Tokugawa settlement of the early seventeenth century. The arrival of Christian missionaries, largely from Spain and Portugal, was the nation's first substantial encounter with European civilization. Although large numbers of Christian converts were made, particularly in south-western Japan, the missionary period ended, early in the seventeenth century, with savage repression, including the expulsion of the missionaries and the persecution of converts. Even though small numbers of converts survived and remained loyal to the faith, the main impact of this period of Western contact may be regarded as negative: the eminent success of the missionaries in propagating their message led to a vicious and durable nationalist reaction on the part of the authorities.

The historical legacy of the Tokugawa period (1600–1868) is of enormous importance. It is important for one apparently negative reason, first of all, namely that strict policies of national isolation meant that Japan, which during the sixteenth century was experiencing substantial European influence, to a very large extent missed out on European developments occurring between the early seventeenth and mid-nineteenth centuries. Obviously, this was a period of crucial economic, political and social change in Europe, including as it did the early stages of the industrial revolution, the formation of early-stage capitalist institutions, the French Revolution, the emergence of a middle class, the Napoleonic wars and gradualist political evolution in Britain and elsewhere.

The omission of these influences was to have a profound effect on Japan. When, finally, in the latter half of the nineteenth century, Japan became open to the outside world, there followed a desperate struggle to catch up with Europe and America, and the emergence of what Ronald Dore has termed the 'late development effect'.[8] But what is truly extraordinary about the Tokugawa period is that this period of almost complete isolation was in practice far from being a period of social and economic stagnation: indigenous developments produced results that remain of importance in understanding contemporary Japan. Indeed, historians now generally refer to it as the 'early modern' period of Japanese history.

The Tokugawa settlement, effected in the early seventeenth century, was based not so much on the principle of absolutism as on that of balance between centres of power, none of which was to be allowed to become overwhelmingly powerful.[9] Even though the means by which these compromises were maintained were specific to the period, it may be possible to see a foreshadowing of much more recent political arrangements based on complex balancing of forces inhibiting bold or wilful leadership from the centre.

The principal power centre of Tokugawa Japan, and nearest approximation to a central government, was the *bakufu* ('military camp government'), based at Edo (now Tokyo), headed by the *shōgun* ('Generalissimo'). Although shogunal territories existed in various parts of the country, the principal power base of the

Shogunate was a coalition of various self-governing and self-supporting *han* (fiefs) situated largely in the northern and eastern parts of the country. Other *han*, principally in the southern and western regions, were regarded by the *bakufu* as potentially less loyal, but were kept in check by a comprehensive set of restrictions designed to reduce to a minimum their physical capacity to challenge the *bakufu*.

This was a regime for which the stability of the existing order was a paramount consideration. What today would seem extraordinary measures were put into effect to ensure that the political order remained intact. The Japanese people were, by deliberate government policy, virtually isolated from contact with the outside world – a policy that began with the expulsion of Christian missionaries and persecution of indigenous Christian converts, but was extended to the virtual closing of Japan to international trade and banning of travel into or out of Japan.[10] The population was divided into four principal, rigidly defined, social strata: *samurai* (warrior-administrators), farmers, artisans and merchants, in that hierarchical order of priority. In practice, there was a certain amount of permeability between these categories, but in principle (and to a large extent in practice) each stratum had its own allotted and unchangeable place in the established order.

The Tokugawa period, which brought peace after centuries of recurrent civil war, was founded in the perception that social, economic and political change, as well as foreign influences, were likely to be highly destabilizing. Therefore, ingenious and at times draconian measures were devised to avoid such destabilization.[11]

Ironically the final collapse of the regime in the 1860s bore out the apprehension of its rulers about the destabilizing character of piecemeal relaxation of controls. Once foreigners had been allowed limited access to Japan and some of the controls over the southern and western *han* had been lifted, the overthrow of the *bakufu* and the collapse of the stable order it had cherished came swiftly. This is not to say, however, that, had the controls been retained, things would have continued indefinitely as before.

Many of the conditions for change had been maturing over the long Tokugawa peace. The rigid hierarchy of social strata, mentioned above, bore less and less relationship to economic reality. Despite the fact that the merchants had the lowest formal status,[12] they had accumulated wealth and were the creditors of many of the *samurai*. The *samurai* had become in many cases, and for a variety of reasons, disgruntled and impoverished. Moreover, peace had brought a degree of national prosperity, which happened to favour the 'outer' (southern and western) *han* rather more than the *bakufu*, whose finances were in poor shape, thus upsetting the delicate balance of power. There was also a slow but steady spread of education[13] and commercial institutions during the Tokugawa period, so that the country was not entirely unprepared for a period of modernization and innovation once the old regime was overthrown.

A most important feature of the Tokugawa period was that for two and a half centuries Japan was almost entirely at peace – a great contrast to the three quarters of a century that was to follow (1868–1945). The legacy of the Tokugawa peace was important in various ways, but we emphazise two. First, the period furnished material for those wishing to embed in the national consciousness the notion that Japan did not have to be constantly at war. Second, and more specifically, it furnished a model of bureaucracy, crucial elements of which continued imprinted in the habits of mind of government bureaucrats right up to the present. This point is important and requires some exploration. As mentioned above, the *samurai* were (apart from the feudal lords, or *daimyō*) the highest of the social orders. Their fundamental function was that of a warrior class, but a consequence of the Tokugawa 'peace dividend' was that their warrior function was no longer required, and in large part they became the administrators of the various *han*. For reasons we do not need to go into, many of them were administering *han* other than those from where they originated. In Inoguchi's formulation, as elite administrators with limited inherent power, they developed habits of self-discipline and devotion to duty, careful cultivation of as wide a segment of local interests as possible, and continuous monitoring of local conditions, with due sensitivity to change.[14] It is possible to trace these elements through into the history of Japan's modern government bureaucracy, right up to the present day.

The 1850s and 1860s were a period of increasing instability, precipitated by the pressures which several Western nations were bringing to bear with a view to opening up Japan to commercial interaction with the outside world. Whether internal change or external pressure was the most crucial cause of the eventual change of regime is hard to say because of the extent to which the various trends and events overlapped each other.[15] What is important is that once the old Tokugawa regime was overthrown (in 1868), and after rearguard actions by supporters of the Shogunate had been defeated, the politics of the status quo was swiftly replaced by the politics of radical innovation. The new rulers had little compunction about discarding most of the shibboleths of the former regime, even though they did not claim to be acting in the name of a radically different ideology. It may be noted in passing that nothing of the sort happened in China until much later (1911) and that as a consequence China found it considerably harder than Japan to lay the foundations of a modern state.

What is termed in Japanese the *Meiji ishin* of 1868 was the event that most obviously marks the transition from the old regime to the new. The usual English translation of *ishin* is 'restoration', but 'renovation' is a rather more accurate translation. Given the root and branch character of the changes which the Japanese people subsequently underwent, the sum total of the changes may well be regarded as revolutionary. Nevertheless, the events of 1868 itself seem to have had a more limited aim. The new leaders were concerned, in overthrowing the Shogunate, to place the *tennō*, and the imperial institution, at the centre of the new political system which they were about to create. This was in great part a matter of legitimizing the new regime, although the ideological drive behind the movement to bring back the *tennō* (Emperor), based on Neo-Confucianist principles, must not be ignored.[16] The *tennō*, though quite powerless, had continued to reside in Kyoto, any real power having been 'usurped' by the shoguns many centuries earlier. There had allegedly been no break in the imperial line, and the Shogunate had continued to acknowledge that its own legitimacy ultimately derived from him. This example of apparently 'indirect' rule, where nominal power is separated from effective power, occurs repeatedly throughout Japanese history.

It was only comparatively late in the process of turmoil and agitation which culminated in the *Meiji ishin* that the imperial institution came to be championed seriously as a substitute for the *bakufu*. Previously many of the revolutionary leaders had been seeking ways of strengthening the Shogun and his government in their struggle to ward off the danger of foreign penetration.

Once, however, the *bakufu* had been overthrown,[17] the newly 'restored' emperor proved to be a powerful weapon in the hands of the revolutionary leaders. As a symbol of the legitimacy of their newly established regime, the emperor was a powerful support for them in the enactment of a range of bold and adventurous reforms. As the most recent in an ancient and unbroken line of sovereigns, he could be manipulated into the supreme symbol of nationhood, and in practical terms could be used as an instrument of the centralizing and modernizing which the new leaders proceeded to take upon themselves.

As a revolution, which it undoubtedly was, the *Meiji ishin* has some surprising features from the perspective of revolutions which have occurred in Western countries. Indeed, theories of revolution derived from Western experience make rather little sense when applied to the Meiji revolution. Japanese Marxists were later to engage in convoluted argument in trying to fit the Japanese revolutionary experience into standard Marxist categories.

What then were its salient characteristics? First of all, most of the revolutionary leaders came from the ranks of the *samurai* administrators who had held effective power at the local level in the old regime. It was not, in Marxist terms, a 'bourgeois-democratic' revolution, since the merchants, no doubt because of their low formal status, seem to have taken no active part. Essentially it was a revolution carried out by dissident elements of the old ruling class: a revolution from above, not below. Geographically speaking, however, the status quo was overturned. Apart from a handful of court nobles from Kyoto, the rulers of the new Japan hailed largely from the southern and western *han* of Satsuma, Chōshu, Tosa and Hizen, which had always been regarded with suspicion by the *bakufu*. Despite the fact that the *han* were abolished as administrative units in 1871, Japan's key political and military leaders were still being identified with these four areas (especially Satsuma and Chōshu) for another 40 years.[18]

The second remarkable feature of the *Meiji ishin* and its aftermath was the essential ambivalence of the new leadership towards change. We must remember here, that the leaders did not always agree among themselves, and different strands of thinking were to appear. But they all faced a common dilemma, namely how to modernize Japan, which for the survival of state and nation they knew they had to do, while preserving the spiritual essence (as they saw it) of the Japanese people. What is amazing in retrospect is the sheer scope and ambition of the modernizing and Westernizing reforms embarked upon over the two or three decades following the *Meiji ishin*. But when such reforms threatened to dilute the essential qualities of what it meant to be Japanese, a reaction would take place in favour of the reassertion of national values. A pattern of alternation between modernizing reforms and reassertion of national essence came to be established in the years between the *Meiji ishin* and the end of the Second World War.

The rationale of this process is easy to discern in the character and background of the Meiji leaders themselves. If one phrase is to be chosen to characterize them they were, for the most part, ardent nationalists. Initially, from the 1850s, incensed by the failure of the *bakufu* to withstand foreign pressures, they took the extreme nationalist stance enshrined in the slogan 'expel the barbarian'. Later, when it became apparent to them that it was futile to attempt to rid the country of foreign influences without the material means to do so, they had the foresight and flexibility of mind to embrace the very enemy they had sought to expel. A new slogan, *fukoku kyōhei* ('prosperous nation and powerful army') became the order of the day, and even if the long-term consequences of making Japan both prosperous and powerful were not universally appreciated, the programme itself had rapid and powerful success.

The sweeping reforms of the early Meiji period (1868–1912) included the abolition of the *han* in 1871 and their replacement by *ken* (prefectures), which formed the principal local unit in an increasingly centralized system of local government. A system of universal conscription removed the old *samurai* monopoly of the right to bear arms and formed the base for the creation of an army with truly national loyalties. It proved itself early by defeating the serious rebellion of Saigo Takamori, one of the original Meiji leaders but a man of notably traditional stamp, in 1877. Universal primary education was introduced as a matter of priority, and a number of universities and other secondary and tertiary educational institutions were set up. The first steps were taken towards industrialization, with the government in several cases setting up an industry on its own initiative and later handing it over to private entrepreneurs. The taxation system was completely restructured, and the government proceeded to obtain much of its revenue from a land tax, the effect of which was to produce a surplus for industrialization at the expense of rural interests. Reforms to the legal system were also initiated, although these did not come to full fruition until much later, when the government was determined to abolish the principle of extraterritoriality, whereby foreigners were able to be tried in their own courts for offences committed on Japanese soil.

The question may be posed: why did the governments of the Meiji period manage to carry out such drastic reforms with comparatively little effective protest from those adversely affected by them? Answers in terms of a culture of deference are hardly convincing in view of the events leading to the *Meiji ishin* itself, but a more satisfying explanation in terms of interests is provided by Stephen Vlastos. His analysis emphasizes the benefits obtained by the better off sections of the community, both agricultural and commercial, as a result of the Meiji reforms, as well as the willingness and ability of government quite ruthlessly to sacrifice the interests of strata that were marginalized by the reforms, most especially traditional *samurai* and small-scale subsistence farmers, who for various reasons lacked the social or political structures to revolt effectively. Nevertheless, a number of rebellions did break out, the most serious of which was that of Saigo Takamori, referred to above.[19]

So far as central government was concerned, the Meiji leaders were content to work for some 20 years on the basis of temporary and *ad hoc* administrative arrangements. Meanwhile, pressures for the wider sharing of political power were building up in some quarters, and embryo political parties made their appearance during the 1870s. A popular rights movement, seeking to enshrine Western notions of popular rights into the polity, was an important feature of politics at this period. The government leaders reacted to and against these developments, which caused considerable dissension and splits within the ranks of the Meiji leaders themselves. When a constitution was finally introduced, after a long period of gestation, in 1889 (effective 1890), it was found to contain severe restrictions upon effective sharing of political power.

Nevertheless, the Meiji Constitution is a landmark in Japan's modern political development. In part, it represented a policy of the Meiji leaders that Japan should have at least the forms of a modern Western-type state. Significantly, they were the most attracted by the constitutional practices of Bismarck's Prussia. Although their motives here were by no means uniform, there is little reason to believe that they saw the Constitution other than as formalizing and thus perpetuating substantially the same sort of regime as had obtained hitherto. That is, the *tennō* (meaning in practice his advisers) should retain effective power, the newly created popular assembly should have only a consultative role, and the political parties should be an impotent opposition rather than a potential alternative government. In practice, as we shall see, things did not quite work out like that, and the government leaders, to an extent at least, found themselves imprisoned by constitutional forms of their own making. It has been argued that their later reluctance, despite these difficulties, to suspend or otherwise grossly override the Constitution derived from the same determination to be seen as an equal of the Western powers which had inspired so many of the reforms from 1868 onwards.[20]

The Meiji Constitution established a parliament, known in English as the Imperial Diet, consisting of two houses: a House of Peers, composed of members of the imperial family, nobles created after the *Meiji ishin* and imperial nominees, and an elective House of Representatives (articles 33–4). The House of Representatives was not to be seen as the more effective house, since each had equal powers of initiating legislation (article 38),[21] and the House of Peers had the right of veto over legislation initiated in the House of Representatives (article 39).[22]

The position of the Parliament as a whole, however, was severely limited by the superior status and powers of the *tennō*, although these were not always easy to pin down in practice. Thus the *tennō* was 'sacred and inviolable' (article 3). In him resided sovereignty (not, of course, in the people), although he was to exercise it in accordance with the Constitution (article 4). It was the *tennō* who exercised the legislative power, though with the consent of the Imperial Diet (article 5), who gave sanction to laws (article 6), had considerable powers over the duration of Diet sessions (articles 7, 42 and 43) and dissolved the House of Representatives, this leading to new elections (articles 7, 45).

Moreover, the *tennō* was able to issue imperial ordinances for a wide range of purposes when the Parliament was not sitting (articles 8, 9), although they were to be submitted for its approval subsequently, at its next session. Since the Parliament was expected to sit for only three months in any year (although prolongations of a session, and also extraordinary sessions, could be held by imperial order), the scope for the imperial ordinance power was obviously considerable. *Ex post facto* review of such ordinances by Parliament was unlikely to be very effective.

The powers attributed to the *tennō* by the Constitution were not expected to be exercised by him as a personal ruler.[23] The preamble stated that the ministers of state, on behalf of the *tennō*, should be held responsible for the carrying out of the Constitution (preamble, para. 6). They were also specified as imperial advisers who were 'responsible' for their advice, while the counter-signature of a minister of state was required on '[a]ll Laws, Imperial Ordinances and Imperial Rescripts of whatever kind' (article 55). The ministers of state, however, were not alone in tendering their 'advice' to the *tennō*. He could also consult a separate body, the Privy Council (*Sūmitsuin*), which was then required to 'deliberate on important matters of state' (article 56). Moreover, an extra-constitutional body called the *genrō* (Elders) – of which more will be said later – occupied a key position of power at certain periods, while the chiefs of staff of the armed services had what was termed 'independent access' to the *tennō* on purely military matters, and certain members of the Imperial Household Ministry occupied positions of great influence at certain times.

The situation of the ministers of state, as well as their relationship with the Imperial Diet, contained a number of uncertainties and anomalies. The Constitution deliberately contained no reference to the term 'Cabinet', and Prince Itō Hirobumi, in his *Commentaries on the Constitution of the Empire of Japan*, of which he was the leading author, specifically rejected the doctrine of collective cabinet responsibility as derogating from imperial sovereignty.[24] Moreover, there was no provision in the Constitution stating that ministers had to be members of Parliament, nor that they needed to be answerable to Parliament.

On both of these issues there was much subsequent controversy, which the extreme ambiguity of the Constitution did little to help solve. The traditionalists continued to support the principle of what were termed 'transcendental cabinets' (*chōzen naikaku*) whose ministers were neither members of Parliament nor dependent upon a parliamentary majority, while those more progressively inclined wanted 'responsible cabinets' (*sekinin naikaku*), which among other things would have to resign if defeated on the floor of the House of Representatives. Something like a British-style relationship between Cabinet and Parliament had been established by the 1920s, but such a fundamental liberal principle enjoyed only a brief flowering at that time.

The working of the Meiji Constitution in practice did not entirely bear out the expectations of the Meiji leaders. The House of Representatives proved anything but docile, and the political parties, which despite their recent origin had already accumulated some experience in regional assemblies, fought hard against the principle of transcendental cabinets. Successive governments applied a variety of weapons, constitutional and otherwise, in an attempt to confine the parties to an advisory role. These included frequent dissolution of the House of Representatives, large-scale bribery at elections and the use of article 71 of the Constitution to override opposition by the parties to the governmental budgetary policies.

This last issue is of particular significance. Article 71 reads: 'When the Imperial Diet has not voted on the Budget, or when the Budget has not been brought into actual existence, the Government shall carry out the Budget of the preceding year.' On the face of it, this presented any government with a cast-iron method of nullifying party objections to government policy in the crucial area of budgetary policy. However, this would have been the case only where the size of the budget did not substantially change from year to year. In a period of rapidly rising government expenditure, such as occurred from the outset of the Sino-Japanese war in 1894, the parties had in their possession a weapon of considerable effectiveness.[25]

The use they actually made of this weapon provides us with a fascinating test of party – government relationships at this period. It also illuminates a much longer-term characteristic of Japanese politics, namely the equivocal nature of both conflict and compromise between governments and oppositions.

In the 1890s the electoral franchise was confined to about 1 per cent of the population of Japan. This meant in effect that a high proportion of the parliamentarians elected in the early general elections represented the landlord interest upon which fell most heavily the burden of the land tax, used by the government as the main means of financing its 'prosperous nation and powerful army' policies. This undoubtedly accounts for the vehemence with which parliamentarians in the mid-1890s called on the government to retrench its spending; and the threat of forcing the government to carry on with the budget of the previous year was a powerful one. It is therefore doubly interesting that by the end of the decade the government leaders had succeeded in breaking the deadlock by a series of deals with Diet members and leading party men, which gave them an entrée into the councils of government while allowing the government to maintain its fiscal policies more or less intact.[26]

The Meiji 'oligarchs' – the powerful and creative political leaders of pre-Constitution days, who continued to dominate governments throughout the 1890s – were ultimately forced to step down into the arena of party politics themselves. When Prince Itō founded the *Seiyūkai* party in 1900 with a membership largely of established party politicians, he was pointing the way to a new style of politics, different indeed from what he himself had envisaged in his *Commentaries on the Constitution*. By going along with this and subsequent arrangements, however, the parties were gaining a limited right of participation in decision making at the expense of their ability to present forthright and effective opposition. Henceforth, the line between government bureaucrats and party politicians was a thin one, as it has remained to this day.

One weakness which political parties continued to manifest to their very great cost was the recurrent venality of party politicians. Their willingness to enter into advantageous 'deals' with outsiders, and their consequent propensity to be 'bought', made it particularly difficult for the parties to maintain cohesion or internal unity of purpose. There is a sociological dimension to this, which will be discussed in chapter 3. At the same time it was also undoubtedly related to the ambiguities inherent in the Constitution itself. According to that document, sovereignty resided in the *tennō*, but the *tennō* did not rule personally (with occasional exceptions) and it was not at all clear who *was* supposed to. The enthusiasm with which the authors of the Constitution sought to ensure a strong executive and a weak legislature led them to downgrade even the position of the cabinet, by providing rival centres of power and inveighing against the principle of collective cabinet responsibility. The *tennō* 'cult', which they assiduously promoted as a means to national discipline, also tended to force overt criticism and opposition under the surface, where it was more likely to become immersed in factional intrigue.[27]

Japanese politics during the first two decades of the twentieth century involved a complex and shifting process of balancing elites. Cabinets, political parties, senior government bureaucrats, the House of Peers, the Privy Council, the *tennō*'s personal advisers in the Imperial Household Ministry, the chiefs of staff of the armed forces and directors of certain big business combines were all jockeying for power in a situation where it was unclear where power really lay. Indeed there were frequent power plays within elites as well as between them.[28] For a time, the ultimate direction of key decisions was in the hands of the *genrō*. This group, whose numbers never rose above seven, furnished senior cabinet ministers from among its own ranks until the turn of the century, when it retired more into the background. It still, however, continued to make important decisions, particularly when the choice of a new prime minister, or a matter of war and peace, was at stake. The influence of the *genrō* had markedly declined by the end of the First World War, when few of them were left and younger politicians resented their 'meddling in politics'.[29]

The *genrō*, though anachronistic, had at least functioned as ultimate political co-ordinators and setters of guidelines. By the 1920s the base of political participation had significantly broadened, but the locus of power at the top remained unstable. The suffrage was broadened by stages, and encompassed all males over 25 by 1925. The period from 1924 to 1932 saw a succession of party cabinets, and transcendental cabinets appeared to be a thing of the past. Mitani identifies six factors accounting for this change: (1) the establishment of the superiority of the House of Representatives over the House of Peers; (2) the emergence of Minobe's constitutional theory (see below) as orthodox; (3) the political neutralization of the Privy Council; (4) party penetration of the civil bureaucracy; (5) party accommodation with the judiciary; and (6) party rapprochement with the military.[30]

The instability of this arrangement, however, soon manifested itself, and by the early 1930s several of the above conditions for party ascendancy had ceased to apply. Indeed, it was fragile even during the 1920s, as indicated by the fact that the same cabinet that introduced universal male suffrage in 1925 also introduced a 'peace preservation law' designed to increase the power of the police against manifestations of political dissent.

During the 1930s the power of the political parties ebbed rapidly as the armed forces came to play a more and more commanding role in the affairs of state. In the Manchurian Incident of September 1931 a gross act of insubordination by the Kwantung Army stationed in Manchuria – connived at apparently by the army high command in Tokyo – went unpunished and uncorrected by the civilian Government. Japan proceeded to take over the whole of Manchuria and set up the puppet state of Manchukuo.[31] A series of political assassinations and attempted *coups* followed, the most serious of which occurred on 26 February 1936, resulting in the deaths of several members of the cabinet. Although those directly responsible for these crimes were not admitted to positions of power, and some of them were severely punished, their actions helped elements in the army high command increasingly to take over the reins of government.[32]

The reasons for this reversal of previous trends are extremely complex and can only be briefly summarized here. Five main factors command attention. The first is social and economic. The world depression bore particularly hard on the Japanese peasantry, and provided fertile soil for right-wing radicalism. Since the army recruited a high proportion of its younger officers from farming areas, ultranationalist agitation spread easily within the armed forces and, given the delicate political balance of power in government circles, exerted a pervasive political effect.

The second factor is international. This was the age of economic protectionism and a fascist example in Europe. Both politically and economically the international situation was very fluid, and this seems to have affected the views of some political leaders. Some others, basically liberal, were eliminated by assassination.

The third relates to ideology and indoctrination. Since the Imperial Rescript on Education in 1890, *tennō*-worship had been officially sanctioned as the keystone of a national ideology, thus blurring in people's minds the true location of decision making. There was a tradition, not confined to the far right, of appealing to the *tennō* against corrupt, tyrannical or remote officials, so that it was easy for ultranationalists in a period of national crisis to gain wide support for acts of insubordination and of revolution taken in the name of loyalty to the *tennō*.[33] It was not difficult for them to pillory members of the existing Establishment as corrupt and disloyal.

Fourthly, as we have seen already, the constitutional arrangements which had prevailed since the Meiji period contained an unsettling element of ambiguity. The attempts by the Meiji oligarchs to prevent the supremacy of the legislature by a series of checks and balances had merely served to obscure the effective location of sovereignty. Nevertheless, a rather liberal interpretation of the Constitution had taken root by the 1920s. According to the 'organ theory' of Minobe Tatsukichi, Professor of Constitutional Law at Tokyo Imperial University, the *tennō* was not an absolute ruler but was dependent on the other 'organs of state', much as a human head cannot live without the body to which it is attached. This did not constitute a Western-style liberal democratic interpretation, and Minobe publicly opposed the new Constitution introduced during the American Occupation. But in the context of the times, it could be used to justify relatively liberal political arrangements. When, however, ultranationalist thinking gained the upper hand from the early 1930s, the organ theory was rejected as heresy, Minobe was dismissed from his university post, and an absolutist school maintaining that the emperor was above the state, not accountable to other 'organs', became the new orthodoxy.

Finally, the special position of the armed forces calls for comment. Ever since the leaders of the *Meiji ishin* had invented the slogan 'a prosperous country and a strong army', priority had been given to military preparedness. Japan had defeated China in 1895 and Russia in 1905. Reference has already been made to the independent access to the *tennō* enjoyed by the chiefs of staff of the armed services. Although this was officially restricted to 'purely military' matters, it could prove a useful means of bypassing cabinet on sensitive issues. Another convention (introduced by the *genrō* Yamagata Aritomo at the turn of the century) held that the war and navy ministers in any cabinet should be serving officers of the highest rank in their respective services. A serving officer is of course subject to military orders and therefore as a member of cabinet would have divided loyalties. In the 1930s this brought about the collapse of several cabinets which were reluctant to let the armed forces have their own way. The resignation of a service minister would be followed by the refusal of the service concerned to provide a replacement, and thus the cabinet would fall.

For these principal reasons, Japan experienced what is sometimes termed 'dual government' in the early to mid-1930s, with the civilian and military establishments pursuing uncoordinated though not always unrelated strategies. From the outbreak of war in China in 1937, the character of Japanese politics had undergone a profound transformation. Nearly all parts of the system had assimilated a militant nationalist ethic, even though the young army officers who participated in the 'incident' of February 1936 and similar instances of bloodletting were little more than a catalyst. It is quite misleading to regard the parties as defeated defenders of the 'liberal' norms of the 1920s and the armed forces and other 'reactionary' groups as the victors. With some rather minor exceptions, party politicians were enthusiastic about many of the developments taking place. Even after all political parties in June and July 1940 were merged into the monolithic *Taisei Yokusankai* (Imperial Rule Assistance Association), sponsored by Prince Konoe, party politicians continued to play an important role in the political structure, and indeed they went on politicking in ways that were familiar to them.[34] In April 1942, with war raging in the Pacific, the Tōjō Government even held general elections for the House of Representatives. The vast bulk of successful candidates were from a list of those 'sponsored' by the Government, but a small number of unsponsored candidates were elected.[35]

Politics during the Pacific and East Asian war have been described as 'totalitarian'. Whether or not the term is appropriate, the regime bent its energies to the task of mobilizing the population for total war. Functional groups (business organizations, labour unions and the like) were made organs of state, a network of 'neighbourhood associations' did the government's bidding at the local level, and the *kenpeitai* (thought police) were pervasive. Under wartime pressures, the involvement of the state in most areas of the life of the people became entrenched. Multiple linkages between government and industry, encompassing habits of regular and close consultation, were a legacy of the 1930s and the early 1940s which was transmitted through the time of the Allied Occupation to the Japan of the 1950s and 1960s.[36]

3

The Influence of Social Norms and Behaviour

In chapter 1, the notion that Japanese politics could be studied without reference to Japanese social norms and behaviour was rejected as much too purist, while the idea that Japanese social behaviour is so different from that in other countries as to nullify the value of the comparative study of Japanese politics was also dismissed. In this book, quite consciously, a middle view is taken, regarding Japanese society and politics as open-ended – that is, capable of encompassing a great variety of different sorts of behaviour – but at the same time bounded by social norms and habits of social and political interaction that have their roots in history. If this seems a trite argument, in the sense that much the same could be said about most countries, it is important to remember that the view of Japanese society as 'different' remains deeply embedded both within Japan and outside, while at the other extreme it has become fashionable in some circles to regard Japan as just another bit of the global village.

In the practical business of trying to understand the dynamics of Japanese politics, one of the most perplexing aspects is the task of giving the correct degree of weight to sociological factors. At every turn there is the problem of ambiguity, in the sense that alternative explanations seem possible. We shall try to illustrate this problem through a number of political vignettes, all of which are taken from the author's personal experience.[1]

1. Sometime in the 1980s I contacted a Conservative member of Parliament in Tokyo and requested an interview. The MP generously invited me to his house in a Tokyo suburb and agreed to meet me in his car at the nearest railway station. On the way from the station to his home we passed a house which had a wreath prominently displayed outside, indicating that somebody living in the

house had died. The MP stopped the car, went to the house and spent about ten minutes paying his respects. Naturally the house was in his constituency.

2. Again in the 1980s and in Tokyo, I had a conversation with a lady whose family, though not wealthy, was obviously comfortably off. She mentioned casually that she was thinking of voting Communist at the next elections. Her reason was that the local Communist candidate was a woman whom she knew slightly and greatly admired. The policies of the party appeared entirely secondary, if she had thought about them at all.

3. Another interview with a Member of Parliament. This time I had arranged to meet the MP at his office in one of the MPs' office blocks opposite the Parliament building in Tokyo. Almost from the start of the interview, we were repeatedly interrupted by parties of visitors calling in, as well as by constant telephone calls. It became evident that most of the callers were from his constituency, some with particular grievances that needed attending to, others just to pay their respects. Towards the end of the interview the MP said to me, in some exasperation: 'you see what life is like for parliamentarians in this country'.

4. I was being taken around an area in northern Japan, quite remote from any city or large town. A visit was arranged to a magnificent concert hall, built to international standards, situated on the edge of rice paddies. We heard a classical concert by a German orchestra, followed by a performance of acrobatics by the local fire brigade.

5. I was researching the foreign policy processes of the Japan Socialist Party (JSP) in the 1950s. In 1955 a difficult series of negotiations repaired a left–right split that had occurred in 1951. In writing a joint platform for the reunited party the Japan–US Security Treaty was one of the most difficult and contentious issues. The right wanted to revise it and the left wanted to abolish it. In the end a perfectly meaningless compromise was reached whereby the party called on the government to 'revise-abolish' the Security Treaty.[2]

6. While conducting the same piece of research, I interviewed a certain political activist, who, unknown to me at the time, had changed political parties some years previously. In the interview the activist made no reference to this crucial shift in his orientation, and gave generally superficial answers to questions. Some time later, I discovered the truth about his background and requested another interview, which was granted. This time, having admitted my ignorance on the first occasion, I was treated to an exhaustive and in-depth account of the activist's political development and views.

7. While talking with a Japanese graduate student studying in Britain, and knowing that at the conclusion of his studies he would return to Japan and join a particular bureaucratic organization where he would be most likely to stay for the whole of his career, spending all or most of his working life alongside the same team of fellow employees, I asked him whether he wouldn't be bored by such a prospect. 'It's fun,' he replied.

8. A British journalist, for whom I was acting as interpreter, was interviewing a group of Japanese university students in the mid-1970s. The journalist asked

the students whether they felt oppressed by the economic power exercised by huge conglomerate groupings such as the Mitsubishi and Sumitomo groups. Did not they feel like rebelling? A student replied to the effect that since so many items of everyday equipment – from pencils to cars – were manufactured by such firms, it was best to accept them and make the best of the system that created them.

9. A Japanese student returned from Britain to Japan to resume to employment in a government ministry. A year or two later, he was posted on temporary secondment to another ministry. In a letter to me, he reported that the people he was now working with were going through his desk drawers when he wasn't there, apparently to check whether he was spying on them on behalf of his original ministry.

10. In the early 1990s, I was able to observe a session of the prefectural assembly in the principal city of a prefecture distant from Tokyo. The prefectural governor was to be questioned on policy matters by elected members of the assembly. Before entering the assembly hall, I was introduced to a number of officials, and was lent a transcript of both the questions and answers that were expected. The course of the discussion, as it turned out, had been anticipated with almost verbatim accuracy by the transcript, which was hardly surprising, since both the assembly members and the prefectural governor had copies of the same transcript, and were, for the most part, reading from it.

Let us examine these ten vignettes, and see what they tell us.

The first story illustrates the importance of personal constituency service on the part of parliamentarians. For an MP, the purpose of paying his respects to a family which has suffered a bereavement is not simply humanitarian. It is part of the process of building up a network of obligation in his constituency. To do the 'done thing' is also to build up personal support. Of course, this kind of activity can lead to various forms of corruption, though we must take care with the definition of that word.

The second story makes a different but related point. The lady who was going to vote Communist was doing so on personality grounds, and possibly to some extent on grounds of personal connection with the candidate, rather than with any real sense of voting for a party. We should not, however, generalize too much from this example, because a high proportion of Japanese voters would react negatively to the idea of supporting the Communist Party.

The third story relates closely to the first and, to a lesser extent, to the second. Members of Parliament are expected to be at the beck and call of their constituents to an extent that would amaze, for instance, the average British or Australian MP. Often the demands on them seem to make little sense in terms of a rational allocation of their time, since many constituents come simply to pay their respects.

The fourth story illustrates an aspect of the results of constituency-oriented politics. The scramble to get elected, especially in rural areas, has led to fierce competition between parliamentary candidates to provide material benefits for their local areas. In terms of provision of local facilities many rural areas in the 1990s are better off than cities, though the role of parliamentarians in this process is only part of the story: redistributive policies by government, especially certain ministries, have played an important part as well.

With the fifth story we move to the area of consensus-creation, and its inherent difficulties. In the particular case given – that of the JSP in the 1950s – the task of reunifying a divided party was a complex matter involving personal relationships as well as ideological and factional differences. The task was so difficult, indeed, that even a meaningless and self-contradictory policy on the Security Treaty seemed to be a price worth paying for reuniting the party.[3]

The sixth story illustrates a perhaps subtle point. By showing ignorance about the background of the person I was interviewing, I was not qualified to be admitted into an 'inner circle' of truth revelation. Once I had remedied this defect, the *tatemae* (surface impression) which had been created in the first interview was replaced by the *honne* (real meaning) vouchsafed in the second.

The seventh story illustrates an attitude of mind which may go some way to explaining the apparently ready acceptance of conditions of employment in bureaucratic organizations (including commercial companies) which from a free labour market viewpoint would be seen as restricting personal freedom to change a person's place of employment. Working within the same team over a very long period is seen as 'fun' presumably because of the psychological benefits stemming from dynamic interaction with others engaged in a closely related set of tasks. Needless to say, not all situations, nor all careers, in Japanese bureaucratic organizations would be regarded by participants as 'fun'.[4]

Story number eight serves to illustrate the point that accommodation to the status quo, and acceptance of the rights of the strong, may be ingrained in Japanese society. In the course of Japanese history there have been periods of political unrest, strikes, demonstrations and general mayhem. But there is a clear pattern of reversion to a state of affairs in which respect is given to those who have power.

The ninth story illustrates the prevalence of interorganizational rivalry, jealousy and battles over 'turf'. This is in a sense the other side of the coin of a system in which permanent employment in the same organization is regarded as the norm.

So far as the tenth and final story is concerned, it suggests a preference within politics and other walks of life to set up arrangements behind the scenes, but to present a common front once the public arena is involved. Lest this seem too much like a copy of the system operative in the former Soviet Union, we should note that probably a great deal of fierce bargaining had gone into the process of writing the transcript in the first place.

Reflecting on these ten cases, care needs to be taken if a sociological explanation is being offered. Apart from the fact that one ought not to generalize from single, anecdotal cases, there is the problem that some of them at least may be explicable by reference to non-sociological factors, such as institutional constraints or rational calculation of advantage.

Let us look once again at four of the stories with this consideration in mind. It is possible that the lady who proposed to vote Communist had been influenced by Marxist lecturers as a student. The parliamentarian swamped by constituency business may, as some have argued, be in such a condition because the former electoral system for the House of Representatives (now replaced)[5] had the effect of creating fierce competition between candidates from the same party, who were forced into competing for votes through personal service to constituents. The political activist who was less forthcoming in the first interview than in the second may simply have been impatient of an ill-prepared researcher in the first interview, but flattered in the second to find that his interviewer had now done his homework about his background. The bureaucrat who had difficulties when posted to another ministry may have simply been replicating the experiences of officials placed in similar situations in bureaucracies the world over.

In other words, explanation is not a simple business since most situations require multifactor explanations. Even so, it is worth searching for generalizable factors in Japanese society, as models to hold up against reality. Even if such generalizations ultimately have to be rejected in the face of some specific situations, the exercise is likely to be enlightening. Let us therefore examine some of the main issues relating to the understanding of Japanese society. It is important to realize that each of the propositions that we shall examine is, to a greater or lesser extent, controversial.

The first proposition is that Japanese society is especially group-oriented. This implies, first of all, that Japanese people experience a more or less intense identification with the group to which they belong and, secondly, that group loyalty brings with it a degree of exclusivity: relationships between people in different groups are sharply distinguishable from those between people within the same group. Some social anthropologists have linked this in with distinction in Japanese between *uchi* (inside) and *soto* (outside). The distinction is said to be symbolically expressed by the *genkan* (threshold) of the typical Japanese house, and the fact that anyone entering the house via the *genkan* removes footwear before stepping into the house proper. In so doing that person has moved from the unclean, polluting *soto* into the clean welcoming and cosy environment of the *uchi*.[6]

The second proposition is that Japanese social relations are essentially based on assumptions of hierarchy, and that Japanese generally find relationships based on strict personal equality of status difficult to manage. Some aspects of the Japanese language appear to bear this out. Japanese contains a complex set of distinctions collectively known as *keigo* (respect language), whereby quite different forms of expression (for instance, forms of common verbs, such as 'see', 'do', 'go') are used depending on the hierarchical relationship of the people conversing. Even though the system has now to some extent been modified so that by using *keigo* one is simply trying to be polite rather than responding to a situation of hierarchy, *keigo* remains a central and integral, not a marginal, part of the language, as anyone who has tried to learn Japanese will be aware.[7] An indicator of hierarchy in family relations is that Japanese has different terms for 'elder brother', 'younger brother', 'elder sister', 'younger sister'.

The third proposition is that Japanese society attributes great importance to norms of mutual obligation, and that this serves both as a motivating mechanism and as a binding mechanism. By common observation, Japan is a gift-giving society, gifts from one person, family or group to another symbolizing both the fulfilment of an obligation which should stimulate further action, and a means of cementing a relationship. The first to recognize the significance of mutual obligation for Japanese social dynamics was the American social anthropologist

Ruth Benedict, writing at the end of the war. Benedict concentrated on the concepts of *on* and *giri*, which she likens to Western-style debt repayment conventions, except that they cover a far broader range of activity and relationships than the purely financial. According to her analysis, *on* could best be translated as 'love' and 'devotion', generally to a hierarchical superior. She speaks of *on* as a set of obligations passively incurred, since every Japanese thinks of himself as a 'debtor to the ages and the world'. *On* can be received from the *tennō*, one's parents, one's lord, one's teacher, and from all the contacts in the course of one's life.[8]

It is now widely accepted that her analysis was too extreme, even for the time at which it was written, and of course far more so for contemporary Japan. Nevertheless, the scrupulous fulfilment of obligations incurred is still common.

 The fourth proposition is that there is a strong preference in Japanese society for reaching decisions by the method of consensus, rather than by simply allowing the view of the majority to prevail. The latter is said to be disliked on the ground that it leaves some members of the group dissatisfied and is therefore potentially disruptive. It is also felt to expose the individual to an uncomfortable assertion of his or her actual views, whereas the final responsibility for a decision should be collective. The practice of consensus decision making, on the other hand, involves a process of adjusting initially differing views, so that everyone having a part in the decision can in the end subscribe to it knowing that his or her views have been taken into account.[9] If, on the other hand, consensus proves impossible to attain, the consequences may be serious, and may include extreme expressions of hostility and frustration on the part of those who feel that their views have been ignored or rejected.

The four propositions together suggest that Japanese society is group-oriented, hierarchical, based on mutual obligation and inclined to making decisions by consensus. But is this really either an accurate or an adequate description of how Japanese behave in social situations?

As a way in to answering this question, we need to focus on the institution of the family, or household (in Japanese *ie*), which is widely regarded as having provided the model for various other types of organization. We shall describe a somewhat idealized model of a more or less traditional family, and it is crucial to be aware that the contemporary family has diverged from the model in various ways. In the 'traditional' family, the perpetuation of the family line was regarded as crucial. The individual was seen as less important than the *ie* to which he or she belonged. The *ie* was male-oriented and paternalistic. Internally it was hierarchical, with the bonds between father and son being accorded the greatest symbolic and practical importance. Relations between those of comparable status, such as siblings, or husband and wife, were regarded as less significant. The head of household was granted supreme respect, but the obligations between the head and other *ie* members were not simply one-way, but contained a strong element of mutuality and paternalism.

Perpetuation of the *ie* was a supreme duty, but succession to the headship did not have to be through the blood line, since it was seen as more desirable to have a competent male head, who might be brought in from the outside to marry a daughter of the family,[10] than to have an incompetent head in the direct line. Inheritance was by primogeniture, which meant that property would be maintained intact and in the hands of the continuing *ie*. Ties with collateral families, linked through marriage, tended to be less strong than in many other societies, though there were exceptions.

The main importance of understanding *ie* dynamics for our discussion is that it has served as the model of other types of organization, including commercial firms. A rather over-generalized view of Japanese social relations, based on the structure of the *ie*, was presented by the social anthropologist Nakane Chie. She argued that the system, especially in its extension to non-family groups, did not, even in the contemporary period, easily permit social pluralism, because it meant that there were few cross-cutting relationships. Individuals belonged to one group only, which combined elements of family and work. As she put it: '... groups become independent of each other with no elaborate or constant network cutting across the different groups, in the way the Hindu caste networks cut across various villages'.[11] The problem with Nakane's analysis is that it does not allow for variation or change over time, and yet plainly there is plenty of both, especially as a result of the rapid and comprehensive urbanization of Japan since the late 1940s.

Nevertheless, an advantage of her model is that it points to the possible significance of certain important social, economic and political phenomena beyond the realm of the actual family. Not only could the *ie* relatively easily incorporate non-blood, as well as blood relationships (as in the case of adult adoption), but it was also extensible in a figurative sense to situations where actual family ties were not involved at all. In Nakane's words: '[t]he piety and loyalty shown by Japanese dependants towards the father was in the nature of that shown to the leaders of a kind of economic corporate group, but combined with family sentiment'.[12] The ready extension of patterns of behaviour within the family to non-family situations gives us some insight into the behaviour of many types of organization, including commercial companies and various political organizations, including parties. Later in this chapter we shall devote some space to discussing specific examples of what may be called 'figurative extensions' of the traditional family system, but we shall also introduce the reader to a body of literature which suggests that it is the manipulation of social norms for political or bureaucratic purposes, rather than the social norms themselves, that we need to concentrate on in order to comprehend political patterns.

To begin with, however, let us take the model of an 'extensible' *ie* system and examine some of its implications. Again, we need to make the caveat that the very term '*ie* system' is an abstraction from a complex and variable reality, but simplification is necessary if we are to remain comprehensible.

First, the system in its more traditional forms was anti-individualistic, and based on vertical ties of hierarchy rather than on horizontal ties of equality. A marriage between members of two families was in one sense a marriage between two families (rather than between two individuals); but at the same time the membership of the two families was exclusive (the name of the bride was taken off her parental family register and entered on to that of her in-laws' family). The links between the two families, though they might be quite important, in no sense amounted to a coalescence of separate nuclear families into one larger group. If we assume that the *ie* is a relevant model for the commercial or industrial firm (an arguable but not irrefutable proposition), then we see a parallel with the hierarchy and exclusiveness of membership evident in many firms. If the focus of loyalties is upon one organization or set of relationships only, then we can see the logic of Nakane's remark, quoted above, that the system largely excludes social pluralism.

It has been suggested that such a system leads to exploitation. Relationships, rather than being contractual, are based on loyalty to the one exclusive group you happen to belong to, and within which your relationship to others is hierarchical.[13] The rationale behind this argument is that where group aims predominate, and relationships are based on personal feeling rather than on any form of contract, those at the top have little to stop them from ruthlessly exploiting those below. On the other hand, given the importance of *ninjō* (literally, personal feeling) in the context of intragroup relationships, some restraint may seem likely to be exercised. *Ninjō* implies not only personal affection between the group leaders, but also obligation that is mutual, not just top-down.

This, however, leaves out of account those who are marginalized, or to a greater or lesser extent excluded from mainstream groups. Temporary or casual workers in large firms, workers in some small firms doing subcontracting work for major firms, and members of various social or ethnic minorities are examples of such marginalization. It is at least partially plausible to explain the generally weak and sporadic (though occasionally violent) nature of both social and political protest movements in recent Japanese history in terms of the difficult choice facing those who feel themselves to be marginalized. One route to improvement of status is by organizing vociferous protest, but what ultimately may be more useful for the people concerned is to 'join the system' – that is, establish themselves in a working relationship with those groups that exercise power in the relevant context. This is often the most effective gateway to improving social and economic status, and is of course greatly preferred and encouraged by the authorities, in most circumstances.[14]

Stemming from the patterns of social interaction that we have been discussing, it is sometimes argued that the Japanese have a view of ethics which is 'situational' rather than universal. Although, once again, it is unwise to overgeneralize about this, behaviour within cohesive groups often visibly contrasts with behaviour between group members and outsiders. In many circumstances, however, social relationships are better encapsulated by the model of a series of concentric circles. Rather than a rigid distinction between in-group and out-group, group membership seems to consist of 'core' and 'periphery'. The core members are those who are privy to all the group's secrets and exercise influence over its direction, while the peripheral members revolve, as it were, in orbit around the core, without ever being fully being involved, and in some cases having loyalties to other groups as well. Political factions, among other organizations, tend to exhibit this feature.[15] An important implication for cohesive group relationships in politics is that these relationships predispose people to act according to particularistic rather than impartial criteria.

At this point it is worth noting a particular theory about patterns of Japanese social interactions that had a big influence, particularly in the 1970s. This is the argument of the social psychologist Doi Takeo that many Japanese exhibit a psychological need to 'depend and presume on another's benevolence' (in Japanese, *amaeru*).[16] Also called by Tsurumi 'dependent collectivism',[17] this suggests that, for whatever set of reasons, Japanese tend to have a desire both to depend on others and to belong. It seems sensible to regard this theory with a healthy dose of scepticism, given the varieties of psychological makeup met with in contemporary Japan, but it has at least the merit of emphasizing that there are alternative attitudes to the Western (especially American) emphasis on personal individualism, which Japanese often denigrate.[18]

If we accept that there is a strong element of collectivist organization and thinking in Japan (and let us not forget that this is neither a simple nor uncontroversial assertion), then we are left with two practical implications of a collectivist ethic to explore. The first is the problem of corruption, and the second is the relationship between collectivism and achievement.

Corruption is a problem in any society, particularly as regards relationships between officials (elected or otherwise) in public life, and participants in the private sector. Japanese politics has a deserved reputation for corruption, and staggering sums of money change hands in an underhand and arguably corrupt manner.[19] While some argue that certain sorts of 'corruption' oil the wheels of administration and contribute to dynamic government (or, more modestly, that corruption doesn't really matter),[20] it clearly does create problems of mis-allocation of resources, dangerous or undesirable weakening of regulations on safety, environmental impact and so on, inequitable treatment of different people or organizations, many types of inconvenience to the public and popular alienation from politics and government. In the politics of Japan in the 1990s, the serious consequences of certain forms of corrupt behaviour have become apparent, and popular political alienation has become quite marked.[21]

A relationship between collectivism and corruption is widely recognized among Japanese, particularly intellectuals. The 'cashing in' of close personal ties and group relationships to set up an arguably corrupt behind-the-scenes deal is seen as widespread, while there is anxiety that dependent collectivism leads to the weakness of the individual in the face of bureaucratic arrogance. How far there is substance in these charges will be examined in later chapters.

The relationship between collectivism and achievement is an intriguing one. A rather fundamental assumption of much Western (especially American) thinking about how to create and sustain an achievement ethic across a society was always that its basic unit of achievement was the individual and his or her interests and aspirations. So long as a system of adequate rewards for achievement could be established and maintained, an achievement ethic would flourish. Few would dispute that Japan in the course of its remarkable economic development since the Meiji period, and especially since 1945, has become an achievement-oriented society. What from a Western perspective appears surprising, however, is that there seems to be a strong collectivist impulse behind the Japanese engine of achievement.[22] Allegedly, Japanese work not for themselves as individuals, but for the good of the group to which they belong. It is necessary, however, to be extremely careful in arguing this kind of position. A popular misconception is that all Japanese workers exhibit a single-minded devotion to their companies, and will normally sacrifice their own interests to promote the company interest. This, however, would be to neglect the considerable degree of union militancy that has manifested itself over the period since the

Second World War in various sectors of the Japanese economy. Perhaps more importantly, it neglects the extent to which the interests of the worker and the interests of the company have in practice coincided. With the firm being the provider of many important welfare services and bonuses for its employees (but most impressively for its core employees – those with long-term contracts), it is in the direct interests of the firm's workforce not to sabotage the capacity of the firm to provide those services. With nearly all labour unions being enterprise unions, there has been a strong tendency for the union to put the interests of the firm as a corporate entity high in its list of priorities, even if it is simultaneously putting pressure on the employers. While there are thus instrumental reasons for acting in a collectivist manner, it is also important to realize that individualism has made some inroads into the collectivist ethic. The values of car, home and leisure are certainly not ignored, and are very often treasured, by the average Japanese family.

In this chapter we have talked extensively about the *ie* system, and foreshadowed a discussion of what we call 'figurative extensions' of the system. Once again, we need to be on our guard against the temptation to assume that the language commonly used in this regard represents an immutable or definitive reality. Contemporary Japanese society is extraordinarily complex, and superficial generalization rarely succeeds in capturing the nuances of any given situation. Having said that, it is important to understand that the *ie* is widely believed in Japan to have formed the model for other types of social and political grouping not necessarily involving family ties. Some of the 'figurative extensions' of the *ie* system are historical, but some of them still persist. It is useful to see how extensively the model has been applied.

The *tennō* system from the Meiji period until 1945 is an obvious case in point. The Meiji leaders imaginatively projected the norms of small face-to-face groups in scattered communities on to a national level in the interests of building national cohesiveness. The language used to describe the relations between the *tennō* and his subjects was deliberately chosen with the norms of the Confucian family in mind.[23]

Another example is the so-called *oyabun–kobun* (or *oyakata–kokata*) relationship, which emerged in the chaotic conditions of the labour market during the Occupation, and drew the interest of some American administrators.[24] *Oya* means 'parent', *ko* means 'child', while *bun* or *kata* means 'standing in place of' or 'quasi'. So it could be translated as 'quasi-parent–quasi-child relationship'. Somewhat similar meanings are conveyed in English by 'boss–henchman' and 'patron–client' relationships, but today it has a distinct whiff of gangsterism about it. Whereas labour bosses (*oyabun*) during the Occupation period after the Second World War would collect labourers (their *kobun*) and farm them out to employers, in contemporary Japan *oyabun–kobun* relationships are largely to be found in *yakuza* (analogous to Mafia) gangs.

Nevertheless, the contemporary Japanese press (particularly its more scurrilous elements) still use terms such as *oyabun–kobun* and *oyakata–kokata* in relation to politics, to indicate that fictive parent status is being attributed to a powerful politician whose coterie of personal followers (*kobun*) are demonstrating family-like loyalty to their *oyabun*. The press generally uses this kind of vocabulary in a critical sense, as old-fashioned and reprehensible, but it is used often enough to indicate that the patterns persist, even though the context has changed.

Another related and commonly used term is *batsu*, used with a variety of prefixes. It signifies 'clique' or 'faction' with overtones of a quasi-familial relationship, but the term is often used vaguely and could be translated 'coterie' or even just 'group'.

In Meiji Japan and after, the *hanbatsu* were the group of leaders from the south-western *han* who led the *Meiji ishin* and remained at the centre of power for the next 40 or 50 years. The group was far from united, but were largely from the same part of Japan and collectively kept a grip on power.

The *gunbatsu* or 'military clique' – a term used often in the 1930s – were the top echelons of the armed forces, which was again a manifestly divided body, but which was distinctly 'cliquish' from at least the time of the Manchurian Incident of 1931.

The term *habatsu*, in common use today and usually translated 'faction', is a group within a political party or other organization comprising a leader (rarely, more than one) and his followers. *Ha* and *batsu* mean essentially the same thing, so that the two reinforce each other when put together as one word. *Ha* on its own is commonly added to the surname of a politician. Thus 'Nakasone-*ha*' means 'Nakasone faction'. *Habatsu* are different from the types of faction most commonly found in European political parties. In Japanese parties, they are less inclined to be based on ideological differences than in Europe (though it depends on the party) – they usually have a strongly personal base and they are often surprisingly durable and well organized.[25] There is some evidence that their importance has declined during the 1990s.

Another related term is *gakubatsu,* which may be translated as 'academic clique' or 'old school tie'. This connotes a narrowly based recruitment, greatly favouring Tokyo University, into the most elite government ministries and, secondly, the strength and importance of personal connections made at university for a person's future career, particularly among those in the same year at the same university.

Finally, the term *zaibatsu* refers to pre-war business combines with interlocking directorates and a common family ownership base. The successors of the *zaibatsu* are called *keiretsu* (perhaps translatable as 'organizational linkage'), which lack the single family ownership element, but typically revolve around a corporate bank and in which there is cross-stockholding between the various constituent companies.[26]

In this chapter an attempt has been made to provide an introduction to politically relevant aspects of Japanese society, first by means of ten vignettes, secondly by examining four propositions (that Japanese society is group-oriented, hierarchical, based on mutual orientation and inclined to the making of decisions by consensus), and thirdly by an examination of the notion of *ie* and concepts derived from it.

In concluding, however, a corpus of literature will be briefly introduced that appeared largely in the 1980s and 1990s, and which challenges much of the reasoning behind the assumption that political behaviour is explained by reference to the norms and behaviour of Japanese society, and emphasizes more strongly considerations of power, bureaucratization, manipulative policies and 'system'. This will necessarily be a most superficial account, but the issues will be touched on again later in the book. Several bodies of writing having different ideological agendas will be discussed, but they have what may be identified as the common purpose of emphasizing the primacy of politics rather than the unmediated influence of society.

One body of writing, with examples among both Japanese and non-Japanese writers, is what one might call 'traditional left wing'. Against the ideas of classlessness, which stem rather naturally from the 'vertical society' theory of Nakane or from the 'new middle mass' idea of Murakami,[27] these left wing writers stress class conflict and exploitation on the part of a ruling class.[28] These writers tend to regard the alleged influence of the *ie* system and the paraphernalia of collectivism and consensus, hierarchy and habits of mutual obligation, as ideological window-dressing devised by the power holders for purposes of political control and class exploitation.

The second is a body of writing that emerged largely in Australia from the late 1970s, which concentrated on deconstructing the body of literature known as *nihonjinron* ('what it means to be Japanese'). Its main proponents were Sugimoto, Mouer (both sociologists) and Dale, whose disciplinary background lay in the humanities.[29] Although Dale's approach was rather different from that of the other two,[30] they were all concerned to demonstrate that there was an ideological purpose behind much of the *nihonjinron* writing. Sugimoto and Mouer were also concerned to argue that it was just as possible to construct a model of Japanese society based on conflict as one based on consensus.[31] Indeed they created a small industry providing alternative models of Japanese society in an attempt to discredit the *ie*-based model.

The third corpus of writing arose in the United States in the 1980s at a time when trade 'frictions' between Japan and the United States were at their most severe. The idea that this was a coherent 'school' was perpetuated by the press, and indeed the writers concerned are surprisingly diverse. What they had in common, however, was an interpretation of Japan emphasizing the divergence of the Japanese model from an economically liberal free-market system, such as the United States. Essentially, four writers were involved, Chalmers Johnson, Clyde Prestowitz, Karel van Wolferen and James Fallows. Johnson's view that the Japanese model was fundamentally at variance with that of the US went back a long way, and can be found in his book *MITI and the Japanese Miracle*, which emphasizes effective bureaucratic agency in economic policy making.[32] Although by the late 1980s Johnson had become extremely critical of aspects of the Japanese system, much of his earlier writing is favourable, even eulogistic. Van Wolferen's 1989 book *The Enigma of Japanese Power* was, by contrast, critical to the point of alarmism.[33] He painted the picture of a system without effective pilot or brakes, where nobody took ultimate responsibility, where accountability was lacking, but where there was a relentless 'system' which ran on regardless of the lack of central direction. The book undoubtedly had a big impact at the time.[34]

While the four writers mentioned were often criticized as 'Japan-bashers', they had a serious purpose in alerting US policy-makers to important problems of communication with Japan. A more recent writer, David Williams, similarly sees Japan as different, but is far more up-beat about it than Johnson, van Wolferen, Prestowitz or Fallows in their writings of the 1980s and early 1990s. Indeed, his purpose is to show that in a post-Cold War world which appears to have only one model of political economy, that of free-market liberalism, Japan provides a second, fundamentally different, and perhaps hopeful, point of reference.[35]

Although the three sets of writers just mentioned differ on many issues, they have in common a particular perception, which is that to make an effective analysis of Japanese society and its essential dynamics, the political dimension must not be left out. Politics in its broadest sense (not just party politics) is of enormous importance, even though the level of political apathy and disenchantment obtaining in the late 1990s suggests that much of the Japanese people may not sufficiently appreciate this. In particular, if we are to understand Japan properly, we should keep at the centre of attention the problems of power. The actual location of power, however, is a more complex matter than most writers appear to appreciate.

4

Post-war Reforms and the 'Time of Troubles', 1945–1960

The three decades following Japan's comprehensive military defeat in 1945 constitute a period of national renewal comparable with the Meiji period from 1868 to 1912. In the later months of 1945 Japan was in a state of physical devastation and psychological despair. The bulk of her industrial plant and infrastructure had been destroyed or put out of action in air raids, her armed forces were in the process of being disbanded, her home territory was occupied by the forces of her erstwhile enemies so that her national sovereignty was suspended, and she had been accorded the dubious distinction of being the first nation in human history to have been subjected to atomic bombing.[1] To many Japanese, in the months after 15 August 1945, it seemed that everything had been destroyed – from their own houses and means of livelihood to the *tennō* ideology – and that it was necessary to begin again from scratch. The term 'spiritual vacuum' is often used to describe the atmosphere of immediate post-war Japan, but most people were simply concentrating on the business of physical survival.

When we move three decades ahead and observe the Japan of the early 1970s, the picture was barely recognizable. As early as 1968 the Japanese gross national product (GNP) had moved ahead of that of West Germany, creating in Japan the third largest economy in the world after those of the United States and the Soviet Union. Most Japanese people had experienced unprecedented increases in their standard of living (though it still lagged well behind that of a number of industrialized countries and it had been achieved at the expense of long hours of unstinted labour from a long-suffering workforce). National sovereignty, formally re-established with the ending of the Occupation in April 1952, but in practice circumscribed by the relationship with the US in the 1950s and into the 1960s, had been gradually becoming firmer and national self-confidence was growing. International pundits were beginning to see Japan as the wave of the future and drawing grandiose consequences from the Japanese economic 'miracle'.[2]

It is tempting (and has tempted many analysts) to assume that the key to understanding the Japanese economic 'miracle' lies in the Allied (largely American) Occupation and its reforms. Even though some of the more extravagant claims by the Supreme Commander, Allied Powers, General Douglas MacArthur, imply that this was the case,[3] in fact the reality is very much more complicated. Indeed, one may well argue that some reforms that the Americans failed to carry out, as well as some that they began to carry out but stopped half way, are as significant in terms of the subsequent course of events as many of the reforms that they actually accomplished. Moreover some reforms that were carried out had later consequences that differed from the original intention of those who put them in place. That is not to say that the Occupation was not important. It was of enormous importance. But in retrospect its impact needs to placed alongside the influence of several other factors which also helped determine how Japan's political economy would be shaped once the Occupation had ended.

The history of Japan between 1945 and 1973 is immensely complex, and it is all too easy to become conceptually lost in its kaleidoscopic and sometimes contradictory developments. It seems helpful, therefore, to make a fivefold distinction between different elements influencing the total picture. These are as follows:

1. Those Occupation reforms having the effect of simplifying and centralizing the location of sovereignty and of power.
2. Those Occupation reforms having the effect of broadening participation in the political arena.
3. Persistent influences deriving from Japanese social traditions and long historical experience.
4. More recent historical influences, deriving largely from political developments in the 1930s and early 1940s – the period of militarization and war.
5. Political innovation in the post-war and post-Occupation period, in particular the establishment of conservative single-party dominance from 1955.

This particular framework for analysis in no way implies that the Japanese economic 'miracle' was inevitable. It required a great effort of political, economic and social engineering to achieve. The process of achieving it involved some clear thinking and enlightened leadership, a certain amount of good luck, and a number of mistakes and false trails. Its path was strewn with political controversy and it was the product of many different hands and minds. But in the end something quite extraordinary was created. Much the same – though some of the parameters were radically different – could be said about the Meiji period.

1. Those Occupation reforms having the effect of simplifying and centralizing the location of sovereignty and power The underlying philosophy of Occupation was, as one might expect, liberal and democratic. 'Democratization' was one of the two great catch-cries of the occupying authorities.[4] Interestingly enough, however, no attempt was made to introduce an American-style system based on the separation of powers, as was done in the Philippines, and although some features derived from US practice were introduced, these did not greatly affect the central structure. The formal institutional framework inherited from the pre-war period was closer to the British model than to the American, even though the actual working of the system had differed radically from either. In any case, the thrust of Occupation reforms ensured that formal relations between the legislature and executive were close to the 'Westminster model', in which the Prime Minister and Cabinet are chosen by Parliament (essentially from within its ranks), and Cabinet exercises executive power.[5]

The Meiji Constitution, as we saw in chapter 2, was vague and ambiguous about the location of sovereignty. According to the Meiji Constitution, sovereignty rested with the *tennō*, but since the *tennō* for the most part in practice did not rule, the effective location of sovereignty was a shifting thing, depending on the balance of power at any one time between the various political elites. This phenomenon of dual (or multiple) government, whereby the armed forces in particular had been able to exercise uncontrolled power by virtue of their independent access to the *tennō*, was inimical to the principle of clarity in the location of sovereignty, and it was to this task of clarification that the occupying authorities addressed themselves.

A number of the main reforms may be grouped under this heading. The clarification of sovereignty and its firm location in the people, through a popularly elected *kokkai* (National Parliament)[6] to which Cabinet was directly responsible, was their principal purpose.

The position of the *tennō* was radically changed. He was persuaded to renounce his divinity on 1 January 1946, a matter of great psychological importance to the people, even though 'divinity' had rather different connotations in the Japanese tradition from those in the Christian tradition, for instance.[7] From 'Head of State' he became 'Symbol of the State and of the unity of the people, deriving his position from the will of the people, with whom resides sovereign power'. The word *shōchō* ('symbol') apparently meant little to many Japanese at the time, although the status of the *tennō* has since gained widespread acceptance.[8] All his special powers, exercised for the most part, in practice, by his advisers, were taken away, including those which could be exercised in time of emergency. His functions as listed in the new Constitution were purely ceremonial.[9]

The peerage was abolished except for the immediate imperial family, and with it the House of Peers was eliminated. Although SCAP (Supreme Commander for the Allied Powers)[10] seems originally to have intended a unicameral legislature, the House of Peers was in the end replaced by a 'House of Councillors', an elective house, though on a different electoral system from the House of Representatives. Although weaker than the latter, its powers of blocking legislation could be important.[11]

The armed forces were completely abolished, and therefore could no longer be a factor in politics. The attempt to make this situation permanent was enshrined in article 9 of the Constitution, which has, however, not prevented the establishment of the *jieitai* (Self-Defence Forces), which are substantial in size and possess sophisticated modern defence equipment.[12] Perhaps in anticipation of such a development, the occupation authorities saw to it that the principle of civilian control was strongly emphasized. Also, it was specifically provided in the Constitution that '[t]he Prime Minister and other Ministers of State shall be civilians' – an apparently superfluous article if there were to be no armed forces of any kind.[13]

In addition to the removal of the emperor and the armed forces from effective political participation, the Privy Council, the Imperial Household Ministry, the *genrō* and the *jūshin* (senior statesmen: in a sense, successors to the *genrō*) were also abolished for this same reason, that they disputed the legislative and executive authority of Parliament and Cabinet.

It was further stipulated in the Constitution (article 68) that the Prime Minister and a majority of his ministers should be members of Parliament. In practice very few ministers indeed have not held a seat in Parliament. Moreover, the prime minister was to be chosen by Parliament from among its own members (article 67). Thus a convincing victory was won over the old principle of 'transcendental cabinets'.

The principle of collective Cabinet responsibility to Parliament, absent from the Meiji Constitution (where the term 'Cabinet', as distinct from 'ministers of state', was nowhere mentioned), was enshrined in article 66, which also clearly and unambiguously vested executive power in Cabinet, though its authority was confined to the execution of legislation enacted by Parliament.

Similar clarity in the location of sovereignty was aimed at in the famous article 41, which states: 'The Diet [Parliament] shall be the highest organ of state power, and shall be the sole law-making authority of the State'. The various articles of the Constitution relating to Parliament sought to reinforce this supreme position. Thus its power over the budget was assured (article 60), as well as over finance (articles 83–91), and the provision of the Meiji Constitution, that if the government's budget was rejected by Parliament the budget of the previous year could come into force, was dropped.

It can be seen that what these reforms had in common was the intention to produce a Parliament/Cabinet system, essentially on the British model, with clear lines of responsibility and an unambiguous statement of where sovereignty actually lay. It should not be assumed, however, that this was exactly the way things worked out in practice. Although there was no reversion to the practice of the Meiji Constitution, neither Cabinet nor Parliament turned out to be in a position to exercise as much effective power as the reforms had anticipated. The unravelling of why this should be will be discussed in later chapters.

2. Those Occupation reforms having the effect of broadening participation in the political arena The following reforms may be regarded as largely or in part connected with the aim of broadening the base of independent participation in politics.

The suffrage was increased to include women, who had never been enfranchised under the pre-war system, and the minimum age for voting was lowered from 25 to 20.

Labour unions and other independent groups were given official sanction and were encouraged to put forward their views and exert pressure on the government without being required to express their views in terms of the interests of the state, as had tended to be the case before the war.[14]

Left-wing political parties, whose existence had been precarious since their formation in the mid-1920s, were granted complete freedom to organize and were given active encouragement by some sections of SCAP as a potential nucleus of an alternative government to the various conservative groups. Communist leaders were released from prison, where they had languished in some instances since the late 1920s, and a vigorous legal Communist party was formed (an illegal party had been founded in 1922), as well as a Socialist Party, which was usually much more successful at the polls than the Communists.

A wide range of civil liberties was written into the Constitution, in order to ensure, among other things, that citizens had proper redress against unjust or illegal actions by government. This helped ensure far greater freedom for the mass media than had existed before the war, and the press in particular is often critical of government action.

Partly in order to enable 'new blood' to flow freely through the political arteries, a large number of politicians were excluded for the time being from all participation in public life. This 'purge' edict extended broadly through the ranks of politicians, former military men, businessmen and bureaucrats, and although there was a fair amount of rough justice in its implementation, it cleared the way, for instance, for Yoshida Shigeru, a former Foreign Ministry official with no previous political experience, to become a forceful and successful prime minister over much of the ten years following Japan's defeat.[15]

Following on article 62 of the Constitution: 'Each House may conduct investigations in relation to government, and may compel the presence and testimony of witnesses, and the production of records', a parliamentary standing committee system was set up, and has become in effect the main forum for parliamentary debate. This represents perhaps the most significant departure from the British model of parliamentary procedure and the closest adherence to the American, since the system of congressional committees was the model upon which it was based. Here again, the aim in part seems to have been to avoid narrow cliquishness in decision making, and throw open the decision making process to a wider audience.

In order to destroy what were regarded as excessive concentrations of economic power, legislation was introduced to break down into their constituent units the *zaibatsu*, or family-based combines, which formed an important element in the Japanese economy of the 1920s and 1930s. Whatever the wisdom or otherwise of this reform, and whatever the degree of success in implementing it, it was undoubtedly conceived as a measure of economic democratization, in that economic power (and so, presumably to some extent, political power) was to be distributed more broadly and more evenly.[16]

Parallel to the programme of economic deconcentration was a measure designed to bring democracy to the countryside, namely the land reform. Rural landlordism, especially absentee landlordism, had been a potent source of discontent during the depression of the rural economy in the 1930s, and the effect of the land reform was, by placing a ceiling of three *chō* (one *chō* was about 2½ acres)[17] on individual land holdings, to create a relatively egalitarian peasantry of small farmers. The land reform has been widely praised, and it undoubtedly acted to 'democratize' the rural area of Japan in a certain sense. In the long term, however, the small size of farms created an enduring problem for agricultural efficiency and had other unforeseen consequences. By removing previous sources of discontent from farming areas (some of which had been hotbeds of radicalism in the pre-war period), it provided a solid base of support for conservative politicians (and also some moderate Socialists). This, reinforced by a continuing electoral gerrymander and government support for rural industries, has greatly strengthened the position of conservative parties in post-war Japan.[18]

Another area of reform which the Occupation authorities saw as an exercise in broadening the base of political participation (rather on the American model) was in local administration. Whereas previously local government had been firmly in the hands of the Home Ministry, and most important positions were appointive, not elective, the Occupation abolished the Home Ministry and set up in its place the Local Autonomy Agency (later Ministry) with greatly truncated powers. Substantial powers were placed in the hands of local authorities, and most of the relevant positions were made elective.[19]

In two areas of administration – police and education – a drastic form of decentralization was carried out, with the aim of taking responsibility in these key sensitive fields away from the central government and putting it into the hands of the newly elective local authorities. This, however, was only one aspect of the 'democratization' of the education system. Syllabuses were substantially revised to remove the emphasis on nationalist mythology and to replace it by a far more internationalist orientation. The pre-war 'ethics' courses were abolished. Moreover, the whole structure of the education system was revamped, and at the tertiary level the number of institutions offering full degree courses was greatly increased.

Some have argued that the Occupation's attempts at administrative decentralization were unfortunate;[20] and so far as political and educational administration is concerned, the decentralizing measures were put into reverse fairly soon after the Occupation ended. In the long term, however, local politics has enjoyed a vigorous and healthy growth, particularly since the appearance of citizens' movements from the 1960s.

Finally, substantial reforms of the judicial system were introduced. These included an attempt to reduce the influence of the Ministry of Justice over the courts and to increase that of the Supreme Court, as well as a revision of the civil code.[21] Another important reform of the judiciary was that the Supreme Court was given the power of judicial review of the constitutionality of legislative and executive acts. This may be seen as another 'American-style' reform potentially conflicting with the principle of single locus of sovereignty on the principle of checks and balances. Significantly, however, the power has been most sparingly used.

At this point it may be useful to summarize the relationship between what have here been singled out as two conceptually separate set of reforms. Essentially, the relationship lay in the desire of SCAP to establish a political system in which the political interests and views of the broad mass of the population should be represented through a government whose lines of responsibility were clear. This desired situation was in turn contrasted with the state of affairs prevailing under the Meiji Constitution, where not only was the political say of the population at large circumscribed in a number of ways (restricted suffrage, officially sanctioned social norms inculcating submissiveness to the state as enshrined in a semi-divine *tennō*, police suppression of 'dangerous thoughts', and so on), but the power relationships existing among the political elite (or elites) were fluid, ill-defined and, as it turned out in the 1930s, dangerously unstable.

Different views are possible about the wisdom or appropriateness of the course of reform undertaken in Japan by the Occupation.[22] In terms, however, of the two broad aims we have identified, success was at best partial. Even though most of the pre-war reasons why lines of responsibility became confused were removed, other factors were to intervene to complicate the maintenance of accountability. While many pre-war restrictions on political participation were eliminated, obstacles of a political, social and psychological kind to the establishment of a fully free society remained for a long time (and still remain to some extent).

On the other hand, seizing the opportunity for change provided by the defeat in war and the imposition of a foreign reformist Occupation, the Japanese people and their leaders created a system which for many years was spectacularly successful in terms of different, but not unrelated, aims, namely those of building the nation into a major economic power.[23] By the 1990s, however, the more equivocal achievements in relation to a system of responsible government and participatory politics were causing serious problems for leaders and people alike.

3. Persistent influences deriving from Japanese social traditions and long historical experience   We suggested above an analogy between the changes that took place between 1945 and the early 1970s, and the reforms of the Meiji period. One obvious difference, however, is that while the Meiji reforms were devised and implemented by Japanese in control of their nation's destiny, the reforms of the Allied Occupation were devised and directed by foreigners. In both cases, however, while there was root and branch reform using foreign models, there was also much in evidence another strand of influence, namely constant or intermittent reference to a body of national experience going back for several centuries. We have already described in chapter 3 some of the sociological and ideological aspects of this tradition, but in addition one may find much reflection upon history and upon historical tradition.

A particular example of this latter aspect is the use by the *tennō*, in the aftermath of the 1945 defeat, of the principles of the Charter Oath of 1868. The Charter Oath had been a formulation devised in the immediate aftermath of the *Meiji ishin* to justify the opening of the country to foreign influences, the break with past customs, and the desirability of wide consultation. The deliberate re-use of a historical document such as the Charter Oath is a fascinating example of aspects of a long historical tradition being used as a key reference point. In this case participants in radical political and social transition were drawing continuities with a previous experience of discontinuity.

Another example is seen in the emergence of impressive bureaucratic influence in postwar Japan. As was suggested in chapter 1, Japan has a tradition of bureaucratic rule which can be traced back at least to the Tokugawa period.

The government ministries emerged strengthened considerably by the Occupation experience, for a number of reasons. One was that the Occupation, lacking sufficient numbers of administrators and interpreters, needed to rely upon the existing bureaucratic structures in order to administer its reforms. Another was that the principal pre-war rivals to the civilian bureaucracy, and most importantly the armed forces, had been removed from the politico-administrative arena. Thirdly, from the end of the 1940s the bureaucracy began to 'infiltrate' the conservative political parties and the corporate sector, so that by the 1960s they were an enormously powerful political force. Ironically, the 'purge' of party politicians too much implicated in wartime policies created a power vacuum which representatives of government ministries were able to fill. For these reasons something that was embedded in the long-term historical experience of Japan emerged from the first post-war decade with its power greatly strengthened.

The land reform succeeded in its aims partly because it was sensitively designed and competently implemented, but also because it fitted in with the priorities of the bureaucracy (or significant parts of it). There had been bureaucratic plans for more or less similar radical land reform before the war, and the ideal of a conservative, productive and small farmer class had deep roots.

By contrast, the programme of administrative decentralization was less successful because it ran counter to a long-standing aim of government policy, and because it was based, arguably, on an inappropriate model. The reforms themselves were based on American tradition of thought which saw elective local government as a vital element in grass-roots democracy. Unfortunately, this thinking incorporated an equation of American and Japanese conditions in the post-war period which was unwarranted. For one thing, the geographical dispersion of centres of population in the US lent itself to genuine local autonomy, whereas in Japan the mass of the population was concentrated along a narrow strip of coast, and thus more prone to centralized administration. Historically, too, the Japanese and American experiences could not have been more different. Whereas the constant extension of the 'frontier' by independent-minded citizens was a key part of the American experience (even though by now a historical memory), progress in Japan since the Tokugawa era had been closely connected with a process of centralizing most aspects of administration. In many ways the centre could be regarded as more progressive and modern than the periphery, even though the extension of rule from the centre might well be felt by many as oppressive.

The introduction of local responsibility for education and the police in particular did not work well because of inadequate finance, so that they rapidly became an intolerable burden for local authorities. Moreover, a tradition of local autonomy was not something that could be created overnight. In the case of the locally elected boards of education, where there was no tradition among the local population of participating in educational traditions, most of those elected to the boards turned out to be teachers. So far as the police were concerned, the operation of an efficient police force on a national scale proved problematic when the responsibility was spread among many impecunious and unevenly motivated local bodies. These particular reforms were speedily reversed by Japanese governments after the Occupation had ended. Although their undoing was resisted by the Opposition parties on the grounds that they were part of an intended full-scale 'reverse course', it is arguable that they were reversed principally because they were not compatible with long indigenous historical experience.

Here, however, we need to introduce an important caveat, namely that even long historical traditions are not necessarily immutable. One aspect of local government reforms which has survived is the introduction of a great many elective positions. Passin's argument that this reform led to a 'cancerlike growth of elective positions, ... a kind of overloading of the political communication circuits',[24] is questionable in the light of developments in local government and politics from the late 1960s. Rather, the local political structures set up during the Occupation ultimately facilitated the vigorous expression of local interests and points of view, and thus provided a crucial counterweight to the centralizing tendencies of Tokyo. Broadly speaking we may characterize the current (1990s) condition of local politics throughout the country as consisting of a series of uneasy compromises between efforts to extend the influence of the centre, local courting of the centre, and local efforts to become more independent.[25]

Finally, let us examine further the implications of the basic political structure that emerged from the Occupation. The determination of SCAP to eliminate 'dual government' has already been mentioned. In order to do so it proved easier to reconcile a single line of authority and responsibility with a British-type fusion-of-powers theory than with American-style notions of the separation of powers. When Parliament is elected by the people, Cabinet is chosen from among the members of Parliament (in practice by a majority party or parties), the prime minister leads the Cabinet, government departments (ministries) have a member of the Cabinet at their head as minister, and legislation is introduced by the government (broadly defined) into Parliament, which it can normally control because of its majority, then the lines of authority and responsibility are fairly clear.

It was probably a correct assessment that this style of government was more likely to solve the problems raised by Japan's ambiguous constitutional tradition than any system based primarily upon a separation of powers. The party-based cabinets of the 1920s – the era of relative liberalism between the two world wars – approximated the British model, even though their status was uncertain and their powers very incomplete. Conversely the 'transcendental' cabinets of the period which predominated between 1890 and 1924, and again between 1932 and the war, looked rather more like the American President in his relations with Congress, although Congress has always commanded far more independent influence than did the Japanese Parliaments of the 'transcendental' eras.[26]

In choosing, therefore, a system for Japanese government based on the fusion of powers, the Occupation authorities ultimately had the effect of further directing Japan along the centralizing path pursued by governments since the mid-nineteenth century. The effect, though not necessarily the intention,[27] of the reforms was thus consonant with long historical experience.

4. More recent historical influences, deriving largely from political developments in the 1930s and early 1940s We have distinguished between long historical influences, discussed in the previous section, and more recent influences from the militarist period, in part because it is all too tempting to see historical influences as all of a piece, whereas certain periods can have a disproportionate influence. This is particularly true for the period of the 1930s and early 1940s.

As Japan became more entangled in the affairs of continental Asia in the 1930s, so her needs for efficient and flexible military production increased. This led gradually to industrial mobilization and, by the time of Pearl Harbour, state direction of industry was pervasive. The habits of interaction between government and industry engendered during this period carried over into the post-war world, and were important in moulding the kinds of relationship between the two that prevailed in the 1950s and 1960s. During the late 1930s in particular the structure of industry itself changed substantially, with a number of new companies (the so-called 'new *zaibatsu*') emerging to prominence. The power and industrial experience of these companies, forged during the particular conditions of war and preparation for war, also had an impact on the shape of the economy in the post-war period.[28]

Also of significance is the development from the 1920s of what has more recently come to be seen as a 'peculiarly Japanese' system of industrial relations, in which firms maintain a permanent workforce of well-paid and highly skilled labour which is led to develop close identification with the firm. Although it was not until after the end of the war that such a system became the norm in large firms (and some smaller ones), the influence of the 1920s and 1930s experience is certainly important in explaining its rise to normality.[29]

Some of the *modus operandi* of the post-war banking system – which the Occupation conspicuously failed to reform – may also be derived from the inter-war period. In particular, close linkages between the banks and the government were maintained, and free competition between banks on the American model was conspicuous by its absence. The Bank Law of 1942, for instance, had confirmed the subservience of the banks to the control of the military, and after the war was over, although the military had been dissolved, the central government continued to exercise a similar kind of control.[30]

5. Political innovation in the post-war and post-Occupation period, in particular the establishment of conservative single-party dominance from 1955 In November 1955 the Liberal Democratic Party was formed out of various competing conservative parties. It is common to regard this as a turning point marking the establishment of what has often been called Japan's '1955 political system', which survived until the LDP lost office in August 1993. In reality, however, this simple term masks a most complex and evolving reality. In this section the element of innovation on the part of Japanese leaders themselves over the years of the Occupation and the period after the regaining of national independence in April 1951 will be emphasized. There were five interrelated areas where seminal and innovative changes took place:

1. The formation of the LDP in 1955.
2. The relative marginalization of left-wing parties and the labour union movement from about 1960.
3. The infiltration by government ministries of political parties and parts of the corporate sector, etc., from the Occupation period onwards.

4.   The realization that US security guarantees provided desirable freedom of manoeuvre in many policy areas, but particularly in the pursuit of economic growth.
5.   The abandonment, from the early 1960s, of attempts at wholesale reversal of the Occupation reforms in favour of directing attention towards economic policies.

These five categories of innovation will be revisited in the concluding section of this chapter, as well as in chapter 5, but meanwhile we need to trace as briefly as possible the salient events of domestic politics for the period covered by this chapter.

The first government following the surrender broadcast by the *tennō* and the war's end on 15 August 1945, lasted until October.[31] The succeeding prime minister was Baron Shidehara Kijurō, a former diplomat regarded as relatively liberal and international in orientation.

The brief life of the Shidehara Government (October 1945 to May 1946) coincided with the initiation by SCAP of a number of its key reforms including the introduction of the new Constitution, the original text of which was announced on 6 March 1946. Treated formally as a revision of the Meiji Constitution, it was debated by the House of Representatives between June and August 1946 and by the House of Peers until October, was formally promulgated by the Emperor in November and came into effect the following May.

General MacArthur was not satisfied with the various drafts submitted by the Shidehara Government towards the end of 1945 and into 1946, on the ground that they remained within the spirit of the Meiji Constitution. In February 1946 he ordered the Government Section of SCAP to prepare a radically new draft (to be known as the GHQ draft) which was done in secret and extremely quickly. Pressure was placed on the Shidehara Cabinet to 'present a draft' based on the GHQ draft, ensuring that 'American pressure' would become one of the sources of controversy in later debates about the Constitution.

The Constitution will be discussed in much greater detail in chapter 10. We need here, however, to introduce article 9, the 'peace clause' or 'no war clause'. It has been of such momentous significance for Japan's foreign policies and domestic politics as to justify quoting it verbatim. It reads:

> Aspiring sincerely to an international peace based on justice and order, the Japanese people forever renounce war as a sovereign right of the nation, and the threat or use of force as means of settling international disputes.
>   In order to accomplish the aim of the preceding paragraph, land, sea and air forces, as well as other war potential will never be maintained. The right of belligerency of the state will not be recognised.

It remains uncertain whether this article (which differs significantly from that in the GHQ draft: see chapter 10) was MacArthur's idea or was suggested to him by Shidehara. The controversy is more than a historical curiosity, and touches upon the relationship between antiwar feeling and nationalism in contemporary Japan.

Another issue that gravely affected the conduct of politics in the Occupation period was the purge which began in January 1946. An ironic effect of the purge was that former career bureaucrats were enabled enter the vacuum created when a high proportion of party politicians were purged from political life. They had to step down into the party political arena in order to do so but, with the Occupation reforms, that was where the political action was going to be.

The outcome of the first post-war general election to the House of Representatives, held in April 1946, was seriously affected by the purge. Although the *Jiyūtō* (Liberal Party) emerged as the largest party in the House, its leader, the veteran politician Hatoyama Ichirō, was purged shortly after the elections. Needing to find a new leader in a hurry, the party chose Yoshida Shigeru, a former career diplomat, who had been Foreign Minister under Shidehara but had no previous connections with a political party.

This was a fateful decision. Yoshida at the time was 67 years old, and was to remain Prime Minister, with one break of about 17 months, for the next eight and a half years. At least until the purge restrictions were lifted on his potential rivals towards the end of the Occupation, he dominated his own party and the political world to an extent that few politicians have managed to do before or since.[32] He provided strong and individualistic leadership at a time when a prime minister, sandwiched between the Occupation authorities and a complex political environment, was in a position of great delicacy. He also nurtured a small band of younger politicians, similarly of bureaucratic origin, who were to play a leading role in politics for many years after his retirement. Although it was not until the 1949 general election to the lower house that former central government bureaucrats became numerically significant in the conservative parties,[33] the unexpected elevation of Yoshida in 1946, like the forming of the *Seiyūkai* Party by Itō Hirobumi in 1900, facilitated that partial fusion of government ministries and ruling party that has been so characteristic of Japanese politics in the post-war period.

New elections were held in April 1947 under a revised system that survived, in essence, until 1994.[34] The *Nihon Shakaitō*, or Japan Socialist Party (JSP), formed less than 18 months earlier, became the largest party. The Yoshida Government was replaced by a three party coalition of the JSP, the Democratic Party (essentially conservative) and the small *Kokumin Kyōdōtō* (People's Co-operative Party), under a Socialist Prime Minister, Katayama Tetsu. Katayama's Government was beset by factional and ideological divisions in its own ranks (including within the JSP), and fell in February 1948 over an abortive attempt to nationalize the coal mines. A Government of almost identical composition, led by the Democratic Party leader, Ashida Hitoshi, succeeded it, but in fell in turn in October 1948 as the result of the Shōwa Denkō corruption scandal.[35]

The 'opening to the left' had resulted in fiasco, and as a result Yoshida's renamed *Minshujiyūtō* (Democratic Liberal Party) took over following general elections held in January 1949, which gave that party an absolute majority.

Apart from the divided nature of the coalition cabinets, they suffered from coinciding with a gradual change in the priorities of the Occupation. With the emergence of the Cold War, the Americans were beginning to see Japan less as a conquered enemy to be reformed, and more as a potential ally in the struggle against 'International Communism'. Other factors were also beginning to affect

US policy. The cost of supporting Japan economically was creating electoral repercussions at home, and there was a perception that the breaking up of industrial combines, as well as demands for reparations by various Allied powers, was delaying economic recovery. Labour militancy was causing concern in SCAP, which banned a general strike planned for 1 February 1947 and in 1948 imposed restrictions on the right to organize and strike of public sector workers. MacArthur imposed a stringent economic stabilization programme known as the 'Dodge Line'[36] in 1949. This stabilized the economy and halted inflation, but left a legacy of bitterness with the Americans on the part of much of the political left.

The outbreak of the Korean war in June 1950, less than a year after Communist victory in China, led MacArthur to authorize the formation of a 75,000-man National Police Reserve, which was to help fill the security vacuum caused by the redeployment of American troops from Japan to Korea. This, together with his New Year message at the outset of 1951 that Japan might consider a measure of rearmament (though he did not call for revision of the 'peace clause'), threw the peace clause into the centre of political controversy, where it has remained ever since.

In October 1951 the San Francisco Peace Treaty was signed, and became effective in April 1952. International circumstances made a simultaneous peace treaty with all the Allied powers out of the question, and so Japan had to make do with a 'partial' peace.[37] Largely at American insistence, the Peace Treaty was a favourable one for Japan. Although she renounced her claims to her former imperial territories, no restrictions were placed on the development of her economy or her trade, nor was she obliged, as some Japanese had earlier feared, to retain any of the Occupation reforms if she should choose not to.

On the same day that the Peace Treaty was signed, the US and Japan signed a bilateral security pact which was to provide for a continuation of an American military presence in Japan after independence. This was to become a matter of acute domestic political controversy. Closely involved was the issue of Japanese rearmament. In early 1951 John Foster Dulles had strongly urged Yoshida to rearm to the extent of building a 350,000-man force. Yoshida, realizing the likely economic and political consequences should such a plan be implemented, resisted. Though he was able to hold off Dulles, the 1951 Security Treaty nevertheless contained a clause to the effect that Japan would maintain forces in and about Japan '... in the expectation ... that Japan will increasingly assume responsibility for its own defense against direct and indirect aggression, always avoiding any armament that would be an offensive threat ...'.[38] Subsequent negotiations were to lead to the formation of the *jieitai* (Self-Defence Forces) in 1954, at a very much lower strength than had been envisaged by Dulles.

Once the Occupation was ended, Yoshida's power within the conservative camp waned as party politicians who had been purged, returned to political life. An intense rivalry developed between Yoshida, trying to hang on to power, and the de-purged Hatoyama, who was working to replace him. Hatoyama succeeded in December 1954, at a time when the conservative side of politics was still split between several parties and splinter groups.

On the other side of the political spectrum, the JSP split over the peace settlement in 1951, but the two halves of the party together made steady electoral progress until well after their reunification in 1955. The Japan Communist Party (JCP) had done well (35 seats and about 10 per cent of the vote) in the 1949 elections (when the Socialists did very badly, reflecting the failure of the coalition governments), but the Communists turned militant on Moscow orders from January 1950, and consequently became a negligible electoral force throughout the 1950s. In 1950 SCAP purged the JCP leadership.

By the mid-1950s, the stage was set for a much clearer polarization of party political forces between right and left than had been seen hitherto. In October 1955 the two Socialist parties were reunited after a series of long and difficult negotiations. Partly under pressure from business interests, which feared further Socialist electoral advances and a possible Socialist government, the Liberal Party and the Japan Democratic Party merged one month later and formed the LDP.

This, in retrospect, was a crucial turning point. Despite factional rivalries, the Liberal Democrats avoided further defections and eventually consolidated their position as a party semi-permanently in power. Socialist unity, on the other hand, was to prove more fragile, and although throughout the 1950s the electorate was moving towards the left, the JSP was unable to maintain the electoral impetus of the mid-1950s. Two-party alternation in power failed to materialize. Hatoyama was succeeded in December 1956 by Ishibashi Tanzan, and he in turn, a mere two months later, by Kishi Nobusuke. Kishi for a number of reasons was a divisive figure, and his period in office culminated in the Security Treaty revision crisis of 1960, which led to his fall from office.[39]

If the period between 1952 and 1960 was one of transition in party politics, it was also one of acute polarization of opinion. The policies of successive conservative governments were often lumped together under the term 'reverse course'. From the Government side, the Occupation reforms were subjected to critical scrutiny, and attempts were made to dismantle or emasculate those which seemed most objectionable. From the Opposition side (left-wing parties, labour unions, academics and much of the mass media) fears were expressed that each new piece of government legislation was part of a planned programme of reversion to the pre-war system.

The main areas in which reform was desired or actually implemented by governments were police administration and powers, labour unions, educational administration and the content of courses, defence and the Security Treaty, and the Constitution.

Police administration and powers, evoking memories of the pre-war period in which the police had been an instrument of political control, were a particularly sensitive issue. In 1952 a Subversive Activities Bill, largely directed against the JCP, was passed by Parliament, and in 1954 the Yoshida Government also introduced a new Police Law, which effectively recentralized police administration. On the other hand, a Police Duties Law Amendment Bill, introduced by the Kishi Government in 1958, designed to increase the powers of the police to control demonstrations, met a barrage of criticism within and outside Parliament, and eventually was allowed to lapse.[40]

Post-Occupation governments continued the restrictive policies towards labour unions which had been initiated during the latter half of the Occupation, especially with the restrictions on the union rights of government workers imposed in 1948 and amendments to the post-war Labour Union Law which were passed in 1949. Following prolonged strikes in the coal and electricity industries in 1952, a Coal and Electricity Strike Control Act went on to the statute books in 1953. The labour unions themselves, after Communist attempts to control them during the Occupation had largely failed, nevertheless retained much of their radicalism during the 1950s. The *Sōhyō* Federation, formed in 1950, split in 1954 into a radical wing (still called *Sōhyō*) and a smaller moderate wing (*Zenrō*, later called *Dōmei*). Relations between the unions and the Socialist parties remained close.

Education policy was also a highly contentious area, in which the conservatives wished in particular to reverse some at least of the policies initiated during the Occupation. In 1956 the Hatoyama Government introduced legislation to recentralize educational administration. The local boards of education ceased to be elective and came to be appointed. The Ministry of Education, under separate legislation, acquired powers of vetting and authorizing school textbooks. In 1958 the Ministry began to use a teachers' efficiency rating system, which was bitterly contested by *Nikkyōso* (the Japan Teachers Union) and other groups, partly on the grounds that it was likely to be used for political ends. The introduction of 'ethics' courses into schools in 1958 also occasioned great controversy. With their memories of what 'ethics' had meant before the war, members of the Japan Teachers Union and others attacked this strongly. Relations between the Ministry and the union (which was strongly Marxist in orientation) became strained to say the least.

Defence and the Security Treaty were the most celebrated area of controversy. Although the Yoshida Government successfully resisted Dulles' demands for massive rearmament by Japan, it authorized the formation of a modest military force known euphemistically as the *jieitai* (Self-Defence Forces) and in 1954 signed the Mutual Security Assistance (MSA) Agreement with the US. It was left, however, to Kishi to negotiate a revision of the original Security Treaty of 1951. His attempts to do so triggered Japan's worst political crisis since the war, leading ultimately to his resignation. Antiwar feeling had increased during the 1950s, and the JSP from 1955 was campaigning on a platform of 'unarmed neutralism'. Any attempt by the Government to enhance national defence capacity or to consolidate its defence relationship with the US was bitterly resisted by the left.

Campaigns against American military bases in Japan were a feature of the politics of the period, and a movement against nuclear weapons, *Gensuikyō* (Japan Council against Atomic and Nuclear Weapons), was able to tap a vast reservoir of antinuclear sentiment in a nation which had undergone – to quote a phrase which gained currency at the time – 'nuclear baptism'. *Gensuikyō* originated in a housewives' petition after a Japanese fishing boat had been showered with radioactive ash from an American test at Bikini atoll in 1954. In the 1960s it was to become a political battleground between the Communist and Socialist parties, and also between the two sides in the Sino-Soviet dispute. It consequently lost much of its appeal, but annual rallies continued to be held every August at Hiroshima.

Finally, the 1946 Constitution was not surprisingly a major field of contention. The Hatoyama Government came to power with a policy of initiating constitutional revision, and in July 1956 a bill passed through Parliament providing for a Cabinet Commission to Investigate the Constitution (*Kenpō Chōsakai*). The Commission began to function in August 1957, by which time Kishi, who also wanted constitutional revision, was Prime Minister. The Socialists and their allies refused to participate in the Commission, which despite this proved not to be the solidly revisionist body that many had feared. The Commission reported finally (at great length, but without unanimity) in 1964, but by that time pressure for revision had receded and no action was taken. The attitude of the Opposition to the whole issue (but especially to article 9, the peace clause) is summed up in a JSP campaign slogan used in the 1960s: 'The Constitution protects you; we protect the Constitution'.

The Security Treaty revision crisis of May–June 1960 was the most serious political fracas since the end of the Occupation. It produced mass demonstrations and riots on an unprecedented scale, led to the cancellation of a state visit to Japan by President Eisenhower, precipitated the fall from office of a Japanese prime minister (but not his party), and seriously strained relations between Japan and the United States. On the other hand, Japan obtained a Mutual Security Treaty which in several respects was an improvement on the old one; and some saw in the crisis itself a realization of democratic participation in the political process. Following the crisis, moreover, Japan entered a period in which political stability was markedly greater, and the temperature of politics noticeably lower, than it had been in the 1950s.

Very briefly, what happened was this. In 1958 the Kishi Government began negotiations with the Eisenhower administration for a revision of the 1951 Security Treaty to make it more acceptable from the Japanese point of view. Essentially, Kishi was trying to increase Japan's independence of action under the Treaty without reducing the value of the American defence commitment or committing Japan to excessive defence responsibilities. To a very considerable extent, he succeeded in these aims.[41]

The left-wing Opposition for the most part objected to the Treaty in any shape or form, and saw revision as perpetuating a dangerous 'military alliance' with the US. In February–March 1959 a People's Council for Preventing Revision of the Security Treaty was formed, to co-ordinate activities. The left at this time was encouraged by the success of the campaign to block the revision of the Police Duties Law Amendment Bill in 1958, where mass demonstrations by unionists, students and others had been a big feature. Their morale was also given a boost by the March 1959 verdict in the Sunakawa case, which held among other things that the presence of American troops in Japan was incompatible with article 9 of the Constitution.[42] The decision, which cast grave doubt on the constitutionality of the Security Treaty (and also of the projected revised Treaty), was reversed by a decision of the Supreme Court in December of the same year.

During the earlier stages of the movement against revision of the Treaty, it was fairly limited in scope and in the number of people involved. The Socialist and Communist Parties, the *Sōhyō* labour union federation and the student movement *Zengakuren* (All-Japan Federation of Student Self-Governing Associations) were the main participants, with some support from academics and the mass media. It was these elements which broke into the Parliament compound on 27 November 1959 and which unsuccessfully attempted to prevent Kishi from leaving Haneda airport on 16 January 1960 in order to sign the revised Treaty in Washington.

In May and June 1960, however, a series of events occurred which broadened the base of the movement to previously uncommitted or apolitical people. It so happened that, as the parliamentary debates on the Treaty were nearing completion, international tension rose dramatically with the U2 incident[43] and the breakdown of the planned summit meeting between Eisenhower and Khrushchev. This gave rise to acute fears of Japan being dragged into an international conflict by virtue of her security links with the US. Eisenhower's world trip was now likely to include only anti-Communist capitals and not Moscow, as had been planned. The symbolism, for the left – and for others too – was unpalatable. Meanwhile, Kishi was faced not only with a continuous series of hostile demonstrations, but also with constant obstruction of parliamentary proceedings by the Opposition parties. Moreover (and this in a sense was the most crucial point) he could not count on the unswerving loyalty to him of several of the intra-LDP factions. While his own factional alliance was loyal, some factions were decidedly equivocal in their support and others were openly hostile and criticized his policies incessantly, no doubt with the expectation that one of their leaders would be able to replace him as prime minister.

Kishi's first tactical defeat was when he failed to have the Treaty passed by the House of Representatives by 26 April. If it had been passed by that date, then it would have been ratified by the House of Councillors without further action on 26 May, and without the necessity of formally extending the regular session.[44] The consequences of this failure were compounded by what in retrospect seems a most unwise decision, namely to invite President Eisenhower to Japan for 19 June, on the assumption that the Treaty would have been formally ratified by that date. This meant it had to pass the lower house by 19 May.

When 19 May arrived and the Treaty still had not passed the lower house, Kishi decided on drastic action. He called police into the Parliament to remove Socialist MPs and their male secretaries who were physically preventing the Speaker from calling a vote on the extension of the session,[45] and then, late at night with only Liberal Democratic members present and with many of them unaware of what was planned, held two votes in quick succession, the first to extend the session and the second to ratify the Treaty.[46]

To public apprehension about the Treaty was now added a widespread fear that Kishi was subverting basic parliamentary procedure and even democracy itself, which, as many realized, was still a fragile plant. The obstructionist tactics of the Socialists (such as imprisoning the Speaker) were regarded more leniently. There followed a month of serious crisis, with a mounting series of demonstrations and strikes. On 10 June Eisenhower's press secretary was mobbed in his car by a crowd of demonstrators and had to be rescued by helicopter. Things came to a head on 15 June, when a massive demonstration outside Parliament led to an invasion of the parliamentary compound and pitched battles with police. There were many injuries and one female student was killed. The next day Kishi cancelled Eisenhower's visit on the ground that he could not guarantee the President's safety. The revised Security Treaty duly passed the House of Councillors on 19 June, and four days later Kishi announced his resignation.

The LDP did not split, although it came close to it.[47] The demonstrators all went home.

A crucial turning point in the evolution of the Japanese political system was reached in 1960. In this brief concluding section of the chapter, we shall look both backwards and forwards at the innovations that were emerging from the maelstrom of political conflict occurring a decade and a half after the defeat. As foreshadowed earlier in the chapter, five such innovations seem crucial, though not all of them were entirely apparent by 1960.

The first, quite obviously, was the unification of the disparate members of the conservative camp into a single party, the LDP, in 1955. In its early years, though, the prospects for the LDP becoming a truly 'ruling party', or even surviving intact, seemed poor. As we shall describe in the next chapter, however, the 1960 crisis was to prove a turning point in its fortunes, after which the habit of simply being in power took hold.

The second key development, foreshadowed by the 1960 crisis, but not wholly evident yet at the time it took place, was the relative marginalization of left-wing parties and the union movement. The term 'relative' should be taken seriously, because the Socialists and the unions were still a force in the land during the 1960s, but the prospects for a change of government bringing them closer to the centre of power receded during that decade. This was, of course, the reverse side of the coin of LDP dominance, but rapid economic growth was taking the edge off radical protest.

The third innovation (which, as we have seen, had inexact though interesting parallels in the pre-war period) was the infiltration by government ministries of political parties and parts of the corporate sector, among other areas. There were cabinets in the 1960s, fully half of whose members had served in the bureaucracy. Thus government and politics alike were given a strongly bureaucratic colouring, and this contributed to a political single-mindedness, which was a characteristic of the period.

This brings us to the fourth innovative development of the post-Occupation period, namely the dawning realization that US security guarantees provided desirable freedom of manoeuvre in many policy areas, but particularly in the pursuit of economic growth. What is sometimes known as the 'Yoshida doctrine', after the post-war Prime Minister, was based essentially on this perception. The approach was to be further developed by the two prime ministers of the 1960s, Ikeda and Satō, but keeping defence spending as low as possible and undertaking as little in the way of international responsibilities as politically feasible, became a hallmark of government policy from this period.

The fifth innovation, which is of enormous significance in retrospect, will be the subject of chapter 5. This is the abandonment, from the early 1960s, of attempts at wholesale reversal of the Occupation reforms in favour of directing attention towards economic policies. The consequences of this change of approach in moving from the 1950s to the 1960s were to be long lasting and far reaching.

5

Politics of Economic Growth and Political Survival, 1960–1989

The suddenness with which the 1960 Security Treaty crisis was over suggests that a strong element of stability underlay the political turbulence. It is true that there were some disturbing instances of political violence in the aftermath of the crisis.[1] The next few years, however, were relatively calm and uneventful. Ikeda Hayato, who followed Kishi as President of the LDP and thus Prime Minister, was also of bureaucratic background and was a protégé of Yoshida. Government remained in the hands of a predominantly conservative and business-oriented political party.

Ikeda, nevertheless, succeeded in projecting an image very different from that of his predecessor. Following a more conciliatory approach to the Opposition, and what he termed a 'low posture' (*tei shisei*), he received a wide measure of popularity. Deliberately, he played down contentious political issues such as revising the Constitution and defence co-operation with the US, and concentrated on the more rewarding area of economic growth. By the early 1960s the economy had already moved to the stage of double-digit growth rates, and Ikeda was able to gain political advantage by issuing a long-term economic plan for 'income doubling' over a ten-year period. He made genuine efforts to restore the normal working of Parliament, the reputation of which had been seriously damaged by the events of the previous months. He obtained for Japan full recognition as an advanced industrial nation. Japan became a member of the

OECD in 1964. Perhaps as a reflection of these efforts, the LDP did well in lower house general elections held in 1960 and 1963.

For a time the conciliatory approach taken by the Ikeda Government met its due response in more moderate policies by the Opposition. The Socialist leader Eda Saburō, newly risen to prominence, promoted a policy of *kōzō kaikaku* ('structural reform') which was reformist rather than revolutionary in its implica-tions. His grip on the party organization, however, was fragile, and by 1965 he had been replaced by leaders of a more extreme and doctrinaire stamp.[2]

For the Socialist Party the 1960s were an unhappy decade. Whereas in the mid-1950s it was confidently believed in many quarters that the JSP would continue to win more votes until it could form a government in its own right, by the late 1950s its level of support had peaked at about one third of the voters. Party unity, forged with much difficulty in 1955, did not prove durable. In 1959 a right-of-centre group led by Nishio Suehiro (prominent in the Katayama and Ashida Governments of 1947–8) broke away in protest against the Party's drift to the left[3] and formed the *Minshatō* (Democratic Socialist Party, DSP). This party did not do particularly well at the polls,[4] but its defection destroyed the ideological balance within the JSP, and for a while made it easier to run that party from the extreme left than from the centre or right.

The JSP was also poorly organized and heavily dependent upon labour unions affiliated with the *Sōhyō* federation. Unlike the German Social Democrats at about the same period, who were successful in broadening their base of support, the JSP appeared to be ever narrowing its appeal to the ranks of organized labour, principally indeed to unions in the public sector. This left the way open to other groups with an eye to the organization of discontent to poach on the Socialists' traditional bailiwick. One was the *Sōka Gakkai*, a proselytizing neo-Buddhist sect (the largest of many new religions which had come to prominence since the war) having astonishing success in attracting members from the ranks of unorganized workers, small shopkeepers and middle-aged housewives in cities.[5] In the late 1950s it began sponsoring candidates for election to Parliament and in 1964 founded a new political party, the *Kōmeitō*, which campaigned on a platform of cleaning up politics and paying attention to the problems of the disadvantaged and unorganized. The party was highly disciplined and won 47 seats in the 1969 lower house general elections. The other rising force was the JCP, which was rapidly recovering from its setbacks in the 1950s and becoming an important political force, especially in the big cities. The JSP, on the other hand, suffered a major defeat in the 1969 elections, losing 50 seats and sinking to a total of 90.

Ikeda was forced by ill health to resign as Prime Minister in November 1964 (he died the next year) and was succeeded by Satō Eisaku, younger brother of Kishi Nobusuke.[6] Sato was another former bureaucrat and protégé of Yoshida, and was to remain in office until June 1972 – a record tenure of office which still stands. He presided over the later stages of the economic 'miracle' which by the late 1960s had given Japan a larger GNP than those of Britain, France and West Germany, and smaller only than those of the US and USSR. Japan was becoming a major force on the world scene, though her economic influence was hardly matched by political initiative.

Satō was a cautious and conservative Prime Minister, even though, in part because of the Vietnam war, relations between Government and Opposition were generally more polarized under Satō than under Ikeda. His most tangible achievements, but also his most notable setbacks, were in the field of foreign policy. Thus in 1965 he finally concluded a treaty with the Republic of Korea, paving the way for close economic links between Japan and that country. In 1970 he gained the agreement of the US for indefinite extension of the Security Treaty, and thus avoided a repeat of the 1960 crisis, which had been widely predicted. In November 1969 President Nixon agreed to return Okinawa to Japan, and this duly took place in May 1972, thus defusing an issue with which the Opposition was making great play.[7] The award of the Nobel peace prize to Satō in 1974 was related to his declaration in 1971 of three non-nuclear principles for Japan: that Japan should not manufacture, stockpile or introduce nuclear weapons on to her territory.[8] Even so, it is clear that the nuclear option, though rejected, was actively discussed by his Government.

The years 1968 and 1969 saw a flare-up of violence on university campuses which for a time confronted the Government (and of course the universities themselves) with a serious situation. Educational and political issues became inextricably confused as the student bodies were increasingly radicalized. Finally the Government, after waiting some time until public opinion was beginning to tire of the student radicals, introduced a Universities Control Bill in August 1969, which had a dramatic effect in returning things to normal.

Satō's final year in office, however, was much more seriously troubled. The startling success of Japanese exports to the US caused a sharp American reaction, and President Nixon's economic measures of August 1971 were designed, among other things, to force Japan to revalue the yen, which had remained at 360 yen to one US dollar since the Occupation. The yen thus embarked on an uneven path of increasing value relative to other currencies, which continued until the mid-1990s.[9]

China policy, however, caused Satō's political demise. In July 1971, President Nixon announced, without prior consultation with Japan, that he was to visit the People's Republic of China (PRC). This, and his economic initiative in August, were known in Japan as the two 'Nixon shocks', and led to much rethinking of Japanese foreign policy positions. Satō was unwilling (or unable) to take real initiatives on China, whereas the mass media were virtually at one in urging a drastic change in China policy, and in calling on Satō to step down if he could not produce one.

Towards the end of his prime ministership the public mood was shifting away from a single-minded pursuit of economic growth towards a concern with environmental pollution, quality of life issues and social welfare. Some appalling environmental disasters had occurred over the high-growth period, and a rise in support for Opposition candidates in the big cities was a symptom of the problems which a rapid growth of affluence had brought and governments had yet to solve.

In July 1972 Satō was replaced as Prime Minister by Tanaka Kakuei, a man of limited formal education and no bureaucratic background, who had made his career in business and in the LDP machine. The tide of disillusionment with Satō was probably what robbed his preferred successor, Fukuda Takeo – a man of similar background and perceptions to his own – of the succession.

Tanaka immediately took bold initiatives in two directions. He moved at once to recognize the PRC, which meant severing formal ties with the Republic of

China on Taiwan. He also produced a plan for the 'Reconstruction of the Japanese Archipelago', which involved dispersal of industry and population to areas of the country away from the existing big cities. Despite its relatively auspicious start, however, the Tanaka regime soon ran into serious difficulties. Reflecting international trends, inflation began to become a problem, and with the publication of the Prime Minister's decentralization plan came a speculative boom in land prices, especially in those areas marked for future development. The scheme had to be shelved. Tanaka also attempted, but failed, to reform the lower house electoral system to the advantage of his party.

The most serious blow to his leadership, however, came with the fourfold increase in the price of oil provoked by the Organization of Petroleum Exporting Countries (OPEC) in late 1973, following the Arab–Israeli war of October. This provided a further stimulus to inflationary trends, and brought economic growth to a sudden halt.

Following adverse (though not catastrophic) results in the upper house general elections of July 1974, and well-publicized revelations about the dubious propriety of Tanaka's financial dealings, the Prime Minister resigned in November 1974.[10] His successor, chosen by a process of behind-the-scenes consultation within the LDP, was Miki Takeo, seen as a has-been by many media commentators at the time, and leader of a small faction on the left of the party. The choice of Miki as Tanaka's successor was no doubt occasioned by a need to choose a 'clean' politician as leader, following the publicity about Tanaka's murky financial affairs. In addition, the fear that Miki, who had hinted at such a possibility in the past, might lead his faction out of the party in protest at its corruption, could possibly have played a role.

Miki's tenure of the prime ministership was to appear fragile and transitory, since he enjoyed only a weak power base in the party. A most interesting feature of his regime, however, was that for a few months in 1975 he actually tried to rely on votes from Opposition parties in support of bills opposed by the right wing of the LDP. He had a modest success with a watered-down revision of the Anti-Monopoly Law, which enabled the Fair Trade Commission to pursue cartels with somewhat greater effectiveness than hitherto.[11] He succeeded in bringing about the ratification of the Nuclear Non-Proliferation Treaty, long after its signature in 1970.

In February 1976 a sub-committee of the US Senate Foreign Relations Committee heard evidence from the Deputy President of the Lockheed Corporation that several million dollars had been given in bribes to unnamed politicians in Japan and elsewhere to influence aircraft contracts. This admission caused a sensation in Japan, and the 'Lockheed scandal' came to dominate the nation's politics for a long period.[12]

Miki, unlike some of his predecessors in similar circumstances, allowed the official investigators a free hand to probe as deeply into the affair as they wished. In a sensational move, Tanaka was arrested in July and made to answer charges about his part in the affair. Though quickly released and still a member of Parliament (he later resigned from the LDP), he had to face protracted court proceedings until an adverse verdict was brought against him in 1983. The case was still under appeal in 1986 when he was incapacitated by a stroke, which ended his political career. Until that point, however, he remained an LDP faction leader (despite being no longer an LDP member!), and during the 1980s his faction was not only the largest in the party, but the one in effect determining who should be prime minister.

The Lockheed scandal brought about the one serious defection suffered by the LDP between 1955 and 1993, that of six parliamentarians led by Kōno Yōhei, who formed a small party called the *Shin jiyū kurabu* (New Liberal Club, NLC) in June 1976. The NLC remained in existence for ten years, never graduated beyond the status of a minor party, but nevertheless probably had a certain catalytic effect on the LDP. It was brought into a coalition government with the LDP in 1983, and most of its members were reabsorbed into the LDP in 1986. Kōno Yōhei was to be LDP President between 1993 and 1995.

At general elections for the House of Representatives held in December 1976, the LDP, having suffered the NLC defection, recorded its worst electoral result hitherto, barely scraping home with a majority of seats. Subsequent analysis was to show that support for the LDP, which had been slowly declining since the late 1950s, was bottoming out, and would gradually recover to somewhat safer levels.[13] Even so, the immediate effects of the near defeat in December 1976 were that the LDP lost control of a number of House of Representatives standing committees, thus complicating its legislative task.[14] An era known as the *hakuchū jidai* (era of Government–Opposition parity) had begun and was to last until June 1980. Some commentators were confidently predicting that the Opposition parties would soon attain a majority and even replace the LDP in power.

Miki resigned following the elections, and was replaced by Fukuda Takeo. Fukuda's Government began to feel the effects of the loss of LDP control over parliamentary committees when it was forced to incorporate tax reductions into its 1977 budget. On the other hand, economic growth had begun to resume, even though at around half the rates achieved in the 1960s. Problems between Japan and the United States over a growing trade imbalance in Japan's favour, which were to become much more serious in the 1980s, were already causing strain in the latter half of the 1970s.

A crucial year in the development of better relations between Japan and the PRC was 1978. In February a large-scale trade agreement was signed, and in August the Sino–Japanese Treaty of Peace and Friendship, long stalled over the issue of 'hegemony' (see chapter 12) was concluded. The reverse side of this same coin was that relations between Japan and the USSR were worsening, and reached a low point following the Soviet invasion of Afghanistan at the end of 1979. Policies of maintaining 'equidistance' between the PRC and the USSR were quietly forgotten by Government spokesmen. The Fukuda Government put considerable effort into improving Japan's image in Southeast Asia and watched the developing ties between the Soviet Union and Vietnam with concern.

In domestic politics, while the LDP faced problems, so did the parties in Opposition. In 1977 a splinter from the JSP formed the *Shaminren* (Social Democratic League, SDL), spearheaded by Eda Saburō, who unfortunately died shortly after its formation. The 1970s were a period of electoral stability (more negatively, stagnation) for the JSP, but the party was still beset by left–right divisions. It was a protest against the continued influence of Marxists within the party that led to the formation of the *Shaminren*. The other parties in the Opposition were, for different reasons, not doing particularly well either.[15]

By the late 1970s there were signs that the electorate was no longer swinging to the left as it had been in the early 1970s, and that conservative electoral support was stabilizing. From the late 1960s left-of-centre chief executives were elected to head local authorities in many urban and metropolitan areas, arriving essentially on the back of a concern with the environment, welfare and quality of living, which had all been seriously degraded during the period of rapid growth in the economy. Though they had a number of achievements to their credit,[16] they had not always proved the most competent of administrators. With the change in public mood towards the end of the decade, most of them were defeated in elections and replaced with essentially conservative coalitions.

The position of the Prime Minister was not rendered more secure by a conservative mood in the electorate. A new method of electing the LDP President, initiated by Miki when he was Prime Minister, provided for a primary election by all party members (not just members of Parliament and one party representative per prefecture, as in the past) prior to the main election. Although heralded as a method of 'modernizing' or 'democratizing' party procedures, it had the effect of extending factional divisions down to the rank and file membership. Central factions competed to recruit new local members, and when the first primaries were held in November 1978, the combined organizational strength of the Ōhira and Tanaka factions proved too much for the current Prime Minister, Fukuda. In a four-cornered contest Ōhira beat Fukuda and the other two candidates by a wide margin, and Fukuda decided not to contest the second-stage run-off election.

Further OPEC oil price rises prompted the second 'oil shock' in 1979, and the Ōhira Cabinet devoted extraordinary efforts to devising an energy policy which would conserve oil, increase oil stockpiles and accelerate the development of alternative sources of energy. The economy, however, had now achieved the capacity to withstand an 'oil shock' more effectively than in 1973–4. Economic growth rates were scarcely affected.

Even so, it had become plain by the end of the decade that the informal power structures within the LDP were going through a period of serious instability, whose roots went back at least to 1972, when Tanaka had taken over the prime ministership from Satō in place of the expected successor, Fukuda. When Fukuda had then been in turn beaten by Ōhira in 1978, relations between intra-party factions became particularly tense. Ōhira in fact turned out to be an innovative prime minister, and a number of policies subsequently taken up in the 1980s by Nakasone can be traced back to the brief Ōhira period. Nevertheless, Ōhira's tenure of the top political position was not an easy one. A general election was held in 1979, in which the LDP performed marginally worse than it had in 1976, though it still managed to hang on to its parliamentary majority. One factor which was widely believed to have contributed to this result was a statement by the Prime Minister, quickly retracted following electoral protests, that his Government planned to introduce new indirect taxation. This same issue was to remain highly controversial throughout the 1980s and into the 1990s, helping depose another prime minister in 1989.

Following the 1979 elections Ōhira's tenure came under challenge from within the LDP, and a '40-day crisis' ensued, which was only resolved when the LDP put forward two candidates, Ōhira and Fukuda, in the parliamentary election to determine the choice of prime minister.[17] Ōhira narrowly won the contest, but this was the first time in the history of the LDP that the party had been unable to decide on a prime ministerial candidate and had had to entrust the selection, in a real not formal sense, to a parliamentary vote.

The second Ōhira Government continued to be plagued by the political circumstances that had led to the 40-day crisis in October–November 1979. On 16 May 1980 the JSP presented to Parliament a motion of no-confidence, citing corruption, proposed defence spending increases and rises in public utility charges as reasons for the House of Representatives to withdraw its endorsement of the Government. Quite unexpectedly 69 LDP parliamentarians, from the Fukuda, Miki and Nakagawa factions, abstained from voting on the motion. The Government was soundly defeated (243 votes to 187) and resigned. For the first time a simultaneous double election was called for both houses of Parliament.

Although at the time of the no-confidence motion many observers thought that the LDP was heading for disintegration, the shock of the Government's resignation created the impetus for a closing of ranks. The desire to unite was further strengthened when on 12 June Ōhira died from a heart condition, no doubt exacerbated by the defeat. Itō Masayoshi[18] became caretaker Prime Minister, and the LDP went to the people on 22 June carrying black-edged posters of its dead leader. In an extraordinary reversal of its fortunes, the Party won a clear victory in both houses and in the House of Representatives secured its safest majority since 1969.[19] The ruling Party was once more in control of all parliamentary committees, and therefore had regained its former power over legislation.

An intriguing feature of the election is that the LDP went to the people leaderless, and was nevertheless granted a resounding endorsement by the people. It was not until after the elections were over that, following intensive negotiations within the Party, Suzuki Zenkō, who had inherited the leadership of the Ōhira faction, became Party President and thus Prime Minister. His name had scarcely been mentioned in speculation about the succession immediately following Ōhira's death.[20]

Suzuki was in some ways a curious choice as Prime Minister. His background was from the fishing industry in northern Japan, scarcely a mainstream industry, and, most unusually for a Liberal Democrat, he was briefly a member of the JSP in the late 1940s. There was a widespread perception at the time that he was not really up to the job.[21] Nevertheless, it is easy to detect a continuity of policy from the Ōhira period (1978–80) through the Suzuki period (1980–2) into the Nakasone period (1982–7), with some important policy departures usually associated with the Nakasone period actually originating during Suzuki's prime ministership.

The most important of these was the inauguration, in March 1981, of the *Rinchō* (abbreviation of *Rinji Gyōsei Chōsakai*, Provisional Commission on Administrative Reform). With only a little exaggeration we may say that the *Rinchō* set the most important guidelines of government economic policy for the next decade. The actual outcome of its deliberations, however, differed sharply from its initial announced purposes. At the outset, the public could have been forgiven for believing that the purpose was to rationalize, and curb, the powers of the government bureaucracy. In practice, however, what emerged was essentially an exercise in budget cutting.[22] The background to this is important and takes us back into the 1970s.

It will be recalled that when Tanaka became Prime Minister in 1972, the LDP was deeply concerned with the prospects of losing power if issues of social welfare, environmental protection and quality of life were not vigorously addressed. The Tanaka administration took this lesson to heart, and initiated a range of new programmes in each of these areas. So impressive were the Government's efforts to improve social welfare provision that 1973 was often referred to in the media as *fukushi gannen* (Year One of Welfare). Naturally, this involved major increases in public expenditure, but with GNP registering annual increments of 9 or 10 per cent, the funding to pay for it was readily available from naturally increasing tax revenues. The first oil crisis of 1973–4 brought economic growth to a complete halt, and though it resumed fairly quickly after the economy had adjusted to a regime of expensive energy inputs, the rate of growth, as we have seen, never regained the earlier levels. In these circumstances, the Ministry of Finance was obliged to resort to the floating of deficit bonds, leading to a progressive increase in the national debt. Even Prime Minister Fukuda, known as a fiscal conservative, was unable to keep costs in check, and it was not until the turn of the decade (and especially the signal victory of the LDP in the 1980 lower house elections) that the political will, and the political means, existed to tackle the perceived problem effectively.[23]

The choice of chairman to head the *Rinchō* was significant. Dokō Toshio, former Chairman of *Keidanren* (the Federation of Economic Organizations, the leading interest group representing big business), already over 80 when appointed, was a convinced and determined advocate of budgetary retrenchment by government. He placed his own indelible imprint on the Commission's deliberations and findings. A second individual of great importance in relation to the *Rinchō* was Nakasone Yasuhiro, Director of the Administrative Management Agency in the Suzuki Cabinet, in which capacity he oversaw the *Rinchō*'s formation. Within a few months of the publication of its final Report, in April 1983, Nakasone was himself Prime Minister and in a position to ensure that its recommendations were implemented.

Before the crucial period in which Nakasone was Prime Minister is discussed, it is first necessary to examine changes that were taking place in the early 1980s in the way in which the LDP was structured.

In retrospect, the LDP seems to have alternated between periods of acute factional conflict over leadership of the Party, and periods in which one faction was able to impose its will, or at least act as arbiter of ultimate control. The late 1950s and early 1960s, as well as the 1970s, were an example of the former, while the Satō period (1964–72) and most of the 1980s were an example of the latter. As we shall see in chapter 6, a split in the dominant faction in 1992 was to lead to a split in the LDP and its fall from power.

The ultimate factional arbiter of power in the ruling party from around 1980 was the Tanaka (from 1986, Takeshita) faction. Ever since the implication of Tanaka in the Lockheed scandal in 1976, he had been actively recruiting new LDP parliamentary members into his faction, which by the early 1980s had become much the largest in the Party. The faction's resources made it a most attractive proposition for any LDP parliamentarian having difficulties funding his election campaigns. Three factors contributed to the emergence of the Tanaka faction as arbiter. One was the disruptive legacy of factional conflict in the 1970s and the near disaster – turned into a resounding success – of the 1980 elections. There was a strong sense in the Party after this experience that it needed to make a new start. The second was the sheer size of the faction. Although it never recruited a clear majority of LDP members of Parliament (no faction in the history of the Party has ever done that), it was big enough that attempts by other factions to combine against it were likely to fail because of lack of numbers. The third reason was Tanaka's political skill, combined with his financial resources. Although Tanaka is usually thought of as a politician principally concerned with the acquisition and application of money for political purposes, he was much more versatile than this stereotype suggests, and in particular he was skilled in the art of motivating others, notably bureaucrats, in relation to policy initiatives.[24]

In October 1983 a long-awaited verdict was handed down by the Tokyo District Court in the Lockheed case. So far as Tanaka was concerned, he was fined 500 million yen and sentenced to four years in prison, though the sentence was not operative pending appeal. It has often been remarked as surprising (some might use stronger language) that Tanaka could continue to exert crucial political influence within the LDP despite the Lockheed trial and its implications for him. In part this reflects the dynamics of politics in Japan, but also the unusual – and fascinating – characteristics of Tanaka as a politician.[25]

In November 1982 Nakasone had succeeded Suzuki as Prime Minister. If evidence were needed of the kingmaker role exercised by the Tanaka faction within the LDP at this juncture, it was provided by the fact that a high proportion of Nakasone's first Cabinet were Tanaka faction members. Although Nakasone was later able to escape from such a situation of dependence, his tenure of office in its early stages appeared to be at Tanaka's pleasure. Nakasone himself, however, was a resourceful political leader, and unlike his five immediate predecessors in the prime ministerial chair (none of whom lasted substantially more than two years in office) he was vouchsafed a full five years, which gave him time to impose his stamp on events.

Until he became Prime Minister, Nakasone had often seemed to be a somewhat maverick politician, outside the mainstream of the LDP, notably nationalist and concerned with defence matters, but at the same time a leader who merited the sobriquet 'the weather vane' (*kazamidori*). His own faction had never been particularly large (though it became larger after he took office as Prime Minister), and never belonged in any reliable fashion to any of the coalitions of factions that were a characteristic of factional manoeuvring within the ruling party. He was known as a politician with presence and charisma in a political system where such characteristics tend not to be well rewarded.

Nakasone was undoubtedly attracted to a presidential style of government, and several years previously had proposed introducing such a system to Japan, with direct election of the president. As Prime Minister, he set up various task forces and commissions to report on important policy areas, following a precedent set by Ōhira before him.

The most important policy initiatives of his period in office concerned privatization, defence, relations with the United States, taxation and education.

It is not easy to determine how far any of these initiatives were his own and how far they were inherited from the past or resulted from reactions to contingent circumstances. The extent to which a Japanese prime minister is able to exercise independent initiative on policy matters is limited, and some non-Japanese commentators at the time fell into the trap of attributing to Nakasone the kind of power that they would have expected based on the norms of their own political systems. Nevertheless, it seems reasonable to argue that there was a Nakasone flavour to most of the policy initiatives undertaken during his period as Prime Minister. To describe this flavour succinctly is difficult, but it may perhaps be summed up as an attempt to increase the sense of national pride, combined with opening the country more to the outside world and liberalizing its domestic institutions and practices.

In embarking on measures of privatization, Nakasone was tuning into a current fashion for market liberalization and the small state which was much in evidence in the United States and western Europe in the mid-1980s. He was ideologically sympathetic to many of the economic prescriptions of Reaganism and Thatcherism, and this was no doubt cemented by the personal rapport that he was able to establish with Ronald Reagan and Margaret Thatcher, especially the former. At the same time, circumstances particular to Japan to an extent informed the privatizations actually undertaken.

The most important privatization undertaken was that of *Kokutetsu* (the Japan National Railways, JNR). Essentially two purposes were to be served by taking JNR out of the public sector. One was because over the years it had accumulated a staggering deficit, in part because of the strategic political influence of the many local communities which were able, through their members of Parliament and other channels, to put pressure on JNR to keep in service many local railway lines which ran at a loss. It was felt that to privatize and split up JNR would make it easier for such pressure to be resisted. In addition, by permitting the successor companies to engage in economic activities other than simply running a railway network, they were expected to acquire the flexibility necessary to operate at a profit. The second purpose was to smash *Kokurō*, the union of workers in the JNR, and replace confrontational with co-operative unionism. With the splitting up of JNR into nine privately run regional companies, the union itself was split, many dismissals were made, and union ability to block policy changes was much decreased.[26] It is important to understand that this was part of a government strategy to extend the co-operative unionism that prevailed in the private sector to what had been the public sector also.

The privatization of Nippon Telephone and Telegraph (NTT) followed a somewhat different path from that of JNR, though the purposes were essentially similar. Rather than being split into separate regional companies, it was transformed from a public enterprise into a joint stock corporation. Even though an element of competition was introduced, NTT was able to retain a near monopoly position in the provision of its service into the 1990s though, as with the privatized railway companies, it was now permitted to enter into lines of business other than those concerning its primary activities. The NTT union, *Zendentsū*, under the able leadership of Yamagishi Akira, adopted a stance of co-operation with the changes proposed, and was thus able to exercise an important influence on the process of privatization.[27]

On matters of defence, Nakasone made a concerted effort to push back the limits of what was permitted. This was an area in which he had a long-standing personal interest, and where most of what he did as Prime Minister was consistent with his earlier positions. In seeking to sum up the rationale for his general approach, he spoke of 'settling accounts with the post-war period' (*sengo jidai no sōkessan*), by which he meant that a good deal of the legacy of the American Occupation had been against the national interest, and that the Government needed to develop a clear and bold set of policies on what constituted the national interest in the 1980s.

Nakasone did not achieve all he wished to in defence matters, since he was challenging a minimal-defence orthodoxy which remained strong.[28] In the words of Aurelia George: 'Nakasone introduced an element of dynamism into the defence policy making process, challenging many of Japan's postwar defence orthodoxies and altering the substance as well as the public perceptions of defence policy.'[29] Specific changes that he succeeded in making while Prime Minister included: the breaking of a limit, established by the Miki Government in 1976, of 1 per cent of GNP for the total defence budget;[30] the breaking of a long-standing ban on sales of military equipment overseas, to the extent of permitting the export of military-related technology to the US; commitments to defend the straits between the main Japanese islands and to protect Japan's vital sea lanes; provision for increased 'interoperability' between Japanese and US forces; and the ending of a restriction making it impossible for US naval forces in the vicinity of Japan to be assisted in a crisis by elements of the Maritime Self-Defence Forces. More generally, Nakasone emphasized more than his predecessors the 'common destiny' of Japan and the United States, and the need for co-ordinated deterrence against the Soviet Union. He sought to project Japan's image on to the world stage and to increase Japan's contribution to the maintenance of the health of the global system. As Prime Minister, he controversially paid an official visit to the Yasukuni Shrine in Tokyo, in which are 'enshrined' the souls of the war dead, including those of several convicted war criminals. His predecessors had not risked alienating antiwar opinion by doing so, but this was part of Nakasone's design of escaping from the restraints imposed on Japan by the post-war settlement.

Not all of these reforms achieved the results desired for them. For instance, the lifting of the GNP 1 per cent ceiling did not lead to the defence budget regularly going substantially above 1 per cent, export of military technology did not amount to much in practice, and the Japanese contribution to sea lane protection was less impressive than initially hoped. Even so, Nakasone was challenging a long-held set of propositions about defence, and he set an agenda of reform which his successors could take up if they so wished.

Most of the defence-related issues involved the promotion of closer military co-ordination with the US under the Security Treaty framework, and this was one crucial aspect of the Japan–US relationship during the Nakasone period. Another aspect, however, was a serious imbalance in trade between the two countries. Japan at this period was fortunate in that the Reagan administration was ideologically opposed to major government interference in trade matters, which it believed should be left to the market. Even so, Japan faced trenchant and increasing criticism from American sources over a range of Japanese practices seen as designed to favour Japanese exporters and inhibit the attempts of Americans to export to Japan. In 1985 an ambitious attempt to solve, or at least mitigate, the problem of the Japanese trade surplus was made with the conclusion of the Plaza Accords in September. Thereby a realignment of currencies was effected, as a result of which the yen strengthened substantially against the US dollar. This, however, was another reform which failed to produce the effect for which it was designed. Making Japanese exports more expensive and imports into Japan cheaper was supposed to reduce the volume of exports and boost imports. This result, however, failed to materialize, because Japanese industry rapidly demonstrated the ability to make itself so much more efficient that it could absorb the extra burden imposed on it by the realignment. Meanwhile, the range of bureaucratic and other (often hidden) controls on imports meant that imports hardly increased.

Nakasone was sufficiently exercised by this situation that he commissioned what became known as the Maekawa Report, which recommended a range of measures to deregulate the economy and decrease government control. Although deregulation was certainly favoured by the Prime Minister, most of the recommendations of the Maekawa Report were to remain unimplemented. Late in his prime ministership, Nakasone promoted a campaign to encourage imports, so as to answer American criticisms about the reluctance of Japan to import manufactured goods, services and so on.

A perennial problem for Japanese governments in the 1980s was the apparent imbalance between direct and indirect taxation, in favour of the former (especially income tax and corporation tax). At the same time the redressing of the balance of taxation in favour of indirect taxes along the lines of a value added tax aroused fierce opposition from affected groups, including small and medium businessmen, who resented the greater scrutiny of their financial affairs that such a tax would entail. Ōhira had been discomfited electorally in 1979 as an apparent result of his early version of an indirect tax proposal, and the Suzuki Government concentrated on reduction of government expenditures rather than increasing revenues by introducing a new tax. When Nakasone produced another version in February 1987 (having pledged in the 1986 general election campaign not to do so), this soon had adverse effects in local elections, and the proposal was withdrawn in May. It was left to his successor, Takeshita, to bring in yet another version of an indirect tax, with political costs that were severe, as we shall see.[31]

Nakasone was also much exercised by problems he identified in the education system, and set up the Ad Hoc Council on Education, normally abbreviated to *Rinkyōshin* in Japanese. There were essentially two elements in Nakasone's unhappiness with the education system and educational practice. One was the fact that the system had been extensively reorganized along American lines during the Occupation, in ways that he considered to go against the grain of Japanese tradition. Secondly, however, and more importantly in terms of the *Rinkyōshin*, he had come to believe that the education system was too uniform in its structures and practices, and lacking in choice. This latter concern was in harmony with his profession of faith in free-market principles, which he thought should be extended to the educational sector. In practice, however, the *Rinkyōshin* turned out to be too closely controlled by the Ministry of Education (*Monbushō*) to recommend radically liberalizing reform.[32]

As is evident from this brief account of major policy issues of the Nakasone Government, the Prime Minister had clear priorities and the will to innovate, he had a certain amount of success in implementing his various programmes, but vested interests and orthodoxies frustrated him at many junctures.

During his tenure of power his party faced two general elections, the first, that of December 1983, for the House of Representatives only, and the second, that of July 1986, for both the House of Representatives and House of Councillors simultaneously. The 1983 elections produced a disappointing result for the LDP, whose seat total was approximately back to the level it had sunk to in 1979. The verdict in the Lockheed scandal trial, against Tanaka Kakuei and others, may have adversely affected the result. Nakasone, however, avoided the problem faced in the 1970s, when certain key parliamentary committees were outside LDP control, by inviting the New Liberal Club (NLC), formed by Kōno Yōhei in the aftermath of the Lockheed revelations in 1976, to join the LDP in a coalition government. Even though the NLC had only eight lower house seats, its adherence was sufficient to give the Government control over all the parliamentary committees. The 1986 elections, however, were a different story from those in 1983. Nakasone was at the height of his popularity, the economy was doing well and, as in 1980, this was a double election, for both houses at the same time.[33] The LDP greatly increased its majority and had its best result for many years. This victory further increased Nakasone's prestige and helped him to rely on a factional power base of his own making, rather than, as initially, relying on the dominant Tanaka faction.

The fortunes of the LDP between its remarkable electoral victory of 1986 and its unexpected defeat in the House of Councillors elections of July 1989 declined to an extraordinary extent. In the remainder of this chapter an attempt will be made to explain why this was so.

The late 1980s in Japan was a time of economic boom, with land prices increasing to wholly unreasonable levels, in part because companies were buying up urban land and using it as security for bank borrowing. It was a time of increasing difficulty in the economic relationship between Japan and the United States, as the US put pressure on Japan to open markets further and threatened retaliation against Japanese products in the American market if barriers to imports into Japan remained intact. Some well publicized Japanese investments and purchases of well-known American companies and institutions fuelled the flames of anti-Japanese feeling in the US. The period saw a new sort of literature about Japan written by Americans or for the American market, claiming that Japan worked to different rules from the rest of the non-Communist world, and that the Japanese economy increasingly represented a threat to American interests. The principal authors representing what came to be called a 'revisionist' approach to the understanding of Japan, Clyde Prestowitz, Karel van Wolferen, James Fallows and Chalmers Johnson, in fact had widely divergent views and concerns, but they were united in criticizing what they saw as American complacency with regard to Japan.

Certainly, under the influence of the apparently invincible strength of the Japanese economy in the late 1980s, American official attitudes towards Japan were toughening, and among the concessions wrung out of the Japanese Government by American pressure was an agreement to lift import restrictions on beef and citrus products. Coupled with intensive pressure, associated with the negotiations for the Uruguay Round of the GATT, for Japan to permit imports of rice for direct consumption,[34] beef and citrus liberalization caused great disquiet among farmers and their organizations, which had always been the bedrock of electoral support for the LDP outside the principal cities.

The internal situation with the LDP was also changing, with important effects upon its fortunes. In February 1985, Tanaka Kakuei, whose appeal against the Lockheed verdict brought down against him in 1983 was still pending, suffered a stroke, which effectively put him out of politics. As leader of much the largest and most powerful faction in the LDP, his retirement created a vacuum of power within the party. After a good deal of manoeuvring one of Tanaka's principal lieutenants, Takeshita Noboru, took over the bulk of the Tanaka faction, though a minority of members would not follow him, and apparently he did not have Tanaka's blessing. The weakening thus caused to the party's kingmaker faction conversely strengthened Nakasone, who thereby became less dependent upon the former Tanaka faction, and could make appointments with less concern for the interests and preferences of that faction. He was thus able to fight the double elections of July 1986 as a domestic leader now fully established in his own right and experienced as an international statesman on the world stage. The election results were, as we have seen, extremely favourable for the LDP, and this positively contributed to his being granted by the party an extra one year extension to his party presidency and thus prime ministership. Thus reinforced, he felt able to propose taxation reform in February 1987 but, as was outlined above, the proposal created a serious electoral backlash, mainly from small businessmen, who, second only to farmers, were normally staunch supporters of the LDP, so that the proposal was later (May 1987) withdrawn.

In November 1987, Nakasone finally stepped down as Prime Minister[35] and was replaced by Takeshita Noboru. Takeshita was not an internationally known politician as Nakasone had become, but as leader of the largest faction in the LDP, a faction which had been able to exercise a determining role in the distribution of power within the party, he should have been well able to consolidate his position as Prime Minister. Indeed, though the Tanaka (now Takeshita) faction had occupied a kingmaking position within the LDP for several years, it had not, because of Tanaka's problems with the courts, held the top job since Tanaka's resignation in 1974.

A combination of events, however, were to frustrate his longevity as Prime Minister. The alienation of the farming population because of the lifting of protection against foreign imports of beef and citrus fruits has already been mentioned. In addition, however, Takeshita tempted fate by grasping the nettle of taxation reform, which had been briefly held, but later dropped, by his predecessors Ōhira and Nakasone. After much deliberation a 'consumption tax' (*shōhizei*) of 3 per cent was scheduled to be introduced on 1 April 1989. Even though in devising this new tax, an attempt had been made to iron out objectionable features of the two proposals which preceded it,[36] it immediately excited intense opposition, particularly from housewives and representatives of small businesses. Nevertheless, unlike the two previous attempts to shift the emphasis of the system of taxation away from direct taxes towards indirect taxes, the third attempt succeeded, and the consumption tax was duly introduced on the announced date.

In the summer of 1988, reports began appearing in the media about a company called Recruit, which was allegedly distributing shares of a newly floated subsidiary, Recruit Cosmos, in an illegal fashion to large numbers of politicians and others. The most important business operation of the Recruit Co. Ltd, was that of matching job opportunities with job seekers, particularly with students in their final year of university. There was evidence that the company had exercised influence in order to obtain some examination results before they were officially announced, with the purpose of informing companies about the qualifications of job seekers ahead of the competition. Apart from this, the gift of unlisted shares of Recruit Cosmos Ltd, to politicians, who would see the value of these shares rise substantially once they were floated on the stock exchange, constituted a technical breach of the law. For several months the media were full of the 'Recruit scandal', to the great discomfiture of many who had accepted the gifts of shares.

Unlike the Lockheed scandal, which only affected a handful of LDP politicians, the Recruit scandal affected a large proportion of the political class as a whole. The ruling party in particular was affected, though some Opposition politicians had also received the shares.

Meanwhile, some important developments had been taking place among the Opposition parties themselves. It will be recalled that from the late 1960s the JSP (always the largest of the Opposition parties) had been electorally stagnant, and appeared to many observers to be stuck in the memory of past debates, and devoid of new ideas. Early in 1986, however, the then JSP Chairman, Ishibashi Masashi, was able to persuade the party to modernize its platform and issue a new basic policy statement, replacing a document of 1964 entitled 'The Road to Socialism in Japan'. The former document was replete with Marxist vocabulary, and ideas which seemed no longer in keeping with the contemporary situation of Japan. Despite this change, the JSP did badly in the July 1986 double elections, where Nakasone's popularity led to a remarkable result for the LDP.

Ishibashi resigned to take responsibility for the election defeat, and in his stead the party elected Doi Takako, the first woman in Japanese history to lead a political party, to replace him. Although Ms Doi did not have great experience in leadership positions within the party, she succeeded, in the particular political and social conditions of the late 1980s, in establishing a notable rapport with sections of the electorate that did not normally vote Socialist. In 1988–9 she succeeded beyond all expectation in exploiting the boiling discontent that had been developing over beef and citrus liberalization, the consumption tax and the Recruit scandal (as well as over other concerns such as skyrocketing land prices), and the popularity of the JSP grew rapidly, eclipsing that of the smaller Opposition parties, some of whose leaders had become embroiled in the Recruit scandal. In an appeal to the female vote, she introduced a policy of endorsing considerable numbers of women candidates for election, and this also proved popular.

In April 1989 Takeshita, whose popularity as recorded in successive public opinion polls had fallen to single figures, resigned as Prime Minister. He was succeeded by Uno Sōsuke, Takeshita's Foreign Minister, who was quickly implicated in a much publicized sex scandal, which did little to establish his popularity. Fixed-term elections (held every three years) for half the seats in the House of Councillors had to be held in July 1989, but the LDP was plainly not in good shape to contest them. In the elections, the LDP was badly defeated (though since only half the members were being re-elected, it retained its majority). In upper house elections electors cast two votes, one for local (prefecture-level) constituencies, and one for a constituency covering the whole country, in which the results are determined by a system of proportional representation. Whereas the LDP was narrowly ahead of the JSP in terms of votes cast for each party in the prefectural constituencies, the JSP was ahead in the proportional representation constituency.[37] Perhaps the most striking aspects of the results, however, related to rural constituencies. The prefectural consti- tuencies included 26 prefectures (mainly in rural areas) to which only two seats were allocated. Since only half the seats were renewed in any election, these prefectures operated as single member constituencies (elected, of course, on the principle of first-past-the-post).[38] Whereas before the elections the LDP held 24 out of the 26, following the elections their seat total in these constituences had been reduced to three. The JSP had won 12 and the *Rengō* labour federation, contesting elections for the first time, had won 11.

Uno resigned after the elections, and was replaced by Kaifu Toshiki, one of the few Liberal Democrats not implicated in the Recruit scandal. In a momen- tous year for world politics, a new era was about to be adumbrated in Japanese politics as well. But for a while at least, the LDP would be granted a reprieve.

6

Demise of the Old System, Groping Towards the New: The Politics of the 1990s

Eric Hobsbawm's creative notion that there was something called the 'short' twentieth century, lasting from 1914 (the outbreak of the First World War) to 1989 (the ending of the Cold War)[1] might in a sense also be applied to Japan, though in Japanese politics, even more than in international politics, many aspects of the system continued much as before. For Japan, 1989 was a momentous year in terms of leadership, in a symbolic as well as real sense. If 1978 was for the Catholic Church the year of the three Popes, 1989 was for Japan the year of the two emperors and the three prime ministers. The Shōwa *Tennō* [Showa Emperor] (known outside Japan as Hirohito)[2] who had been terminally ill (though this was officially denied) since the previous autumn, died on 7 January 1989. Although the *tennō* under the 1946 Constitution has no political power, the death of the Shōwa *Tennō* was highly symbolic in a nation the great majority of whose people had known no other *tennō* for the whole of their lives. Becoming *tennō* in 1926 (and having been Regent for his incapacitated father for two years before that), he embodied so much of Japan's modern history that his passing was seen by many as a historic turning point. The Shōwa *Tennō* was, of course, a highly controversial figure, as much within Japan as he was abroad,[3] despite official efforts to play down the fact. Indeed, the official management of the final illness and death of the Shōwa *Tennō* forms an interesting study, since different interpretations of both official policies and public reactions are possible. They range from conspiracy-theories holding that officialdom was intent on re-instituting an emperor-cult, to almost equally implausible interpretations that the solemn music, mass signatures of condolence books and restrictions on some of the more garish manifestations of urban bar culture during the mourning period were entirely a natural reflection of popular sadness and dismay at the passing of the Emperor.[4]

The inauguration of the new *tennō*, 55 at the time of his accession, marked a clear break with the past, as indicated by his inauguration speech. Instead of archaic court language he used everyday expressions, addressing his audience as *minasan* (literally, 'everybody', but perhaps best translated as 'Ladies and Gentlemen'), and boldly declared that he supported the post-war Constitution of Japan, which was the only one he had known.[5] It seems unlikely that he would have been permitted to say such a thing had Nakasone still been Prime Minister. Even though court bureaucracy in the 1990s was apparently continuing to inhibit efforts to modernize the *tennō* institution, the fact of having a *tennō* who was essentially post-war-educated gave a quite different feel to the *tennō* institution.

The three prime ministers who came in quick succession during 1989 were, as we have seen, Takeshita, Uno and Kaifu. Like Suzuki nearly a decade earlier, Kaifu was an individual who would never have been considered for the party presidency and thus prime ministership had it not been for wholly exceptional circumstances. In Kaifu's case it was the discrediting of so many senior political leaders by the Recruit affair, that made it imperative that the party find a 'clean' leader, at least before the dust settled and things could return to normal. Kaifu was a second-ranking member of the smallest faction in the LDP, namely the faction led by Kōmoto Toshio, an elderly former shipping executive (Kōmoto had inherited the leadership of the Miki faction). He had had some ministerial experience (notably as Minister of Education) but not in senior posts. He became Prime Minister, therefore, with hardly any power base of his own and with less experience than would normally be required for the position. His advantages, on the other hand, were that he enjoyed the support of the Takeshita faction, and that he had avoided the problems caused for so many other LDP leaders by having accepted shares from Recruit.

In constructing his first Cabinet, Kaifu included two women, in a clear attempt to counter the appeal to women of the JSP under Doi Takako. Indeed, for his first few months in office he was clearly making a rather favourable impression on the electorate, and the JSP was failing to maintain the level of support which it had obtained in the July elections for the House of Councillors. There is evidence that the *Nōkyō* (Agricultural Co-operative Association) – the main organization representing farmers' interests – having in many parts of the country advised its members to vote against the LDP as a protest against the lifting of protection for beef and citrus fruits, was now returning to its normal conservative loyalties. It knew that it could in this way punish the LDP at an upper house election, since the House of Councillors did not determine the composition of a government.[6]

General elections were held for the House of Representatives on 18 February 1990. Any predictions, based on the 1989 debacle in the Upper House, that the LDP might lose its parliamentary majority proved wide of the mark, since the ruling party won a comfortable majority of 275 out of 512 seats, even though a few seats less than the number won in 1986. The Socialists, though they came nowhere near beating the LDP, much improved their position by comparison with 1986, winning 136 seats as against 83 at dissolution. Their percentage of the vote improved by more than seven points over 1986 (24.4 per cent as against 17.2 per cent), much of this being at the expense of the smaller parties. No less than 56 'new faces' were elected, providing an important rejuvenating element in a party which had been dominated by older members. Of the 12 women elected to the lower house – traditionally a male bastion[7] – seven belonged to the JSP (and none to the LDP).

Much the most important international issue, and indeed probably the most important issue of all, which the Kaifu Government had to deal with during its two years in office was the Gulf Crisis and Gulf war of 1990–1. As the first international crisis following the end of the Cold War, it tested the emerging parameters of new international relationships, now that world affairs were not dominated by mutual hostility between the US and the USSR. For Japan, it was a particularly difficult issue to handle for several reasons which we shall now explore. These included the constitutional restraints on sending military contingents overseas, the situation of political flux which was currently being experienced and, in particular, the loss of the LDP majority in the House of Councillors.

Japanese political reactions to the Gulf crisis occasioned much international criticism, and in order to understand what was happening, we need to run through the chronology of events in some detail.

A few days after Iraq invaded Kuwait on 2 August 1990, the Kaifu Government banned all oil imports from Iraq, something which its predecessor had been unwilling to do in 1979 when the Americans imposed an embargo upon Iran. For Japan, this was a substantial cutback, since around 12 per cent of her oil imports originated from Iraq and Kuwait, whereas the 1973 oil crisis had resulted in an oil import cut of only 5 per cent. The situation had changed in that, whereas in 1973 Japan had stockpiled a mere 60 days of oil, now her oil supplies were estimated at 142 days. The Government also froze ¥400 billion-worth of Iraqi assets in Japan.

In mid-August the Prime Minister decided to postpone what would have been the first Middle Eastern tour by a prime minister for 12 years, although his Foreign Minister was to go in his stead. The reason given for postponement was that, with large numbers of Japanese nationals stranded in Iraq and Kuwait, a prime ministerial visit to the region might worsen their plight. At the same time Government officials were being urged by their US counterparts to take financial and political, if not military, steps to assist in the search for a resolution of the Gulf Crisis.

A little later in August Watanabe Michio, Nakasone's successor as head of his faction, suggested that the Government might send a contingent of mine-sweepers to the Persian Gulf. This was an option that had been rejected in 1987, during the Iran–Iraq war, when Nakasone was Prime Minister. At the time of the Watanabe statement, various other options were under consideration, including yen loans to Egypt, Turkey and Jordan, the regional states most severely affected by the conflict, technical assistance to states abutting the Gulf and financial assistance to the UN. No proposals appeared to be coming forward which would involve any participation by the Self-Defence Forces.

On 30 August the Kaifu Government announced a package of $1 billion towards the costs of the multilateral force that was being assembled, and in addition offered to provide civilian aircraft and ships to ferry non-military supplies to the region, as well as to send 100 medical personnel. In any case, it became quickly apparent that President Bush was not satisfied with the scale of the contribution, so that late in September a new package was announced totalling $4 billion, comprising $2 billion to the frontline states (Egypt, Turkey and Jordan), and a further $2 billion towards the expenses of the multinational force.

During October the pace of events quickened, as the Kaifu Government sought to put through Parliament a United Nations Peace Force Co-operation Bill. This would have set up a Peace Co-operation Corps, which would have included personnel from the Self-Defence Forces (SDF). While they were seconded to the Corps, however, they would no longer officially be members of the SDF. Elaborate arrangements were foreshadowed for their management in order to ensure that they should not be confused with serving SDF personnel but that they should nevertheless retain their pension and other rights. Moreover, because of widespread fears both about their safety and about giving the impression that Japan would be sending participants to a war, their functions were to be restricted to such non-combat roles as election monitoring, ceasefire supervision, help with transport, medical activities and telecommunications. They were expected never to be in a position where they could use or threaten the use of force, and they were to be issued only with sidearms for their own protection.

The press speculated that Kaifu was a reluctant participant in the devising and presentation of this bill, that he originally had opposed the incorporation of SDF elements into the Peace Co-operation Corps, and that it was pressure from elements in the LDP more powerful than himself that had forced him into it. In particular, the high profile LDP Secretary-General, Ozawa Ichirō, was said to have persuaded, or forced, him into acceptance.

In any case the evident contradictions and absurdities of this bill brought a torrent of criticism from those whose co-operation was essential if the bill were to pass through the House of Councillors, where the LDP now lacked a majority in its own right. The Democratic Socialist Party (DSP) and especially the *Kōmeitō* were critical, and even some in the LDP were unenthusiastic. The *Asahi Shinbun* published the results of a questionnaire it had administered to members of the House of Representatives. Of the 181 (65 per cent) LDP parliamentarians who replied, only 115 supported the bill. A higher proportion would have supported a bill despatching SDF personnel (rather than quasi-non-SDF personnel), provided they would not be involved in the exercise of military force.[8] Public opinion was also highly critical of the Government's performance, as can be seen from a public opinion poll administered early in November (see table 6.1).

As can be seen from this poll, the public still had grave doubts about the desirability or propriety of 'overseas despatch', in whatever form, was unhappy about co-operating with a basically American military venture, but was relatively positive about sending financial aid to the frontline states.

On 8 November the bill was withdrawn, the announcement being made at a meeting of the secretaries-general of the LDP, JSP, *Kōmeitō* and DSP. There followed a series of meetings between the parties at which a substitute proposal was discussed, for the establishment of a peacekeeping organization which

Table 6.1   *Asahi* telephone poll, 3 and 4 November 1990 (*n* = 1500).

Do you support overseas despatch of the SDF?	
Support conditionally	15%
Oppose	78%
Do you support overseas despatch of a basically civilian peace co-operation organization?	
Support	30%
Oppose	54%
Do you support the UN Peace Co-operation Bill?	
Support	21%
Oppose	58%
Do you think that the overseas despatch of the SDF is in accordance with the Constitution?	
Constitutional	15%
Unconstitutional	67%
Do you support the Government's decision to send $2 billion to the 'frontline states' (Egypt, Turkey, Jordan)?	
Support	45%
Oppose	39%
Do you agree with the Government's policy hitherto of co-operating with the US, which is the core element in the multinational force?	
Agree	27%
Oppose	56%
Do you think that Mr Kaifu has adequately performed his prime ministerial role in the Middle Eastern crisis?	
Yes	19%
No	69%
Do you support the Kaifu Cabinet?	
Yes	33%
No	50%

Source: *Asahi Shinbun*, 6 November 1990.

would be completely separate from the SDF. The JSP soon withdrew from these discussions, a decision which later events were to suggest was a serious mistake. The three remaining parties were able to come together on an agreement in principle that Japan would provide financial and material assistance to the UN, as well as personnel within the constraints of article 9 of the Constitution. Japan would set up a force separate from the SDF to assist UN-sponsored peacekeeping operations, as well as humanitarian and disaster relief activities.

Towards the end of 1990 public discussion of the Gulf Crisis was focused to a large extent on the hostages issue, as well as on the attempts to keep the Japanese Embassy in Kuwait open against Iraqi pressure. A succession of politicians visited Baghdad with a view to persuading Saddam Hussein to release his Japanese 'guests of the Iraqi Government'.[9] Even after the UN made 15 January 1991 its deadline for Iraqi withdrawal from Kuwait, there seems to have been a widespread expectation in Japan that Saddam Hussein, as a practitioner of real-politik, though he might indulge in brinkmanship, would at least effect a last-minute withdrawal, thus demonstrating that multinational pressure short of actual war would bring a peaceful solution to the crisis.

When such an expectation was dashed by the intransigence of Saddam Hussein, the reaction of the Japanese political system was notably more urgent and co-ordinated that it had been the previous autumn. Without delay, an additional $9 billion was pledged to the multinational peacekeeping efforts in the Gulf, making a total of $13 billion. By any standards this was a large sum of money, and Japan ended up paying a large part of the total cost of the expedition. President Bush's cool reaction of the previous autumn was replaced by a response from the President which seemed genuinely grateful.

Even so, the Kaifu Government still faced a potentially serious obstacle. For the bill to become law it had to pass both houses, but the LDP was substantially short of a majority in the House of Councillors. If the bill was to pass the upper house as well as the lower, it was absolutely essential that the *Kōmeitō* should vote for it. If it failed to pass the upper house, that house's veto could only be overruled by a two thirds majority of the House of Representatives, which the LDP did not have, and probably never would. The *Kōmeitō*, however, was not happy with the proposals that the Government was making for raising the revenue necessary to pay the extra $9 billion. The Government proposed to increase the levels of taxation on certain items, such as company tax and tax on cigarettes, as well as by floating bond issues (a practice that had been rejected by the more austere governments of the early 1980s). The Kaifu Government wished to avoid reducing any items of Government expenditure, whereas the *Kōmeitō* insisted that some compensatory reduction in Government spending be brought about, including a reduction in the defence budget, and resisted the proposed increase in cigarette tax. Negotiations took place in which a compromise was reached, based on token reductions in defence and other Government expenditure, more modest increases in taxation and a smaller bond issue.

Despite the more co-operative atmosphere induced by the fact that war had actually broken out, the Kaifu Government found itself embroiled in another controversy of its own making. It now proposed to send five C140H transport aircraft to help with the transport of refugees in the region. These are military, not civilian, aircraft, and the Government's justification for this apparent breach of the Constitution-derived ban on overseas despatch was a clause in article 100 of the Self-Defence Force Law which had been drawn up quite specifically to provide for the use of SDF planes to carry visiting VIPs from place to place within Japan when there was thought to be a security risk. Speaker after speaker from the opposition benches waxed eloquent about the inappropriateness of using such a narrowly designed clause as precedent-setting leverage to prize open the Constitutional ban on overseas despatch. The Gulf war was over before this issue was resolved, and in the meantime some private – mainly religious – groups actually chartered private aircraft to help in the transport of refugees.[10]

The final episode in the story occurred in April 1991, when the Kaifu Government managed to obtain parliamentary approval for the despatch of minesweepers to the Gulf. The decision met with predictable opposition, but was justified in terms of an argument that the purpose of their despatch was peaceful, not military, and therefore not in breach of article 9. It did, however, represent a breach with precedent, in that previously vessels of the Maritime Self-Defence Forces (MSDF) were sent overseas only for ceremonial visits to foreign ports or for participation in joint exercises with the US Navy.

The ways in which the Kaifu Government attempted to deal with problems posed for it by the Gulf crisis and war have been treated in some detail, because it seems clear in retrospect that they had crucial short-term and medium-term effects on the development of political change in the 1990s. The effects, however, are far from easy to summarize and appear to some extent contradictory.

The first effect which we should concentrate on is the impact of the loss of the LDP's majority in the House of Councillors at the 1989 upper house elections. As we have suggested earlier, the difficulties created for the Kaifu Government by these elections are an underestimated but absolutely crucial key to understanding the Japanese Government's behaviour. Without a majority in the House of Councillors, an LDP Government lacking a two-thirds majority in the House of Representatives is only able to pass its bills into law (apart from the budget and treaties) if it can persuade other parties to join it in support of its legislation and thus create a composite majority. The debacle of October–November 1990, when the Government had to withdraw its UN Peace Force Co-operation Bill, occurred principally because it lacked an upper house majority, and failed to persuade the *Kōmeitō*, which held the balance of power in that house, to back the bill. From that time on, however, the *Kōmeitō* (and also the DSP, though with some differences of emphasis) began to come round to the Government's position. Although the *Kōmeitō* naturally extracted a political price for its support, that party was the essential element in ensuring the success of the $9 billion package once the war had begun.[11]

A key actor in this process was the Secretary-General of the Kaifu Government, Ozawa Ichirō, who will be encountered again later in this chapter. Being acutely aware of the stakes involved, and determined that Japan should play an international role consistent, so far as possible, with its economic size and importance, Ozawa entered into extensive negotiations with the leadership of the *Kōmeitō*, from which it became apparent to him that the *Kōmeitō* was unhappy with the performance of Suzuki Shunichi, Governor of Tokyo Prefecture since 1979, who had been elected already for three four-year terms with both LDP and *Kōmeitō* support. At Ozawa's initiative, therefore, the LDP abandoned its support for the octogenarian Suzuki, and gave its backing to another candidate in the elections scheduled for 7 April 1991. Suzuki, however, being of a feisty disposition, refused to withdraw his candidacy, stood as an independent, and went on to humiliate his LDP-backed rival, as well as all other candidates. Ozawa promptly resigned as LDP Secretary-General to take responsibility for this debacle, but he had performed a signal service to his Prime Minister in bringing the *Kōmeitō* on to the side of the Government in relation to the approval of a huge financial contribution to the operation in the Persian Gulf. In the longer term this was also significant in consolidating links between Ozawa and the *Kōmeitō* (as well as the DSP), which would become of great future importance.

Even more striking than the Kaifu Government's ultimate policy success (which was in any case heavily qualified)[12] was the adverse electoral effect of the Gulf Crisis and war upon the JSP. By mid-1991 the JSP appeared to have fallen to levels of support reminiscent of the elections of 1986 rather than of 1989 or even of 1990. The Party's handling of the Gulf Crisis and war cost it even more dearly than it cost the Kaifu Government. Despite public opinion polls which, as we have seen, showed a majority against most of the Government proposals for participation in, or contribution to, peacekeeping activities, the hard line taken by the JSP against all such proposals (and its refusal to negotiate with other parties) struck a discordant note with the electorate. The popular leader of the party, Doi Takako, the first woman to lead a Japanese political party, and a major celebrity in 1989, saw her popularity fade in 1990–1 as she continued to reject as unconstitutional any sort of participation in effective peacekeeping.[13] The competence of the leadership came into serious question when it proved incapable of picking a credible candidate for the Tokyo governorship elections in April. The candidate chosen, late in the day, won less than 7 per cent of the vote and trailed even behind the Communist candidate.

When we examine the effects of the Gulf Crisis on Japanese politics, we come up against multiple contradictions. The political and bureaucratic performance of the Kaifu Government became the target of much international and domestic criticism, even though *in the end* Japan provided $13 billion – a huge sum – to the operation. It failed in its attempt to provide a real physical contribution in terms of personnel on the ground. But at the same time it went some way towards nullifying the LDP loss of its House of Councillors majority by bringing the *Kōmeitō* (and DSP) rather provisionally into the camp of its allies. This alliance, however, had sown the seeds of the LDP split which was to lead to its downfall in August 1993, when it was to lose office to a multiparty coalition. In retrospect it is evident that LDP dominance had always relied on essential exclusivity, but when parties outside the fold had to be given a say in policy in order that the LDP remain able to function as an effective policy-making body, the structure risked becoming fragile and even collapsing.[14]

So far as the JSP was concerned, its resurgence in the late 1980s with Doi Takako as leader had previsaged an evolution of the political system away from single-party dominance, but its credibility had been sorely damaged by the uncomfortable exposure of its negative attitudes in the Gulf Crisis. Even so, in retrospect we can see that the shaking up of long-standing expectations caused by the ending of the Cold War and the Gulf Crisis that so quickly followed this, had created a situation in which both the JSP and the newly reorganized labour union movement, as well as the Buddhist-based *Kōmeitō*, were potential allies in alternative government-coalition arrangements. There is a further irony in respect of the JSP, however, namely that though it was incorporated into government in 1993, and remained part of a government coalition for all but nine weeks of the period August 1993 to October 1996 (even providing the prime minister for more than 18 months of that period), yet the ultimate result of its excursion into government was to be its virtual collapse.

In November 1991 Kaifu resigned as Prime Minister. Having a weak power base within the LDP, he had always occupied the position at the pleasure of other factions, and notably the powerful Takeshita faction. The occasion of his resignation, however, was an attempt to reform the electoral system of the House of Representatives. Reform of the electoral system was a recurrent theme of party and parliamentary politics, for several interconnected reasons which we shall explore in more detail in chapter 8. The changes proposed in 1991 – a mixed system of single-member constituency seats and seats elected by proportional representation – was not unlike the system ultimately put in place in 1994.

The ostensible arguments for it were to root out corruption, to correct mal-apportionment of votes, and to move from a system of personality voting to one where competition over policy really mattered. In the minds of some, at least, of the reformers was a programme of consolidating LDP (or more broadly, conservative) rule by bringing in a reform wherein multi-member constituencies would disappear and single-member constituencies (in which the LDP was likely to be strong) would predominate.

However this may be, the proposed reform was used as a pretext for ending the prime ministership of Kaifu. It was now generally accepted in the Party that sufficient time had elapsed for memories of the Recruit scandal to have faded, and for the many LDP leaders implicated to have purged their offences. The new Prime Minister was Miyazawa Kiichi, leader of the faction that had produced the Prime Ministers Ikeda, Ōhira and Suzuki, a former official of the Ministry of Finance, one of the few Japanese politicians who had near total fluency in English, and in policy preferences a centrist.

In retrospect it seems ironic that a man with such impressive credentials should have presided over the downfall of the LDP, after nearly 38 years in office, in August 1993.

The Miyazawa Government proved a lacklustre affair, and its last year was punctuated by the emergence of that very fragmentation of the LDP that was to precipitate its fall from office. Nevertheless, the Government had one considerable achievement to its credit, namely the passage through Parliament of the Peace Keeping Operations (PKO) bill in June 1992. Even though it was limited in its scope, and fell far short of unqualified participation by Japan in UN peacekeeping missions, it marks a crucial turning point in the development of Japan's foreign policies towards greater international engagement (See chapter 12).

The question that immediately arises is why the Miyazawa Government succeeded in passing the PKO bill in June 1992, whereas its predecessor failed in a similar endeavour in November 1990. The simple answer to this question is that whereas in 1990 Kaifu did not have the numbers in the House of Councillors, by mid-1992 a coalition of forces had been constructed which gave the Miyazawa Government its required majority. Specifically, the Kōmeitō and the DSP were persuaded to abandon their objections to any Japanese participation in UN peacekeeping operations, and to vote for the bill. Behind this, however, lie two crucial factors. The first was the fact that the Gulf War had intervened and Japan had received an uncomfortable measure of international opprobrium for her failure to send substantial contributions other than financial. Public opinion had consequently swung round in favour of the new bill. A poll conducted in September, at the time when Japan sent a contingent to the UN peacekeeping mission in Cambodia, showed 52 per cent support for this operation and 36 per cent opposition.[15] The second factor was a history which we have already touched on, in which Ozawa Ichirō was a major player. Using the foreign pressure upon Japan to contribute to the expeditionary force to the Gulf, he did deals with the two aforementioned parties so as to restore the Government's upper house majority (at least on this particular set of issues). But crucially, in so doing, he was also able to sow the seeds of a cross-party political relationship that was to change the face of Japanese politics from 1993.

Meanwhile the JSP seems to have further alienated the electorate by practising its time-honoured *gyūho* ('cow-walking') tactic, whereby Socialist parliamentarians walked with deliberate slowness through the voting lobbies. In the regular three-yearly elections for half the seats in the House of Councillors, held the following month, the JSP only won 22 seats, as against 69 won by the LDP.[16]

By far the most important party political event to occur in 1992 was the split in the hitherto dominant Takeshita faction of the LDP. A precipitating factor was the political disgrace of the faction's effective leader, Kanemaru Shin. The most important of several financial scandals aired in the press during the year, was that involving a road delivery company called Sagawa Kyūbin. In September Kanemaru – a politician famous for a traditional style of political manipulation – admitted breaking the Political Contributions Control Law (*Seiji shikin kisei hō*) and paid a 200,000 yen fine. Previously the police had raided his house and discovered a huge cache of money, including gold bars. There was a public outcry at the derisory value of the fine, given the magnitude of the offence. Kanemaru resigned all his political offices, including headship of the Takeshita faction, and resigned his parliamentary seat in October. In November Takeshita himself was called upon to testify before Parliament in relation to a curious case whereby in 1987 he had allegedly had contacts with a gangster organization (*bōryokudan*).[17] These cases shook the faction to the core, and brought into relief existing strains within it over its future leadership. In December, Hata Tsutomu and Ozawa set up a breakaway group, known as Reform Forum 21. About half the Takeshita faction joined this group and the rest coalesced around a more orthodox leader, Obuchi Keizō.

Two further events occurred during 1992 that were to feed in to the floodtide of change that came rushing in during the summer of the following year. The first was the formation of a completely new party (as distinct from parties formed by splinter groups from existing parties), entitled *Nihon Shintō*[18] (Japan New Party or JNP), in mid-1992. The party's founder was Hosokawa Morihiro, who was to become one of the most significant politicians of the 1990s. Hosokawa, who some years previously had been an LDP member of the House of Councillors, was currently Governor of Kumamoto Prefecture in Kyūshū, the most south-westerly of Japan's four main islands. His maternal grandfather was Prince Konoe Fumimaro, Prime Minister immediately before the Pacific war, and even though the country had lacked an aristocracy since the Occupation abolished it (apart from immediate relatives of the *tennō*), Hosokawa's aristocratic background was seized upon in certain sections of the mass media as a fresh and attractive feature in the staid and stolid world of party politicians. The newly formed *Nihon Shintō* won four seats in the House of Councillors elections held in July 1992.

The second development was the foundation in November by Eda Satsuki, head of the minor party called *Shaminren*, of a 'study group' called 'Sirius', consisting of 27 parliamentary members from the JSP, *Shaminren* and the *Rengō* union contingent in the upper house. Sirius was in a direct line of descent from the New Wave Society, referred to above. The establishment of Sirius created a force on the moderate left which was favourable to the kinds of reforms which came on to the agenda with the formation of a new government in August 1993.

As an unsettling, but also opportunity-creating, backdrop to the developments that were to unfold in 1993 we should not ignore either the state of the economy or the radical changes that were taking place in the international system. There is no space to go into these in detail, but a brief note of the general relevance of each needs to be made.

In the late 1980s the Japanese economy had experienced boom conditions, leading to asset inflation, severe trade frictions with the United States, and what turned out in retrospect to be unwise investment decisions by banks, funds of various kinds and companies. In 1991 the 'bubble economy', as the mass media soon came to call it, collapsed and the economy entered a period of relative stagnation, with barely positive growth rates – a situation that was to last for several years. This led to the need for painful economic adjustment and a readiness to question existing institutions and practices – particularly the role of government ministries – which in turn created an atmosphere in which political reform came to seem attractive. The seemingly unstoppable flow of media reports detailing allegedly corrupt linkages between businessmen, national and local politicians and (increasingly, later in the decade) government officials, was also no doubt linked with economic fluctuations and uncertainties, and it fed into a spreading view that the *system* needed to be looked at more critically than hitherto.

The period 1989–91 saw the most far-reaching changes in international politics since the late 1940s. So far as Asia was concerned, the changes were less profound than for Europe (see chapter 12), but for Japan the removal to all intents and purposes of the Soviet threat to her north created a situation with altered parameters. This was important for political change in one crucial respect: the domestic political divide which had closely mirrored themes from the Cold War was coming to an end (though it had not completely ended by 1993), and this also permitted the shaping of new forms of political alliance. There was now, for instance, much less inhibition about having moderate labour unions as part of the ruling structure.

The immediate issue which brought about the downfall of the LDP was electoral law reform. The Miyazawa Government had put forward proposals for a lower house electoral system based entirely upon single-member constituencies, with candidates elected according to the principle of first-past-the-post. This was countered by a proposal from the JSP and *Kōmeitō* close to the German system, giving a heavy emphasis to proportional representation. Attempts at compromise made little headway, and in June the Government announced that it was shelving its proposals. Events moved fast from that point on.

All the non-Communist opposition parties combined to put forward a no-confidence motion in the Miyazawa Government, and on 18 June a vote on the motion was taken in the House of Representatives. Miyazawa's attempts to win over the Hata-Ozawa group failed, and 39 LDP members, including 34 from this group, voted in favour of the motion, while a further 16 deliberately absented themselves from the voting.[19] The Government had no choice but to dissolve Parliament. Over the following few days, not one, but two groups of LDP parliamentarians decided to form new parties, outside the LDP. On 21 June, a small party was formed under the leadership of Takemura Masayoshi, and inclined to the centre-left on a number of policy issues. It called itself the

Shintō Sakigake (New Harbinger Party) [henceforth *Sakigake*] and comprised 10 former members of the LDP. The second party was formed two days later by the Hata-Ozawa group itself, consisting of 44 former LDP parliamentarians (from both houses), and chose the name *Shinseitō* (Renewal Party) [henceforth *Shinseitō*]. In these confused circumstances a general election for the House of Representatives was held on 18 July 1993, and the LDP, for the first time since its foundation in 1955, found itself well short of a majority.[20]

An important factor behind the collapse of LDP rule seems to have been the complacency of the Miyazawa Government, no doubt born of long years in office. There appears to have been an assumption that even if groups defected from the party, it would still be possible to persuade them to enter a coalition government of which the LDP would be the leading party. The LDP desperately attempted to construct such a coalition in the days following the election, but was frustrated by the adroitness with which the other non-Communist parties were able to put together a coalition government of their own.

A new eight-party coalition government was formed on 9 August 1993, excluding the Communists and the LDP, whose uninterrupted reign of nearly 38 years was thus brought to an end. The Prime Minister was Hosokawa Morihiro, who, along with the other members of his *Nihon Shintō* had been elected to the House of Representatives only the previous month. A new start seemed possible for the political system, which had become so discredited by the endless stream of corruption allegations throughout the previous years.

The parties participating in the Hosokawa Government, in order of lower house strength, may be read off from table 6.2.

It will be observed from table 6.2 that the JSP, though it was the largest party in the coalition government, had suffered a stunning defeat at the elections, losing nearly half its seats. By any measure it had outperformed the LDP in the comprehensiveness of its electoral reverse, but by the irony of strategic numbers the JSP found itself in government for the first time in nearly 45 years. Its period

Table 6.2 Composition of the Hosokawa Government.

	Seats	*% of total vote*
Government parties		
JSP	70	15.4
Shinseitō	55	10.1
Kōmeitō	51	8.1
JNP	35	8.0
DSP	15	3.5
Sakigake	13	2.6
Shaminren	4	0.7
(In addition the *Minkairen*, having representation in the House of Councillors, participated in the Hosokawa Government)		
Independents	30	6.9
Opposition parties		
LDP	223	36.6
JCP	15	7.7

Source: *Asahi Shinbun*, 19 July, 8 August 1993 (evening).

in office (with one short break) over the next three years was not to be a happy one.

It is hardly surprising that the leadership of the LDP should have been sceptical about the ability of the other non-Communist parties to coalesce into a coalition, and it required skill and foresight on the part of a number of individuals to create such an unlikely arrangement. Prominent among them were Ozawa Ichirō, Hosokawa Morihiro, Yamahana Sadao and Yamagishi Akira.

It is probably correct to say that Ozawa was the most important strategic thinker and actor in the process of constructing the Hosokawa coalition Government. He had a vision of reform and the political skill to put together the political arrangements necessary for its realization. In the summer of 1993 it was clearly Ozawa who had the initiative, as is clearly seen by the fact that it was his own newly formed *Shinseitō* that took the lion's share of key positions in the new Cabinet.[21] Hosokawa was essential to the new Government in terms of the image he was able to project of a new kind of politician leading a new party formed from outside the political Establishment. The JSP Chairman Yamahana was important in that he was committed to the idea of Socialist participation in the coalition and was able to deliver on this commitment. The JSP, after all, despite its disastrous election, was the largest party to participate, and the coalition could not have been formed without it. One interesting innovation was that Ms Doi Takako, the former Chair of the JSP, became the first woman President (Speaker) of the House of Representatives. Yamagishi had created the *Rengō* union federation, whose most vital function was to bring together the previously divided union movement. This in turn created the conditions for reconciling the JSP and the DSP – previously backers of rival union federations – and allowing them to coexist in the same coalition.

Unfortunately, as we shall see, all these leaders turned out to have inherent weaknesses, and their schemes ultimately could not hold.

The Hosokawa Government began with an astonishingly high level of popularity, and the Prime Minister recorded an unprecedented 71 per cent support in early public opinion polls.[21] A programme of apparently radical reforms was quickly announced, covering reform of the lower house electoral system, anti-corruption legislation, proposals for substantial deregulation of industry, commerce and banking, and for the devolution of some central government functions to local authorities. There was, initially at least, a degree of coherence in these proposals taken as a whole. In the terms put forward by Ozawa, the key strategist of the Government in its early stages, Japan ought to be run by politicians responsible to the electorate rather than by unelected elitist bureaucrats, truly competitive party politics (he preferred the two-party alternating model) should replace dominance by a single party, an overregulated economy should be radically deregulated, and the individual endeavour of ordinary people should be encouraged. More power should be given to local regions and local authorities, at the expense of central control by government ministries. In order to achieve a politics of competition between parties over matters of policy, to replace the politics of factions, money politics and personality voting, the electoral system should be radically restructured. In foreign policy, according to Ozawa, Japan ought to evolve into a 'normal state' possessed of the right to defend itself, and the means to do so.[23]

It was, however, not entirely surprising that as a rather shaky coalition of seven parties and one upper house political grouping, the Hosokawa Government should prove to contain diverse views on the desired direction of reform. Trouble emerged early within the ranks of the JSP, at whose September Congress the party Chairman, Yamahana Sadao, one of the chief architects of the coalition, was forced to assume responsibility for the poor JSP showing at the July elections by stepping down as Chairman. (Importantly, however, he retained his Cabinet post as Minister without portfolio in charge of electoral system reform.) Whereas Yamahana, broadly speaking, represented the right wing of the party, his successor, a 70-year-old politician from Ōita in Kyūshū, Murayama Tomiichi, was identified with the left.

For Hosokawa, who had declared shortly after taking office as Prime Minister that he would take responsibility (that is, resign) if the reform package were not passed by the end of 1993, the attempt to reform the electoral system for the lower house was to prove a particular burden. We shall cover the details of the successive reform proposals in chapter 8, but here it will suffice to summarize what happened in broad outline.

Reforming the electoral system was not something that could be done without taking the views of the LDP into account, but views predominating within the LDP were incompatible with those widely held on the left wing of the JSP, on which the Prime Minister was dependent if he wished to maintain his majority. The reform announced in August 1993 proposed an equal number of seats to be filled by first-past-the-post in single-member constituencies and seats to be filled by proportional representation (i.e. 250 and 250). Whereas the LDP (and indeed elements within the coalition) wanted the bulk of seats to be in local, single-member districts, there was strong support in the JSP for maximum emphasis to be placed on proportional representation. Similarly in respect of proposed anti-corruption legislation, a spectrum of opinion existed concerning its desired severity, with a relatively relaxed regime preferred within sections of the LDP, but rigorous measures against business-based 'money politics' most strongly supported in the more left-wing parts of the coalition.

A compromise package was with difficulty agreed in mid-November 1993 between the Prime Minister and the recently elected President of the LDP, Kōno Yōhei, and passed the House of Representatives on 18 November, based on 274 single-member seats and 226 proportional representation seats.[24] Two months later, however, the same package was defeated in the House of Councillors, with 17 JSP members voting against it and three being absent. There were also five LDP votes in favour. A few days later, Doi Takako, President of the House of Representatives, negotiated a compromise proposal between Hosokawa and Kōno, the essence of which was a system based on 300 single-member, first-past-the-post seats, and a further 200 elected from 11 regional constituencies by proportional representation. The proposed legislation passed a joint session of both houses on 29 January 1994.[25]

If divisions within the JSP had been the principal 'problem' within the coalition Government hitherto, strains between other of its constituent parties were now appearing. In particular it was widely reported in the press that relations between Ozawa and the *Sakigake* leader Takemura Masayoshi, the Chief Cabinet Secretary, had deteriorated. Moreover, while the press in 1993 had been reporting that Hosokawa's *Nihon Shintō* and Takemura's *Shintō Sakigake* were so close in spirit that a merger between them was likely, in February 1994 the Prime Minister, pressured by the Ministry of Finance, moved unilaterally to increase the level of consumption tax from 3 to 7 per cent, and when Takemura as Chief Cabinet Secretary strongly objected, he attempted, unsuccessfully, to reshuffle his Cabinet so as to remove Takemura from his post. At this juncture there appeared to be a close political alignment between Hosokawa and Ozawa in favour of vigorous policies of economic and financial reconstruction regardless of the objections of vested interests. The Prime Minister in retrospect placed great emphasis on his achievement in December 1993 of relaxing the previous total ban on rice imports for direct consumption as the price of signing up to the Uruguay Round of global trade liberalization. Reducing the power of the agricultural lobby in favour of rational market economics fitted closely with his political philosophy.[26]

Despite these difficulties and strains, the Hosokawa Government was expected to survive into the medium term. It therefore came as a great surprise (and was regarded by some reformers as a tragedy), when in April 1994 Hosokawa announced his resignation as Prime Minister, for reasons which remain in part unexplained.[27]

Despite its brief duration and somewhat chaotic character, the Hosokawa Government must be considered one of the most important Japanese governments of recent times. Not only did its formation force the long-ruling LDP into opposition, but it set an agenda of reform across a range of areas, which no subsequent government could easily ignore. It opened up the possibility of alternative kinds of government, and thus in various ways affected and altered prevailing habits of political behaviour. It succeeded, against the odds, in rewriting the lower house electoral law, not, it is true, in such a way as to produce a perfect law (that would have been impossible), but having the effect of shaking up long-standing forms of political activity and organization. Even though early experience with the new law in operation suggests that many early expectations for it have failed to materialize, it may be regarded as one step along the path to more representative and responsible politics than had prevailed before its advent.

The Hosokawa Government did not, of course, measure up to its initial promise, nor was it likely to do so. Government ministries and their officials, after their initial shock at finding they had to deal with a (partially) different set of politicians from those they were used to dealing with, discovered that a set of relatively or completely inexperienced ministers were in many cases easier to manipulate than those from the LDP's pool of 'ministrables'. A programme of reform also gave bureaucrats new things to administer, and since they could choose to a great extent what had to be 'deregulated', they excluded the things that were really important to them. The various parties and personalities in the Government bickered and squabbled a good deal, especially in the later stages, but at the same time they exhibited a determination to set an agenda for reform and embark upon implementing it that had rarely been seen in governments composed of LDP ministers.

The Hosokawa Government was succeeded by a minority administration led by the head of the *Shinseitō*, Hata Tsutomu. It was initially supposed to consist of the same parties that formed the Hosokawa administration, but the JSP quickly pulled out and the *Sakigake* refused to co-operate. The reason for the withdrawal of the JSP was that Ozawa had devised a scheme to unify all the parties of the coalition, *except the Socialists*, into a single party to be called *Kaishin* (Renovation).[28] On the scheme becoming public knowledge, the recently elected JSP Chairman, Murayama, promptly led his party out of the coalition, thus depriving the Hata Government of its parliamentary majority.

The consequences of this episode took most observers by surprise. During the nine weeks (April–June 1994) of the Hata Government, it was permitted to exist by the Socialists and *Sakigake* essentially for the purpose of passing the budget, which had been stalled during the last weeks of the Hosokawa administration. Once the budget passed through Parliament, the coalition leaders engaged in intensive negotiations with leaders of the two parties that had defected, in an attempt to tempt them back into the coalition and restore the Government's majority. This was in vain, however, since the two parties were simultaneously talking with the leadership of the LDP, and on 29 June a new government was announced, combining the LDP, the JSP and *Sakigake*. Although the LDP was much the largest party in the new coalition, the JSP Chairman, Murayama Tomiichi, became Prime Minister and the finance portfolio went to the *Sakigake* leader, Takemura Masayoshi.

The arrangement caused astonishment for a number of reasons. First of all, Japan found itself with a Socialist Prime Minister for the first time since the resignation of Katayama Tetsu in 1948, nearly 45 years earlier. Secondly, the new Prime Minister was from the left wing of his party, and had been little known to the public before he became party Chairman a mere nine months before he found himself as leader of his nation. Surprising as these points were, however, they could easily be explained as part of the price exacted by the Socialists for allowing the Liberal Democrats back into office. Much more surprising was the very fact that the LDP and JSP, sworn political enemies for so many years and apparently far apart in their political ideologies, were now prepared to run a government together. Since the LDP/JSP/*Sakigake* coalition Government was to prove more durable than most had expected, and indeed turned out to be the ruling force in Japan throughout the middle 1990s, we need to dwell a little on the rationale for its formation.

From the point of view of the LDP, deprivation of office had been an extraordinary shock. Since the 1950s the party had woven itself into the fabric of both legislation and administration so seamlessly that to be in opposition was hard to tolerate. The party's appeal had rested to a considerable extent in being able to convince a notably parochial electorate that it was more advantageous to support a party which was at the centre of government, and could therefore deliver material benefits, than to support opposition parties which were only capable of delivering empty rhetoric. To be out of office for a long time, therefore, risked potential disaster at the polls. Moreover, if the forces which had constituted the Hosokawa and Hata governments had been able to consolidate themselves in office, the LDP would have risked further defections as some of its parliamentarians repositioned themselves to 'get with the strength', and the party became thus further weakened.[29] The JSP may have seemed an unlikely bedfellow, but together with the LDP and *Sakigake* it had sufficient numbers for a comfortable majority in both houses, and, since the Cold War ended, the LDP–JSP ideological polarity was no longer so acute (though important differences of policy and emphasis remained). Moreover, some strategists in the LDP seem to have believed that to persuade the JSP to join a coalition with it would ultimately constitute the kiss of death for the JSP.[30] In this they would be proved uncannily perceptive.

The great temptation for the JSP was to be offered the post of Prime Minister, together with other more or less significant cabinet and party positions.[31] In policy terms, the new coalition made more sense than was immediately apparent. During the Hosokawa Government period the JSP (especially its left-wing factions) had become seriously disillusioned with the reformist instincts of Ozawa, and indeed of Hosokawa himself, given that these politicians gave first priority to deregulation and to reducing the influence of vested interests. The strongest traditional base of support for the JSP had always lain in the labour movement, and particularly in those unions whose membership was in the public sector. The old conservative attitudes of excluding labour involvement in decision making had become to some extent eroded with the formation of the *Rengō* union federation at the beginning of the decade, so it was less surprising to find the Socialists co-operating with the Liberal Democrats than it would have been a few years earlier.[32]

Nevertheless, to be in office and to have their own leader as Prime Minister did not provide the rewards that the party may have expected of it, even though Murayama had a number of modest legislative successes.[33] In August 1994, not long after the formation of the Cabinet in June, the Prime Minister announced a drastic revision of some long-standing JSP policies. Henceforth, the Self-Defence Forces would no longer be regarded as unconstitutional, the party would cease to oppose the Japan–US Mutual Security Treaty and would no longer campaign against the compulsory raising of the rising sun flag and the singing of the national anthem, *kimigayo*, in schools.[34] These new policies were endorsed by majority vote at a JSP Congress in September. The fact that the policies were proposed by the leader of the party's left wing no doubt helped their acceptance among those elements in the party most likely to have opposed such tampering with holy writ. Even so, strains within the party were extreme during this period and, as we shall see, it very nearly split apart in January 1995.

After the fall of the Hata Government in June, most of its constituent parties engaged in negotiations to form a single large party in opposition to the Murayama Government. The middle months of 1994 witnessed a kaleidoscopic scene of defections from parties (especially the LDP), the formation of small splinter parties, party amalgamations and, even more significantly, failed attempts at amalgamation. In December 1994, however, a major new party was born, known in Japanese as *Shinshintō* and in English as 'New Frontier Party'.[35] Into it were merged the Democratic Socialist Party (DSP), which split from the JSP in 1960, the *Kōmeitō*, founded in 1964,[36] Hosokawa's *Nihon Shintō* (founded 1992), Ozawa's *Shinseitō*, which split from the LDP in 1993, and the *Jiyū Kaikaku Rengō*, formed late in 1994 by the former Prime Minister Kaifu Toshiki and a handful of defectors from the LDP. Kaifu was elected head of the new party by a wide margin. The *Shinshintō* at the time of its foundation had 178 members in the House of Representatives and 36 members in the House of Councillors.

It was thus much the largest party of opposition (for the first time since the 1950s the JSP had lost that position) but somewhat smaller than the LDP.

Meanwhile, on the government side, the Prime Minister was facing a crisis within his own party, as moves gathered pace to form a new party which would either replace the JSP altogether or else involve the defection of a great part of it. Various names were used to describe the new movement, including 'social-democratic-liberal',[37] and by January 1995 a new party to be led by the former JSP Chairman, Yamahana Sadao, was ready to be launched. On 17 January, however, a quite unexpected event occurred which led to a moratorium on political disputation for several months, and destroyed, for the time being at least, the momentum of the new movement.

The event came to be known as the Great Hanshin-Awaji earthquake.[38] Early in the morning of 17 January a major earthquake hit parts of the city of Osaka, Awaji island and, most severely, the city of Kōbe. The earthquake caused over 6000 deaths, many injuries, and enormous property damage, particularly in the older areas of Kōbe along the harbour front, where the quake was strongest and where fires raged out of control for many hours. A large section of overhead road collapsed, and rail links between the east and west of Japan along the Pacific coast were cut, taking several months to restore. Some thousands of people, many of them elderly, were still living in temporary prefabs in the early months of 1997.

The political impact was complex. On the one hand, as we have seen, Murayama was given a reprieve from the threatened split in his own party. On the other hand, the reaction of the various authorities charged with disaster relief was widely criticized as being slow and badly co-ordinated, and the Government was expected to take at least some of the responsibility for this. In particular, many observers felt that the death toll would have been much lower if a better rescue effort had been mounted more quickly.

This issue became linked with that of political and administrative reform. Many critics argued that political checks and balances, combined with vertically articulated administrative structures having poor horizontal co-ordination, resulted from a system that was badly in need of restructuring. Some ventured to speculate that the current government was not the best equipped to carry out such a task.[39]

Not many weeks had gone by before another disaster, this time man-made, occurred, not in a provincial city but in the central government district of Tokyo. On 20 March several people planted canisters containing the highly toxic sarin gas in underground railway stations and trains. Over 5000 victims were made ill and at least 10 died. Suspicion quickly fell on a religious sect known as *Aum Shinrikyō* (translatable as 'Supreme Truth Religion'),[40] led by a nearly blind heavily bearded guru who went under the name of Asahara Shōkō. The sect, which had many members in Russia as well as in Japan, required total dedication and full-time involvement from its members and apparently commanded for-midable financial resources. It was one of a number of 'new, new religions' that had emerged since the 1970s and 1980s. It came to be accused of a similar, though smaller scale, sarin attack in the city of Matsumoto (Nagano Prefecture) the previous year; the kidnapping in 1989 and (as it later turned out) murder of a lawyer who had been investigating the sect's activities, together with his wife and child; other kidnappings; and the serious but non-fatal shooting of a senior police officer in Tokyo.[41]

This affair became a media sensation, and led to much soul-searching about the goallessness of contemporary society when it was discovered that a number of the sect's leading members were highly educated, having science degrees from leading universities. It also brought to the forefront of the political agenda the relationship between politics and religion (see chapter 11). There was evidence that the sarin gas attack in Tokyo might have been part of a bizarre scheme to mount a *coup d'état*. In any case, in December 1995 the Murayama Government set up a commission to investigate whether a case for the dissolution of the *Aum Shinrikyō* could be made under a controversial 1952 law against 'subversive activities' (*hakai kōdō bōshi hō*). When the commission reported in February 1997, however, its conclusion was that the *Aum* had become so gravely weakened that it no longer constituted a threat.[42]

The *Aum* affair also served to highlight how fundamental religion had become in the struggle for political power between the parties. In July 1995 a regular three-yearly election was held for half the seats in the House of Councillors. In this election the *Shinshintō* won 19 seats more than at the elections three years previously, whereas the LDP won 18 less than the previous time and the JSP also did badly.[43] The key to this result was thought to be the record low turnout of 44.52 per cent, reflecting a trend of alienation from politics and political parties for which there was much other evidence.[44] Central, however, to the electoral strategy of the *Shinshintō* was the impressive electoral organization developed by the former *Kōmeitō*, part, though not all, of which had been absorbed into the new party, as we have seen. The great majority of those who had voted for the *Kōmeitō* had been members of Japan's largest 'new' religion, the *Sōka Gakkai*. Since the motivation to turn out to vote – and to vote 'correctly' – was far higher in the case of *Sōka Gakkai* members than with the general population, the electoral showing of the *Kōmeitō*, and thus subsequently of the *Shinshintō* into which it had been partly absorbed, was much benefited by a low general turnout.[45]

There was a good case for arguing, therefore, that the upper house election results were essentially a perverse result of the low turnout. Although precipitated by the *Aum* crisis, there is little doubt that when the LDP in October 1995 presented a bill to Parliament entitled the Religious Corporate Body Law (*Shūkyō hōjin hō*), this electoral factor was paramount. The LDP attempted to have Ikeda Daisaku, revered head of the *Sōka Gakkai*, testify to Parliament, but this was fiercely resisted by the *Shinshintō*, and a lesser official was brought in to testify instead. Eventually a compromise bill was agreed on, in which the original wording was much watered down.

Two other issues preoccupied politicians during 1995: the effect on economic recovery of currency fluctuations; and the fiftieth anniversary of Japan's defeat on 15 August 1945.

The yen rose during the middle months of 1995 briefly to a rate of about 80 yen to the dollar, causing great difficulties for Japanese exporters and tending to accelerate a tendency for companies to relocate in Southeast Asia and elsewhere where costs were cheaper. Economic growth had been very slow since the collapse of the boom in 1991, but the high value of the yen made economic recovery more difficult and compounded the already widespread disquiet about the economy.

An important aim of the Prime Minister and his party in the early months of 1995 was to persuade Parliament to pass a resolution expressing regret and apology for Japan's actions during the war. After much negotiation, the three parties constituting the coalition Government agreed to a compromise form of wording in which the Liberal Democrats made concessions to the JSP position. The resolution, voted by Parliament on 9 June, fell well short of what many critics of Japan's war record would have liked, but the resolution had a certain symbolic force. This, however, was weakened by the fact that the *Shinshintō* members, disagreeing with its wording, absented themselves *en bloc* from the vote. On 15 August, the Prime Minister made an official statement including the following words: '[Japan] brought great damage and suffering on the peoples of many nations, and particularly on the nations of Asia, by its colonialism and aggression'.[46]

A related issue which came to the fore at this period was that of former so-called 'comfort women' (*ianfu*), from Korea and other (mainly Asian) nations, who had been forced to serve as prostitutes for the Japanese armed forces during the war. As more and more evidence emerged of how widespread and degrading this practice had been, the Government resisted demands for apology and compensation to the women who still survived, maintaining that the issue of compensation had been settled in earlier treaties between Japan and other Asian states. The issue was still causing friction between Japan and (in particular) South Korea in the early months of 1997.

In the later months of 1995 both of the main parties changed their leaders. In September, Kōno Yōhei, who had become party Chairman in the aftermath of the collapse of the Miyazawa Government in 1993, withdraw from the scheduled party leadership contest when it became clear that the Minister for International Trade and Industry, Hashimoto Ryūtarō, would inevitably beat him. Hashimoto, widely seen as a more traditional conservative than the centrist Kōno, easily fought off a challenge from the much younger Koizumi Junichirō (a rare 'Thatcherite' in Japanese politics), and was elected. In December, an election was held for the leadership of the *Shinshintō*, with the election thrown open to any member of the general public willing to pay one thousand yen for the privilege of participating. As a result, Ozawa Ichirō polled about twice as many votes as his opponent, the former Prime Minister Hata Tsutomu, and was easily elected.

Early in January 1996, Murayama stepped down as Prime Minister and was replaced by Hashimoto. There was now a certain sense that both the three-party coalition Government and the main opposition party had new leaders who were the central strategists of the two alternative regimes contending for government office, rather than leaders to some extent peripheral in each case.

Whereas 1995 had seen electoral advances by the *Shinshintō*, its challenge to the LDP lost momentum in 1996, and there were signs that the coalition of parties and very disparate leaders which it contained was beginning to unravel. Politics in the early months of the year were dominated by a Government plan to rescue a number of housing loan companies (the *jūsen*) which were in effect bankrupt as a result of non-performing loans negotiated during the boom period of the late 1980s and early 1990s. This in turn threatened the viability of a number of major banks to which they were indebted. Although the Government's proposal to inject large amounts of taxpayers' money into an ambitious rescue plan created fierce and widespread criticism, the *Shinshintō* in turn found itself unpopular after staging a lengthy sit-in in Parliament in an attempt to block the legislation. Moreover, it became increasingly evident as the year went on that the *Sōka Gakkai* might not automatically support *Shinshintō* candidates at the next lower house elections.

Meanwhile, attempts continued to create a viable political third force on the moderate left. Although negotiations in the latter half of 1995 between the JSP and the *Sakigake* did not ultimately succeed, complicated manoeuvres continued through much of 1996 to form a new party. This eventually emerged, in September, as the *Minshutō* (Democratic Party), which included members from the *Shakai minshutō* (Social Democratic Party – the new name adopted in Japanese by the JSP in January 1996), *Shinshintō*, *Sakigake* and elsewhere. Its leaders included the two brothers Hatoyama (grandsons of Hatoyama Ichirō, who was Prime Minister between 1954 and 1956), and Kan Naoto, who as Minister for Health and Welfare in the first Hashimoto Government early in 1996 had dramatically apologized, on his knees, to the families of haemophiliacs who were victims of transfusions of blood contaminated with the HIV virus during the 1980s. Certain officials in the Ministry were accused of having knowingly supplied contaminated blood, but for a Minister to apologize on behalf of the Ministry in this manner was unusual to say the least. Kan consequently became enormously popular with the electorate, and his involvement in the formation of the *Minshutō* ensured it a degree of success. The contaminated blood issue, and also the *jūsen* rescue, symbolized an important political development, namely that whereas for years corruption had been seen as the province essentially of politicians and businessmen, both corruption and maladministration were now perceived to be occurring also in the government bureaucracy. Government officials now felt themselves to be under redoubled attack from the political reformers.

On 20 October 1996 the first lower house elections were held under the new system. The results will be examined in more detail in chapter 9, but to summarize them in brief: the LDP gained nearly 30 seats, but still fell short of a majority in its own right, *Shinshintō* fell slightly short of its pre-election total, *Minshutō* did respectably but not stunningly well, the SDP, now once again chaired by Doi Takako, suffered its worst ever defeat, and *Sakigake* came close to being wiped out. Meanwhile the Japan Communist Party, which had long refused to join any political grouping or coalition, came close to doubling its representation. Hashimoto formed a minority administration supported by the much reduced SDP and *Sakigake*.

A few weeks after the elections, in December, *Shinshintō* suffered the defection of Hata Tsutomu and a few of his followers. Since the leadership contest a year earlier, relations between Hata and Ozawa had become difficult to manage on either a personal or an ideological level. Hata founded a new party called *Taiyōtō* (the Sun Party). Another small group of *Shinshintō* defectors founded a party called *21 seiki* (21st Century). It seemed plain that the process of party reshuffling was not at an end, but in the early months of 1997 the LDP was vigorously attempting to restore a majority in its own right by tempting either individuals or groups of parliamentarians to join it. This was achieved in early September.

The second Hashimoto Government put forward various programmes of reform, including a substantial liberalization of the Tokyo financial market, so that it could compete on an equal footing with New York and London, a plan to reduce the budget deficit to 3 per cent over a number of years and plans to cut down the number of government ministries. In the eyes of many commentators, however, the Government's real aim was to consolidate its own power by restoring the LDP majority, and if the old system of *yuchaku* (close and corrupting relations between politicians, bureaucrats and business interests) was re-established, the prospects for real reform of the system were dim. Indeed, the principal change effected by the confused politics of the 1990s up to 1998 seemed to be the near disappearance of the political left, rather than genuine system reform. The electorate's increasing alienation from politics seemed understandable.

By the middle of 1997, however, signs were emerging of a new and ironic twist to the political scene. In a series of announcements and proposed measures the Hashimoto Government appeared to be adopting the main points of the reformist agenda put forward by the Hosokawa Cabinet earlier in the decade. Particularly in the field of financial services, the Government announced an ambitious programme of deregulatory reforms, to be accomplished over a period of four years. Evidence was accumulating that the bureaucratic and business worlds were taking these proposals extremely seriously. It seemed like a replay of a game played successfully by the LDP in the past, that of stealing the clothes of the Opposition. Meanwhile, Ozawa and others in the disintegrating *Shinshintō* were working hard for a 'conservative–conservative coalition' (*ho-ho rengō*), though meeting resistance from within the LDP. Hosokawa defected from the *Shinshintō* in June and became, for the time being, an Independent. Hashimoto was re-elected President of the LDP, unopposed, in early September,[47] and in the same month the LDP at last, through defections from other parties, clawed back its independent majority in the House of Representatives. This did not, however, signal the immediate end of the coalition arrangement between the LDP, SDP and *Sakigake*, given that the LDP still needed the support of its two small allies to form a majority in the House of Councillors.

At the end of December 1997 Ozawa announced the dissolution of the *Shinshintō*, which split up into no less than six mini-parties. The next few months were spent in an attempt to forge a new viable party of opposition to the LDP. In April 1998, several *Shinshintō*-successor parties and other minor groups merged with the *Minshutō* to form a party accounting for nearly 100 lower house members. The new party retained the name *Minshutō* and was headed by the popular Kan Naoto. Absent from the new party were various groups backed by the *Sōka Gakkai*, and a small party of close supporters of Ozawa called *Jiyūtō* (Liberal Party).[48]

Japanese politics from the latter half of 1997 was overshadowed by a series of financial crises affecting several East and Southeast Asian nations, and collectively known as the Asian economic crisis. Severe economic effects were felt in Thailand, Malaysia, Indonesia and South Korea, and in Indonesia a near-revolutionary situation developed in the early summer of 1998, leading to the resignation of President Suharto after 32 years in office. Given that the Japanese economy was by far the largest in the region, it was expected that Japan would help its neighbours return to economic health. Japan itself, however, was in severe economic difficulties, which some analysts maintained would become much worse before they improved.[49] Several factors contributed to these difficulties. One was a huge overhang of debt, affecting the financial sector, from the collapse of the bubble. Since the banking sector had been geared to economic expansion and worked on the basis of high debt-to-equity ratios, in an economic recession it was peculiarly vulnerable. Distortions also were caused by the political power of numerous vested interests – for instance, the construction industry – which were able to call upon government protection. Macro-economic management had been generally poor during the 1990s, and, in the face of imminent recession, taxes were actually increased in 1997. Finally, consumer confidence was low, with consumers showing their lack of faith in the future by saving rather than spending.

One symptom of the crisis was a severe fall in the value of the yen, which declined from around 80 yen to the US dollar in 1995, to 145 yen to the dollar by early August 1998. The Hashimoto Government had acted cautiously, though various deregulation plans were initiated. A four-year plan for financial de-regulation (called 'Big Bang', on the British model) was introduced in 1997, in a bid to make Tokyo as a financial centre competitive with New York and London. Whether 'Big Bang' would, as Asher and Smithers argue, turn into 'Big Bankruptcy', remained to be seen.[50] Meanwhile, however, there remained many areas of strength in the 'real' economy, which was highly competitive in many sectors.

On 12 July 1998, the LDP suffered a severe blow in elections for the House of Councillors. Needing to win 60 seats of the 126 contested, simply to maintain its pre-election strength, Hashimoto's party retained only 44 seats, doing particularly badly in the big cities. The main beneficiaries were the Democratic Party of Kan Naoto, the JCP and Independents, leading to comparisons with the LDP defeat in the upper house elections of 1989. Reflecting, no doubt, the anxiety of voters about worsening economic conditions, voting turnout was over 14 percentage points higher than in 1995. Hashimoto promptly resigned, and was replaced as LDP President and Prime Minister by Obuchi Keizō, heir to the Takeshita faction but lacking evident reformist credentials. Though the least popular candidate in the country at large, he scored 225 votes, against 102 for the feisty Kajiyama Seiroku and 84 for the radical Koizumi Junichirō. For Finance Minister he chose the former Prime Minister, Miyazawa Kiichi, already 78 but widely experienced in financial matters. It remained to be seen whether Obuchi's strong factional backing within the LDP would enable him to carry out the drastic measures needed to restore the economy to health, whether vested interests would continue to frustrate reform, or whether the LDP would either split or suffer further electoral defeat, leading to another bout of coalition government. A period of intense debate about politico-economic reform could be expected to continue into the next millennium.

7

The Structure and Process of Central Government: Is Japan a Bureaucratic Polity?

In the previous chapter we have seen how reform of the political (more broadly, politico-economic) system became a central part of the agenda of many politicians and political movements during the 1990s, but how difficult it was proving to implement. One of the problems with the whole process was that there were different – and at times contradictory – understandings of reform, but the theme which tended to dominate discussion was that of deregulation. Advocacy of deregulation presupposed that the economy, and perhaps society as well, were over-regulated, and that government was too inclined to interfere in what ought to be free-market processes.

The assumptions underlying such advocacy reflected the experiences of several major advanced economies from the 1980s, where government controls on various aspects of economic activity had been considerably reduced, taxation levels had been cut back, social services provided by the public sector pared, the power of unions attacked and 'flexible' use of labour encouraged. Government policies in the United Kingdom, the United States, New Zealand, Australia and elsewhere, were a reaction against actual or perceived economic problems stemming from government over-spending and excessive burdens placed on the private sector in the 1960s and 1970s, so that the pursuit of economic efficiency – by ruthless means and extremely inegalitarian policies if necessary – became the watchword of reform in the much changed international atmosphere of the 1980s and 1990s. The collapse of Soviet-style Communism at the beginning of the 1990s gave a further boost to this movement, and led to the extraordinary degree of credence granted to the arguments of the American social critic Francis Fukuyama that the end of Soviet Communism somehow constituted the 'end of history'.[1] The emergence of globalizing tendencies in financial markets and economic transactions of all kinds, as well as the enormous growth of multinational corporations that appeared to lack national loyalties and often to dictate the terms of economic policies pursued by national governments, gave some plausibility to the view that there was basically only one viable model of economic organization. States which ignored the realities of the global market and its imperatives risked creating a sluggish or declining economy with high rates of unemployment and the danger of social unrest.

The question which underlies the argument of this chapter is whether and to what extent Japan constitutes an exception to these prescriptions. Is Japan, in other words, a fundamentally different model, and if so, is it a viable model, principally of course for Japan itself, but also for other political economies in East and Southeast Asia (or elsewhere) which have pursued, or might pursue, policies influenced by Japanese practice?

There seems little doubt that the most commonly given answer to this question when it was asked at the end of the 1980s was to affirm both the difference and the viability of the Japanese model, even though it was widely decried, especially in the United States, for being different, and even threatening. The theme of much so-called 'revisionist' commentary on Japan from the middle 1980s onwards was that Japan played her part in the international economy by her own rules, which were unfair to those who played by otherwise generally accepted rules.

Given that, from early in the 1990s, the Japanese economy was performing much less impressively than in earlier decades, does it follow that the lustre of the 'Japanese model' has irretrievably faded and that there is no alternative but to switch to a model (based on deregulation) now regarded as 'universal'? Is that indeed the direction in which Japan is moving?

The answers to these questions are highly problematic and at this stage it is only possible to offer qualified and equivocal answers. Before attempting, however, to describe the salient features of the structure and process of central government as they have developed in the post-war period, there is a need to anticipate some very broad conclusions to be recapitulated at various stages in the rest of the book. The argument is in three parts: first, that for strong historical and cultural reasons Japan is unlikely simply to assimilate a model whose parameters are set elsewhere; second, that Japan will continue to learn from external models and adopt certain features of them, as she has done in the past; and third, that in adapting to external pressures created by a 'globalizing' economy, Japan is likely ultimately to create a new (or partly new) model capable of responding effectively to such pressures while retaining many features that are *sui generis*. Using a simile to elucidate this argument, Japan may be compared to a sailing boat experiencing the same wind conditions that affect the rest of a fleet that tends to stick together, but within the serious constraints provided by those conditions, pursuing her own course and following a different strategy.

Even despite the changes that have occurred during the 1990s, many of the principal features of the structure and process of central government have remained intact. It seems important, therefore, at this stage in the book to describe and elucidate these features in a rather schematic and generalizing form. An attempt will then be made to set out the ways in which some features have evolved since the 1950s, including the changes which have been emerging in the 1990s. Finally, certain key features of formal and informal structures will be examined in greater detail – focusing especially on the government bureaucracy, but also on interactions between government, politics and interest groups. Two working principles underlie the analysis in this chapter: first, a sceptical position regarding grand theory, especially theory developed in relation to political systems other than Japan; and second, the assumption that the structure and process of central government in Japan needs to be analysed as a whole before reliable judgements can be made about particular parts of it. The second principle does not imply that all parts of the structure and process work in a uniform manner, which indeed is very far from the case, but it does mean that without some understanding of the nature of the whole, it is difficult to understand the parts.[2]

The Basic Structure of Politics and Government, 1955–1993

1. The structure of power and legitimacy as embodied in the 1946 Constitution was strongly reminiscent of the patterns found in what is often referred to as the 'Westminster model'. That is, in contrast to an American-style separation-of-powers system, there is a marked degree of fusion between legislative and executive power built into the basic constitutional structure. In regular elections to the House of Representatives,[3] the electorate chooses members of Parliament. From these members a government is formed which to be viable must have the confidence of the house. In practice this means either that it is formed by a party (or coalition of parties) commanding the allegiance of a majority of members, or (as during the short-lived Hata Government in 1994, or following the general elections of October 1996) by a party lacking a majority but tolerated by a sufficient number of parliamentarians (belonging to other parties or to none) to guarantee its survival at least for a while. Throughout the whole period from 1955 to 1993 the electorate returned a single party (the LDP) to power.[4] From 1993, coalition governments predominated. In both cases, however, the government of the day not only was in a position to control the legislature by virtue of its parliamentary majority, but also exercised ultimate executive power through the cabinet, since every ministry had a cabinet minister (*daijin*) at its head. If it lost its parliamentary majority and were defeated in a motion of no-confidence, a government was constitutionally required to resign, dissolve the House of Representatives and hold new elections.[5]

2. Within the parameters of what we are calling the 'Westminster model', government ministries have evidently played a role which in certain respects and in certain periods has been at variance with the accepted norms of this model, giving rise to one of the most interesting controversies about Japanese

politics, namely whether it is right to call it a 'bureaucratic polity'. Several features of the government bureaucracy seem to lend weight to this view, and some of these we have touched on in earlier chapters. Government officials after the war were heirs to a long historical tradition of self-identification as a carefully selected, highly educated elite, dedicated to service of the state (and in the pre-1945 period, service to the *tennō*). The removal of the armed forces from political significance after the war conversely reinforced the influence of the civilian bureaucracy, while, as we saw in chapter 4, the American Occupation forces treated government officials – unlike politicians and businessmen, for instance – rather gently because they needed their services in the implementation of the Occupation reforms. A third explanation, however, for the great influence wielded by the government bureaucracy since the 1950s, is of concrete and measurable significance. Since the Yoshida Governments of the late 1940s and early 1950s, there has been a tendency for substantial numbers of government officials to 'colonize' the LDP (though the term should not be taken too literally). In the late 1960s around a quarter of lower house LDP parliamentarians had retired from government ministries in order to stand for Parliament, and been elected using the LDP label. The proportion was even higher in the upper house, and at that time, most significantly, as many as one half of cabinet ministers had experienced public service careers.[6] It would be easy to conclude from this phenomenon that bureaucrats run politics, but in fact, as we shall see later, the reality is a great deal more complicated than this. For one thing the persistence of interministerial rivalries brings about acute jurisdictional and policy disputes, so that the bureaucracy ought not to regarded as a monolithic whole.

3. Bureaucratic influence is also projected into the commercial and business sector through a practice known in Japanese as *amakudari*, translated literally as 'descent from heaven', but known in the United States as 'parachuting'. This practice, which has become highly controversial but is still widespread, involves public officials on their retirement or shortly thereafter, taking positions on the boards of companies or other institutions, usually those related to the area of jurisdiction of their former ministry. Unlike the case in Britain and elsewhere, where priority is given to preventing 'unhealthy' relationships between ministries and private sector organizations, in Japan the practice is very lightly policed. Indeed, within the ministries and the private sector it is often seen as a useful device, both to give able bureaucrats rewarding post-retirement careers, and to enlist top bureaucratic expertise in order to further private sector profitability. Needless to say, it receives criticism on grounds of potential for corruption.

4. If items 2 and 3 suggest the projection of bureaucratic influence into the political and private sector spheres, item 4 involves, in principle at least, a mechanism for the assertion of political influence within the bureaucracy and the private sector. Since at least the 1970s groups of LDP parliamentarians known collectively as *zoku* (literally 'tribes') have coalesced around particular policy areas, such as education, defence, telecommunications, transport and construction, and operate in conjunction with their similarly interested counterparts in ministries, companies, think tanks and so on. There is some similarity here to

the American phenomenon of 'iron triangles', in the sense that the *zoku* endeavour to exercise ultimate control over a particular area of policy. It would be too simple to argue that *zoku* merely represent a means whereby politicians extend their own influence into other spheres. For instance, it is understood that the tobacco *zoku* has greatly assisted the tobacco industry to avoid the kinds of restrictions on advertising that their counterparts in other advanced industrial countries have increasingly had to face in recent years as a result of public pressure and the huge cost to health services of treating tobacco-related illness. In this, as in most other comparable cases, what we are dealing with are complex processes of mutual and reciprocal influence.

5. During the 1950s and 1960s powerful oligopolistic structures of industrial and commercial concentration were put in place, despite the antimonopoly law, which was substantially emasculated during the 1950s. The period of rapid economic growth between the late 1950s and the early 1970s was premised on the concentration of huge economic power in the hands of vertically integrated *keiretsu*-type firms, which, through a variety of mechanisms, exercised great influence on government economic policy. Other interest groups, such as those representing agriculture and small and medium-sized industry, were also important, but the big firms occupied the most central position.

If the first four characteristics we have just listed suggest concentration of power, the next two constitute evidence of its dispersal.

6. Whereas in the classic British case the Westminster model has been found to be compatible with a dominant prime minister (though not all prime ministers have been makers and shakers), in Japan the prime minister has typically been a cautious figure, constrained by complex political forces, seeking influence through the assiduous cultivation of consensus, and usually having limited tenure.[7] We should not of course over-generalize here. Several prime ministers have plainly had a conspicuous influence on events. Prime ministers in certain periods appear to have enjoyed more auspicious circumstances in which to promote their policies than others. But very broadly speaking it seems reasonable to describe Japanese prime ministers as ranging between weak and moderately effective. Moreover, the Japanese cabinet has not been the central locus of decision making that one would expect from the British model, though again there are differences between time periods and issues.[8] Not only prime ministers but also cabinet ministers as a whole have tended to have rather short tenure of office, giving them little time to impose their personal imprint on the portfolio. Here in fact, we are citing important examples of a broader phenomenon, namely the tendency for decision making to be dispersed through an often time-consuming process of consultation and consensus-building. This naturally results in conservative outcomes, though once a decision has been taken implementation is likely to be reasonably smooth.

7. During the period of one-party dominance and the multi-member single non-transferable vote electoral system for the House of Representatives, an important and widely analysed aspect of politics in the LDP was the phenomenon of *habatsu* (usually translated 'faction', but in fact rather different from political factions as known in much of Western Europe). *Habatsu* were quite

complex and often long-lasting organizations within the party[9] which normally (there were exceptions) centred on a single leader who was a senior politician. The *habatsu* leader would bargain with the prime minister over the distribution of posts before each cabinet reshuffle, and indeed one of the reasons for rather frequent reshuffles was that the prime minister needed to ensure his own position by satisfying the factions who were competing for as many cabinet and party positions as possible. *Habatsu* were also organized for the collection of political funding, typically but not only for electoral purposes. While the LDP was stably in power, *habatsu* could paradoxically even serve as a binding force (though there were conspicuous examples of the opposite) because, not being primarily policy groups, they served to keep power contests at one remove from policy disputes. Also, through some bitter experiences in its early years and also in the 1970s, the LDP assimilated the Hobbesian message that a consensual distribution of power between the various *habatsu* was the best way of preventing disruptive power struggles. In 1992–3, this lesson was again unlearnt, with disastrous results.

8. Styles and methods of electioneering were another crucial feature of the political structure and process. In great contrast to the British situation for much of the twentieth century, personality and local connections were central to voting behaviour, and politicians tailored their campaigns to the realities of this facet of electoral behaviour. One reason for this was a severe distortion of the electoral system in favour of rural areas, resulting from a chronic failure adequately to redraw constituency boundaries to take account of movements of population to the cities in the post-war period. Any shift of emphasis from rural-style voting patterns to more urban ones thus occurred unexpectedly slowly, and personality voting remained entrenched. Another reason was the fact that each constituency, until the system was changed in 1994, elected several members, whereas each voter exercised a single, non-transferable vote.[10] Particularly in the case of the LDP, which was strong enough to endorse more than one candidate in most constituencies, each candidate set up or inherited a *kōenkai* (personal support association) as the main basis of his campaign. The *kōenkai* was in no sense a party branch, but was the exclusive preserve of the candidate concerned. This type of organization in turn reinforced the localistic and personalistic nature of elections. The impact on the structure and process of government was important. Members of Parliament were snowed under with constituency business, but much less pressured by the electorate on matters of national or international importance. This in turn meant that parliamentary interventions into policy making tended to take on a local 'pork barrel' character, and with certain regular and important exceptions, parliament did not much interfere in the affairs of state.

9. A further aspect of the way things worked was corruption, or, to use a rather politer term translated from Japanese, 'money politics'. Where the borderline lay between corrupt and non-corrupt political relationships was a matter of controversy, but observers were agreed that the causes of money politics were both structural, in the sense that it was extremely difficult for a parliamentarian to run his political machine in all its aspects without seeking and obtaining funding of dubious provenance, and legal, in the sense that the anticorruption laws were

so full of loopholes that it was easy to evade them. In 1994, however, they were substantially tightened.

Here again we find a pervasive aspect of the way politics operated, having the effect of diverting media and voter attention away from national policy matters towards corruption scandals, which though a matter of concern, essentially affected particular individuals and their behaviour rather than anything that could be called the national interest. In the 1990s, moreover, the tide of corruption scandals as reported in the media seem to have become a factor in the widespread alienation from politics reflected in declining voting turnout rates.

10. One often neglected part of the dynamics underlying the structure and process of government in Japan during the period of single-party dominance was the relative weakness of the opposition parties. There were periods (such as the 1970s, and in 1989–90) when they appeared to constitute a threat to the LDP monopoly of power but, for most of the time, a government composed of opposition parties seemed a remote possibility. Nevertheless, the opposition parties between them were able to exercise important veto power over potential or actual right-wing attempts to tamper with the Occupation settlement. Such a veto was absolute in relation to constitutional revision (as distinct from reinterpretation of the 1946 Constitution) because the LDP lacked the required two-thirds majority in both houses separately, without which a revision procedure could not begin. But it also existed to some extent in relation to other matters, as a result of arrangements made between the LDP and parties in opposition to further the smooth running of Parliament. At times this had the effect of making some opposition parties act like clients of the LDP, rather than opponents of it, but it had the long-term conservative effect of keeping intact the principal features of the Occupation settlement, much against the wishes of right-wing members of the ruling party.[11]

11. Finally, there is a real sense in which the structure and process of government and politics over the era of single-party dominance was held in place by the Japan–US relationship in the context of the Cold War. This is an issue we shall return to once again in chapter 12.

Evolution Between 1955 and 1993

The elements outlined above constitute a broad description of the structure and process of Japanese government and politics in the period from the 1950s to the early 1990s, but it should not be assumed that nothing changed over that period. Although from the early 1960s stability was a conspicuous feature, adaptations and incremental changes were constantly occurring. The following evolutionary factors were most important.

1. If the rapid economic growth period of the 1960s was the high point of bureaucratic dominance, thereafter it was possible to detect a gradual rise in the relative influence of the LDP, although we need to be somewhat hesitant in this judgement. The LDP *zoku*, mentioned under item 4 above, became conspicuous from the 1970s, and began to compete with the ministries by

acquiring relevant expertise. The length of time that the LDP had been in power gave it an increasing edge in terms of the ability of experienced Liberal Democratic parliamentarians to 'sew up' policy in particular areas. Analytically, however, the long-running argument about bureaucratic versus political power may well lead to misleading conclusions, from whichever side the argument is approached. While it may be possible to observe a certain erosion of bureaucratic power, what is more significant is the growth of co-operative relationships involving government officials, politicians and interest group representatives focusing on particular areas of policy, and often ranged against other such mixed groupings. The analytical problem is that it is by no means clear – or indeed necessarily significant – who within such a grouping is influencing whom.

2. Between the 1950s and the 1990s, the corporate sector grew enormously in size and wealth, and with the removal of many bureaucratic controls which had existed in the earlier post-war period, attained much greater independence. Big *keiretsu* firms became far less dependent on raising capital through the banking system, over which the Ministry of Finance and the Bank of Japan exercised substantial control, when they had the means to raise capital on the international money markets. This change did not mean the breakdown of relations between the corporate sector and government ministries, but the balance of power had certainly shifted.

3. As has been already seen in earlier chapters, by the early 1990s the great ideological divisions that existed in the earlier post-war period between the LDP Government and left-wing Opposition parties had gradually diminished, and significant linkages had been established across the divide. This paved the way for the political changes that took place from 1993.

4. Subtle changes also took place in the relations between government and interest groups, matching the maturing of the economy between the 1950s and the 1990s. Whereas in the period of high economic growth the corporate sector tended to dominate access to government policy making and could be regarded as a central part of the real structure of government, by the 1990s many other sectors were in a position to exert significant pressure on government, leading to what Inoguchi has called 'mass-inclusionary pluralism'.[12] Although governments of the early 1980s proved able to resist interest group pressure and maintain for a while the principle of 'zero-ceiling' budgeting, it was noticeable that the Hashimoto Government in compiling the budget for 1997 found it necessary to resort to tax increases in order to finance public works, which benefited interest groups of various kinds, rather than engage in the drastic budget cutting programme demanded by the opposition *Shinshintō*.[13] This indeed accelerated the economic downturn of 1997–8.

5. A further change that has taken place is the greater unpredictability of the electorate and increasing fluidity in voting behaviour. Whereas up to the 1980s the behaviour of electors at the voting booths could be predicted with reasonable accuracy, by the 1990s this was no longer the case. There were signs of greater fluidity even during the 1980s, while in the 1990s many electors have reacted to an unstable party situation by abstaining from voting in large numbers. Although, as we have emphasized in chapter 6, party splits were more to blame

for the LDP's fall from power in 1993 than changes in voting behaviour, by the late 1990s it was proving difficult for any one party to maintain a majority on its own.

6. Although corruption scandals had been a more or less constant feature of the political scene throughout the period since the war, from the Recruit scandal of the late 1980s they seemed so pervasive, and were attracting so much media attention, that this in turn began to affect political attitudes within government, led to passage of the anti-corruption laws of 1994, and made the flow of money for political purposes a good deal more problematic. Moreover, by the second half of the 1990s, suspicion of corruption was affecting not just politicians and businessmen, but also some in the public service. By early 1997 the media was treating alleged improper behaviour by public officials as a major issue,[14] and the practice of *kan-kan settai* (lavish entertainment of officials at public expense by other officials) was being targeted for criticism.[15] Even though the Hashimoto Government was widely regarded as being more favourable than some Opposition parties (notably the *Shinshintō*) to the interests of the government bureaucracy, it too was having to talk the language of financial retrenchment and organizational 'slimming' in relation to the public sector.[16]

7. Finally, the nature of the promotion system within the LDP had changed gradually over the time of single-party dominance, and in particular it had become uncomfortably rigid for the interests of younger LDP parliamentarians. Partly in order to stabilize the party, which had been wracked by dissent between factions during the 1970s, a system was devised whereby virtually no ruling party parliamentarian would have obtained a full cabinet post until he (rarely she) had been elected for his (or her) fifth term, but almost all of them had experienced one cabinet post by their sixth term. Beyond the sixth term, only high flyers could be expected to be given successive cabinet posts, but the *habatsu* were in this manner able to be satisfied.[17] Since five successive terms in Parliament usually meant about 15 years (assuming the member was not defeated in any election), this was understandably frustrating to ambitious younger members, and was an important factor motivating the defections from the LDP which have taken place during the 1990s. To an extent generational groups of parliamentarians have come to replace *habatsu*.[18]

This factor, however, also proved important in another sense. As we have previously seen, up to the late 1960s, former public officials made up a substantial proportion of LDP parliamentarians, and frequently enjoyed a dream run into cabinet. These tended to be public officials who had attained high positions in their ministries, positions which they could not be expected to reach until their fifties. If, when they moved into a political career they then had been required to wait around 15 years for their first cabinet post, in many cases they would have been too old to fulfil their political ambitions. This led to a lowering of the age of transfer from the bureaucracy to Parliament. By the 1980s those effecting such a move successfully were of a younger age group, and the ultimate course of their careers would include a longer political component and a shorter bureaucratic component than in the case of their predecessors. It may not be fanciful, therefore, to see in this further evidence of a certain shifting of the balance from bureaucratic to political in the governmental process as a whole.

The Structure of the Government Bureaucracy

The present structure bears comparison with the system set up in the late nineteenth century. When a cabinet was first instituted in 1885 (preceding by four years the Meiji Constitution), its ministers respectively held the portfolios (each corresponding to a ministry) of foreign affairs, home affairs, finance, army, navy, justice, education, agriculture and commerce, and communications. When the new Constitution came into effect in 1947, the following ministries existed: Foreign Affairs, Home Affairs, Finance, Justice, Education, Welfare, Agriculture and Forestry, Commerce and Industry, Transport, and Communications. Today the Ministries of Foreign Affairs, Finance, Justice, Education and Transport still remain, but in addition there is a Ministry of Labour and a Ministry of Construction. The Ministry of Commerce and Industry has been replaced by the Ministry of International Trade and Industry, often referred to in English as MITI. The former Ministry of Communications is now the Ministry of Posts and Telecommunications (though the Japanese title has not changed), the Ministry of Welfare is the Ministry of Health and Welfare (again, no change in Japanese), and the Ministry of Agriculture and Forestry has had 'Fisheries' attached to its title, to make it the Ministry of Agriculture, Forestry and Fisheries. The former Ministry of Home Affairs was replaced during the Occupation by the Local Autonomy Agency, a branch of the Prime Minister's Office, but in 1960 it became the Ministry of Local Autonomy, and now uses 'Ministry of Home Affairs' as the English translation of *Jichishō* (Ministry of Local Autonomy), thereby seeking to make an important point about its status.

It has proved very difficult since the Occupation to increase the number of ministries or basically change their structure, although the Hashimoto Government early in 1997 was talking about a drastic reform of the bureaucratic structure which might take the form of a reduction in the number of ministries. In addition to the 12 ministries (*shō*), however, a variety of commissions (*iinkai*) and agencies (*chō*) are grouped under the Prime Minister's Office (*Sōrifu*), which has a formal status equivalent to a ministry. These include the Fair Trade Commission (*Kōsei torihiki iinkai*), the National Public Safety Commission (*Kokka kōan iinkai*), the Imperial Household Agency (*Kunai chō*), the Administrative Management Agency (*Gyōsei kanri chō*) the Hokkaidō and Okinawa Development Agency (*Hokkaidō Okinawa kaihatsu chō*), the Science and Technology Agency (*Kagaku gijutsu chō*), the National Land Agency (*Kokudo chō*), the Defence Agency (*Bōeichō*) and the Economic Planning Agency (*Keizai kikakuchō*).

The Constitution, in article 66, defines cabinet membership as consisting of the prime minister and the other ministers of state. Article 2 of the Cabinet Law places an upper limit of 20 ministers of state, plus the prime minister, within cabinet. All ministers are members of cabinet, and there is no provision for an inner cabinet. Since, however, a cabinet restricted to 13 members (the numbers of ministries plus the Prime Minister's Office) would be too small for the breadth of government responsibilities, advantage is taken of article 3 of the Cabinet Law, which permits ministers without portfolio. Several of the more important commissions and agencies of the Prime Minister's Office have therefore been designated as requiring a minister of state to head them, thus giving them full representation at cabinet level. The Chief Cabinet Secretary, and the Director-General of the Cabinet Legislative Bureau have also been elevated to cabinet membership status in this way. Formally speaking, the ministers of state concerned remain ministers without portfolio, despite the fact that their departmental responsibilities may be as great as those of some ministers heading actual ministries. This explains why, for instance, the Director-General of the Defence Agency (*Bōeichō*) is a minister of state with full entitlement to sit in cabinet, despite the fact that efforts to raise the status of the Agency to that of a ministry have so far failed. Cabinets have generally comprised 21 or 22 members, so that some ministers have to take on more than one portfolio.

In its task of co-ordinating the functions of central government, the Cabinet has the assistance of the Cabinet Secretariat (*Naikaku kanbō*), the Cabinet Legislative Bureau (*Naikaku hōseikyoku*), the National Defence Council (*Kokubō kaigi*) and the National Personnel Authority (*Jinjiin*).

The role of the Cabinet Secretariat overlaps somewhat with the functions of the Secretariat of the Prime Minister's Office. The Chief Cabinet Secretary (*Kanbō chōkan*) is always a most powerful figure within the government, and a close confidant of the prime minister, acting as cabinet spokesman on many issues, and as a channel of communication with both government and opposition parties. The Cabinet Secretariat itself is principally concerned with the preparation of matters for cabinet discussions, policy research and co-ordination between different ministries.

The Cabinet Legislative Bureau was abolished on American insistence during the Occupation but was revived later. Its main task is to investigate and oversee legislative technicalities, including drafting of legislation, throughout the civil service.

The National Defence Council is more like a cabinet committee than an advisory bureau of cabinet. It consists of the Prime Minister, the Foreign Minister, the Finance Minister, the Director-General of the Defence Agency and the Director-General of the Economic Planning Agency. It was originally set up by the Defence Agency Establishment Law (*Bōeichō setchi hō*) of 1954 as a safeguard for civilian control over the Self-Defence Forces, and the Prime Minister is supposed to refer to it important matters of defence policy, including draft defence plans.[19] There are sometimes accusations that it is being bypassed by cabinet.

The National Personnel Authority was established during the Occupation in an attempt to rationalize the recruitment and conditions of civil service personnel, and bring them under some sort of centralized control, thus reducing bureaucratic sectionalism. It was deliberately given the status of an independent advisory bureau of cabinet so that it could exercise authority in personnel matters over the civil service as a whole. The influence of the National Personnel Authority was much resented by the established ministries, which were used to controlling their own affairs in matters of personnel, so that various attempts to emasculate it were made once the Occupation had ended. Nevertheless, although its influence is far inferior to that of the major ministries, it has survived, and continues to make recommendations to cabinet on matters affecting civil servants. In the past it has touched upon some politically sensitive matters, such as the bargaining rights of civil servants, and it has tried to maintain (without much success) the relativities between civil service and private sector salaries. With reform of the government bureaucratic structure high on the political agenda in the 1996–7 period, the National Personnel Authority is called upon to draft legislation on a range of matters relating to the ways in which civil servants are supposed to operate.

We have mentioned earlier that for much of the post-war period cabinets appeared to have allowed many decisions to be taken in reality elsewhere, and to have rubber-stamped many decisions essentially taken by the bureaucracy. This appears to be rather less the case in the 1990s, because of enhanced role of various political pressures upon cabinet. Even so, we should not neglect the importance of one extremely important body, the *jimu jikan kaigi*, or Conference of Permanent Vice-Ministers. Even though this body has no formal legal status, it meets regularly under the chairmanship of the Chief Cabinet Secretary. A permanent vice-minister (*jimu jikan*) is the highest career position in any ministry, and the Conference represents an attempt by ministries to smooth out their differences and reach a high degree of consensus before submissions are made to cabinet. On certain items, notably the draft budget and high personnel appointments, it is normal to bypass the Conference of Permanent Vice-Ministers, while issues so controversial that no administrative compromise is likely to emerge may also go to cabinet for a political decision.[20] There is also a less important *seimu jikan kaigi* (Conference of Parliamentary Vice-Ministers). The *seimu jikan* are political appointees – junior ministers who are required to resign if the cabinet is replaced, and there are one or two of them to assist the minister in each ministry. By comparison with the United Kingdom, there are rather few political appointees (ministers and junior ministers) attached to any given ministry.

Of the ministries themselves, those most closely associated with national economic policy making have carried most weight politically and in terms of status. Throughout the whole half century from the end of the Second World War until the mid-1990s a career in the Ministry of Finance (*Okurashō*) was difficult to match for prestige and influence. During the 1990s, however, that ministry came to be the target of trenchant criticism for its allegedly negligent handling of the issue of bankrupt housing loan companies (*jūsen*) and other matters. Members of opposition parties, among others, argued loudly that it ought to be split up and its influence reduced. Nevertheless the Ministry of Finance fought back strongly and could be expected to survive at least the more radical of reform proposals directed at it.

The Ministry of International Trade and Industry, which was formed out of the former Ministry of Commerce and Industry after the war, is no doubt Japan's best known government ministry. A classic study of it by the American political scientist Chalmers Johnson, published in 1982, may well be the most quoted book on the Japanese political economy published in English.[21] In it he developed the influential notion of Japan as a Developmental State, with the government bureaucracy (and most importantly, MITI) orchestrating the direction of economic change, but in concert with the corporate sector and in a market-conforming fashion. Although a great advance on the 'Japan Incorporated' approach associated with the name of James Abegglen, which preceded it by more than a decade,[22] Johnson's book has been criticized by writers who point to significant examples of failure in MITI's efforts to 'pick winners',[23] argue that MITI's influence has declined since the 1970s,[24] and emphasize the other side of that coin, namely the greatly increased financial independence of the corporate sector in relation to government,[25] or focus on the clientelistic and often economically irrational nature of much government intervention in the private sector.[26] On the other hand, despite these criticisms there is plenty of evidence that bureaucratic regulation, whether economically rational or irrational, whether developmental or regressive in effect, whether desired by those regulated or not, whether in the national (and international) interest or not, remains much more extensive than in most comparable states.[27]

Other ministries will be discussed more briefly. The Ministry of Agriculture, Forestry and Fisheries was until the 1990s one of the most successful ministries in terms of its ability to protect its clientele, the farmers, from competitive pressures through subsidy and through opposition to trade liberalization. With Japan's agreement in December 1993 to adhere to the Uruguay Round settlement, the ban on rice imports was partially lifted. The new electoral system introduced in 1994 was also less rurally biased than the old, so that the Ministry in the late 1990s was fighting to retain its influence, which had, of course, been cemented through the disproportionate number of LDP parliamentarians representing rural constituencies.

The importance of the Ministry of Foreign Affairs (MOFA) has gradually increased as Japan's international role has grown, and the posting of officials of other ministries in embassies abroad facilitates communication between the MOFA and other parts of the bureaucracy. Nevertheless the MOFA, like its counterparts in other countries, lacks a domestic constituency, which weakens its impact upon politics at home.

The Ministry of Education in the post-war period and for several years thereafter was locked in confrontation with the Japan Teachers Union (*Nikkōyso*), and had a strongly reactionary reputation among intellectuals and others. In the 1980s it gained international notoriety as a result of reports about its control of school history textbooks and the allegedly distorted accounts it authorized of Japanese military actions in Asia during the Asian-Pacific war. Although the textbook issue is still alive in the 1990s, the MOE appears to have revised some of its earlier priorities, partly no doubt because the union has become much more conformist and society more pluralist.

The other full ministries are the Ministries of Justice, which oversees the judicial system, the Ministry of Health and Welfare, the Ministry of Transport, the Ministry of Posts and Telecommunications, the Ministry of Labour, the Ministry of Construction and the Ministry of Home Affairs. Of these, the Ministry of Home Affairs (*Jichishō*) was broken up during the Occupation period, though up to 1945 its officials had ranked alongside those from the Ministries of Foreign Affairs and Finance as the most prestigious within the bureaucracy, and Home Affairs was the background for many successful political careers. In 1960 a rather minor successor agency called the Local Autonomy Agency (*Jichichō*) was elevated to the status of a ministry as the *Jichishō*). Some time thereafter it took to using its old title of 'Ministry of Home Affairs' in English language literature. It has never managed, however, to regain fully its pre-war status.

The powerful ministries of War (concerned with the army) and the Navy completely disappeared as a result of the Occupation, thus excising what had been a crucial instrument of bureaucratic control. Although they were eventually replaced by the Defence Agency (significantly never a ministry) within the Prime Minister's Office, it has far less influence and status than its predecessors were able to enjoy.

The pre-war bureaucratic ethos has been described – possibly with some exaggeration – by the term *kanson minpi* ('reverence for the government and disdain for the people'). Government officials saw themselves as privileged servants of the *tennō*, and implementing policies designed to extend government authority, not to restrict it.

The Occupation attempted to bring democratic principles to bear upon the status and behaviour of the bureaucracy. The term 'government official' was changed to 'public servant' (*kōmuin*), and new legislation was brought in to regulate their status and conditions.[28] Article 15 of the 1946 Constitution states, in a complete break with the former tradition of subservience to the *tennō*, that 'the people have the inalienable right to choose their public officials and to dismiss them. All public officials are servants of the whole community and not of any special group.' This did not mean, of course, that all civil service (public service) positions were to be the subject of popular election, but that the civil service was to be subject to popular control through Parliament, to which Cabinet was responsible. Moreover, article 73 of the Constitution stated that: '[t]he Cabinet ... shall ... [a]dminister the civil service, in accordance with standards established by law'.

Nevertheless, it is widely agreed that the impact of the Occupation upon the bureaucracy was considerably less than it was in other areas. The Americans needed the expertise of the existing bureaucrats to help implement their extensive programmes of political, social and economic reform, and this meant that reform of the bureaucracy itself had to take second place in the scale of priorities. Post-Occupation developments, most notably the rapid economic development from the 1950s, gave the bureaucracy ample opportunity to exercise influence because of the scope and rapidity of the changes taking place. In these circumstances old patterns of behaviour and the newly prescribed patterns sometimes seemed to be confused. A confusion that was particularly prevalent related to the connotations of 'public' in 'public servant'. The character *kō* (公) in *kōmuin* has the standard meaning of 'public'. Thus *kōkai* means 'public disclosure'. But it can also mean 'official', as in *kōyō* ('official use'). The confusion is illustrated by a trivial but amusing example: At a provincial state university there was a notice at the entrance to a special section of the car park. A notice read in Japanese: *kōyōsha senyō* ('reserved for official vehicles'). Underneath, in English, it read: 'public use only'. The example comes from the 1990s.[29]

It is often remarked that civil servants are widely seen as neutral and impartial by contrast with the venality and self-centredness of politicians.[30] This was certainly true in the 1950s, when one of the results of the promotion of local democracy was the emergence in many areas of a particularly undemocratic form of boss politics. In the late 1960s and early 1970s, however, serious problems relating to the quality of life and environmental pollution created significant disillusionment with a bureaucracy that was seen as promoting economic growth with scant regard for the consequences. In the 1990s, as we saw in chapter 6, a series of scandals involving various ministries led for the first time to a real questioning of the alleged uncorruptibility and impartiality of civil servants. Public anger at the contaminated blood scandal involving the Ministry of Health and Welfare, and at the alleged poor supervision, by the Ministry of Finance and the Bank of Japan, of the bankrupt *jūsen* (housing loan companies), fed into the political movements of the 1990s calling for genuine reform of the bureaucracy and serious deregulation.

It would, however, be difficult to interpret this as a clear preference by the public for party politicians over bureaucrats. Indeed, the two are seen as interlocking, and the two issues just mentioned coincided with a sharp trend of popular alienation from politics, shown in declining turnout rates at elections and low support rates for political parties.

Japan is not the only country about which it has been argued that the civil service exercises dominant influence over parties in power, but it is one of the few in which senior civil servants actually enter politics in considerable numbers after retirement. This phenomenon, referred to above under the second element we identified in the basic structure of politics and government, is also closely analogous to the third element, namely *amakudari*.[31] Although, as we saw, there has been a certain decline in the impact, age profile and number of former civil servants within political parties (primarily, but since 1993 not exclusively, the LDP), the phenomenon of *amakudari* remains of absolutely crucial importance in the structure of the political economy.

According to the National Personnel Authority, in 1996 134 retired public servants, having an average age of 55 years and 10 months, were permitted to be re-employed in the private sector. This figure was down by 55 on the figure for 1995, and includes 27 from the Ministry of Finance (a drop of 32 from the previous year), 18 from the Maritime Safety Agency, 17 from MITI, 15 from the Ministry of Education, 14 from the Ministry of Transport and 13 from the Ministry of Construction. The reduction in the numbers, particularly in the case of the MOF, reflects the intense criticism of *amakudari* experienced in the wake of the *jūsen* and other scandals involving former public servants. Nevertheless, these figures conspicuously leave out of account those re-employed in state-run corporations and other public entities.[32]

The practice of *amakudari* has been widely and trenchantly criticized within the political reform camp during the 1990s, but, equally, tenaciously defended within the bureaucracy. How, then, ought we to interpret its significance? Broadly speaking it seems possible to explain it through two contrasting, if overlapping, paradigms. The first of these emphasizes the functionality of this practice in terms of the smooth implementation of government policy or, more specifically, the policies of particular ministries. Without *amakudari*, it is argued, it would be much more difficult to ensure the smooth running of the system as a whole because individual companies would be inclined simply to follow their own selfish interests according to the dictates of the market, rather than following the national interest, as interpreted through government policy. Needless to say, such attitudes are roundly attacked by those reformers who want to open up the economy decisively to the discipline of the market, but at least the argument suggests a dedicated mandarinate, selflessly devoted to the task of serving the national interest according to enlightened calculations.[33]

The second paradigm is less flattering but possibly rather more realistic. It emphasizes the much narrower interests of ministries and agencies of government, as well as the interests of individual civil servants. The argument is based on the basic structure of career paths in a ministry and also on patterns of remuneration of career civil servants. The career structure in a ministry may be likened to a tall house with a gabled roof. That is to say, those entering the elite career track at the bottom advance in seniority and status with their age cohort on an equal basis until they reach a certain age, typically 45. Thereafter, promotion opportunities rapidly narrow, until the top position of *jimu jikan* is reached. At that point – the 'apex of the gable' – since only one person from the relevant cohort can occupy the position, the others need to seek employment elsewhere. This creates a need to find employment opportunities for considerable numbers of able, active men (and a few women) in early middle age, who are intimately informed about the policies of their ministries. In 'parachuting' into the private or quasi-private sectors, they typically earn considerably more than than they had done during their bureaucratic careers, thus achieving 'postponed income' as a reward for loyal service to the government.[34] Accounts may even be found of regulatory bodies being set up in a particular industry, serving the essential purpose of providing post-retirement positions for retired civil servants, and incidentally adding to the overall costs borne by the industry concerned.

It can be seen from this discussion of *amakudari* both that it is an entrenched institution, driven by structural bureaucratic interests, and also that it is a central feature of the way politics and government work in Japan. While, however, its abolition or fundamental reform is naturally a key target of the free-market reformers, it is important to analyse the actual nature of its impact, which is not entirely as one might expect.

First of all, there is no doubt that *amakudari*, together with other bureaucratic practices such as *gyōsei shidō* (administrative guidance),[35] have led to the emergence of an economy which is unusually highly regulated by government. This remains the case despite a considerable degree of deregulation in certain areas of the economy that has taken place in recent years. Persistent and often angry overseas complaints that Japanese bureaucratic regulation operates to the disadvantage of foreign enterprises doing business with Japan are matched by grumbling within Japan itself that many of the regulations devised within the bureaucracy are onerous, expensive to fulfil and at times nonsensical.[36] It is nevertheless true that despite the considerable cost to the economy of the totality of bureaucratic regulations, much of the private sector has been not unhappy with the kind of regulated environment that is created because it is seen as providing stability and predictability, as well as protection from 'excessive' competition, both domestic and foreign. Given that until recently, at least, the economy as a whole outperformed most of its competitors, regulation seemed an acceptable price to pay for these benefits.

Secondly, however, and returning to the logic of *amakudari,* it seems necessary to modify this picture when we discover which are the principal target companies of the practice of *amakudari*. Rather than the leading *keiretsu*-type (i.e. vertically integrated) companies or major banks, retired bureaucrats most usually 'descend' on to the boards of second ranking companies, whose ability to compete with the larger firms may well thereby be enhanced. Calder even argues that this tends to '··· *co-opt* and to *undermine* [his italics] bureaucratic efforts at strategic dirigisme'.[37] This in turn may well relate to broader politico-economic networks with which, typically, *zoku* parliamentarians are also connected. The effect, therefore, of *amakudari* as a whole is exceedingly complex. It helps ministries to enforce a regulatory regime, which may be in the interests of promoting economic rationality, of encouraging national objectives, of fostering greater equality between sectors, of maintaining clientelistic networks, of rewarding retired officials for under-recompensed public service, or some combination of all these. To repeat a formula used elsewhere, the structure of government and politics in Japan is an almost inextricable mixture of dynamic and immobilist practices and outcomes, which is what makes it so difficult to describe.[38]

Taking the post-war period as a whole, on balance the system has produced dynamic and innovative government, while the immobilist aspect has often been positively regarded as some guarantee of stability. Countries which have experienced frequent changes of government accompanied by drastic changes of policy might regard not only the innovative, but also some of the immobilist features of Japanese government and politics as not wholly disadvantageous. Whether these features can or should survive in the face of enhanced international competition and the emergence of a 'global' economy remains to be seen. The outcome probably rests on how far immobilist and clientelist practices come to develop tangible disadvantages for those party to them as much as on the capacity of government to provide leadership.

Economic and other Interest Groups and their Interaction with Government and Politics

To understand the role of government in the Japanese economy, and conversely the attitudes of major economic interest groups towards government, it is essential to appreciate the extent to which this has changed over time. In the Meiji period the government laid the foundations of certain industries for which immediate profit opportunities were not apparent, and then, when they were functioning properly, handed them over to private enterpreneurs. During the military period of the 1930s and early 1940s, the autonomy of private industry was greatly reduced as it came to operate under close official supervision and control. Industry, commerce and trade were also hemmed in by all kinds of regulations during the Occupation period, and into the 1960s businesses needed government authorization for several purposes, including the supply of foreign exchange. Liberalization of foreign capital imports was late in coming, but by the mid-1970s *official* restrictions on the operation of foreign firms in Japan were about on a par with those in other comparable countries, though agriculture remained highly protected. On the other hand, *informal* restrictions continued to be pervasive, so that the cost and uncertainties of doing business in Japan meant that by the mid-1980s foreign investment in Japan was far outweighed by Japanese investment overseas. Japan's current account surplus also grew from US\$11 billion in 1980 to US\$87 billion in 1987, while in the same period the US merchandise trade deficit increased from US\$10 billion to US\$60 billion.[39] This led to severe trade frictions between Japan and the United States, which became a salient feature of the politics of the 1980s. The much slower growth of the economy in the 1990s, combined with some further liberalization on Japan's part has dampened these frictions, but complaints from abroad about the 'closed' nature of the Japanese market still continue.

To a very large extent these stem from the more or less constant interactions between government on the one hand and industrial, commercial and banking organizations on the other. Apart from the practices of *amakudari* and *gyōsei shidō* already mentioned, ministries maintain considerable numbers of advisory committees (usually termed *shingikai*, though other names are also used), reporting on matters of current concern to the ministry, and these committees usually include significant representation from the business world. In addition, there are of course a host of informal government–business contacts of all kinds.

During the long period of LDP dominance up to 1993, the majority party received (either directly, or through factional and individual channels) huge amounts of political funding from the business world. The larger firms tended to spread their contributions across more than one faction, as a kind of insurance policy to take account of the vagaries of factional politics. This contrasted with the pattern in the 1920s and 1930s, when the major conservative parties became heavily dependent financially on particular *zaibatsu* (business conglomerates). That did much to discredit political parties at that time, and although the more recent pattern was associated with many corruption scandals, the sources of finance were so diverse that influence was by comparison thinly spread.

In general, it is true to say that the business world was happy to allow the LDP and officialdom to get on with the business of running the country. It was generally assumed that the government would deliver relative political stability and economic policies that were favourable to business. While, therefore, the business world was prepared to fund the majority party, it would only rarely interfere in the way the LDP ran its affairs. At times, in the mid-1970s, the business world would show reluctance to underwrite the majority party – usually in response to corruption scandals – but it was not until the fall of the LDP from power in 1993 that *Keidanren* (the Federation of Economic Organizations) announced that it would no longer provide funds for political parties. This policy was later somewhat relaxed.

The business world has a variety of organized channels for making its views known on particular policy matters and for exercising influence. Each industry has its own independent organization, which among other things may be an important contributor of political finance. These include, for instance, the Japan Steel League (*Nihon tekkō renmei*), the Electrical Manufacturing Federation (*Denki jigyō rengōkai*), and the Automobile Industry Association (*Jidōsha kōgyōkai*). There are also associations based on geographical areas, such as Tokyo, Osaka or Nagoya. Some associations specialize in labour relations, others in more general matters of policy affecting their members. Others are meeting grounds for the top leaders of a single *keiretsu*-type combine such as the Mitsui or Sumitomo groups. There is a Central Association of National Medium and Small Industry Groups (*Zenkoku chūshō kigyō dantai chūōkai*). Although small and medium-sized industry does not have the financial clout of the large combines, by being a very large sector of the economy in terms of the numbers employed, it has great voting power, and exercises influence over many parliamentarians from various parties. In the 1980s it mounted a concerted and at least partly successful campaign against emasculation of the Large Stores Law

(*Daiten hō*), which protected small shops against the incursion of large super-markets. Much the same can be said of agriculture, whose central organization is the Union of Agricultural Co-operatives (*Nōgyō kyōdō kumiai* or, more commonly, simply *Nōkyō*). Even though the influence of *Nōkyō* has declined with the drastic reduction in the agricultural population since the war, it is a classic example of a pressure group which, by means of symbiotic links with the Ministry of Agriculture, Forestry and Fisheries, its own development as a huge industrial combine, providing all manner of services to farmers, and its network of linkages with politicians, managed to delay by many years the kinds of agricultural liberalization that strict economic rationality would have dictated.

The most important and influential associations representing Japanese industry as a whole (but chiefly the major firms and industries) are four 'peak associations', namely: *Keidanren* (the Federation of Economic Organizations), which can be regarded as the key spokesman for big business; *Nikkeiren* (the Japan Federation of Employers Associations), having much the same membership as *Keidanren*, but concerned largely with matters of employment, including the annual *shuntō* (spring struggle) mounted by labour unions; *Nisshō* (the Japan Chamber of Commerce and Industry), the only one of the four to have existed before the Second World War; and *Keizai dōyūkai* (known in English as the Japan Committee for Economic Development, though this is not a direct translation of the Japanese). The *Keizai dōyūkai* differs from the others in being based on individual, not corporate, membership. After its foundation in 1946 it had a progressive, even radical reputation, but is hardly so distinguished from the other groups in the 1990s.

There are many professional groups, representing doctors, dentists, lawyers and so on, which are treated seriously by government in relation to their professional spheres. The best known, perhaps, is the *Nihon ishikai* (Japan Medical Association), which has exercised great influence in relation to a host of health service matters.

We shall deal with labour unions in a later chapter, but simply note here that they have increasingly been incorporated into a government Establishment that previously tended to keep them at arms length. Since the late 1960s there has been a proliferation of so-called citizens movements (*shimin undō*), and the more localized residents movements (*jūmin undō*). Although these have had a considerable impact since the 1970s in relation to a variety of environmental and quality of life issues, they have generally found difficulty in maintaining a universalistic approach, tending as they do to consist of people concerned with essentially parochial problems.

One notable omission from this list is that of consumer groups. This is not because they do not exist, but rather because they have been both weak and generally conformist. We do not have the space to examine consumer groups in detail, but it is worth noting that the weakness of consumer movements is the other side of the coin of the strength of producer interests. Ever since the Meiji period, it has been the thrust of government policy to organize the state and the economy for production and, beginning in the 1930s but most successfully in the half century since the end of the Second World War, that aim has been largely realized. This central fact of course explains much of the factual material that we have presented hitherto in this chapter. In so far as Japan is a 'bureaucratic polity', it is such because of the perceived imperatives in earlier periods to organize the state and nation as a production machine given Japan's isolation and lack of resources except for human skills (which themselves had to be cultivated as a central part of government policy: hence the great emphasis given to universal education since the Meiji period). It is less obvious whether the statist methods used to promote production over several decades are appropriate to Japan in the global situation of the 1990s, which would explain the slow and painful process of reform that is being fought over during the present decade. Nevertheless, the evidence is on balance against the view that Japanese government will simply move into conformity with American or European models.

The relationships between the different parts of the structure are deeply entrenched, and depend in part on strongly held strategic principles, and in part on habits of mind which fall most easily into complex clientelist relationships. The structure is a complex of interlocking elements. We may illustrate this by a kind of caricature: politicians persuade the electorate to elect them, form governments and get legislation through Parliament and thus enable bureaucrats to realize their policies; politicians also provide post-retirement political careers for some ex-bureaucrats; bureaucrats provide much of the legislative initiation and drafting expertise needed by politicians, and implement the policies passed though Parliament (as well as measures not requiring parliamentary sanction); bureaucrats regulate the economy in such a way to benefit businessmen, and in turn are rewarded by *amakudari* positions after retirement; businessmen find electoral funding for politicians and support them in electoral campaigns, while in turn relying on politicians to create a benign policy environment for their activities.

This is, we repeat, a caricature, some elements of which have in any case been evolving in the challenging circumstances of low economic growth and a disillusioned electorate that have characterized the 1990s. But like the sailing boat that cannot escape the conditions affecting the rest of the fleet, but which still charts a course at some remove from the rest of the fleet, Japan may be regarded as being in the process of groping towards a new approach owing something to external conditions and much to her own historical experiences, habits of mind and deep-rooted structures.

8

Parliament and Parliamentary Elections

Parliament

Although Japan has had what could strictly be called a parliamentary system of government only since the Occupation, she has had a parliament since 1890, and the traditional nature of the institution has no doubt contributed to its ready acceptance over the past half century. The position of parliament in the political system is a blend of historical influences. The Meiji Constitution was strongly German in inspiration, and German influences can be easily found even among post-war constitutional lawyers. At the same time the constitutional relationships between emperor, prime minister, cabinet, parliament and the bureaucracy are highly reminiscent of British arrangements, while the structure and role of parliamentary committees are American-inspired. Japanese social norms, a long period of dominance of parliament by a single party, and the self-confidence of the government bureaucracy, have all put their stamp on the functioning of parliament in practice.

The key position which the *Kokkai* (Parliament) was expected to occupy in the whole system of politics and government was forcefully presented in article 41 of the 1946 Constitution, where it was given the title of 'highest organ of state power' and 'sole law-making authority of the State'. There are two houses, the House of Representatives (*Shūgiin*), and the House of Councillors (*Sangiin*), which are often referred to, respectively, as the 'lower house' and the 'upper house'.[1] Both houses are elected (whereas the pre-war upper house, the House of Peers, had an appointed membership) and 'representative of all the people',[2] a phrase which can be interpreted to mean 'elected by universal suffrage'. The term of the lower house is four years, although it can be ended prematurely by dissolution.[3] Its membership rose from 464 at the time of 1946 general election to 512 in the late 1980s, stood at 511 at the time that the system of election was radically changed in 1994, and under the new system has been reduced to 500, although there are calls from some conservatives to reduce it further. There is a fixed term in office for upper house members of six years, with half the membership being elected every three years.[4] Its membership remained at 250 during the post-war period, but rose to 252 with the return of Okinawa prefecture to Japanese sovereignty in May 1972. Nobody can be a member of both houses simultaneously.[5]

Relations between the two houses are complex, and reflect the fact that the initial (GHQ) draft of the Constitution envisaged a unicameral legislature, so that the addition of a second chamber was one of the few really significant changes which the Japanese Government of the day was able to effect in the course of its discussions with SCAP on the drafting of a new Constitution. The constitutional position of the House of Councillors is inferior to that of the House of Representatives. Early hopes that the upper house might differentiate itself from the lower house either by speciality of function or a difference in the quality and background of members have hardly been fulfilled.

On a number of matters the two houses have identical powers.[6] Each independently judges disputes about the qualifications of its members,[7] keeps and publishes records of its proceedings,[8] selects its president (speaker),[9] establishes its own rules and punishes its own members,[10] receives petitions,[11] and conducts 'investigations in relation to government'[12] (a power which is the basis of the committee system of each house). The members of each house enjoy freedom from arrest (except in cases provided for by law) while Parliament is in session,[13] and freedom from liability outside the house for speeches, debates or votes cast inside the house.[14] There is also no difference in the rights of the two houses concerning revision of the Constitution.[15]

On the other hand, only the House of Representatives has the power to force a cabinet resignation by passing a no-confidence resolution (or rejecting a confidence resolution).[16] Also, dissolution of the House of Representatives means that the House of Councillors must be closed as well,[17] whereas the latter operates on the basis of fixed terms and cannot be dissolved prematurely.

The House of Councillors possesses one attribute which is peculiar to it, namely that it may be convoked in emergency session in a time of national emergency. The lower house, however, has to agree to measures taken by such a session within ten days after the opening of the parliamentary session, or they become null and void.[18]

The constitutional inferiority of the House of Councillors is manifest in the restricted nature of its power to reject or delay the passage of legislation originating in the House of Representatives. In the case of ordinary bills, where the upper house differs from the lower house (in other words, when it rejects or amends the proposed legislation), the bill nevertheless becomes law if passed a second time by the lower house by a two-thirds majority of the members present.[19]

On the other hand, in such a case another road is open to the House of Representatives, namely to call for a joint committee of both houses to resolve the issue.[20.] In order to avoid the possibility of indefinite delay by the House of

Councillors, a bill on which that house fails to take action within 60 days of its receipt from the lower house (time in recess excepted) may be regarded by the lower house as having been rejected by the upper.[21]

Between 1955 and 1989, these provisions were largely academic, because the LDP controlled both houses and maintained tight party discipline, at least so far as voting in Parliament was concerned. When, however, the LDP was defeated in the House of Councillors elections of July 1989, this caused severe problems for the Kaifu Government during the period of the Gulf Crisis, as we saw in chapter 6. Since in practice it has normally been impossible for any government to muster a two-thirds majority necessary to override an adverse vote in the House of Councillors, the only practicable strategy available was to seek to *create* an upper house majority, by doing deals with parties in opposition there. Much of the politics of the early 1990s was concerned with this problem, and indeed the cross-party linkages formed as a result of the need to forge a new coalition in the upper house were an important factor in the fall of the LDP from power in 1993 and its replacement by an eight-party coalition government under Hosokawa.

In the case of matters regarded as of outstanding importance, namely the budget, treaties and the designation of a new prime minister, the supremacy of the House of Representatives is more marked than with ordinary bills. The relationship between the two houses is also much simpler. The annual budget, unlike other bills, must first be submitted to the House of Representatives.[22] In the case of a disagreement between the two houses, reference of the budget to a joint committee is mandatory (not voluntary, as is the case with ordinary bills); but if the House of Councillors has taken no action within 30 days, the decision of the House of Representatives is considered the decision of Parliament.[23] Until 1990, the budget had never been referred to a joint committee, although at least once (in 1954) the upper house failed to take action and the budget automatically came into force after 30 days.[24]

Treaties fall under the same provisions as the budget, except that the Constitution does not forbid a treaty being submitted first to the upper house (though this is very unusual).[25] It will be recalled (see chapter 4) that in the case of the revised Mutual Security Treaty in 1960, Kishi needed to force the Treaty through the House of Representatives on 19 May if the Treaty was to be ready in time for President Eisenhower's projected visit, because it required 30 days in the House of Councillors before it would automatically receive parliamentary endorsement.[26]

The rules are similar for the designation of a prime minister, except that this takes precedence over any other business, and the decision of the House of Representatives becomes the decision of Parliament if there is no agreement between the two houses or if the House of Councillors fails to make designation within a mere ten days of action by the House of Representatives.[27] In February 1948, the composition of the two houses was sufficiently different to produce different candidates from each. After a joint committee had failed to agree and ten days had elapsed, the candidate of the lower house, Ashida, prevailed over the candidate of the upper house, Yoshida, and became prime minister. In July 1989 Kaifu prevailed over Ms Doi Takako in a similar way.

While the House of Councillors can be used against the government to good effect by an opposition enjoying an upper house majority, another powerful weapon at the disposal of the Opposition has been the rigidity of the parliamentary timetable. The 1960 crisis is only one of many instances in which the government of the day has been gravely embarrassed by Opposition filibustering, premised on the Government's lack of control over the timetabling of parliamentary business. This in turn has meant that the Management (Steering) Committee (*unei iinkai*) of the House of Representatives has at times become crucially important, and paradoxically relations between the management committee chairmen of government and opposition parties have been a subtle but crucial factor in maintaining a working relationship between the various parties within Parliament.[28]

Provision is made for three types of parliamentary session (apart from the emergency session of the House of Councillors mentioned above). The first is the ordinary or regular session (*tsūjō kokkai*) which is held once every year.[29] This session is normally convoked in January (before 1991, in December) and lasts for 150 days.[30] Since the revision of the Parliamentary Law in 1955 it may be extended once only, although previously an indefinite number of extensions was permitted.[31] The second is the extraordinary session (*rinji kokkai*), which may be called by the cabinet, or must be held when a quarter or more of the total members of either house makes the demand.[32] The third is the special session (*tokubetsu kokkai*), called in fulfilment of the constitutional provision that after a lower house dissolution, a lower house general election must be held within 40 days, and Parliament must be convoked within 30 days of the date of the election.[33] Both extraordinary and special sessions may now be extended up to twice;[34] and with all three types of session, if there is disagreement between the two houses on, say, the length of the extension, the House of Representatives prevails.[35]

The importance of the length of session is considerable because of the principle in the Parliamentary Law that: '[a]ny matter not decided during a session shall not be carried over to the following session', except that in certain circumstances parliamentary committees can continue their deliberations into the adjournment, and matters entrusted to them can then be carried on into the next session.[36] For the most part, however, the government is under strong pressure to complete its legislative programme by the end of the session (extensions included), and this task is not made any easier for it by the fact that the order in which legislation is to be discussed is in the hands of the management committee of each house. Particularly for much of the 1970s, when the balance of parliamentary forces between government and opposition was nearly even, and for periods of coalition and even minority government that have intervened in the 1990s, the management committee provides another forum in which delaying tactics can be applied.

Indeed, the Opposition parties have a variety of means at their disposal to delay the passage of legislation, so that the length of a particular session may assume magnified importance. During the earlier post-war decades, the left-of-centre Opposition parties, most notably the JSP, were famous – or notorious – for obstructionist tactics of various kinds, including 'cow-walking' (*gyūho senjutsu*), which is a tactic of deliberate slowness in recording their votes, presenting a large number of amendments and (in May 1960) physically preventing the President of the house from taking a vote. In the 1980s and 1990s such tactics have become much less common, and when the JSP engaged in 'cow-walking' in 1992, seeking to delay the PKO bill, it met a hostile public reaction. Rather similarly, when early in 1996 the *Shinshintō* organized a sit-in of its members in the parliamentary corridors in protest against the Hashimoto Government's proposed use of public money to help rescue bankrupt housing loan companies, it seems to have harmed its reputation with the electorate. (See chapter 6 for an account of these two episodes).

There continue to be episodes, however, where parliamentary timetabling is a problem for a government. In 1994, for instance, the Hosokawa Government's budget was seriously delayed, and its passage had to await the minority Hata Government. By the time it was passed under the Hata Government, it had been substantially modified. Since 1947 there have been many instances where, faced by opposition party obstruction, the government decides to make concessions to the opposition by modifying its legislation, simply in order to have the relevant bill or bills passed by the end of the session. If, however, as has also happened many times, the government assumes an intransigent position, the opposition parties may decide to boycott the remainder of the session (either the plenary session or the session of the relevant parliamentary committee). The government is then faced with a choice between bargaining with the parties in an effort to persuade them to resume their seats, or brazening it out and pushing the legislation through unilaterally. Experience on a number of occasions, particularly in the earlier post-war years, showed that the latter course carried with it the danger of precipitating a serious political crisis, with the government standing accused of having 'broken consensus', or of having exercised the 'tyranny of the majority'. It should be noted perhaps, that the ideal of 'consensus' serves both as a cultural norm and a political excuse: a cultural norm in the sense that 'winner-take-all' majority decision making does not sit easily with Japanese social practice, and a political excuse in that parties long excluded from power (principally the left-of-centre parties in the long period of single-party dominance) have managed to hold the line on some issues important to them by invoking the principle of consensus and arguing that they should be part of it. In the more fluid politics of the 1990s, however, the option of actually participating in a government has become a reality for nearly all parties, which creates a new environment for them, and reduces the attractions of the old forms of obstructionism.

As in the British House of Commons, the overwhelming majority of bills are government-sponsored. Private members' bills are not uncommon, but in contrast to Britain, where private members' bills often concern social issues which are not part of the government's agenda, in Japan they more typically concern constituency matters. Some of them, however, originate in a government ministry which has been successful in finding a parliamentarian prepared to pilot a piece of legislation through the house.

In contrast, the most 'American' feature of the operation of Parliament is its system of standing and special committees. Based on the constitutional right of each house to 'conduct investigations in relation to government',[37] the system replaces the pre-war practice of taking bills through three successive readings on the floor of the house. Bills initiated by individual parliamentarians, by Cabinet or referred from the other house, are normally sent straight to the appropriate committee. The committee has the power of 'killing' any bill referred to it (with the exception of bills transmitted from the other house), but it is a comparatively simple matter to pull a bill out of a committee. If, within seven days of a decision by the committee not to submit a bill to the plenary session, its release is demanded by 20 or more members of the house, then it must be submitted to the plenary session.[38] In this respect, at least, the power of Japanese parliamentary committees is much less than that of their American counterparts, the committees of Congress.

Initially, there were as many as 20 standing committees of each house. In January 1995 there were 20 standing committees of the lower house and 17 of the upper. All parliamentarians are obliged to belong to at least one standing committee. Before the 1955 revision of the Parliamentary Law, parliamentarians were not allowed to belong to more than two standing committees and, if they belonged to two, the second had to be chosen from a restricted list. Since 1955, however, this restriction has not applied, and the president (speaker), deputy president, prime minister, ministers and other cabinet officials are no longer obliged to belong to any committees.[39] Membership of standing committees and special committees is allocated in proportion to party strengths in the house, with the Management Committee being the arbiter.[40] Chairmen of standing committees are formally elected from the committee membership by a vote of the plenary session,[41] but in practice they are selected by the president (speaker) according to the distribution of party strengths in each committee.[42] Chairmen of special committees, on the other hand, are elected by the committees themselves from among their members, not necessarily according to their relative strengths.[43]

Table 8.1 is a list of the standing committees of each house, with the number of members and the chairman's party affiliation in each (as of January 1995).

Until the elections of 1974 for the upper house and 1976 for the lower house, the LDP provided the chairman and a majority of members of each committee. Following those elections, however, it faced a less favourable situation. Since membership of committees was allocated to each party on the principle of proportionality to its house membership, the LDP lost undisputed control of many committees. In January 1980, for instance, the LDP provided 261 members, and the Opposition parties 257 members, of the standing committees of the House of Representatives (there were also two vacancies). Of the 16 standing committees, the LDP held a majority in four, the LDP and Opposition parties had equal numbers in 10, and the Opposition parties were in a majority in two. A committee chairman, however, could not vote, and since the LDP continued to provide a majority of committee chairmanships (though it no longer monopolized them), effective committee control in the above example was distributed in the following way: LDP 6; equal numbers 2; Opposition 8.

After the double elections of June 1980 the LDP regained control of all standing parties of both houses. Then in December 1983 lower house elections the LDP fared poorly again, and Nakasone's desire to ensure his Government's control of all parliamentary committees was a principal reason why he brought the New Liberal Club into a coalition government with the LDP. As a result of the 1986 double elections, the LDP once more gained control of all committees of both houses, but in the July 1989 House of Councillors elections lost

Table 8.1 Standing Committees of the House of Representatives and House of Councillors (January 1995).

Name of committee	Party of Chairman	
	House of Representatives	*House of Councillors*
Cabinet	JSP	LDP
Local Administration	LDP	JSP
Judicial Affairs	LDP	*Heiseikai**
Foreign Affairs	*Sakigake*	*Heiseikai*
Finance	LDP	LDP
Education	LDP	LDP
Social Welfare	JSP	JSP
Agriculture, Forestry and Fisheries	JSP	LDP
Commerce and Industry	LDP	LDP
Transport	JSP	*Heiseikai*
Communications	LDP	JSP
Labour	*Shinshintō*	*Shin Ryokufūkai*[†]
Construction	*Shinshintō*	LDP
National Security	*Shinshintō*	(no committee)
Science and Technology	*Shinshintō*	(no committee)
Environment	*Shinshintō*	(no committee)
Budget	SDP	LDP
Audit	*Shinshintō*	SDP
House Management (Steering)	LDP	SDP
Discipline	LDP	*Heiseikai*
Total	**20**	**17**

*The *Heiseikai* was a grouping comprising the *Shinshintō* and *Kōmei* members in the House of Councillors.
[†]The *Shin Ryokufūkai* was an upper house grouping that takes its name from the grouping of independent minded members called *Ryokufūkai* ('Green Breeze Society') that existed in the 1950s.
Source: *Asahi Nenkan,* 1996, pp. 242–3.

control both of the house itself and of many of its committees. With the formation of multi-hued coalition governments from 1993, the control of committees became an exceedingly complicated business, with the result that inter-party compromise and accommodation over bills submitted to committees became the essential condition of the success of a government's legislative programme. (See table 8.1.)

In January 1995 the special committees of the House of Representatives covered the following areas (party affiliation of chairmen in brackets): disaster policy (JSP); revision of the public election law (LDP); coal policy (*Shinshintō*); consumer issues (*Shinshintō*); road safety policy (*Shinshintō*); Okinawa and the northern territories (LDP); the relocation of Parliament (LDP); local decentralization (*Shinshintō*); deregulation (*Shinshintō*). Of these all except the committees on relocation of Parliament, local decentralization and deregulation had existed from at least 1980, except that 'consumer issues' had changed its name from 'prices policy and related problems'. Two special committees that were in existence in 1980 – those on science and technology and on the environment – were both elevated to the status of standing committees in 1981. The House of Councillors had special committees on the following questions (party of chairmen in brackets): science and technology (*Heiseikai*); the environment (JSP); disaster policy (LDP); political reform (JSP); Okinawa and the northern territories (LDP); local decentralization and deregulation (*Heiseikai*); small and medium industry policy (LDP).[44] The LDP, lacking a majority in both houses, had also lost control of a majority of the committees, standing and special, of both houses. What is also interesting is how little the committee structure had changed over the previous decade and a half. The only lower house committee that had completely disappeared since 1980 was the special committee to look into the import of aircraft, which had been set up after the Lockheed scandals of the 1970s.[45]

The committees of each house are much the most important forum for parliamentary debate. This is particularly true of the lower house standing committees on the budget and on foreign affairs, wherein debates of major national importance take place. As with US Congressional committees, the Japanese parliamentary committees are empowered to hold public hearings 'in order to hear the views of interested parties or persons of learning and experience'.[46] Whereas in the US, however, government officials have no right to speak on the floor of either house of Congress, but appear before Congress committees in a more privileged capacity than expert and interested witnesses, in Japan, where Cabinet is within Parliament, ministers of state have a right to speak both in plenary session and in committee. They also appear frequently at the request of a particular committee, in order to answer questions (the cumbersome word 'interpellations' is used) on particular bills for which they are responsible. This activity may take up a good deal of a minister's time.[47] Much more surprising than this from a British parliamentary perspective is that senior civil servants also are allowed, and expected, to be present and answer questions in committees. On one occasion a minister, having been asked a difficult question is alleged to have replied: 'This is a *very* important matter, so I must ask Mr X [a civil servant standing beside him] to answer it'. A frequent complaint of senior civil servants is the amount of time they have to spend in Parliament in the expectation of being required to answer questions. Needless to say, this practice is widely regarded as downgrading Parliament, and some 1990s reformers would like to abolish it.[48]

The committee system of Parliament needs to be seen in the context of the evolving history of the structure and process of politics. For much of Japan's post-war history the committees have been firmly in the hands of the LDP, but even when that has been the case they have given parties out of power some opportunity to check parts of the government's legislative programme, or at least its legislative aspirations. In periods where committee control was mixed, the government was sometimes forced into complex bargains and deals with the opposition in order to salvage what it could of its legislative programme. During the 1990s even more difficult inter-party relations developed in the committees.

Quite apart from the question of the balance between the parties in parliamentary committees, during the earlier post-war decades many LDP parliamentarians whose careers began in government ministries gravitated to committees most relevant to their former ministries, and from there they maintained close liaison with their former colleagues. Since the 1970s the committees have also been a focus for *zoku* parliamentarians, using them as a base for the development of control over their chosen areas of policy. Indeed, the two things are not unrelated, since *zoku* parliamentarians are also in some cases former civil servants (or, reversing the order, some former civil servants are *zoku* parliamentarians). As this shows, it is extremely difficult to determine how far the influence flows from the bureaucracy into the parties, and how far from the parties into the bureaucracy, since the two are so closely woven together. A more relevant question may well be to ask what is the balance of influence between different policy networks based in part on separate parliamentary committees.

Finally, many commentators have assumed that the Japanese Parliament is an inherently weak body, having little autonomous power, and a comparative irrelevance within the total political and governmental structure and process.[49] Our analysis suggests that this is an exaggerated view. Certainly it is true that many vital decisions affecting the lives of citizens are made elsewhere than in Parliament. As in most other industrialized countries decisions taken in boardrooms of major corporations may well have more impact than legislative decisions taken within Nagata-chō.[50] It is also true, as we have seen in chapter 7, that the government ministries have more discretion over many areas of policy than they are allowed in the British and some other similar political systems. Key policy networks include Parliament but also stretch far beyond it. Nevertheless, there are important counter-arguments.

First of all, it is important not to confuse the Japanese Parliament with the US Congress, which is a far more autonomous element in a system designed consciously on the principle of separating powers rather than fusing them.[51] Secondly the long period of LDP dominance tended to mask the significance of Parliament since the dominant party was generally able to get its own way on policy issues. Even so, our analysis has shown that during certain periods at least, the LDP needed to manoeuvre with finesse, particularly through the committee system, in order to realize even the important parts of its legislative programme. Up to 1960, to some extent in the 1970s, and most significantly from 1989, its control of Parliament was decidedly problematic. Thirdly, and most importantly, the constitutional description of Parliament and its functions, though idealized in some aspects, is far from a dead letter. Although there are various devices whereby government can go beyond legislation,[52] government cannot do without legislation, and for this Parliament is necessary. Indeed, it is perhaps best to regard Parliament as the *arena* in which power is contested and laws are made, rather than as an independent body exercising power. This is, very broadly, also the way many parliaments function elsewhere. Even so, the arguments, emerging with some force in the 1990s, that Parliament needs to be further strengthened, and indeed that in some parts of the system the rule of law needs to be reinforced, are persuasive. This will be discussed further in chapter 10.

Parliamentary Elections

It seems likely that more ink cartridges have been used up on the topic of electoral systems in Japan than on any other topic except the government bureaucracy. The issues involved are complex and rather technical, but extremely important for an understanding of the structure and process of politics. Over the whole period since the war, the electoral system and associated issues have been enmeshed in a tangled web of controversy, which even in the second half of the 1990s does not seem to have been entirely or satisfactorily unravelled.

The House of Representatives and the House of Councillors have different electoral systems, and this has been the case throughout the post-war period. The system for the House of Representatives was established in 1947,[53] and lasted with occasional modifications until 1994, when it was changed to a wholly different system. In all, 18 elections were conducted under the 'old' system (which was similar to the system used between 1925 and the war). One – that of October 1996 – has so far been held under the 'new' system.

The former lower house electoral system can be briefly described as one based on a single, non-transferable vote (SNTV) in multi-member constituencies (MMC). We shall refer to it as 'SNTV in MMCs'. In Japanese, however, it is known somewhat crudely as the 'medium constituency system' (*chūsenkyokusei*), to distinguish it from the 'large constituency system' (*daisenkyokusei*) – the system used in the 1946 and in some pre-war general elections – and the 'small constituency system' (*shōsenkyokusei*), in other words first past the post in single-member constituencies. The essence of SNTV in MMCs was as follows: Each elector has one vote, and no possibility of expressing preferences beyond his or her first preference. Each constituency, however, elects several members. Until the 1980s all constituencies except one[54] elected (in approximately equal proportions) three, or four, or five members. The number of seats increased from 466 in 1947 to 511 in 1994 when the system was replaced.[55] At the time of the 1993 elections (the last under this system) there were 129 constituencies throughout the country, two electing six members, 47 electing five members, 33 electing four members, 39 electing three members and eight electing two members.[56] Since each elector had one single vote, this was not a preferential voting system, as in Australia, nor a two-stage voting system, as in some French elections, nor was it, strictly, a form of proportional representation, though the number of seats mirrored more closely the number of votes (and thus small parties were less disadvantaged) than in the British-type system. A feature of the system was that the voter had to write the name of the candidate of his or choice on the ballot paper.

The system that replaced SNTV in MMCs in 1994 was entirely different. The number of constituencies was reduced from 511 to 500. Of these 300 elect one member each, and the remaining 200 seats are elected by the d'Hondt list system of proportional representation from 11 regional constituencies. The elector has two votes, one for the local constituency and one for the regional (proportional representation) constituency, so that vote-splitting is permitted. The elector marks two names (one for each constituency), already printed on the ballot paper. In a highly controversial provision, candidates may stand for *both* constituencies, and take a seat if elected in the one, even if defeated in the other.

The House of Councillors is elected on a different system, which apart from one important change in the early 1980s, has remained virtually unchanged since the upper house was established after the war. Of its 252 members, 100 are elected from a 'national' constituency (the whole nation considered as one single constituency) and 152 (150 before the reversion of Okinawa to Japan in 1972) from multi-member constituencies which are coincident with the prefectures.

The term of the House of Councillors is a fixed six years, but elections are staggered, with half the seats (50 from the national constituency and 76 from the prefectural constituencies) being contested every three years. As in the 'new' lower house electoral system, each voter has two non-transferable votes, in this case one for the 'national' constituency and one for the local prefectural constituency. Candidates, however, may only stand for one constituency. Whereas, unlike the House of Representatives where, under the SNTV in MMCs, some attempt was made over the years to adjust the constituencies to take account of population shift, the upper house prefectural constituencies remain entirely unchanged, except for the addition of two seats for Okinawa prefecture, and a slight readjustment of seats in the early 1990s. Two seats were taken away from Hokkaidō and one each from Hyōgo and Fukuoka, while one each was added to Miyagi, Saitama, Kanagawa and Gifu. The basis of election to the 'national' constituency, however, was radically changed in August 1982. Since in each (staggered) election 50 seats are contested in this constituency, the pre-1982 method of election could be described as 'first fifty past the post'. The great expense and uncertainty of campaigning as an individual candidate in an electorate with more than 80 million voters led to a reform whereby the d'Hondt list system of proportional representation was used to elect the 50 'national' constituency seats. As in the lower house proportional representation seats under the 'new' system, candidates have to be grouped in party (or quasi-party) lists, so that the voter cannot directly vote for a named candidate.

The electoral law which governs elections for both houses of Parliament, as well as for governors and assemblies of prefectures, mayors and assemblies of cities, towns and villages, is the Public Offices Election Law (*Kōshoku senkyo hō*).[57] The purpose of the law given in article 1 is 'to establish an electoral system ... based on the spirit of the Japanese Constitution, to ensure that these elections are conducted fairly and properly according to the freely expressed will of the electors, and thus to aim at the healthy growth of democratic politics.' Any citizen having reached the age of 20 may vote after three months' residence in a constituency (there are some exemptions from this limitation), provided that he or she is not an incompetent or serving a prison sentence. The minimum age for candidacy to all the offices covered by the Election Law is 25, except for membership of the House of Councillors, where it is 30.[58] Voting is not compulsory.

Several types of problem have arisen with the electoral systems in Japan, relating to perceived or actual deficiencies in the Law, to the characteristics of voting behaviour and candidate behaviour, and to broader issues concerning the structure and process of politics as a whole. Electoral system reform was almost constantly on the political agenda of government. Four prime ministers between the 1950s and the 1990s (Hatoyama, Tanaka, Kaifu and Miyazawa) proposed radical reform of the system for the House of Representatives, but all of them failed. Even with the collapse of LDP rule in 1993, reforming the system was fraught with difficulty, though it was achieved in 1994. Moreover, the new system introduced in 1994 itself seems riddled with problems, and calls for it to be radically reformed were widespread in the late 1990s.

The problem with electoral reform proposals, in Japan as elsewhere, is that the nature of the reform proposed differs depending on the kind of political system (especially party political system) that its proponents wish to achieve.

In Japan there is the additional problem that electoral systems having a particular kind of effect elsewhere are apt to have a significantly different effect in Japan, given certain indigenous patterns of social interaction. The following discussion will look first at the particular effects of SNTV in MMCs, second at the personalizing of elections and the related issue of corruption, third at malapportionment (the 'negative gerrymander'), and finally at the particular effects emerging from the new electoral system. Our discussion will concentrate on the House of Representatives, but we shall also discuss briefly the House of Councillors.

The problems to which the SNTV in MMCs system has given rise for political parties may be illustrated by the example of Chiba No. 1 constituency in the three successive elections of 1986, 1990 and 1993. The results are shown in tables 8.2, 8.3 and 8.4. From these tables it can be seen that for the smaller parties the system was rather uncomplicated. Either they enjoyed enough support in the constituency or they did not. This was particularly true of the two 'organized' parties, the *Kōmeitō* and the JCP, each of which could count on a highly motivated base of committed supporters (see chapter 9). Thus, Torii, the *Kōmeitō* candidate, polled a nearly even number of votes across the three elections, and his votes were sufficient to have him elected by a comfortable margin, at position number 3, 4 and 3 respectively. Having represented the constituency since 1969 (except for the period between 1972 and 1976) personal contacts and name recognition would have helped him, on top of the organizational backing provided by the *Sōka Gakkai* religion.

For the Japan Communist Party, Chiba No. 1 was plainly a marginal constituency, which they won twice out of the three elections, but each time in the number 5 position. In 1990, when they were defeated, they were nevertheless in the sixth position. The retirement of Shibata in 1993 and his replacement by the young and dynamic Shii (who not long afterwards became Secretary-General of the JCP) shows that a new candidate was not – as in most other parties – a liability (because of absence of name recognition and the time to establish networks), nor necessarily a great advantage. It is worth noting that vote of the highly organized Communist Party only varied in this constituency by a tiny 620 votes over the three elections, and paradoxically the party's best vote performance was in the election in which their candidate was defeated. By contrast to the *Kōmeitō* and the JCP, the DSP (Democratic Socialist Party), which had a much

Table 8.2   House of Representatives election 1986: Chiba No. 1 constituency.

		Times elected	Party	Votes
Elected	Usui, H.	3	LDP	124,074
Elected	Eguchi, K.	1	LDP	119,055
Elected	Torii, K.	6	*Kōmeitō*	114,824
Elected	Okajima, M.	1	LDP	98,276
Elected	Shibata, M.	5	JCP	97,900
Not elected	Ueno, K.		JSP	92,993
Not elected	Kojima, T.		DSP	88,557
Not elected	Wakimoto, K.		Independent	4,382

Source: *Asahi Nenkan*, 1987, p. 103.

Table 8.3 House of Representatives election 1990: Chiba No. 1 constituency.

		Times elected	*Party*	*Votes*
Elected	Ueno, K	2	JSP	221,216
Elected	Usui, H.	4	LDP	132,238
Elected	Eguchi, K.	2	LDP	127,689
Elected	Torii, K.	7	*Kōmeitō*	109,241
Elected	Okajima, M.	2	LDP	106,202
Not elected	Shibata, M.		JCP	97,917
Not elected	Kojima, T.		DSP	76,075
Not elected	Wakimoto, K.		Independent	3,776
Not elected	Sakai, K.		Minor party	2,227
Not elected	Sato, S.		Minor party	2,187

Source: *Asahi Nenkan*, 1991, p. 92.

Table 8.4 House of Representatives election 1993: Chiba No. 1 constituency.

		Times elected	*Party*	*Votes*
Elected	Noda, Y.	1	JNP*	175,671
Elected	Okajima, M.	3	*Shinseitō*	151,163
Elected	Torii, K.	8	*Kōmeitō*	113,706
Elected	Usui, H.	5	LDP	108,613
Elected	Shii, K.	1	JCP	98,297
Not elected	Eguchi, K.		LDP	97,277
Not elected	Yoshimine, K.		JSP	82,633
Not elected	Watanabe, T.		DSP	22,935
Not elected	Wakimoto, K.		Independent	4,853

*JNP = Japan New Party – the party founded by Hosokawa in 1992.
Source: *Asahi Nenkan,* 1994, p. 127.

more traditional and personalized labour union vote base, was gravely affected by a change of candidate between 1990 and 1993, losing over 53,000 votes between the two elections!

Remarkable fluctuations were also characteristic of the JSP performance in this constituency. The party's candidate, Ueno, who had first been elected in 1983, fell behind the Communist into sixth place in 1986 – a poor election generally for the JSP. But then in 1990, benefiting no doubt from the Doi Takako boom, he jumped right into first place, with much the highest number of votes won by any candidate over the three elections. Indeed, as it turned out he won enough votes to justify the candidacy of a second JSP candidate, assuming that the Socialist vote had been split more or less evenly between them. The assumption, however, was not one that could easily be made, and in any case it was difficult for the party to predict in advance how many votes it was going to obtain. The danger of splitting the vote and having both candidates defeated (*tomodaore*, 'going down together') was fresh in the minds of the party from bitter experiences in earlier elections. In 1993 – once again a poor election for the party nationally – a new candidate found himself in seventh place, well over 15,000 votes behind the Communist.

Much the strongest party in the constituency was of course the LDP, which won three out of the five seats in both 1986 and 1990. In 1993, however, it fared disastrously, winning only one seat. One seat was lost because one of its previous members, Okajima, belonged to the Hata faction and defected to the newly formed *Shinseitō*. Another, that of Eguchi, was lost because of the successful intervention of a candidate from Hosokawa's fashionable Japan New Party, who came top of the poll, forcing Eguchi into sixth place. Significantly, however, the combined votes of Usui, Eguchi and Okajima across the three elections were remarkably consistent: 341,405 (1986); 366,129 (1990); 357,053 (1993). Okajima's defection reduced the LDP total in 1993 to 205,890. This suggests that all three candidates had built up a strong and fairly predictable 'hard vote'[59] in the constituency. In 1986 and 1990 the order remained the same: Usui, Eguchi, Okajima, with several thousand votes separating them, but the fact that Okajima overtook both of them by a wide margin in 1993 suggests that his recent defection to the newly formed *Shinseitō* added a substantial 'image vote' on top of his hard vote. Historical experience suggested, however, that the former was far less reliable in the long term than the latter.

Our analysis of the election results in Chiba No. 1 constituency leads us to some significant if tentative conclusions. The first and most important is that Japan's long experience with SNTV in MMCs was highly consistent with (whether or not it had caused) the personalizing of electoral campaigns. The *Kōmeitō* and JCP were largely exceptions to this rule in the sense that they were tightly organized and projected an appeal to *party* loyalty. At the other extreme, the party which most consistently and most successfully based its campaigning on the cultivation of a 'hard vote' was the LDP. How far it was the multi-member electoral system that led the LDP to cultivate the hard vote, and how far it was culturally conditioned patterns of social interaction that induced LDP candidates to run their own highly personalized campaigns within the framework of the multi-member constituency system, is essentially a chicken and egg question.[60] What is important is that the LDP methods were so successful for so long that it was normally able to resist demands for radical change. Only when the party itself split in 1993 did the introduction of a new electoral system become a realistic possibility, though of course the split itself was connected both with concern about widespread corruption and the frustration of younger parliamentarians with what many of them saw as the straitjacket of the existing system. Another factor was the urbanization of Japan, making the rural social element in politics seem anachronistic.

Two particular issues concerning the old system were addressed in the reforms of 1994: corruption and malapportionment.

Whereas the regulations on political corruption under the old system had been lax and full of loopholes, a serious attempt was made in 1994 to introduce much tighter legislation. In outline, the measures introduced were as follows.[61]

Requirements for the disclosure of financial contributions were made much more strict. Political parties and other political organizations now had to declare all contributions in excess of ¥50,000.[62] Previously, a distinction had been made between the two, with parties required to declare contributions over ¥10,000, but other political organizations not having to declare contributions less than ¥1,000,000. This had led to parties being bypassed, and bodies set up by factions, individual parliamentarians or parliamentary candidates becoming the principal channels of political funding.

Companies, labour unions and other bodies could now contribute funds to a maximum of ¥500,000 for political activities to *only one* financial control body (*shikin kanri dantai*) representing a party, a political funding body (*seiji shikin dantai*) or an individual politician.[63] Previously almost unlimited funding had flowed into the political world because politicians could evade maximum limits by setting up several separate funding organizations.[64] In cases of infringements of this provision, both the contributor and the receiver of funds would be liable to punishment, including suspension of civil rights.[65] The principle of complicity (*renzasei*) was also established, so that a candidate could be penalized for illegal fund raising activities by members of his family or of his secretarial staff, if the candidate had been privy to these activities.[66] If an elected candidate were convicted, this would not only invalidate his election, but would mean that he could not stand for election in the same constituency again for a period of five years after his conviction.[67] The establishment of this principle was in order to plug a gaping hole in the Election Law, which had permitted candidates to escape the consequences of wrongdoing by members of their staff or their families, and to regard any fine that they did incur as part of the costs of campaigning, because it did not bar them from further candidacy.[68]

It had long been established wisdom that a good part of the reason for such widespread corruption in Japanese elections (and in politics generally) stemmed from the extraordinarily high cost of campaigning and, more broadly, of establishing and servicing political organizations. Given the candidate-centred electoral organizations under the old electoral system, much of the cost of maintaining an extensive staff and engaging in political activities had to be borne by the candidate himself (or herself). Since one of the objectives of the 1993–4 electoral system reforms was to shift the emphasis from candidates to parties, some provision needed to be made to establish party financing on a firm footing. The Hosokawa Government therefore embarked upon the controversial path of public funding of elections, and this came to be embodied in the revised legal structure. The amount of money needed to finance public funding of elections was calculated on the basis of ¥250 per head of population per annum,[69] and in 1994 slightly exceeded ¥30 billion. Much debate went into the question of eligibility to grants from the fund, and in particular on the definition of an 'eligible party'. 'Eligible party' came to be defined in the following way: (a) a party containing not less than five (*gonin ijō*) members of Parliament; or (b) a party which, at the most recent lower house or upper house general election, and in either the single-member or proportional representation constituencies, has received at least 2 per cent of the total valid vote.

In order to avoid the proliferation of minor parties excessively reliant on public funding, it was further provided that the amount calculated for a party (to be paid normally on 1 January) should not amount to more than two thirds of its total income. In order to be eligible for public funding, a party also had to be registered as a 'legal person' (*hōjin*).

Another widely discussed problem with the old election system was that of malapportionment. The 1947 Election Law contained no effective provision for regular and impartial redrawing of electoral boundaries to take account of movements of population. Between the late 1940s and the late 1990s, however, enormous numbers of people moved from the countryside to the cities, as the result of urbanization attendant upon rapid economic growth. Despite the efforts of the Election System Deliberation Commission, it proved extremely difficult to rectify the resultant 'negative gerrymander'. It was not difficult to discover political reasons for this failure, since the firmest base of support for the LDP was in rural parts of Japan, and in an era of single-party LDP governments, the political will to reduce rural over-representation and urban under-representation was largely absent. The effect was quite extreme. For instance, at the lower house general elections held in October 1979, there were 3.87 times more electors per seat on the electoral role in the most under-represented constituency (Chiba No. 4) than in the most over-represented constituency (Hyōgo No. 5).[70]

Even though no comprehensive reform of the malapportionment was undertaken under the old electoral system, palliative measures were taken from time to time. In the 1960s and 1970s reforms consisted in adding numbers of seats in major conurbations. This, however, resulted in an expansion in the size of the House of Representatives, to the point where it was realized it could not be continued indefinitely. It was not until the 1980s that the Government grasped the nettle of reducing in some regions the number of rural sets, to match a parallel increase in big city seats. By the 1980s the courts were interesting themselves in the question of malapportionment, from the standpoint of equality of rights, and a judicial guideline was established that no set of voters should find the value of their votes worth more than three times the value of the votes of any other set of voters. The courts, nevertheless, refrained from invalidating any election.[71] The only practicable way to approach voter equality was by cutting back the number of seats in country areas. This, however, resulted in the emergence of a number of two-member and six-member constituencies, in addition to the three-, four-, and five-member constituencies which still accounted for the great majority of seats. By the early 1990s the system appeared even more complicated than before, while the vote value discrepancy kept creeping up to beyond the judicially prescribed three-to-one limit.

The complete redrawing of boundaries required by the new electoral system in the mid-1990s provided an opportunity to eliminate the 'negative gerrymander'. Even when the new electoral boundaries were announced, however, there was already a discrepancy – slightly over two times – between most- and least-well represented single-member constituencies, which increased with further movements of population. It seems possible that a certain amount of political pressure from rural interests was exerted on the Boundaries Commission, and there were particular problems in those prefectures which stood to lose much of their previous (inflated) representation. In fact, however, the rural over-representation was concentrated in a few constituencies, so that the broad picture was one of a substantial shift in the voting balance towards the cities and away from the countryside. In addition to the 300 single-member seats, the 200 seats elected by proportional representation were essentially lacking in malapportionment. In the medium term, at least, this had not inconsiderable implications for changes in policy. In the medium-to-long term, moreover, it may have an impact on the ways in which politics is conducted. Putting together the arguments about the highly personalized nature of elections and the degree of malapportionment under the old system, it would seem to follow that substantial reduction in the vote-value imbalance should give to the cities, which have more modern and fluid modes of social interaction, a greater say in national politics and thus the capacity to change the patterns of political interaction. This needs, however, to be qualified by the fact that the contrast between urban and rural social patterns has narrowed since the war, partly through the modernizing influence on the countryside of television, fast transport networks and so on, but also because in some ways the cities have never completely urbanized their social patterns.

There remained one part of the national electoral system which was nearly unreconstructed in respect of unbalanced vote values, namely the prefectural constituencies of the House of Councillors. As seen above, out of 252 House of Councillors seats, 152 (76 at each three-yearly election) are elected from constituencies continuous with the 47 prefectures. In any one election, Tokyo, the most populous prefecture, elects four members, whereas Tottori, on the Japan Sea coast of Western Honshū, elects one. This meant a discrepancy in vote value of 5.26 to 1 at the time of the Upper House elections of July 1977.[72]

The October 1996 General Elections for the House of Representatives

In the rest of the chapter we shall briefly examine the first general election to the House of Representatives under the new electoral system, that of 20 October 1996. The main feature of the elections that stands out is a surprising degree of continuity with the kinds of result that obtained under the old system.

Let us return to the area of Chiba Prefecture that, under the old system, was Chiba No. 1 constituency (see tables 8.2, 8.3 and 8.4). Under the new system more or less the same geographic area was divided into three constituencies, known as the first, second and third constituencies of Chiba. The results in these three new constituencies in October 1996 was as shown in table 8.5.

What is striking in these results is that in these successor constituencies exactly the same well-established conservative candidates were elected (Usui, Eguchi and Okajima) as in the single multi-member constituency under the old system.

Table 8.5 House of Representatives election 1996 (new system): single-member constituencies.

		Times elected	Party	Votes	
Chiba No. 1					
Elected	Usui, H.	6	LDP	77,679	+PR*
Not elected	Murai		*Shinshintō*	40,094	
(+1 DP, 1 JCP, 2 minor party, candidates)					
Chiba No. 2					
Elected	Eguchi, K.	3	LDP	75,939	+PR*
Not elected	Nakamura		*Shinshintō*	60,401	
(+1 DP, 1 JCP, 1 minor party, candidates)					
Chiba No. 3					
Elected	Okajima, M.	4	*Shinshintō*	84,846	
Not elected	Murano		LDP	73,254	+PR*
(+1 JCP, 1 DP, 1 minor party, candidates)					

*Candidate standing also in proportional representation constituency.
Source: Asahi Nenkan, 1997, p. 188.

Table 8.6 House of Representatives election 1996 (new system): Proportional representation constituency: Shikoku block (total seats = 7).

		Times elected	*Order*	*Margin**
LDP (3 elected, 783,589, 41.6%)				
Elected	Ochi	10	1	
Elected	Nishida	7	2	
Elected	Morita	6	3	
Not elected	Shichijō		4	
Not elected	Sanseki		5	
Not elected	Miki, S.		6	94.36%
Not elected	Miki, T.		6	87.41%

(In addition, 10 LDP candidates who stood for the Shikoku block also stood for and were elected in single-member constituencies in Shikoku. All were ordered as '6')

Shinshintō (2 elected, 455,269, 24.2%)				
Elected	Endō	5	1	
Elected	Nishimura	6	2	
Not elected	Mizuta		3	

Minshutō (DP) (1 elected, 245,323, 13.0%)				
Elected	Gotō	3	1	93.64%
Not elected	Manabe		1	50.31%
Not elected	Asami		4	
Not elected	Utsunomiya		5	

(In addition 1 DP candidate was elected for a single-member constituency in Shikoku. He was listed as '1')

JCP (1 elected, 227,014, 12.1%)				
Elected	Haruna	1	2	26.79%
Not elected	Matsubara		3	

(In addition 1 JCP candidate was elected in a single-member constituency in Shikoku. He was listed as '1')

SDP (0 elected, 132,868, 7.1%)
(4 candidates, all listed as '1', stood in the Shikoku block. All stood in single-member constituencies, where their margins of defeat were, respectively, 47.85%, 22.74%, 20.70% and 16.30%)

Minor party (omitted)

* 'Margin' = percentage margin of defeat in a single-member constituency. Thus in Kōchi No. 1, Gotō (DP) won 31,391 votes, or 93.64% of the vote of the winning (JCP) candidate, who polled 33,523 votes. This put him ahead of Manabe, who only managed to win 31,501 votes, or 50.31% of the vote of the winning (LDP) candidate, who polled 62,612 votes in Kagawa No. 1.
Source: Asahi Nenkan, 1997, p. 198.

Two of them had remained with the LDP, while the third, Okajima, having defected to the *Shinseitō* before the 1993 elections, subsequently joined the *Shinshintō*. All, however, seem to have applied time-honoured methods of electioneering to the single-member constituencies created by the electoral reform. While not all such constituencies followed exactly this pattern, the result was far from atypical.

When we turn from the 300 single-member constituencies to the 200 proportional representation (PR) constituencies, a most interesting pattern emerges.

According to the new election rules, a candidate could stand both in a single-member, and in his or her regional PR constituency, but in the latter, it had to be as a member of a party list. In constructing its list of candidates for the PR constituencies, a given party could list its candidates for a given regional block in order of preference: 1, 2, 3, 4, 5 ... . But, if it wished, it could list them all equal: 1, 1, 1, 1, 1 ..., or partly in preference order and partly equal, e.g.: 1, 2, 3, 4, 4, 4 ... . Where candidates were listed as equal by their party, who was elected in the PR constituency depended on the margins of defeat of those same candidates in single-member constituences, assuming they were standing in both. The effect of this can be seen by referring to table 8.6, giving the result of the Shikoku regional block. Candidates who failed to be elected in a single-member constituency, nevertheless, could be given a second chance, and the determination of that second chance could depend on their performance *in the single-member constituency*, not just in the PR constituency.[73]

This, in effect, created conditions not entirely unlike those of the old multi-member constituencies and further rewarded *kōenkai*-based electioneering, much as in the old system. When we consider the actual working of the new system, therefore, it is hardly surprising that there should have been such evident continuity with the pattern of elections before the change.

9

The Politics of Party:
The Liberal Democrats
and their Rivals

The Party System

The formation of the Liberal Democratic Party in 1955 was a political achievement whose significance can hardly be exaggerated. It led to more than three and a half decades of single-party dominance, covering a period in which Japan moved from relative poverty to being the second-largest economy in the world. Many observers and some participants came to believe that single-party dominance, and the network of power relationships which accompanied it, was more or less immutable, and that the '1955 political system' would last, with occasional fine tuning, into a future so distant that alternative arrangements did not need to be seriously considered.[1] With hindsight, however, it seems evident that the 1955 system was less secure than often supposed, and that what happened in 1993 might well have happened much earlier. Indeed, a principal argument of this chapter is that fluid multi-party politics is as much a natural political condition in Japan as single-party dominance, that both of them have a logic that is particular to Japan, and that there may even be a dialectical relationship between them. Moreover, it will be seen that there is an important relationship between the strength of control *within* the dominant party, and the strength of control *by* the dominant party. In none of the periods covered has there been anything that properly fits the description of a two-party system, despite a widespread normative assumption that it ought to be the norm in democratic party politics.[2] Determined efforts to create a working two-party system in the 1990s have met with little success. On the other hand, the principle of 'winner take all' that is embedded in many theoretical models of party politics, also does not fit the Japanese experience well.[3]

It has already been seen in chapter 6 that between 1955 and 1993 the structure and process of central government underwent significant change in various of its aspects. In this chapter we shall attempt to show that in the narrower world of party politics there were a number of discrete phases, each having a partially distinct logic, though the dividing line between each phase is difficult to define exactly. The interesting point that emerges from this exercise is that historically there have been patterns of correlation between dominance and cohesion within the party or parties in office, dominance and cohesion within the party system as a whole, and lack of dominance and cohesion within the opposition parties. To some extent also the reverse of these factors correlate with each other.

The findings are summarized in table 9.1, where 12 historical phases between 1946 and 1997 have been isolated. In this schema three phases of political dominance may be found, and, more tentatively, a fourth which may be beginning in 1997–8. The first (phase 2) was the period of dominance by Yoshida Shigeru during his second administration, from the electoral victory of his Liberal Party in 1949 to the end of the Occupation in 1952. This occurred during the exceptional period of the Occupation, when many of his potential political rivals were excluded from active participation in politics by the purge edict. The second was in phase 6: the period of Satō's prime ministership between 1964 and 1972. Satō was able to establish unprecedented dominance by his own faction over the LDP, and, particularly after the LDP victory in the 1969 general elections, dominance over the party system as a whole. The third period of dominance occurred during phase 8, principally during the Nakasone prime ministership (1982–7), but more generally throughout the period 1980–9 because of the combination of Tanaka (later Takeshita) faction dominance over the LDP and LDP dominance over the party system. The fourth period of dominance may have begun in October 1996 with the improvement in LDP fortunes at the first lower house general elections held under the new electoral system. Although the LDP did not win a majority at the elections, it put itself in a sufficiently strong position to start attracting to its ranks politicians from other parties, disillusioned with their remoteness from office while languishing in opposition. Enough of these had joined the LDP to give it a lower house majority by September 1997.

We can see from this analysis that periods of political dominance have recurred since the end of the war, but have never lasted more than a decade. It is therefore instructive to examine how it has been possible to establish such dominant regimes, and why they eventually collapse.

In all dominant regimes so far, a constant factor has been the presence of a powerful personality: Yoshida in the case of the first period of dominance, Satō in the case of the second, perhaps Hashimoto in the case of the fourth. The third case is rather more complicated, since Tanaka, having lost the prime ministership in 1974 and subsequently becoming embroiled in the Lockheed investigations and trial, worked to expand his *habatsu* in a kingmaker role. First Suzuki, and then Nakasone, were beneficiaries of his kingmaking, but after doing well in the 1986 general elections, Nakasone was able – at least for a rather brief period – to be much more his own man than when he had first been prime minister.

Table 9.1 Patterns of dominance and cohesion within the party system, 1946–1997.

Phase	Within government party(-ies)		Within party system		Within opposition	
	Dominance	Cohesion	Dominance	Cohesion	Dominance	Cohesion
1. 1946–49	C	C	C	C	C	C
	Post-war confusion and uncertainty; coalition governments					
2. 1949–52	A	A	B	C	C	C
	First period of dominance: dominance of Yoshida over Liberal Party and over politics generally					
3. 1952–5	B	C	C	B	B	B
	Yoshida–Hatoyama struggle; fluid party politics in general					
4. 1955–60	B	B	A	C	B	B
	Mostly Kishi period; only two significant parties, with LDP dominant, and polarised politics; factionalism emerges as major force in LDP					
5. 1960–4	B	B	A	B	B	B
	Ikeda period; still strong factions in LDP; relative quiescence between LDP and opposition parties					
6. 1964–72	A	A	A	C	C	C
	Second period of dominance: tight control by Sato of LDP factional situation, and electoral dominance, especially after the 1969 general elections; oppostion disarray					
7. 1972–80	C	C	B–	B	C	B
	Factional struggle between Tanaka/Ohira and Fukuda; severe disruption within LDP, 1979–80; near-parity between government and opposition; opposition cohesion slightly improved					
8. 1980–9	A	B	A	B	C	C
	Third period of dominance: the Tanaka (later Takeshita) faction as kingmaker; Nakasone five-year term as prime minister; good LDP election results in 1980 and 1986; opposition poorly co-ordinated					
9. 1989–92	A–	B	B	B	B	B
	LDP loss of control over House of Councillors; JSP temporary resurgence, followed by loss of support during the Gulf Crisis					
10. 1992–4	C	B	B	B	C	B
	Split in Takeshita faction, followed by split in LDP; formation of Hosokawa and Hata cabinets					
11. 1994–6	B	C	B	C	A–	B
	Murayama three-party coalition government with comfortable majority, followed by same coalition led by Hashimoto, JSP/SDP problems of cohesion					
12. 1996–8	A	B	B	C+	C	C
	Fourth period of dominance?: LDP minority government under Hashimoto following 1996 elections, supported by SDP and *Sakigake*, continuous attempts by LDP to re-establish single-party dominance. LDP regaining of lower house majority in September 1997, reformist initiatives, but terminal difficulties for the Prime Minister. Turmoil among the parties out of power, with *Shinshintō* collapse and formation of expanded *Minshutō*					

Key: A = dominant/cohesive;   B = semi-dominant/semi-cohesive;   C = not dominant/not cohesive.

Personality, however, though a necessary factor, has not been a sufficient one to establish dominance. Apart from endorsement by the electorate (important in all four cases), the relative absence of effective rivals has been significant. Thus Yoshida had a free hand after his party's victory in the 1949 elections, largely because many of his potential rivals were banned from participating in politics because of the Occupation's purge edict. Satō benefited from the fortuitous deaths of no less than three of his factional rivals (Ikeda, Kōno and Ōno) within a year of taking office. With Tanaka, by contrast, dominance over the LDP was carefully planned over a considerable period, by the application of ample funding in the service of expanding the membership of his *habatsu*. In the case of Hashimoto, where at the time of writing it was too early to identify with confidence the existence of a dominant regime, the political incoherence and eventual collapse of the *Shinshintō* (the principal party to emerge from the 1993–4 coalition governments), made his task a great deal easier, despite severe economic problems. An adverse result, however, in the July 1998 upper house elections ended his prime ministership prematurely.

Why, then, have such dominant regimes faced collapse after a few years? In the case of Yoshida, the return to active politics of rivals such as Hatoyama once the purge restrictions on them had been lifted, together with the turbulent atmosphere of immediate post-Occupation politics, quickly eroded his political dominance. With Satō, the Nixon 'shocks' of July and August 1971, and particularly President Nixon's *volte face* on China policy, seriously wrong-footed Satō and led to his conservatism on the China-recognition issue being used against him by rivals to good effect. The Tanaka–Nakasone–Takeshita dominance of the 1980s is once again more complicated, and indeed the dominance of the Takeshita *habatsu* lasted until it split in 1992. But Nakasone was not politically strong enough in his own right to last beyond the end of 1987 as Prime Minister, and his successor, Takeshita (who now combined the prime ministership with leadership of the dominant *habatsu*), fell foul of corruption scandals arising from the euphoric economic conditions of the late 1980s, as well as reaping the consequences of taking unpopular policy decisions on taxation and agricultural protection. All this led to an unprecedented LDP defeat in the 1989 upper house election.

If dominant regimes, though recurring from time to time, have enjoyed limited tenure, regimes based on a more even balance of forces have been relatively unstable. If we take the whole of the period since the end of the war, we find too much variety of pattern for easy generalization, but some useful comparisons may be made.

Before the formation of the LDP in November 1955 (except, perhaps, for phase 2 – the period of Yoshida's dominance), politics was extremely unstable and confrontational. In the Kishi period (1957–60) confrontation became even sharper, but the formation of a single dominant party led to the development of the LDP *habatsu* system as the principal method of power allocation within the party. It was at this period that the enormous cost of party politics became a matter of major public concern. Nevertheless, with the removal from the scene of Kishi and his confrontational politics in 1960, another implication of the *habatsu* system became evident, namely that it was a mechanism for power broking and power sharing that was not primarily based on *policy* differences

Table 9.2 Members of the House of Representatives, by party, October 1996 general elections.

	Total number	Average age at time of election	% of new members	Average no. of times elected	Average age of new members when elected
LDP	240	56.7 (1980 = 56.5)	20.4 (1980 = 7.3)	4.8 (1980 = 5.6)	48.3
Shinshintō	155	52.4	23.3	3.5	49.7
Minshutō	52	50.8	32.7	2.8	46.0
JCP	26	59.9 (1980 = 53.3)	19.2 (1980 = 6.9)	4.5 (1980 = 3.6)	46.4
SDP	15	57.9 (1980 = 53.3)	26.7 (1980 = 7.5)	4.3 (1980 = 4.9)	47.2
Sakigake	2	58.0	0	4.0	—
Independent	10	48.6	40.0	3.3	48.7

Source: Asahi Nenkan, 1997, pp. 186–99, + bessatsu pp. 184–97.
Kokkai Binran, No. 97 (February 1997), pp. 106–69.
Figures for the 1980 elections are taken from J. A. A. Stockwin, *Japan: Divided Politics in a Growth Economy*. London, Weidenfeld, 2nd edn, 1982, tables on pages 120, 188 and 191.

between *habatsu*. Thus power and policy with the LDP became separated from each other to a considerable extent, with a consequent reduction in instability. The effects of this became evident in the Ikeda period (phase 5: 1960–4), when distribution of cabinet and party posts was based on a finely tuned balancing of interests between rather evenly matched alliances of *habatsu*. This phase was not a period of dominance by a single *habatsu* (as phase 6 was), but it was an absolutely crucial turning point in foreign and economic policy, as we saw in chapter 5. The political checks and balances established as a norm in phase 5 may be seen as part and parcel of the 'low profile' policies of the Ikeda era, which also bequeathed a legacy of 'immobilism', or deliberate playing down of confrontation, to later periods.

Phase 7 (1972–80) is different from phase 5 in that a situation of near parity (*hakuchū*) was reached between the LDP and the Opposition parties, which had established a position of considerable dominance in the local politics of urban areas. Here *habatsu* confrontation took a bitter personal turn, with the Tanaka–Fukuda rivalry as its axis. Economic change from rapid growth to slow growth also added to the tensions of the period, but paradoxically helped the LDP by creating the more conservative political mood in the electorate that became evident towards the end of the decade. Although it is dangerous to engage in hypothetical history, it seems not improbable that a continuation of 10 per cent annual economic growth rates for a few years beyond 1973 would have resulted in the electoral defeat of the LDP within one or two elections.[4]

Phases 9–11 once again find the LDP in trouble from a variety of causes. Various approaches to reform of the political system were much in vogue. But much the biggest cause of the LDP defeat at the lower house elections of 1993 was that it had split. Even at the nadir of its fortunes, when it had suffered considerable erosion of its parliamentary membership, it remained much the largest party. Back in power from June 1994 as the largest party in a coalition government, it was able to act gradually to re-establish and consolidate its power base. As of 1996–8 a new party system appeared to be developing, based on one dominant (but not necessarily majority) party and several other parties of which the Democratic Party had major potential for growth.

A Profile of the Parties following the October 1996 Elections

The parties which emerged from the first elections to be held under the new electoral system were of course much influenced by the turbulent events of the preceding period. A close analysis, however, of the parties and their parliamentary memberships reveals rather less change in composition than one might imagine from the character of those events.

Table 9.2 gives the number of seats won by each party, the average age of parliamentarians at the time of the elections, the percentage of members taking their seats for the first time, the average number of times members had been elected (including the 1996 elections), and the average age of new members at the time of their election. If we compare the ages of members with those for the lower house general elections held in 1980, we find rather little change. The average age of LDP members in the two elections was almost exactly the same, as was that for the SDP (JSP in 1980), while the average age of Communist members had significantly increased. The *Shinshintō* and *Minshutō*, which had no exact counterparts in the 1980 elections, had a younger age profile, particularly in the case of the latter. On the other hand, the percentage of new members to total members elected in 1996 had much more than doubled when compared with the 1980 results, in the cases of the LDP, JCP and SDP. For the *Shinshintō* and *Minshutō* – parties formed within the previous two years – the percentage of new members was at the 20 per cent and 30 per cent level respectively. When we compare these figures, at first sight, the most surprising finding is the extraordinarily low percentage of new members elected in the 1980 elections, particularly in the case of the LDP, for which those elections were particularly successful. Indeed, come-backs by previously defeated members were more numerous in 1980 than entry by new members. This is easy to understand, however, given that the previous elections were less than a year earlier. Although more than twice as many first-timers were elected in the 1996 elections (more than three years after the 1993 elections), the figures are not such as to indicate a wholesale renewal of the parliamentary membership. Moreover, the average age of new members across the parties was surprisingly high, as can be seen from column 5 of table 9.2.

This point needs further exploration, as is attempted in table 9.3. In this table we analyse the 'survivability' of LDP parliamentarians newly elected over the five lower house elections between 1980 and 1993. For reasons of space and complexity we here confine the analysis to the LDP,[5] and ignore other parties. We can see from table 9.3 that while a majority of those first elected in a particular election went on to win a series of subsequent elections, defeat was an ever-present risk, especially for those candidates who found it difficult to establish an adequate *kōenkai*, or personal support organisation in a given constituency.

Table 9.3   The subsequent success rate of LDP parliamentarians newly elected in the 1980, 1983, 1987, 1990 and 1993 lower house general elections*.

1st year elected	1980		1983		1986		1990		1993	
	no.	%	no.	%	no.	%	no.	%	no.	%
Elected first in this and all subsequent elections to 1996	9	50.0	8	44.4	25	69.4	19	51.3	22	84.6
One defeat	2	11.1	3	16.7	10	27.8	10	27.0	3	11.5
Two defeats	2	11.1	3	16.7	0	0.0	2	5.4	—	
Three defeats	1	5.6	0	0.0	0	0.0	—		—	
Four or five defeats	1	5.6	0	0.0	—		—		—	
Did not stand in some later elections	3	16.7	6	33.3	3	8.3	5	13.5	1	3.8
Total	18		20		38		36		26	

*Candidates are here counted as LDP even where they changed party in later elections.
Source: *Asahi Nenkan*, 1981, pp. 236–40; 1984, pp. 103–7; 1987, pp. 102–16; 1991, pp. 91–5; 1994, pp. 126–32.

The figures indeed reflect a wide range of possible electoral careers. At one extreme is the case of Nakagawa Shōichi, first elected in the 1983 elections for the fifth constituency of Hokkaidō, having inherited his late father's constituency. He was elected in the first position in his five-member constituency in the 1983, 1986, 1990 and 1993 elections, and when the electoral system changed became the member for the eleventh (single-member) constituency of Hokkaidō. By contrast Uetake Shigeo was first elected to the second constituency of Tochigi in the 1980 general election, in fourth position out of five seats, was defeated in the 1983 and 1986 elections, came back in fifth position in 1990, was defeated again in 1993, and then obtained the seventh out of eight places in the North Kantō regional bloc in 1996. Both of these, however, were extreme cases, with the bulk of members having to work hard to consolidate an initially tenuous hold on a constituency through subsequent elections. A particularly interesting finding of table 9.3 is that no less than 22 out of 26 LDP members elected first in 1993 found seats under the new electoral arrangements in 1996. Even though the number of LDP members newly elected in 1996 was higher than usual, clearly incumbents were still favoured under the new system of election. Moreover, the number of times a member had been elected, as of the 1996 elections (table 9.2, column 4) came down slightly in the case of the LDP from 5.6 to 4.8 since 1980, but was still much higher than the figures for the newly formed parties, *Shinshintō* and *Minshutō*.

A related question concerns the degree of local commitment evidenced by parliamentarians. One of the great problems of transition from the old electoral system to the new in 1996 was to find seats in their own areas for sitting members. Since the new constituencies were much smaller than the old ones, it was often possible to accommodate members who had previously 'shared' a multi-member constituency as strong candidates for single-member constituencies which at least in part fell within the boundaries of the old districts. Where this was not possible a member could be placed in a high position in the party list for the local regional bloc. There are almost no instances, however, of a defeated member for a constituency in one part of the country standing for election in a quite different region.[6] Even when we examine 'place of origin' (i.e. birthplace) we find that the great majority of parliamentarians hold seats in the region in which they were born, though the JCP is an important exception to the general norms of Japanese politics in emphasising party rather than local ties. (See table 9.4.)

Another aspect of this profile of parties and party politicians is educational background. Data have been compiled on the educational attainments of

Table 9.4 Local or non-local origin of parliamentarians elected in October 1996 lower house general elections (%).

	LDP	Shinshintō	Minshutō	JCP	SDP	Sakigake	Independent
Local	87.9	80.7	86.5	50.0	66.7	100.0	80.0
Not local	12.1	19.3	13.5	50.0	33.3	0.0	20.0

Note: Some flexibility has been used in the definition of 'region'. Thus, for instance, a member representing a constituency close to the boundary of another formally defined region where he or she was born is treated as 'local'.
Source: *Asahi Nenkan*, 1997, bessatsu, pp. 184–97.

parliamentarians elected in the October 1996 elections. The most striking thing to emerge from these figures is the extremely high percentage of parliamentarians of all parties who had attended (and in nearly all cases graduated from) university. Moreover, the percentage was higher across the board than it had been in the 1980 lower house general elections.[7] No doubt this reflected the passing of generations that had been educated before the war, when a much smaller proportion of the population was able to enter tertiary institutions.

Secondly, as in earlier elections such as that of 1980, more LDP members had attended university than members representing any other party. Indeed, when we exclude the diminishing number of elderly parliamentarians still remaining who were educated under the pre-war educational system, we find that university graduates account for almost the totality of the LDP parliamentary contingent. The *Shinshintō* and *Minshutō* were not far behind, and the fact that 91.6 per cent of *Shinshintō* members had been to university is interesting when we consider that in the 1980 elections a mere 39.4 per cent of those elected under the *Kōmeitō* label could claim university attendance.[8] Since the *Sōka Gakkai* and former *Kōmeitō* element within the *Shinshintō* was widely considered to be its organizational core, this seems a most significant finding.[9] As in 1980, the only party which appeared to have a significantly lower educational attainment record was the SDP, but its numbers were now too small for percentages to have much meaning.

Thirdly, for the three main parties at least, around three quarters had attended one of the many universities in the Tokyo area, and this was especially true for the LDP. (The JCP is a conspicuous exception.) Even though the percentage of LDP members attending the prestigious Tokyo University had fallen from 30.0 per cent in 1980 to 21.2 per cent in 1996, it appeared to have risen in the case of the other parties (though comparison is difficult). No less than 67.9 per cent of LDP members, and 53.5 per cent of *Shinshintō* members, had attended one of Tokyo, Waseda, Keiō, Chūō, Nihon, Meiji or Kyoto universities, which are arguably the best known tertiary institutions in the country.

Finally, by comparison with other East Asian countries, the proportion of Japanese parliamentarians who have attended foreign universities is extremely low at a mere seven out of 500. This might perhaps be taken as evidence of a parochial outlook among Japanese parliamentarians, though such a conclusion would need to be advanced with caution.

When we turn from the educational to the professional background of members, we encounter problems of information, definition and interpretation. Much less information is readily available on the previous career backgrounds of those who have been members for a long time than on more recent members, while in many cases it is difficult to disentangle occupations pursued in parallel with a parliamentary career from those which preceded it. Many members list multiple careers, meaning that the number of occupations much exceeds the number of parliamentarians. Nevertheless, our tentative findings are presented in table 9.6. From this it can be seen that much the most common career backgrounds for members, especially in the case of the LDP, are local politics and having been a secretary to a parliamentarian. The proportion of former bureaucrats appears to have declined, though it remains much higher in the LDP than in other parties. A substantial number are found to have worked in companies, either as executives or employees, though the variety of industry and size of company represented is great. Employees of the mass media (journalists, newscasters etc.) are also to be found, though not in great numbers, and there are a small number who have worked in educational and medical establishments of various kinds. In a very considerable number of cases, however, it seems best to consider the member as a professional politician, for whom any other career has at best been secondary. This is particularly true of politicians who have taken over a *kōenkai* from a relative. Finally, the contrast appears less sharp than it used to be between the career patterns of LDP members and members from other parties, though an appreciable number of labour unionists may still be found in the *Shinshintō, Minshutō*, JCP and SDP (none in the LDP). There are more lawyers in the *Minshutō* and *Shinshintō* than in the LDP, and the *Minshutō* includes a significant number of citizens' movement activists.

The final topic in this profile of parties following the 1996 elections concerns regional distribution of support. This can be determined with accuracy from the results of the regional bloc elections conducted by proportional representation (see table 9.7). From this we can see that, with the exception of Hokkaidō in the north, the distribution of votes between the parties was reasonably even across the country. As in previous elections, the LDP generally performed better in areas away from the big cities than in the big cities themselves, but the difference was not extreme. The *Shinshintō* won a fairly even share of the vote in the various regions, ranging from 24 per cent to 33 per cent, except in Hokkaidō, where it did badly. The regional flatness of distribution in the case of the *Shinshintō* is no doubt a product of its combination of urban and rural elements, since the former *Kōmeitō* had a predominantly urban following; the former LDP/*Shinseitō* component reflected a typical rural weighting and the former Democratic Socialist Party elements fell somewhere in between.

The *Minshutō* exhibited a slightly less flat regional distribution, since it did well in the Tokyo area and exceptionally well in Hokkaidō, where it inherited almost the whole of the old Socialist Party machine, and where some its most famous names were located. It was weakest in areas away from the big cities. The JCP did best in the Tokyo and Osaka/Kyoto areas and in Hokkaidō and was weakest in the countryside. The proportion of the vote gathered by the SDP was in single figures almost everywhere (except in the Hokkaidō regional bloc, where it did not present candidates), and none of the minor parties won any seats in the regional blocs. Hokkaidō and Tokyo were the only two regional blocs which maintained a significantly left-of-centre profile, with 'progressive' parties winning 46.9 and 46.6 per cent of the vote in the two blocs respectively. Over most of the rest of the country conservative dominance was overwhelming, even though conservatives were now weakened by being split into two different parties. With the partial exception of Hokkaidō, it was difficult to discern significant regional (as distinct from urban/rural) differences in voting patterns, and even urban/rural differences, though still significant, appeared to have diminished by comparison with previous decades.

Overwhelmingly the most important change revealed by this profile of political parties in the October 1996 elections is the weakening of left-wing parties by comparison with previous elections. Even though the JCP had substantially improved on its previous position, it seems most likely that a high proportion

Table 9.5 Educational background of parliamentarians, October 1996 lower house general elections.

Highest educational level	LDP	Shinshintō	Minshutō	JCP	SDP	Sakigake	Independent
University	218 94.6%	142 91.6%	46 88.5%	22 84.6%	10 66.7%	2 100.0%	10 100.0%
Graduate school*	16 6.7%	15 9.7%	4 7.7%	2 7.6%	0 –	0 –	1 10.0%
Senior high school	7 2.9%	7 4.5%	3 5.8%	1 3.8%	2 13.3%	0 –	0 –
Junior high school	2 0.8%	2 1.3%	1 1.9%	0 –	0 –	0 –	0 –
Pre-war school	13 5.4%	4 2.6%	1 1.9%	3 11.5%	3 20.0%	0 –	0 –
No information	2 0.8%	0 –	1 1.9%	0 –	0 –	0 –	0 –
University in Tokyo area	189 78.7%	112 72.2%	36 69.2%	7 26.9%	6 40.0%	2 100.0%	10 100.0%
University outside Tokyo area	28 11.7%	43 27.7%	9 17.3%	15 57.7%	4 26.7%	0 –	0 –
Tokyo University	51 21.2%	27 17.4%	7 13.5%	6 23.0%	2 13.3%	1 50.0%	1 10.0%
Waseda	40 16.7%	18 11.6%	12 23.1%	–	2 13.3%	–	–
Keiō	29 12.1%	12 7.7%	3 5.8%	–	–	–	2 20.0%
Chūō	15 6.2%	8 5.1%	4 7.7%	–	1 6.7%	–	4 40.0%
Nihon	13 5.4%	6 3.9%	–	–	–	1 50.0%	1 10.0%

Meiji	8 3.3%	6 3.9%	—	—	—	1 6.7%	—	—
Kyoto	7 2.9%	6 3.9%	—	—	—	3 11.5%	—	—
Sōka	—	5 3.2%	—	—	—	—	—	—
Kansai	5 2.1%	5 3.2%	—	—	—	—	—	—
Other state universities	13 5.4%	10 6.4%	6 11.5%	7 26.9%	4 26.7%	—	—	
Other private universities	40 16.7%	32 20.6%	10 19.2%	6 23.1%	—	2	—	
Foreign universities	3	3	1	—	—	—	—	

(LDP: Georgetown 1, University of California 1, Harvard 1;
Shinshintō: Cambridge 1, University of Cairo 1, Michigan State 1;
Minshutō: Princeton 1.)

* The very small number who dropped out of university or school without graduating are here counted as though they had completed that level of education.

Source: Asahi Nenkan, 1997, bessatsu, pp. 184–97.

Table 9.6 Career background of parliamentarians, October 1996 lower house general elections.

Career	LDP	Shinshintō	Minshutō	JCP	SDP	Sakigake	Independent
Local politician	62	39	14	7	3	1	3
	25.8%	25.2%	26.9%				
Secretary to MP	48	19	5	1	0	1	4
	22.8%	12.2%	9.6%				
National government official	36	15	2	0	0	1	0
	15.0%	9.7%	3.8%				
Company employee	25	12	5	0	1	0	2
	10.4%	7.7%	9.6%				
Company executive	17	9	2	0	0	0	2
	7.1%	5.8%	3.8%				
Mass media employee	13	6	5	1	2	0	0
	5.4%	3.9%	9.6%				
Labour union official	0	6	7	2	1	0	1
	—	3.9%	13.5%				
Lawyer	8	10	8	5	0	0	0
Other	50	26	23	9	6	0	2

Note: Totals do not tally with the number of parliamentarians elected per party, both because of multiple careers and because of lack of information in some cases. Where a member has listed more than one career, all are counted.
Source: *Asahi Nenkan*, 1997, bessatsu, pp. 184–97.

of the new votes it obtained came from voters who had previously supported the JSP/SDP, which was now reduced to a shadow of its former self. Other Socialist votes had undoubtedly gone to the *Minshutō*, which had inherited part of the Socialist tradition and personnel. But it seems plain from the data here presented that most features of the conservative side of politics remained intact, except that 'conservatism' was now represented by two large parties, not one. Following the 1996 elections, however, the *Shinshintō* suffered a succession of defections, and it was beset by scandals in the early months of 1997, so that its effectiveness was reduced, and it collapsed entirely at the end of the year. The LDP, by contrast, seemed on the way to recovering its earlier strength, without – as our data indicate – having undergone anything that could be regarded as sweeping reform. It is to the LDP that we now need to turn.

The Liberal Democratic Party (Jiyūminshutō, Jimintō)

The LDP is in a unique position in the politics of Japan in that for most of its existence it has been entrenched at the very centre of the ruling structure of the state. Between August 1993 and June 1994 it found itself performing the unaccustomed role of political opposition, but even in that brief period the Hosokawa Government could not avoid consulting it on the crucial issue of electoral system reform, and indeed the LDP exerted an important influence on the outcome of that exercise. Since June 1994 the LDP has been steadily working to restore its old position of political dominance, no doubt suitably chastened by its temporary loss of office, followed by a period when power had to be shared with other parties. The collapse of the left and the failure of the *Shinshintō* has eased its task.

Like any party long accustomed to ruling the state in a democratic system, the LDP has been skilled at adapting itself to new circumstances and appealing to new sources of electoral support.[10] The 1970s were a conspicuous example of the party's ability to adjust to an electorate that was rapidly changing in composition following the high economic growth rates that persisted from the late 1950s right up to the first oil shock of 1973–4. The proportion of the electorate voting for the LDP was in continuous decline over that period, and a further projection of existing trends would have seen the party either out of office or having to share power if imaginative action were not taken to stem the tide. Fortunately for the LDP, a leader was on hand in the early 1970s, who was capable of broadening the party's appeal beyond the ranks of farmers and the old middle class who had been the central core of its support in previous years. By bringing in policies to improve welfare provision, tighten up environmental standards, reduce the population pressure on cities and generally shift policy emphasis from a single-minded pursuit of growth towards a concern with the quality of life, Tanaka Kakuei made a timely contribution to his party's survival. Although, for reasons we have outlined, he did not last long as Prime Minister, by the early 1980s it seemed clear that the tide had turned. In particular, the LDP had not entirely lost the big cities, as seemed quite possible from the perspective of the early 1970s, when the party was becoming uncomfortably dependent on a continuation of electoral malapportionment for its parliamentary majority. During the 1980s, in consequence, the LDP government was able to embark on fairly stringent policies of financial retrenchment, secure in the knowledge that its base of support was both firm and widely spread in many different segments of society.

While sensitivity to the policy preferences of strategic segments of the electorate was a *sine qua non* for continuing majorities, the methods of campaigning were also an important part of the picture. As we saw earlier in this chapter, turnover of LDP parliamentarians from election to election was conspicuously low, even though it appeared to have increased significantly by the late 1990s. Perhaps the most important reason for this was the crucial role played in any candidate's campaign by a network of supporters, or *jiban* ('constituency', or 'base of support').[11] A particular manifestation of *jiban*, which emerged in the post-war period, is the *kōenkai*, or personal support group.[12] In one form or another, *kōenkai* have been adopted by virtually all political parties (even the JCP), but the *kōenkai* of LDP candidates have become the central feature of that party's grass-roots campaigning.

The most crucial point to understand about LDP *kōenkai* is that they are organized by and for the *candidate*, not the party. This is in part a function of

Table 9.7 Percentage of the total vote, and seat total, of the various parties in the regional blocs, October 1996 lower house general elections.

Regional bloc	LDP % vote	seats	Shinshintō % vote	seats	Minshutō % vote	seats	JCP % vote	seats	SDP % vote	seats	Other % vote	seats	Total seats
Hokkaidō	28.2	3	21.1	2	31.8	3	15.1	1	—	—	3.8	0	9
Tōhoku	35.3	6	33.2	6	11.1	2	9.6	1	8.3	1	2.6	0	16
North Kantō	34.9	8	26.7	6	17.2	4	12.8	2	5.0	1	3.4	0	21
South Kantō	29.0	7	26.6	7	21.2	5	14.0	3	6.4	1	2.7	0	23
Tokyo	27.0	5	24.6	5	23.4	5	17.8	3	5.4	1	1.8	0	19
Hokuriku-Shinetsu	36.1	5	30.3	4	12.7	2	9.9	1	6.2	1	4.7	0	13
Tōkai	32.0	8	33.0	8	15.0	3	11.9	3	5.9	1	2.1	0	23
Kinki	28.4	10	29.2	10	13.9	5	17.5	6	6.2	2	5.0	0	33
Chūgoku	42.8	6	24.0	3	12.6	2	9.7	1	6.4	1	4.6	0	13
Shikoku	41.6	3	24.2	2	13.0	1	12.1	1	7.1	0	2.1	0	7
Kyūshū	35.6	9	28.2	7	10.8	3	9.7	2	10.1	2	5.5	0	23
Total seats		70		60		35		24		11		0	200

Source: Calculated from *Asahi Nenkan*, 1997, pp. 194–9.

the former electoral system, which in turn explains why this institution became more developed in the LDP than in other parties. In nearly all constituencies, apart from those in the largest cities, the LDP could credibly expect to elect more than one candidate. While it was the function (formally) of the party to determine how many candidates a given constituency could take without risking *tomodaore* ('all being defeated together'), it became the function essentially of each individual candidate to organize his (or rarely, her) individual campaign. The electoral system worked in such a way as to give one LDP candidate almost no stake at all in the success of another LDP candidate standing for the same constituency. Rather, that person was a rival claimant on more or less the same pool of conservative-inclined votes. In order to ensure that LDP votes were cast in favour of LDP candidate X and not LDP candidate Y, candidate X maintained a formal association of family connections, school and university friends, business associates, representatives of local interest groups and local notabilities, as well as people falling into none of these categories, charging them with the task of drumming up support for his campaign. In terms of composition, this was the essence of a *kōenkai*. In terms of function, many of its activities were essentially social rather than overtly political (though political discussions of course occurred), and the candidate would typically organize (at his expense) trips for *kōenkai* members to Tokyo, or to a hot spring resort.

Several consequences flowed from the functioning of *kōenkai* under the former electoral system. Firstly, the creation, maintenance and servicing of a *kōenkai* (whose members might be in the hundreds) was expensive, and was one of the principal reasons for the seemingly inexhaustible need for electoral funds, which led in turn to so many corruption scandals as candidates took desperate and dubiously legal methods to raise the necessary funding. Secondly, the *kōenkai* system was hardly compatible with strong local party branches. Even though the party became adept at keeping the number of candidates formally endorsed to a safe minimum,[13] the influence of entrenched candidates within party branches was overwhelming, and also hardly conducive to the fostering of new candidates outside the ambit of those already in place.

A third aspect of the *kōenkai* system is that the effort and expense of maintaining an existing concern was a great deal less than of setting one up from ground zero. Moreover, this was particularly true in the majority of electorates where several *kōenkai* of long standing already existed. Indeed, the easiest way to enter Parliament under the LDP label was to *inherit* a *kōenkai*. The figures on 'inheritance' of seats are truly astonishing. Of all LDP parliamentarians elected in the lower house general elections of October 1996, 37.2 per cent had inherited a *kōenkai* previously controlled by a parent (28.9%), parent-in-law (2.5%), grandparent (2.5%), other relative (2.9%), or spouse (0.4%).[14] Perhaps an extension of the same phenomenon is where a person who has served as the secretary (*hisho*) of a deceased or retired parliamentarian takes over his *kōenkai*.[15]

Fourthly, under the old electoral system, *kōenkai* were closely bound up with *habatsu* (factions). It was rare (though not unknown) for LDP members belonging to the same *habatsu* to sit for the same constituency. An important part of the reason why an LDP candidate needed to join a *habatsu* was to obtain the funding needed to service his *kōenkai*. This meant the setting up and maintaining over a long period of a complex pattern of linkages connecting *habatsu* leaders with various parts of central government and major interest groups, members of Parliament (and candidates), *kōenkai*, and all the local organizations having connections with *kōenkai*.

A final implication of *kōenkai* under the old electoral system was that the focus of LDP parliamentarians was highly parochial. So much time and effort was needed to keep the *kōenkai* organization in working order and its members satisfied that the average member had rather little time to focus on matters of national concern. This point ought not to be exaggerated, for reasons we shall outline below (under *zoku*), but it seems reasonable to make the generalization that Japanese conservative politics has been unusually constituency-focused.[16]

Much has been written, both in Japanese and in English, about the phenomenon of *habatsu* in Japanese politics, and especially in the politics of the LDP. Though usually translated into English as 'faction', *habatsu* exhibit some characterstics that are not necessarily typical of factions as commonly experienced in major European political systems, notably their longevity, and their concern with political funding and power-broking rather than policy.[17] A question of great contemporary importance is whether and to what extent the abolition of multi-member constituencies in favour of a mixed system of single-member and proportional representation constituencies has reduced the importance of *habatsu* within the LDP. If, as is often suggested, it was the intra-party competitive element in the old electoral system that led to the prevalence of *habatsu*, then the abolition of that system should have led to the demise of *habatsu*. Some Japanese scholars, on the other hand, argue that *habatsu* run deeper than might be suggested by an institutional factor of this kind, and stem from basic Japanese social norms. Shinobu, for instance, maintains that the persistence of factionalism can be readily seen in the politics of the LDP since the 1996 elections.[18]

If, however, we compare factionalism within the LDP and other political parties, it seems evident that the way LDP *habatsu* have in the past behaved is materially different in certain respects from the way such organizations behave in other parties. Part of this no doubt stems from the multi-member electoral system, since multiple candidacies were mainly a reserve of the LDP given its dominant electoral position throughout much of the country.[19] In addition, the sheer number of cabinet and party positions to be filled from LDP ranks, as well as the huge cost of LDP politics, ensured that *habatsu* became major political actors in their own right, and in a sense 'parties within a party'.[20] The evidence after the new electoral system came into force suggests that LDP *habatsu* atrophied to a considerable extent, without disappearing entirely.[21] Some of what used to be struggles between rival *habatsu* became inter-*party* struggles following the 1993 split, while the introduction of public funding of elections, tighter anti-corruption laws and the disappearance of multi-member constituencies has removed some of the rationale for *habatsu* activity. Even so, with the LDP once more having a lower house majority, a modified *habatsu* system is back in place, essentially as a means of brokering power distribution. The alternative of a strong top-down leadership whereby a prime minister personally controls appointments to cabinet without having to be unduly concerned with satisfying rival interests still seems remote.

The implications of the *habatsu* system take our discussion beyond the narrow field of party politics. The imperative for prime ministerial survival of satisfying rival factional claims on cabinet and party posts led, from the Kishi period onwards, to frequent cabinet reshuffles having the principal purpose of providing as many posts to the various *habatsu* as would satisfy their ambitions. The result was to weaken the effectiveness of cabinet and to strengthen the individual ministries, since cabinet ministers did not have enough time to master their portfolios before being replaced.[22] Ironically, by trying to ensure their own survival by satisfying the *habatsu* through frequent cabinet reshuffles, prime ministers in the long run tended to weaken their own ability to control the policy agenda because ministries were easily able to control cabinet ministers rather than the other way round.[23]

By the 1980s, this procedure was so formalized that it had led to what amounted to seniority promotions of LDP parliamentarians along lines very similar to those within government ministries. Each *habatsu* leader would maintain a seniority list of its members which it would present to the prime minister preceding a cabinet reshuffle, and the latter would adjust the claims as best he could so as to maintain an equitable balance between the competing claims. Although there were variations in the way the system worked between different periods, broadly speaking it operated in such a way that 'accelerated promotion' was extremely hard to achieve, even for the exceptionally hard working and ambitious. This created at times severe tensions between 'generations' of ruling party parliamentarians, and frustration felt by younger members was in turn one of the factors that contributed to the split in the party that occurred in 1993.

Managing relations between *habatsu* is a matter that has been discussed earlier in the book. Without attempting to cover this ground again, we need simply to note that whether it was managed through a balance between groups of competing *habatsu,* or by a single dominant *habatsu* exercising a 'kingmaker' role, mechanisms for choosing the party president (who inevitably became prime minister when the LDP was dominant) remained controversial within the party. For a period in the latter half of the 1970s and first half of the 1980s the party experimented with primary elections, involving an electoral role for party 'members and friends' at the local level, but this merely had the effect of spreading factional competition from the central to the local level. It also appeared to accentuate the unpredictability of the outcome, as when Ōhira through the primary system unexpectedly replaced Fukuda as party President (and thus Prime Minister) in 1978, so it was quietly dropped in the 1980s. The inter-relationship between rival *habatsu* interests and frequent turnover, not only of cabinet ministers, but of prime ministers as well, is illustrated by the fact that between 1945 and 1998 Japan experienced 25 changes of prime minister (Shidehara to Obuchi), 20 of whom were from the LDP or its predecessor parties, whereas in Britain there were only 11 (Attlee to Blair).

The central organizational structure of the LDP has changed rather little over the years. In late 1996 and early 1997 the top four posts in the party were distributed as follows: *sōsai* (President), Hashimoto Ryūtarō, who was also Prime Minister; *kanjichō* (Secretary-General), Kato Kōichi; *sōmukaichō* (Executive Council Chairman), Mori Yoshirō; and *seimu chōsakaichō* (Policy Affairs Research Council Chairman), Yamasaki Taku. In most historical circumstances the occupants of these four party posts, together with the *kanbō chōkan* (Chief Cabinet Secretary) – who in early 1997 was Kajiyama Seiroku – in effect constituted the 'directorate' of the current government. Given the strong pull of bureaucratic interests over ministers representing specific portfolios, it is important to stress the predominant party component in the five posts listed above. The five politicians mentioned constituted much of the public face of the Hashimoto Government, in that they all received constant media exposure, and they also worked together to hammer out the broad lines of policy that should motivate the government as a whole. This, of course, needs to be seen in the context of a total government structure in which competing bureaucratic and political interests normally tended to fragment and blunt policy initiative, so that the impact of the 'directorate' ought not to be over-stated. Nevertheless, as a long-standing response to the structural problems of fragmentation, this group of posts is of great importance.

A further mechanism for enhancing LDP input into policy making, which has been much commented on since the 1980s, is the phenomenon of *zoku* (tribes). Whereas *habatsu* have been principally concerned with distribution of money and positions, but relatively less concerned with specific policy issues, *zoku*, which cut across *habatsu* boundaries, are groups of LDP parliamentarians with an interest in a specific area of policy.[24] Examples of *zoku* interests include tele-communications, education, construction, transport and defence, though they are also to be found in respect of narrower policy areas, such as the tobacco industry. It seems probable that *zoku* were originally conceived as a response to a perceived lack of political influence over many areas of policy where bur-eaucratic interests prevailed, often (as, for instance, in agriculture) in close con-junction with the sectional interests concerned. Typically, *zoku* parliamentarians do not confront bureaucratic and sectional interests so much as work in conjunction with them. This had led to the widespread designation of *zoku* as 'iron triangles' on the American model, which aim to 'sew up' a particular area of policy by asserting a politico-bureaucratic-sectional control over policy-making initiatives in that area. There are in fact, however, many different pat-terns of operation, which means that generalization should only be attempted with great caution.

Finally, even though it may appear from what we have written so far about the LDP, that it is little changed in structure and approach from what it has been over several decades, in fact the period from its loss of office on 9 August 1993 to its near-victory in the lower house general elections of 25 October 1996 was a learning experience for the party. For the first ten months of that period it was out of office altogether, meaning that its members had to cope with the loss of political influence thus entailed. In retrospect, however, this was too short a period to effect a fundamental rethinking and restructuring. Following the party's return to office on 30 June 1994 in coalition with the JSP and *Sakigake,* under a Socialist Prime Minister, the LDP gradually resumed many of its former practices. The change of LDP President in September 1995 from Kōno Yōhei, who had reformist instincts, to Hashimoto Ryūtarō, who repre-sented much more mainstream sections of the party, may be seen as a crucial stage in the return to a more traditional pattern of operation. The experience of working with the JSP and *Sakigake* meant that some power – and a number of cabinet positions – had to be conceded to the other two parties, but in retro-spect it now seems clear that the LDP came to treat its coalition partners much as specific factions had long been treated within the LDP itself, namely as discrete elements within a 'broad church' that needed to be accorded sufficient largesse to keep them locked within the bounds of the coalition government arrangements.

In sum, the LDP had been forced to adjust to a series of unprecedented political situations during the 1990s, and had suffered severe reverses from 1993. Nevertheless, by 1997 it had returned as the central political element in a power structure that still continued essentially intact, and *fundamental* reform of that power structure seemed not to figure high in the party's list of priorities.

Parties other than the LDP

The sub-heading 'Parties other than the LDP' has been chosen, rather than 'Opposition Parties', here to take account of the fact that at least in the 1990s formal and informal alliances and arrangements between parties have to some extent replaced outright confrontation and opposition. Nevertheless, for the earlier post-war years, the term 'Opposition' seems appropriate.

It is easy to dismiss the forces of opposition in post-war Japanese politics as an irrelevance. Until the 1989 House of Councillors elections they failed to win a majority in any election, though they came close to doing so during the 1970s. More significantly, perhaps, no other party has ever succeeded in challenging the LDP as a single party capable of winning an outright majority of seats in the House of Representatives. Until the 1990s, the only party that ever seemed capable of playing this role was the JSP, which in the 1958 lower house elections won 166 out of 467 seats, at a time when for a brief period there were only two significant parties. That was, however, the high point of its fortunes, apart from its spectacular but temporary boom in 1989 and 1990. Even so, in terms of seats in the House of Representatives, it remained the second largest party in every election until that of October 1996, when it came close to extinction, following a split which led to the formation of the *Minshutō*.

The Japan Socialist Party (*Nihon Shakaitō*); Social Democratic Party (*Shakaiminshutō*) from January 1996

The JSP (SDP from 1996) went through a number of phases in its long and chequered history.[25] The party formed shortly after the end of the Second World War derived from a fragmented socialist and social-democratic movement that had existed before the war, and inherited most of its ideological and factional divisions. Ideologically, the party covered most of the spectrum from a kind of Kautskyite Marxism to Fabian-style democratic socialism. Its early experience of participation in government during 1947–8 (see chapter 4) was premature and unfortunate. The party split no less than four times between 1947 and 1951, and remained as two separate parties (one left-wing socialist, the other moderate democratic socialist) between 1951 and 1955. Though united and at the height of its influence in the latter half of the 1950s, the turbulent politics of that period ultimately made it impossible for the JSP to maintain its cohesion. In 1960 the Democratic Socialist Party (DSP) was formed, comprising most, though far from all, of the Right Socialist Party of the early 1950s. By this time both wings of the movement were entrenched in the labour unions, but the unions themselves had split into the predominant left-wing union federation *Sōhyō* and the less confrontational federation *Dōmei*.

The departure of its centrist and right-of-centre elements in 1960 made it more difficult for the JSP to adapt its policies to the newly emerging world of economic growth of the 1960s, and it thus lost the opportunity to replace its revolutionary Marxist rhetoric by appeals that were relevant to families struggling with new challenges and opportunities in a rapidly changing Japan. The result was that during the 1960s it lost votes in successive elections, but lost votes particularly rapidly in the big cities where its main appeal might have been expected to lie. The LDP was also in electoral decline in the cities at this period, and the slack was being taken up by a number of third parties that were making headway by appealing intelligently to the needs of city people. Reliance for electoral organizational support on the labour union movement, which had helped the party progress electorally during the 1950s, now acted as a drag on its further expansion, since the *Sōhyō* unions were essentially a narrow band of interests concentrated among employees of the public sector.

During the 1970s the JSP stabilized somewhat, though attempts to modernize its organization and policies led in the late 1970s to a minor split, and the formation of the *Shaminren* party. In 1986 the party modernized its platform, Doi Takako became party Chairperson and under her leadership it achieved remarkable results in the 1989 upper house and 1990 lower house elections. The party's decline has already been traced through the Gulf Crisis, its participation in the Hosokawa and Hata governments, the Murayama prime ministership, the fateful but long-delayed split which finally took place in September 1996, and the disaster of the October elections.

Despite its manifest and manifold weaknesses, the party has one long-term achievement to its credit. For many years it was able to keep the issue of the post-war Constitution, and in particular article 9, the peace clause, on the active political agenda. Even though it is very arguable that concentration on this one issue inhibited the party for many years from modernizing its platform in other areas, nevertheless the peace issue was one where genuine achievement was politically possible. This was because the party (at times on its own, at times together with minor parties) had the numbers to block constitutional revision, and, knowing this to be the case, successive LDP governments lost interest in the cause of constitutional revision. The turning point was the Ikeda Government period of the early 1960s, when the report of the *Kenpō chōsakai* (Constitutional Research Commission) was quietly buried.[26] The fostering of a pro-Constitution and antiwar mood in the electorate was something to which the JSP made a long-term contribution with most important consequences for fundamental policy.[27]

The Democratic Socialist Party (*Minshatō*)

Of the other parties in opposition to LDP governments up to 1993, the DSP is the oldest. Formed in 1960 by Nishio Suehiro in protest against Marxist influence within the JSP during the dispute over revising the Japan–US Security Treaty, it never became more than a minor party. Much of its welfare state policies of the 1960s were taken over by LDP governments from Tanaka onwards, and its base in the *Dōmei* labour union federation was a relatively narrow base of core support (concentrated especially in the Nagoya and Kansai areas) beyond which it found it difficult to expand. By the 1970s it had developed rather hawkish views on defence policy, which put it in sharp confrontation with the JSP. In the late 1980s, however, moves to unify the union movement into a single federation, *Rengō*, brought the DSP and JSP into closer contact. The fact that they could both be incorporated into the Hosokawa coalition government in 1993 owed much to this factor. Such co-operation proved temporary, however, and the formation of the Murayama Government placed them on opposite sides of the political fence. The DSP was dissolved into the *Shinshintō* when it was formed in December 1994, but emerged again as *Shintō yūai* (New Party Amity) with the collapse of that party four years later, although in April 1998 it merged with the expanded *Minshutō*.

The Kōmeitō

This party was formed in 1964 by the *Sōka Gakkai* religion, the most successful of many 'new religions' that sprang up in response to social change and the disestablishment of state *Shintō* after the war. The religion grew rapidly until about 1970 and then its membership stabilized at several million households. In its earlier years it appealed to the less educated, less well-off and less well-organized sections of mainly big city populations, but in recent years with rising prosperity both the religion and the party have cultivated a more middle-class image, placing a strong emphasis on education. Despite early fears that it might be fascist or extreme nationalist, the *Kōmeitō* turned out to be for the most part moderately conservative in its policies, and until the political realignments of the 1990s it generally occupied a centrist position between the LDP and the parties of the left.

Perhaps the most remarkable feature of the *Kōmeitō* and its parent religion is its capacity for effective organization. When the *Kōmeitō* still existed as an independent party, as much as 90 per cent of its vote was believed to come from *Sōka Gakkai* believers, and such was the discipline that was exercised over them that the party became remarkably skilled in optimizing the effectiveness of its vote.[28] This made it particularly valuable as a potential component of any new party when realignment was taking place in 1994. By the same token, however, its organizational cohesion and separateness created severe problems of absorption into a new party. When the *Shinshintō* was formed in December 1994, the *Kōmeitō* merged with it, but most upper house members and local branches were careful to retain a separate existence. With the collapse of *Shinshintō* in December 1997 it re-emerged under the name of *Shintō heiwa* (New Party Peace).

The Japan Communist Party (*Nihon Kyōsantō*)

The JCP is Japan's oldest political party, founded in 1922. It led an illegal and clandestine existence until 1945, when it was legalized by the American

Occupation. It had a brief flowering (particularly within the nascent union movement) in the Occupation period up to 1949, sank into electoral insignificance during the 1950s, but from the late 1960s until the late 1970s experienced a resurgence. This was based upon careful cultivation of a close-knit grass-roots organization, in which members' economic and other problems would be addressed, and upon a moderation of the party's previously hard line ideology. From the late 1970s until the 1990s it stagnated under an aging leadership, but in the October 1996 elections was resurgent once again, winning 26 out of 500 seats in the lower house. Such a success by an apparently 'unreconstructed' Communist party in the post-Cold War world was indeed remarkable, and seems to have reflected a combination of disillusionment with other parties (notably the SDP) and a reflection of unfavourable economic conditions. In 1997–8 it was doing rather well in some elections, including those for the upper house in July 1998.

The JCP is now unique among Japanese political parties in avoiding entanglements with other parties, just as the other parties avoid entangling themselves with it.

The New Liberal Club (*Shinjiyū kurabu*), and the *Shaminren*

Two minor parties were formed in 1976 and 1977 respectively, the NLC as a splinter from the LDP, and the *Shaminren* as a splinter from the JSP. Neither became substantial parties, but both obtained a handful of parliamentary seats, and sought to act as a catalyst for change in the parties from which they had split. The NLC went into a coalition government with the LDP following the 1983 lower house elections, but most of its members were absorbed into the LDP in 1986, while the *Shaminren* lasted until 1994, when its members joined other parties. The NLC leader, Kōno Yōhei, went on to become President of the LDP after that party's fall from power in 1993, until being replaced by Hashimoto in 1995, while from the *Shaminren* Eda Satsuki became Minister for Science and Technology in the Hosokawa Cabinet, and Kan Naoto became an outspoken and popular Minister for Health and Welfare in the first Hashimoto administration formed in January 1996, and then one of the two co-Chairmen (later sole Chairman) of the *Minshutō* formed in September 1996, and Chairman of the expanded *Minshutō* formed in April 1998.

The Japan New Party (*Nihon shintō*)

The JNP, founded in mid-1992 by Hosokawa Morihiro, is most unusual in the recent history of Japanese political parties in having been composed almost entirely of political outsiders. The average age of the 35 of its members elected to the House of Representatives in the elections of the following July was only 42, and a number of them were graduates of the Matsushita School of Politics and Economics (*Matsushita seikei juku*), a private college endowed by the founder of Panasonic in order to train new political leaders. Once the Hosokawa Cabinet began to get into difficulties and fell from office in April 1994, the popularity of the JNP rapidly waned. Most of its parliamentary members ended up in the *Shinshintō,* and some, later, in the *Minshutō.*

The Japan Renewal Party (*Shinseitō*)

This was the party formed by Hata Tsutomu and Ozawa Ichirō in June 1993 following the split in the Takeshita faction. The defection of this group from the LDP was the most important factor leading to the ruling party's defeat in the July elections. No doubt a principal motive for the formation of the JRP was Ozawa's desire to shake up the political system and form the nucleus of a credible alternative to continuing government by the LDP. He has also been widely accused – especially by sections of the press which are hostile to him – of creating the JRP as the opening move in a long-term strategy to further his own power ambitions which were being frustrated so long as he remained within the LDP. The JRP took the bulk of senior cabinet posts in the Hosokawa cabinet formed in August 1993, and through it clearly Ozawa's influence appears to have been dominant in policy making within that cabinet. The party went into opposition with the formation of the Murayama Cabinet and was absorbed into the *Shinshintō* in December 1994.

The New Party Harbinger (*Shintō Sakigake*)

This party was formed by Takemura Masayoshi two days before the formation of the JRP in June 1993, and as part of the splintering of the LDP which was occurring at that time. Its views were more 'progressive' than those of the JRP and initially it appeared likely to merge with the Japan New Party. Tensions between Takemura and Hosokawa which appeared over tax policy in February 1994 made this impossible, and *Sakigake* subsequently found common ground with the JSP, joining it as the third and smallest member of the Murayama coalition Government in June 1994. Unusually for the times, *Sakigake* retained its integrity as a single party into 1996–8 (though it suffered some defections), but was reduced to a mere two lower house seats in the October 1996 elections. Takemura himself had lost popularity as Finance Minister in 1996, having to take responsibility for poor handling by the Ministry of the failed *jūsen* (housing loan company) problems.

The New Frontier Party (*Shinshintō*)

This party was formed from no fewer than nine parties and groupings in December 1994.[29] Its specific purpose was to challenge the LDP for power, and the long-term aim, as expressed by Ozawa and others, was to create the conditions for an alternating two-party system. In pursuit of this aim, the party instituted a shadow cabinet system, or 'tomorrow's cabinet', as it was known. Another innovation was that in electing the party leader any member of the public could vote on payment of a small fee. This ensured that Ozawa was elected leader by a large margin as its second leader (the first was Kaifu Toshiki) in December 1995.[30]

The party did well in the July 1995 upper house elections, but various political factors including disputes among the leadership tended to erode the party's popularity and it performed less well than expected in the lower house elections of October 1996. Following these elections, the *Shinshintō* suffered a series of defections, including that of the Hata group (13 parliamentarians) in December 1996. In the early months of 1997 the party was gravely embarrassed by investigations for alleged corruption of one of its former upper house members, Tomobe Tatsuo, who had apparently been endorsed as a party candidate with scant probing into his background.

Even though it collapsed in December 1997, the *Shinshintō* was in some ways a cleverly devised party structure, in that it combined the extraordinary organizational and financial capacity the *Sōka Gakkai* and former *Kōmeitō* with groups originating in the LDP mainstream. The importance of the former *Kōmeitō* element may be seen from an analysis of the origins of *Shinshintō* members elected in the regional blocs at the 1996 elections. Of the 60 *Shinshintō* members elected from the regional blocs, no less than 28 (46.7 per cent) were former members of *Kōmeitō*. Only one ex-*Kōmeitō* candidate was defeated, giving a 95.6 per cent success rate.[31]

Democratic Party (*Minshutō*)

The *Minshutō* was founded in September 1996. Of the 52 members elected from this party in the October 1996 lower house elections, 26 came from the JSP/SDP (predominantly from its right wing), 15 from *Sakigake*, two from the former Japan New Party and one (Hatoyama Kunio) from the *Shinshintō*. The party sought to project a progressive, ideologically centrist, image, as symbolized by such former Socialist Party luminaries as Yokomichi Takahiro, who had been Governor of Hokkaidō, and Yamahana Sadao, Chairman of the JSP until Murayama replaced him in September 1993. The *Minshutō* innovatively adopted a leadership structure based on two co-equal chairmen, and elected Hatoyama Yukio and Kan Naoto, both from *Sakigake*, to fill these posts. In the early months of 1997 Hatoyama and Kan publicly disagreed about whether and to what extent the party ought to co-operate with the LDP Government of Hashimoto, with Hatoyama arguing that the party ought to remain essentially in opposition, but Kan urging that the party should endeavour to place itself in a position where it could participate in government decision making. Kan eventually demonstrated his dominance, and when the *Minshutō* absorbed several other groups in April 1998, Kan was elected Chairman.

The Sun Party (*Taiyōtō*)

This was a small group of 13 parliamentarians, led by the former Prime Minister Hata Tsutomu, that broke away from the *Shinshintō* in December 1996, disillusioned with the leadership of Ozawa. It interacted substantially with other 'progressive' parties, notably the *Minshutō* and the SDP.

Twenty First Century (21 seiki)

This was another small group of *Shinshintō* members that broke away and formed a new mini-party between September and December 1996.

Party Developments from December 1997

From December 1997 until around April 1998 parties out of power split and regrouped like raindrops in a thunderstorm. On 31 December the *Shinshintō* dissolved into six separate parties: *Jiyūtō* (Liberal Party, led by Ozawa Ichirō); *Shintō heiwa* (New Party Peace, including most of the lower house ex-*Kōmeitō* group); *Shintō yūai* (New Party Amity, comprising most of the ex-DSP members); *Reimei kurabu* (Daybreak Club, consisting of the upper house *Kōmei* group); *Kokumin no koe* (Voice of the People, led by Kano Michihiko); *Kaikaku kurabu* (Reform Club, led by Ozawa Tatsuo).[32]

On 8 January, a loose parliamentary grouping called *Minyūren*[33] was formed out of *Minshutō, Shintō yūai, Minkairen,*[34] *Kokumin no koe, Taiyōtō, From Five.*[35] The last three of these, on Hosokawa's initiative, formed a genuine party on 22 January, calling it, on the pre-war model, *Minseitō*. Finally, in April, the rest of the groups constituting the *Minyūren,* together with the *Minseitō,* and the *Minshutō* of Kan Naoto, merged as a major party with over 100 lower house members. This is what has been earlier referred to as the 'expanded' *Minshutō*.

Shortly after the new party was launched, Hosokawa, who from August 1993 had led the first non-LDP administration in nearly four decades, announced his retirement from politics. Meanwhile, three parties or party families outside the LDP ambit remained aloof from the new *Minshutō*: the radical free market *Jiyūtō* of Ozawa Ichirō; the various successors of the former *Kōmeitō* (backed by the *Sōka Gakkai*), and the Japan Communist Party, independent as ever, and experiencing a certain resurgence in an era of confusion.

We can see from this survey of political parties that in 1998 the situation remained confused and apparently lacking in direction. The LDP had made a comeback which was not yet complete, and an LDP Prime Minister was attempting to regain the political initiative by donning the garments of deregulatory reform. Ozawa's aim of forming a second modernizing conservative party to challenge the LDP had failed and the forces of the centre-left had come together but were uncomfortably weak. In these circumstances opportunistic political manoeuvring prevailed for the most part, and clear leadership was generally lacking. Not surprisingly, the electorate was responding to this situation by showing disinterest in party politics and staying away from elections in increasing numbers, though this trend was suddenly reversed at the July 1998 upper house elections.

Table 9.8 House of Representatives election results, 1946–1996

	10/4/46*	25/4/47	23/1/49	1/10/52
Progressive Party	94 (20.3)			
(*Shimpotō*)	10,351 (18.7)			
Democratic Party		121 (26.0)	69 (14.8)	
(*Minshutō*)		6,840 (25.0)	4,798 (15.7)	
Reformist Party				85 (18.2)
(*Kaishintō*)				6,429 (18.2)
Liberal Party	140 (30.2)	131 (28.1)		240 (51.5)
(*Jiyūtō*)	13,506 (24.4)	7,356 (26.9)		16,939 (47.9)
Democratic Liberal Party			264 (56.7)	
(*Minshujiyūtō, Minjitō*)			13,420 (43.9)	
Hatoyama Liberal Party				
(*Jiyūtō* (Hatoyama-ha))				
Yoshida Liberal Party				
(*Jiyūtō* (*Yoshida-ha*))				
Liberal Democratic Party				
(*Jiyūminshutō, Jimintō*)				
New Liberal Club				
(*Shin Jiyū Club*)				
Co-operative Party	14 (3.0)			
(*Kyōdotō*)	1,800 (3.2)			
People's Co-operative Party		29 (6.2)	14 (3.0)	
(*Kokumin Kyōdōtō*)		1,916 (7.0)	1,042 (3.4)	
Japan Socialist Party	92 (19.8)	143 (30.7)	48 (10.3)	
(*Nihon Shakaitō*)	9,858 (17.8)	7,176 (26.2)	4,130 (13.5)	
Social Democratic Party				
(*Shakaiminshutō, Shamintō*)				
Left Socialist Party				54 (11.6)
(*Nihon Shakaitō*, (*Saha*))				3,399 (9.6)
Right Socialist Party				57 (12.2)
(*Nihon Shakaitō* (*Uha*))				4,108 (11.6)
Labour Farmer Party			7 (1.5)	4 (0.9)
(*Rōdōshanōminto, Rōnōtō*)			607 (2.0)	261 (0.7)
Democratic Socialist Party				
(*Minshushakaitō, Minshatō*)				
Kōmei Party				
(*Kōmeitō*)				
Japan Communist Party	5 (1.1)	4 (0.8)	35 (7.5)	0 (0)
(*Nihon Kyōsantō*)	2,136 (3.8)	1,003 (3.7)	2,985 (9.7)	897 (2.6)
Social Democratic League				
(*Shakaiminshurengō,*				
Shaminren)				
Renewal Party				
(*Shinseitō*)				
New Harbinger Party				
(*Shintō Sakigake*)				
Japan New Party				
(*Nihon Shintō*)				
New Frontier Party				
(*Shinshintō*)				
Democratic party				
(*Minshutō*)				
Democratic Reform League				
(*Minkairen*)				
Independent	81 (17.4)	13 (2.8)	12 (2.6)	19 (4.1)
	11,325 (20.4)	1,581 (5.8)	2,008 (6.6)	2,355 (6.7)
Others	38 (8.2)	25 (5.4)	17 (3.6)	7 (1.5)
	6,473 (11.7)	1,490 (5.4)	1,602 (5.2)	949 (2.7)
Total	464	466	466	466
	55,449	27,362	30,593	35,337

*The electoral system at the 1946 election differed from that of all later elections.
Note: For each entry: number of seats (% of total seats)
number of votes, in thousands (% of total votes).

19/4/53	27/2/55	22/5/58	20/11/60	21/11/63	29/1/67
	185 (39.6) 13,536 (36.6)				
76 (16.3) 6,186 (17.9)					
	112 (24.0) 9,849 (26.6)				
35 (7.5) 3,055 (8.8) 199 (42.7) 13,476 (39.0)					
		287 (61.5) 22,977 (57.8)	296 (63.4) 22,740 (57.6)	283 (60.7) 22,424 (54.7)	277 (57.0) 22,448 (48.8)
		166 (35.5) 13,094 (32.9)	145 (31.0) 10,887 (27.6)	144 (30.8) 11,907 (29.0)	140 (28.8) 12,826 (27.9)
72 (15.4) 4,517 (13.1) 66 (14.2) 4,678 (11.6) 5 (1.1) 359 (1.0)	89 (19.1) 5,683 (15.3) 67 (14.3) 5,130 (13.9) 4 (0.9) 358 (1.0)				
			17 (3.7) 3,464 (8.8)	23 (4.9) 3,023 (7.4)	30 (6.2) 3,404 (7.4) 25 (5.1) 2,472 (5.4)
1 (0.2) 656 (1.9)	2 (0.4) 733 (2.0)	1 (0.2) 1,012 (2.6)	3 (0.6) 1,157 (2.9)	5 (1.1) 1,646 (4.0)	5 (1.0) 2,191 (4.8)
11 (2.4) 1,524 (4.4) 1 (0.2) 152 (0.4)	6 (1.3) 1,229 (3.3) 2 (0.4) 497 (1.3)	12 (2.6) 2,381 (6.0) 1 (0.2) 288 (0.7)	5 (1.1) 1,119 (2.8) 1 (0.2) 142 (0.3)	12 (2.6) 1,956 (4.8) 0 (0) 60 (0.1)	9 (1.9) 2,554 (5.5) 0 (0) 101 (0.2)
466 34,602	467 37,015	467 39,752	467 39,509	467 41,017	486 45,997

Sources: *Asahi Nenkan*, various dates.

Table 9.8 *Contd.*

	27/12/69	10/12/72	5/12/76	7/10/79
Progressive Party (*Shimpotō*)				
Democratic Party (*Minshutō*)				
Reformist Party (*Kaishintō*)				
Liberal Party (*Jiyūtō*)				
Democratic Liberal Party (*Minshujiyūtō, Minjitō*)				
Hatoyama Liberal Party (*Jiyūtō* (Hatoyama-ha))				
Yoshida Liberal Party (*Jiyūtō* (*Yoshida-ha*))				
Liberal Democratic Party	288 (59.2)	271 (55.2)	249 (48.7)	248 (48.6)
(*Jiyūminshutō, Jimintō*)	22,382 (47.6)	24,563 (46.8)	23,654 (41.8)	24,084 (44.6)
New Liberal Club			17 (3.3)	4 (0.7)
(*Shin Jiyū Club*)			2,364 (4.2)	1,632 (3.0)
Co-operative Party (*Kyōdotō*)				
People's Co-operative Party (*Kokumin Kyōdōtō*)				
Japan Socialist Party	90 (18.5)	118 (24.0)	123 (24.1)	107 (20.9)
(*Nihon Shakaitō*)	10,074 (21.4)	11,479 (21.9)	11,713 (20.7)	10,643 (19.7)
Social Democratic Party (*Shakaiminshutō Shamintō*)				
Left Socialist Party (*Nihon Shakaitō*, (*Saha*))				
Right Socialist Party (*Nihon Shakaitō* (*Uha*))				
Labour Farmer Party (*Rōdōshanōminto, Rōnōtō*)				
Democratic Socialist Party	31 (6.4)	19 (3.9)	29 (5.7)	35 (6.3)
(*Minshushakaitō, Minshatō*)	3,637 (7.7)	3,661 (7.0)	3,554 (6.3)	3,664 (6.8)
Kōmei Party	47 (9.7)	29 (5.9)	55 (10.8)	57 (11.2)
(*Kōmeitō*)	5,125 (10.9)	4,437 (8.5)	6,177 (10.9)	5,283 (9.8)
Japan Communist Party	14 (2.9)	38 (7.7)	17 (3.3)	39 (7.6)
(*Nihon Kyōsantō*)	3,199 (6.8)	5,497 (10.5)	5,878 (10.4)	5,626 (10.4)
Social Democratic League				2 (0.4)
(*Shakaiminshurengō, Shaminren*)				368 (0.7)
Renewal Party (*Shinseitō*)				
New Harbinger Party (*Shintō Sakigake*)				
Japan New Party (*Nihon Shintō*)				
New Frontier Party (*Shinshintō*)				
Democratic Party (*Minshutō*)				
Democratic Reform League (*Minkairen*)				
Independent	16 (3.3)	14 (2.9)	21 (4.1)	19 (3.7)
	2,493 (5.3)	2,646 (5.0)	3,227 (5.7)	2,641 (4.9)
Others	0 (0)	2 (0.4)	0 (0)	0 (0)
	81 (0.2)	143 (0.3)	45 (0.1)	69 (0.1)
Total	486	491	511	511
	46,990	52,425	56,613	54,010

Note: For each entry: number of seats (% of total seats)
number of votes, in thousands (% of total votes).

22/6/80	18/12/83	6/7/86	18/2/90	18/7/93	20/10/96
284 (55.6)	250 (48.9)	300 (58.6)	275 (53.7)	223 (43.6)	239 (47.8)
28,262 (47.9)	25,983 (45.8)	29,875 (49.4)	30,315 (46.1)	23,000 (36.6)	21,836 (38.6)
12 (2.3)	8 (1.6)	6 (1.2)			
1,766 (3.0)	1,341 (2.4)	1,115 (1.8)			
107 (20.9)	112 (21.9)	85 (16.6)	136 (26.6)	70 (13.7)	
11,401 (19.3)	11,065 (19.5)	10,412 (17.2)	16,025 (24.4)	9,687 (15.4)	
					15 (3.0)
					1,241 (2.2)
32 (6.3)	38 (7.4)	26 (5.1)	14 (2.7)	15 (2.9)	
3,897 (6.6)	4,130 (7.3)	3,896 (6.4)	3,179 (4.8)	2,206 (3.5)	
33 (6.5)	58 (11.3)	56 (10.9)	45 (8.8)	51 (10.0)	
5,330 (9.0)	5,746 (10.1)	5,701 (9.4)	5,243 (8.0)	5,114 (8.1)	
29 (5.7)	26 (5.1)	26 (5.1)	16 (3.1)	15 (2.9)	15 (3.0)
5,804 (9.8)	5,302 (9.3)	5,313 (8.8)	5,227 (8.0)	4,835 (7.7)	7,097 (12.6)
3 (0.5)	3 (0.6)	4 (0.8)	4 (0.8)	4 (0.8)	
402 (0.7)	381 (0.7)	500 (0.8)	567 (0.9)	461 (0.7)	
				55 (10.8)	
				6,341 (10.1)	
				13 (2.5)	2 (0.4)
				1,658 (2.6)	728 (13)
				35 (6.8)	
				5,054 (8.0)	
					156 (31.2)
					15,812 (28.0)
					52 (10.4)
					6,002 (10.6)
					1 (0.2)
					149 (0.3)
11 (2.1)	16 (3.1)	9 (1.7)	21 (4.1)		9 (1.8)
2,057 (3.5)	2,769 (4.9)	3,515 (5.8)	4,807 (7.3)		2,509 (4.4)
0 (0)	0 (0)	0 (0)	0 (0)		0 (0)
109 (0.2)	62 (0.1)	121 (0.2)	58 (0.1)		1,110 (2.1)
511	511	512	512	511	500
59,029	56,780	60,449	65,704	62,804	55,569

10

Some Problems of the Constitution

Japan cannot be said to have developed a national consensus about the present Constitution, although it has now lasted entirely unaltered for more than half a century. Its basic provisions are widely supported but, although successive conservative governments have learnt to operate within its framework, there is a substantial body of opinion in and close to government that would like to revise certain aspects of it.

Debate over the Constitution was at its height in the 1950s and early 1960s. The Hatoyama and Kishi Governments aimed at constitutional revision, and the *Kenpō Chōsakai* (Commission on the Constitution), set up in 1957, was charged with making proposals for revision. When it reported in 1964, however, the political mood had changed, economic goals had taken precedence over such political issues as revising the Constitution, and its proposals, which in any case were not unanimous, were quietly forgotten. In the 1980s, with conservatism of a somewhat nationalistic stamp emerging again, interest in constitutional revision revived to some extent, but no concrete action was taken to revise (as distinct from attempting to re-interpret) the Constitution. The unstable multi-party politics of the mid-to-late 1990s is also hardly conducive to a coherent revisionist campaign, but the decline of the JSP/SDP – previously the Constitution's most determined defender – quite possibly opens the road to revision attempts in the future. A particular straw in the wind is the publication by the *Yomiuri Shinbun* (a right-of-centre daily newspaper with the highest circulation figures in Japan) in 1994 of a revised constitutional draft for general discussion.[1] We shall discuss this later in this chapter.

The politics and political history of the current Constitution abounds with paradox. The Liberal Democrats, in power for most of period between the 1950s and the 1990s, have been staunch supporters of the security relationship with the United States, but lukewarm about their 'American-imposed' Constitution. The left, on the other hand, has often been anti-American, but strongly supportive of a constitution whose American inspiration was clear. In so far as it is a product of the American Occupation (and of its notably conservative Supreme Commander, General MacArthur), it was full of New Deal concepts and contained the 'peace clause' (article 9), which on the face of it banned armed forces in perpetuity. But soon after the Occupation was over, an American Vice-President (Richard Nixon) was, in 1953, calling on Japan to scrap the peace clause. Even though the Constitution has been so politically divisive that politicians cannot even agree on whether they should celebrate 'Constitution Day', it is now one of the 20 or so oldest national constitutions in the world, out of a current total of about 180,[2] and, unusually, remains completely unrevised. Finally, although the Constitution has enormous significance for having shifted the political institutions and practices of Japan away from domination by the emperor-institution and the armed forces towards democratic norms and values, a large proportion of the controversies that have raged over the Constitution relate to one single article, article 9, the 'peace clause'.

The origins of the Constitution are crucial to an understanding of the subsequent controversies about it. The allegation that General MacArthur 'imposed' the Constitution on Japan while creating the fiction that it was an indigenous Japanese product, has been the most emotive and powerful charge levelled against it by its opponents.[3] The work of the Commission on the Constitution (*Kenpō Chōsakai*) between 1957 and 1964 includes searching investigation of this question.[4] The Potsdam Declaration gave positive sanction for a major reform of the Meiji Constitution. It was hardly surprising, therefore, that the Americans, left virtually in complete charge of the Occupation of Japan because of the conflicts that emerged among the former Allied powers once the war in Asia and the Pacific had ended, should have placed constitutional change high on their agenda. It was also obviously desirable that a matter so fundamental as constitutional reform should emanate from the Japanese political process itself, and should benefit from adequate popular discussion.[5] In accordance with the latter principle, the Shidehara Government was invited to submit proposals for reform late in 1946. A committee was set up under a Cabinet minister, Dr Matsumoto Jōji, and had worked out the draft of a revised constitution by the beginning of February 1946.[6] This, however, conceded few changes in the text of the Meiji Constitution, and was rejected by SCAP as too conservative.

On 7 January 1946 General MacArthur had received a document called SWNCC-228 from the State-War-Navy Co-Ordinating Committee in Washington. This document urged that the Japanese should be encouraged to reform the Constitution along democratic lines, but warned the Supreme Commander against a coercive approach, on the unimpeachable grounds that this would seriously prejudice the ultimate acceptability of a constitution introduced under pressure from the occupying power.[7]

At the beginning of February, the pace of events suddenly quickened. On 3 February, the Supreme Commander summoned his Government Section and gave them instructions to prepare, with the utmost despatch, a draft constitution to be used as a 'guide' to their work for constitutional revision. Among the items which MacArthur specifically ordered to be included in the draft were a clause to the effect that the *tennō* should be 'at the head of state', but that his duties and powers should be 'exercised in accordance with the Constitution and responsible to the basic will of the people as provided therein', and one specifying that the right to wage war and to maintain the means of waging it should be abolished.[8] The Government Section, under Major-General Courtney Whitney, but with Colonel Charles Kades effectively in charge, worked under great pressure from 4 February and completed their draft (now known as the 'GHQ' draft) in no more than six days. It was presented on 13 February to Cabinet, which accepted it 'in basic principle' on 22 February.[9]

We need, however, to return to the mid-winter of 1945–6, and examine why it was that MacArthur moved with such speed in early February 1946. It seems that a precipitating factor was the prospective establishment of the Far Eastern Commission in Washington, decided upon at the Big Three summit conference in Moscow in December 1945. The Far Eastern Commission, on which representatives of 11 nations were to sit, could have its decisions vetoed by any of the US, the UK, the USSR or China, which on the face of it gave the Americans a fairly free hand if they were prepared to use the veto. From MacArthur's point of view, however, the crucial difficulty lay in the following provision: 'Any directives dealing with fundamental changes in the Japanese constitutional structure or in the regime of control, or dealing with a change in the Japanese Government as a whole, will be issued only following consultation and following the attainment of agreement in the Far Eastern Commission.'[10]

As late as 30 January 1946, General MacArthur met the Far Eastern Advisory Commission (precursor of the Far Eastern Commission) and told them that, because of the Moscow Agreement, he no longer had authority to take action on constitutional reform, which he hoped would be carried out on Japanese initiative.[11]

What exactly happened when the GHQ draft was presented to a shocked and disbelieving Cabinet on 13 February has never been completely cleared up. What is certain is that substantial pressure was brought to bear upon the Cabinet by the officials of Government Section, including Whitney himself. The precise nature of that pressure, however, has been a subject of some dispute, and upon it hangs in part the controversy about whether the Constitution was 'imposed' or 'written in co-operation'. According to one account that gained wide currency, Whitney told members of the Cabinet that if the Japanese Government did not present a revised constitution similar to the GHQ draft, the *person* of the *tennō* could not be guaranteed.[12]

This account was the basis of the later charge by Dr Matsumoto, whose constitution-drafting efforts have already been mentioned, that the Americans threatened to indict the *tennō* as a war criminal if Cabinet did not accept the GHQ draft as the basis for a new constitution. If the statement was actually made, however, a more likely interpretation would appear to be that it was meant as a warning, to the effect that without drastic action to forestall the Far Eastern Commission, SCAP would find it difficult to stave off demands from the Soviet Union and other countries for the Emperor to be tried in person.[13] It has, moreover, been doubted whether Whitney ever spoke in such terms. Whitney in his own published account of the meeting nowhere mentions it,[14] and Professor Takayanagi Kenzō, later Chairman of the Commission on the Constitution, casts doubt on the reliability of the original account.[15]

Even if Takayanagi's doubts can be sustained, however, it is not quite so easy to agree wholly with his thesis, courageously and persistently argued during the hearings of the Commission on the Constitution, that the Constitution was a 'collaborative effort' between the Americans and the Japanese. Even though the Beer and Itoh point is well taken that Japan had a 'lame duck' cabinet in February 1946, the attempt to coerce – or at least strongly pressure – that Cabinet seems manifest. (Such pressure may, of course, have been well justified, but that is a different point.) Even Whitney's own account reveals a calculated plan of coercing the Cabinet into virtually accepting the GHQ draft as its own, effected with relentlessness and precision. Apart from his gratuitous remark about 'atomic sunshine' (see note 14), Whitney by his own account threatened to place the draft before the people over the heads of Cabinet if they refused to accept it.[16] As Ward commented in 1956: 'Given the traditional distrust of Japanese officials for popular sovereignty in any form, rendered particularly acute by the country's desperate and tumultuous economic and social circumstances and the unprecedented scale of left-wing political activities, it is difficult to conceive of any more ominous development from the standpoint of Japanese officialdom than a constitution formulated in the "marketplace"'.[17]

After the meeting on 13 February, the Cabinet made one more attempt to persuade SCAP to accept the Matsumoto draft as a basis for negotiation, but this was flatly rejected.[18] Finally, the Cabinet capitulated and hammered out a draft constitution, following closely the GHQ draft. This was delivered to SCAP on 4 March. There followed an extraordinary session, some 30 hours long, in which Cabinet and the Government Section arrived at a mutually acceptable draft. Here also the Americans kept up a relentless pressure upon the Japanese Government. Whitney gave an ultimatum that he would 'wait until morning' for a final draft to be produced, and then proceeded to reverse most of the changes which the Japanese had attempted to introduce into the GHQ draft. The only significant concession made at this point by the Americans was the substitution of a bicameral for a unicameral assembly.[19] The document was published on 6 March, and subsequently went through an intensive process of debate in Parliament. The House of Representatives passed it on 24 August by 421 votes to eight (six of the dissenters being Communists), it was agreed to by the House of Peers on 6 October and the Privy Council on 29 October. During this process, some changes were made in the text, but for the most part they were not of great importance, and in any case they were all cleared with SCAP. Beer and Itoh emphasize the importance of the fact that it was a largely new body of parliamentarians, rather than the Cabinet left over from the war, that debated and approved the constitutional draft in the House of Representatives.[20] The overwhelming affirmative vote certainly reflected the mood of the times and the enthusiasm with which democratic reforms were being embraced by many Japanese. It was also true that by this time many of the more conservative parliamentarians had been removed by the purge edict. Also, some who may have had qualms about the new Constitution may have calculated that no real alternative course of action was possible in conditions of Occupation control other than to accept it.

There is thus much force in the argument that the post-war Constitution was imposed on a reluctant Japanese political Establishment, even though, following Beer and Itoh, it is also arguable that that Establishment was discredited and about to be replaced, in part if not in its entirety. SCAP undoubtedly twisted the arm of the Cabinet by writing a constitutional draft based on popular sovereignty and threatening to take it to the people if Cabinet should fail to sponsor it as its own creation. An official view was then maintained that the new Constitution was a Japanese product, and the press was forbidden to make critical comment.[21] Whether and to what extent the course of action taken by SCAP was justified by pressing political circumstances – in particular the opportunities which the establishment of the Far Eastern Commission appeared to create for Soviet interference – is a matter for argument. In so far as this bears on the legitimacy of the Constitution, there is a strong argument that its subsequent history is a more important factor than its origins. As Beer and Itoh put it: 'The intent of the SCAP framers seems to matter little now. Japanese interpretations and judgements will determine whether or not constitutional change is advisable.'[22]

One way in which the survival of the Constitution was facilitated was by making it very difficult to revise. The accusation that it was imposed by the Americans has never gained sufficient impetus as the basis of a political move-ment to surmount the legal obstacles to revision. On the contrary, from the 1950s an impressive degree of support developed among diverse sections of the population for its fundamental principles, even though aspects of it have remained controversial.

A second argument often used by revisionists is that the Constitution was too hastily written, that this is reflected in some of its wording, and that some aspects of the document are basically ill-considered, and ill-suited to Japanese social and political reality. To this it can be replied that Japan in 1946 was ripe for radical political change, and that a dramatic new approach was needed. In any case, successive governments have not found it all that difficult to interpret its provisions with flexibility.

The most controversial parts of the Constitution, dividing revisionists from its supporters, are those relating to the location of sovereignty (including the role of the *tennō* and aspects of the principle of popular sovereignty), the human rights provisions (chapter 5), and the peace clause (article 9).

Since more ink has been spilled and heat generated on the third of these than on any other aspect of the Constitution, we need to dwell on it at some length. For many, the peace clause is the Constitution's very essence, often leading to the neglect of other important parts of it. The fact that it is frequently called the 'Peace Constitution' attests to the dramatic impact and controversial nature of this particular clause.

Both the origin and the subsequent history of the peace clause are interesting and important. It is apparent that it did not originate in instructions received by MacArthur from Washington. The document SWNCC-228, for instance, merely required that 'the civil be supreme over the military branch of the government.'[23] It was natural to assume, therefore, that the author and originator of the clause was MacArthur himself. The idea of having Japan renounce war and the means of waging it through a clause in the body of her Constitution[24] could perhaps be seen as appealing to the visionary element in MacArthur's temperament, and also as part of the calculated attempt to forestall interference from the Far Eastern Commission, mentioned above. With the USSR and other powers calling for the *tennō* to be put on trial as a war criminal, a Constitution which was so radical that it not only replaced imperial by popular sovereignty, but even went so far as to remove from Japan the right to engage in military activities, *and yet retained the tennō* (something which MacArthur apparently regarded as vital to the success of the Occupation), was an attractive stratagem. If this version of events and motivations were correct, the revisionists could argue with force that the obnoxious peace clause was very specifically 'imposed'.

Unfortunately for this version, MacArthur in his testimony to a US Senate Committee in May 1951 claimed that not he, but Shidehara, who was Prime Minister in early 1946, was the originator of the peace clause.[25] According to MacArthur, Shidehara had come to see him on 24 January 1946, and had proposed that a new Constitution should incorporate a renunciation of war. This was substantially corroborated in Shidehara's biography,[26] and was used by Takayanagi in his argument against the 'imposed Constitution' thesis.[27] Shidehara allegedly said nothing of this at the time to his Cabinet colleagues, and since no third person was present at the meeting (and both parties to it have died), it is impossible to be sure exactly what happened. Not all of Shidehara's colleagues were prepared to accept this account of events.[28]

The wording of the peace clause went through a number of changes between its initial enunciation by MacArthur in his instructions to the Government Section on 3 February 1946, and the final version. All the versions contained two paragraphs, the first renouncing the right to war, and the second stating that armed forces would not be maintained.

General MacArthur's initial version read as follows:

War as a sovereign right of the nation is abolished. Japan renounces it as an instrumentality for settling its disputes and even for preserving its own security. It relies upon the higher ideals which are now stirring the world for its defence and protection.

No Japanese Army, Navy or Air Force will ever be authorised and no rights of belligerency will ever be conferred upon any Japanese force.[29]

In the GHQ draft worked out by the Government Section and presented to the Japanese Cabinet on 13 February 1946 the sentence about 'higher ideals' was dropped, as, more significantly, was the phrase 'even for preserving its own security'. There was a further change in the text of the agreed draft published on 6 March, the first paragraph of which read: 'War, as a sovereign right of the nation, and the threat or use of force, is forever renounced as a means of settling disputes with other nations'. This version, in which, instead of war being simply abolished as a sovereign right of the nation, it is renounced *as a means of settling disputes with other nations,* could conceivably be regarded as permitting defence against invasion, or participation in international sanctions.[30]

The most important change to the wording of the article was introduced on the initiative of Ashida Hitoshi (later to be Prime Minister, in 1947–8) during the course of debates in Parliament. An additional phrase was attached to the beginning of each of the two paragraphs of the article, ostensibly to reinforce and clarify its pacifist purpose. The final version, therefore, read as follows:

> Aspiring sincerely to an international peace based on justice and order, the Japanese people forever renounce war as a sovereign right of the nation and the threat or use of force as means of settling international disputes.
>   In order to accomplish the aim of the preceding paragraph, land, sea and air forces, as well as other war potential, will never be maintained. The right of belligerency of the state will not be recognised.

The real significance of the additional phrases (as Ashida admitted later) was one of qualification rather than reinforcement. Now that the 'aim' of the first paragraph was 'an international peace based on justice and order', the ban on land, sea and air forces in the second paragraph could be regarded as qualified in so far as it was now designed to 'accomplish the aim' of the first. Presumably in an imperfectly peaceful world, other aims, such as defence preparedness against aggression, might be regarded as legitimate.

There is evidence that this interpretation was understood at the time by SCAP, which did not disapprove.[31] If this is the case, it goes some way to supporting the conclusion that article 9 was initially intended as a stratagem, to forestall criticism and interference from the Far Eastern Commission, and that later on, even before the onset of the Cold War had started to change American foreign policy priorities, SCAP was content to see the original purport of the article emasculated. It is ironic indeed that despite this it should have become a potent weapon in the hands both of left-wing opponents of American foreign policy within Japan, and of conservative politicians such as Yoshida, who could use it to combat American pressure for heavy Japanese defence spending, exerted during the period of economic recovery in the 1950s.

The existence of article 9 has not prevented the emergence of the euphemistically named Ground, Maritime and Air Self-Defence Forces (*Rikujō, kaijō, kōkū jieitai*), formed under their present names in 1954. As we shall see in chapter 12, their existence, size, cost, location, equipment and permitted roles have attracted recurrent controversy. The debate in the early 1990s over the Gulf Crisis, which led eventually to the passage of the PKO bill in 1992, heralded a certain evolution of public opinion on defence issues, as well as on constitutional issues generally. The state of public opinion concerning the Constitution is a most complex matter, but a few reasonably firm generalizations seem applicable.[32]

First of all, when the question is asked, in the 1990s as in earlier periods, whether the Constitution should be revised in order formally to permit the existence of armed forces, the response remains firmly negative.[33] Secondly, where respondents are asked which of a number of given aspects of the Constitution most concern them – with multiple answers permitted and the total coming to more than 100 – the peace clause always comes out top, though by slowly decreasing margins.[34] Thirdly, where a broad question is asked about the value of the Constitution as a whole, support remains generally strong.[35] Fourthly, however, support for some form of constitutional revision appears to have moved from a minority to a majority position.[36] Finally, of those expressing a revisionist view, a majority in all recent polls cited the difficulties, springing from the peace clause, of making an international contribution (multiple answers permitted), though the percentage declined slightly between 1994 and 1996.[37]

It may tentatively be concluded from this that while the Constitution continues to attract widespread support in general, inhibitions about revising it have to some extent declined. Moreover, no doubt stimulated by the intense domestic debate over the Gulf Crisis and war of 1990–1, a considerable body of opinion now regards the peace clause as problematic. We should nevertheless remember that the clause is supported with intensity by widespread, if now minority, sections of opinion.

Discussion of the peace clause takes us on to the proposals for constitutional reform put forward by the *Yomiuri* in the mid-1990s. Sensing a public mood shifting to some extent in favour of considering the option of constitutional revision, the *Yomiuri* published in November–December 1994 a revised constitutional text. For ease of reference, the existing text and the proposed text, with revisions, were printed in parallel.[38]

The proposed revision of the peace clause made it much longer than the original, and it was divided into two articles, marked '10' and '11' (sections altered or added are underlined):

10. Aspiring sincerely to an international peace based on justice and order, the Japanese people shall never recognise[39] war as a sovereign right of the nation and the threat or use of force as means of settling international disputes.
   Seeking to eliminate from the world inhuman and indiscriminate weapons of mass destruction, Japan[40] shall not manufacture, possess or use such weapons.

11. Japan shall form an organisation for self-defence to secure its peace and independence and to maintain its safety.[41]
   The prime minister shall exercise supreme command authority over the organisation for self-defence.
   The people shall not be forced to participate in organisations for self-defence.[42]

The explanation given for the proposed change is as follows:

'… when we consider constitutional revision, we first of all need a form of words which establishes clearly in the constitution the existence and significance of the Self-Defence Forces. Secondly, even so, in order to continue to defend the spirit of "eternal peace" in the present article 9, a firm brake must be placed on [any tendency for Japan] to become a great militaristic power.[43] This is necessary in order not to create needless anxiety in the world, and especially in Asian countries near to Japan.'[44]

The key element in the proposed revision is of course the elimination of the second paragraph of article 9, which on the face of it bans 'land, sea and air forces, as well as other war potential', and de-recognizes the 'right of belligerency of the state'. In its place a specific ban on weapons of mass destruction is introduced.[45] In the second article, recognition of the legitimacy of the Self-Defence Forces is introduced with the task of securing Japan's 'peace and independence and to maintain its safety', 'the supreme command authority' being specifically placed in the hands of the prime minister. This would place firmly in the text of the constitution the principle of civilian control. The final section is intended as a ban on conscription, which the commentary explains as a means of putting a brake on any tendency to become a militaristic great power.[46]

In addition to the revised peace clause, the *Yomiuri* proposed a new chapter, consisting of three articles, and entitled 'International Co-operation'. This was designed to ensure that in case of natural or man-made disasters occurring outside Japan (including 'military conflicts'), Japan would be constitutionally able to make a positive contribution. This could include despatch of 'a part of its self-defence organization'.[47]

From the point of view of other countries lacking any equivalent of the peace clause, the *Yomiuri* proposals may not appear particularly radical, given that the Japanese people were still not to recognize war as a sovereign right, nor the use of force to settle international disputes. Moreover, certain categories of weapon were to be constitutionally banned, as was conscription. So far as nuclear weapons were concerned, the proposals appeared to add an inhibition that had not existed before. Successive prime ministers had declared that nuclear weapons were not necessarily unconstitutional, while denying any intention to develop them.

On the other hand, in the context of the long-running debate in Japan, the proposals implied quite major change. A 'self-defence organization' (presumably the existing Self-Defence Forces) would for the first time be specifically recognized and the responsibility of the prime minister for them would be written into the constitution. Moreover, abolition of the existing article 9, paragraph 2, would presumably restore the 'right of belligerency of the state', and remove the ban on sending troops abroad. In addition, a new chapter was proposed setting out Japan's obligations in respect of international peace-keeping and associated matters, which had been the subject of fierce domestic debates precipitated by the Gulf Crisis of the early 1990s. Even under the 1992 PKO bill, Self-Defence Force participants in UN peacekeeping missions were severely restricted in what they could actually do.

Whatever the fate of the *Yomiuri* proposals on the peace clause, the existing article continues to shape the parameters of debate on defence policy. How far Japanese governments have been inhibited in their defence policies by the existence of article 9 is a more complicated question than it might seem, because governments have used the existence of the article and the popular support it has enjoyed as a means of countering American pressure for increased expenditure on defence. In retrospect the 1980s, when defence expenditures increased substantially, now seems an exception in this regard. Apart from the defence and foreign policy aspects of this issue (see chapter 12), it raises the crucial question of the constitutional relationship between the various branches of government. One of the most important innovations of the post-war Constitution was the granting to the judiciary of the power of judicial review. Article 81 of the Constitution reads:

> The Supreme Court is the court of last resort with power to determine the constitutionality of any law, order, regulation or official act.

Given the doubtful constitutional position of the Self-Defence Forces, it has often been asked why, in view of article 81, the Supreme Court has apparently been reluctant to take a strong stand on the matter. To answer this we need to examine briefly the relationship between the political and judicial branches of government and the use made by the Supreme Court of its power of judicial review.

Under the Meiji Constitution, the courts had no power whatever of reviewing governmental acts. Constitutional issues were politically, not legally, determined. The introduction of judicial review in the post-war Constitution had a strong American ring about it, and was obviously derived in large measure from Marbury vs. Madison. In the Suzuki case of 1952, which related to the constitutionality of the National Police Reserve (precursor of the Self-Defence Forces)[48] it was determined that the Supreme Court should not act as a constitutional court to determine matters of constitutionality in the abstract, but should act 'only where a concrete legal dispute exists between specific parties'. Otherwise the Supreme Court would be in danger of assuming 'the appearance of an organ superior to all other powers in the land, thereby running counter to the basic principle of democratic government: that the three powers are independent, equal, and immune from each other's interference'.[49] In practice, the Supreme Court has been consistently reluctant to exercise its power of judicial review, and the contrast with the American situation could hardly be more extreme. The *Yomiuri* proposals envisage the establishment of a separate constitutional court, rather on the German model, to examine acts of the executive and legislature involving issues of constitutionality. Such a court could take up issues referred to it by one-third or more of the members of either house of Parliament, by request from another court, or in relation to appeals against Supreme Court decisions.[50]

Cases have been brought to the courts where the peace clause has been at issue. In a number of cases the Supreme Court has been reluctant to declare unconstitutionality where it judges that what is at stake is a 'political question'. The 'political question' first became an issue in the seminal Sunakawa decision of 1959, which was the first to involve the peace clause directly. In 1957 seven demonstrators were charged with breaking into the US Air Force base at Tachikawa, in the western suburbs of Tokyo, following a protest against the extension of a runway on to agricultural land. The penalty they faced, under a law derived from the Administrative Agreement accompanying the Japan–US Security Treaty of 1951, was heavier than it would have been had they been found guilty of trespass on to other property.[51] The Tokyo District Court acquitted the defendants, on the specifically constitutional grounds that the Security Treaty, and thus the Special Criminal Law based on the Administrative Agreement, was illegal under article 9. The Tokyo Public Prosecutors' Office immediately appealed to the Supreme Court, which quashed the lower court decision.

There was a wide variety of opinions expressed by the 15 judges, but the formal judgment used the doctrine of the 'political question'. The judgment pointed out that the Security Treaty was of a 'highly political nature' in the context of the present case, and possessed 'an extremely important relation to the basis of the existence of our country as a sovereign nation'. Arguing, therefore, that it was Cabinet, Parliament and ultimately the 'sovereign people' that should decide on matters such as this, the Court concluded that 'the legal decision as to unconstitutionality ... falls outside the right of judicial review by the courts, unless there is clearly obvious unconstitutionality or invalidity'.[52]

Four successive cases in the 1970s and 1980s – the first, second and third Naganuma Nike Missile Site cases (1973, 1976 and 1983) and the Hyakuri Air Base case (1989) – permitted further testing through the courts of the constitutionality of military bases.[53] The three Naganuma cases related to the reclassification by the Ministry of Agriculture and Forestry of reserved forest land in Hokkaidō to make way for an antiaircraft missile base. In 1973 the Sapporo District Court held, *inter alia*, that '... insofar as the SDF [Self-Defence Forces] and the related laws and regulations violate the Constitution, the construction of defence facilities for the SDF is not in the public welfare as prescribed by the Forest Law'.[54] This was the first time that the SDF had been found to be unconstitutional by a district court. Subsequently, however, both the Sapporo High Court, in 1976, and the Supreme Court, in 1982, managed to avoid the issue of constitutionality in passing judgment in the Naganuma Nike Missile Base case. The 1989 Hyakuri Base case concerned the sale of a parcel of land to the Defence Agency. The sale was challenged on constitutional grounds, but the Tokyo High Court in 1981 and the Supreme Court in 1989 found technical grounds on which to avoid the issue of constitutionality.

In a further case, in 1990, a group of citizens of Okinawa failed in a bid to overturn on constitutional grounds expropriation of property for American military bases, since the Naha District Court held such seizure to be in accordance with the Constitution.[55] As we shall see in chapter 12, the issue of American bases in Okinawa was to become a matter of sharp political dispute and tension from 1995 onwards.

The bulk of controversies surrounding the Constitution have concerned the peace clause, and this has often meant that other parts of the Constitution have been relatively neglected. Even so, some key aspects of dispute remain, outside the specialized realm of article 9.

One of the most interesting and important is Chapter 3 of the Constitution, concerning rights and freedoms. The rights guaranteed in that chapter are both more extensive and less qualified by concomitant duties of the individual than in the corresponding section of the Meiji Constitution. Of the 31 separate articles in Chapter 3, only four are qualified by consideration of the 'public welfare'. Articles 12 and 13 provide general qualifications, and read as follows:

> Article 12: The freedoms and rights guaranteed to the people by this Constitution shall be maintained by the constant endeavor of the people, who shall refrain from any abuse of these freedoms and rights and shall always be responsible for utilizing them for the public welfare.

> Article 13: All of the people shall be respected as individuals. Their right to life, liberty and the pursuit of happiness shall, to the extent that it does not interfere with the public welfare, be the supreme consideration in legislation and in other governmental affairs.

Whereas the 'public welfare' in articles 12 and 13 presumably refers to the whole of Chapter 3, in articles 22 and 29 it qualifies specific freedoms, namely that of choosing one's place of residence and occupation (article 22), and the right, as defined by law, to own property (article 29).

In the earlier years of the Constitution, the Supreme Court was sometimes inclined to use the 'public welfare' as a reason for qualifying certain constitutionally guaranteed freedoms. These included freedom of expression,[56] the right to choose one's occupation and the right to move to a foreign country. In the politically confrontational atmosphere of the 1950s and 1960s, an important area on which the Supreme Court was called upon to pronounce was the regulation of demonstrations. Given the widespread use of demonstrations by dissenting groups as a means of expressing opposition to government policies, the guarantee of freedom of assembly contained in article 21 of the constitution gave rise to much contentious argument.

From the late 1940s a series of cases arose involving regulations of local authorities governing demonstrations. The main issue in contention was whether local authorities should maintain a system of licensing demonstrations, allowing the possibility of demonstrations being banned or severely curtailed, or merely a system of notification. What eventually emerged as a result of litigation was a compromise between the two principles, whereby in broad terms the freedom to demonstrate was maintained, but local authorities retained the means to control demonstrations which threatened to get out of hand or become violent.[57]

More recently, however, litigation in respect of human rights has centred on different issues from this. Beer and Itoh, following the custom of Japanese constitutional lawyers, subdivide human rights cases into six categories: (1) Equality of rights under the law; (2) Freedom of economic activities; (3) Rights related to quality of life (social rights); (4) Rights of political participation; (5) Procedural rights of the person; (6) Rights and freedoms of the spirit.[58]

The first category, equality of rights under the law, includes the famous Aizawa patricide case of 1973, in which the Supreme Court overturned a much earlier (1950) Supreme Court ruling upholding more severe punishment for killing one's father than for other kinds of murder or manslaughter. The issue may appear recondite outside Japan, but within Japan it bears on the Confucian prescription of respect and reverence for lineal ascendants, and the apparent contradiction between this principle and constitutional principle of equality of rights under the law. Within the first category also fall cases concerning discrimination against women in employment conditions, and discrimination against employees on grounds of belief.[59]

In the second category, that of economic freedoms, there have been a succession of cases where individuals and companies have invoked constitutional guarantees of freedom to conduct business, against various forms of bureaucratic regulation by public authorities at national or local level. It also includes cases relating to property disputes stemming from the post-war land reform. All these concern issues where economic freedoms, most notably property rights and rights to engage in private enterprise clash with *raison d'état*, or, more commonly, the sectional interests of a particular department of the government bureaucracy. Where what is presented as the public welfare appears to be at loggerheads with freedom of economic activity, including property rights, the normally conservative-minded Supreme Court has often found it difficult to reconcile two conservative principles which in the Japanese context tend to conflict.[60]

Cases under category 3 – those related to the quality of life – touch on a number of politically sensitive issues, including those concerning the rights of employees in the public sector, such as teachers and local public servants, to engage in union or other protest activity, particularly that having political content. The Supreme Court has tended to take a restrictive view of such rights.

The fourth category, which concerns rights of participation in electoral politics, is of crucial political importance and touches issues at the core of democratic practice. As has been seen in previous chapters, under the former electoral system for the House of Representatives, severe malapportionment had been allowed to develop between the value of a single vote in the most over-represented rural constituencies and the most under-represented urban ones, since no adequate mechanism had been put in place regularly to redesign constituencies so as to secure reasonable voter equality. Rather, although some seats had been from time to time added in city areas since the 1960s, it was not until the 1980s that any reduction in the number of rural seats was effected, and that quite inadequate to eliminate the malapportionment (negative gerrymander).

Until 1976, the Supreme Court had not seen fit to rule unconstitutional the vote imbalance existing in either house of Parliament, and in relation to the House of Councillors elections it could still issue a judgment in 1983 that a discrepancy of 526 per cent (5.26 times) between the best and worst represented constituencies was acceptable. In 1976, however, the Supreme Court held unconstitutional the 1972 lower house general elections in Chiba prefecture, close to Tokyo, given that the best–worst discrepancy in those elections was 4.99 times (499 per cent). To avoid political instability, however, it did not invalidate the elections as such. This pattern was repeated in cases relating to the House of Representatives in 1983 and 1985, in such a way that sufficient pressure was placed on the politicians to make some modification to the gross discrepancies that had been allowed to develop. Even so, up to the time when the electoral system was changed to a new system in 1994, the best–worst discrepancy remained more than 300 per cent.[61]

Category 5, concerning procedural rights, touches on a range of issues, some of which have political implications, such as the role of confessions in criminal investigations by police, other aspects of police investigations, problems of delay in judicial proceedings, and court procedures in the trial of political dissidents.[62]

The final category, that of rights and freedoms of the spirit, constitutes a rich vein of judicial interpretation on a wide range of issues, many with political overtones. Their range is summarized by Beer and Itoh in the following words: 'government seizure of allegedly obscene publications, visa denial in relation to political speech, press disclosure of untruths classified as state secrets, the newsman's privilege to refuse to identify confidential sources, published response to a newspaper advertisement attacking a political party, press defamation of public figures, the legality of vote canvassing, discriminatory restraints on courtroom note taking, separation of the *Shintō* religion from the state, and the downplay of unpleasant wartime history in high school textbooks certified by the Ministry of Education, Science and Culture'.[63]

The last two of these deserve brief elaboration, since they relate to contentious political issues of great moment. The separation of state and religion, embodied in article 20 of the 1946 Constitution, was designed to guarantee freedom of religious belief and avoid the kind of state manipulation of *Shintō* that had occurred up till 1945 (see chapter 11 for further elaboration). For various reasons, however, complete separating of religion and the state is difficult to achieve, so that when the municipal authorities of the city of Tsū in Mie Prefecture participated in a *Shintō* ground-breaking ceremony, they no doubt assumed that they were engaging in a customary social activity rather than something that might fall foul of the constitutional prescription that '[t]he State and its organs shall refrain from religious activity'.[64] A case was nevertheless brought against them, and in 1977 it reached the Supreme Court, which found in a majority verdict that the ceremony in question, though connected with religion, was in essence social and secular, and 'will not have the effect of promoting or encouraging *Shintō* or of oppressing or interfering with other religions'.[65]

In 1988 the Supreme Court pronounced on a case in which the Christian widow of a deceased member of the Self-Defence Forces had challenged the constitutionality of a decision to 'enshrine' the soul of her late husband, without her permission, in a *Shintō* shrine. Her case, however, failed in the Supreme Court on complex grounds. Both these cases illustrate the difficulty of maintaining the letter of article 20 in the Japanese social environment where *Shintō* shrines play a set of community functions which tend to involve local authorities and ordinary individuals as part of their membership of society. They also show, however, that the wartime and pre-war associations of State *Shintō* ensure a continuation of political controversy surrounding the former official religion of Japan.

Constitutional guarantees of rights and freedoms have not surprisingly provided the bulk of judicial case law relating to the Constitution, though opinions differ about how effectively the courts have sought to uphold the rights and freedoms embodied in Chapter 3. Broadly speaking, the Supreme Court (unlike some lower courts) interpreted Chapter 3 cautiously and from a conservative perspective. On the other hand, by the 1990s the accumulation of case law constituted a solid basis for constitutional interpretation in the area of rights and freedoms.

It seems significant that the revisions proposed by the *Yomiuri* left most of Chapter 3 intact. Articles were added on protection of the environment and on the right of privacy, while freedom to conduct one's business was added to the clause concerning freedom to choose one's occupation. On the other hand, the present article 18, prohibiting bondage and involuntary servitude, was eliminated. The article, which the *Yomiuri* argues derived from an American concern with the problem of slavery after the Civil War, has been used in Japan as an argument against conscription, but the *Yomiuri* draft, as we have seen, includes a specfic prohibition of conscription in the articles that replace the peace clause.[66]

Arguably as important as the parts of the Constitution discussed so far, the powers of and relationships between the two houses of Parliament, Cabinet, the Prime Minister and the *tennō* are tackled in a somewhat revisionist fashion in the *Yomiuri* draft. Perhaps the most radical proposal is an attempt to distinguish the House of Representatives from the House of Councillors by giving to the latter sole powers of appointing the Justices of the proposed Constitutional Court, as well as the right to impeach judges. On the other hand, the lower house was to have the sole right to designate the Prime Minister, who should only be chosen from its ranks. In the interests of role-sharing between the two houses, it was further proposed by the *Yomiuri*, that whereas, as in the present Constitution, the budget should be first presented to the House of Representatives and in case of disagreement, the lower house should prevail, on the other hand treaties should be first presented to the House of Councillors, and where the two houses disagreed, the upper house should prevail.[67]

The *Yomiuri* proposals also sought to strengthen the powers of the Prime Minister, in particular in relation to article 66, paragraph 1, of the 1946 Constitution, which reads as follows: 'The Cabinet shall consist of the Prime Minister, who shall be its head, and other Ministers of State, as provided for by law.' The corresponding article 74 of the *Yomiuri* draft read, in its relevant sections:

(1)   The Cabinet shall consist of the Prime Minister and other Ministers of State, as provided by law:

(2)   The Prime Minister shall represent (*daihyō shi*) the Cabinet and exercise control and supervision over Ministers of State (*kokumu daijin o tōsotsu suru*).[68]

There was also a concomitant strengthening (though difficult to represent in English) of the wording in the current article 72, where the statement that the Prime Minister '... exercises control and supervision over various administrative branches (*gyōsei kakubu o shiki kantoku suru*)' was pulled out into a separate paragraph and made to read:

The Prime Minister shall exercise general control and supervision over the various departments of the executive branch (... *gyōsei kakubu o tōkatsu suru*).[69]

In the same article prime ministerial control and supervision was specified in relation to the budget, which is not mentioned in this context in the present Constitution. In addition, the *Yomiuri* proposed that the Prime Minister should be given the specific power to dissolve the House of Representatives (there being an ambiguity over the dissolution power in the present Constitution between articles 7 and 69), and to designate in advance a temporary successor in case of prime ministerial incapacity. In addition to strengthening the powers of the Prime Minister, an attempt was made in the *Yomiuri* draft to bolster the wording of article 73 in order to increase to some extent the power of Cabinet. Apart from changes of wording that are difficult to render in English, the Cabinet was to have the additional power to convoke Parliament and to decide on the conferment of honours added to its existing powers.[70]

Under the existing Constitution, the Emperor (*tennō*) had of course been reduced to a purely symbolic and ceremonial role, by comparison with what the 1889 Constitution said about his position. Nevertheless, it was in the very first article of the 1946 Constitution that he was identified in a famous phrase as: '... symbol of the State and of the unity of the people, deriving his position from the will of the people with whom resides sovereign power'.

The *Yomiuri* draft preferred to relegate the articles concerning the *tennō* to a second chapter of the constitution, and devoting the strategically placed Chapter 1 to a statement of popular sovereignty, from which principle the position of the *tennō* derived. Thus the new article 1 would read: 'Sovereign power in Japan resides with the Japanese people'.[71]

In the second chapter, relating to the *tennō*, he was, as in the current Constitution, specifically given no powers related to government, and his principal role was still defined as that of 'symbol'. In order, however, to meet long-standing objections to his apparent inferior status to foreign heads of state, he was to 'represent the State' (*kuni o daihyō shite*) when receiving foreign ambassadors etc.[72]

The role of the *tennō* as envisaged in the *Yomiuri* draft was far closer to that embodied in the 1946 Constitution than in that of 1889. Even so, there were those who argued that even under the 1946 Constitution the institution provided some scope for manipulation by a government minded to exploit it in the interests of a reactionary programme.[73]

The final point to be noted in the *Yomiuri* draft concerns the provisions for constitutional revision. The current provision – regarded as too difficult by those in favour of flexibility but as a protection against undesirable revision by others – requires a concurring vote of two thirds or more of the *members* of each house, followed by a simple majority in a referendum of the people. The proposed change would substantially ease this provision. Revision could proceed at a vote of each house of Parliament where two thirds or more of members were present. If a simple majority voted for revision, it would be incorporated in the Constitution provided that it was subsequently passed in a national referendum. If, however, the two houses of Parliament passed a revision proposal by a two thirds majority, no referendum of the people would be required.[74]

What are we to make of the *Yomiuri* proposals as a whole? Ronald Dore argues in a recent book that they signify the passing of an older generation of revisionists, who in the politically tense 1950s and 1960s were nostalgic in certain respects for the pre-war Constitution, and the emergence of a new generation of revisionists, more attuned to contemporary needs and conditions.[75]

There is much truth in this observation, but it also seems important to note that there is continuity between some of the proposals for constitutional revision made in the immediate post-war decades and those put forward in 1994 by the *Yomiuri Shinbun*. Robert Ward summarized the general effects of the proposals of the Commission on the Constitution (*Kenpō chōsakai*), which met between 1957 and 1964, in the following terms (thus abstracting from differing and even contradictory proposals within the revisionist group): to strengthen the prime minister and Cabinet at the expense of the Diet and political parties; to strengthen the national government at the expense of the localities; to strengthen public and collective rights against private and individual rights and claims; to expand and legitimize the present powers of the national government in the conduct of military and political aspects of foreign relations; to change the relationship of the two Houses by enhancing the House of Councillors; and to diminish somewhat the ambit of judicial powers through administrative courts, and perhaps also to circumscribe somewhat the powers of judicial review.[76]

While some of the earlier revisionist agenda has plainly been superseded, some of it remains in the *Yomiuri* proposals, although there may be a subtle shift in significance because of a changed context and altered perceptions. For instance, the *Yomiuri* draft also seeks to strengthen the powers of the prime minister and Cabinet, though whether this would be at the expense of Parliament and the parties is an open question.[77] There is an obvious continuity in respect of proposed changes to article 9, in that both sets of proposals call for the full legitimization of the Self-Defence Forces and the clarification of lines of responsiblity in respect of them, even though bans on weapons of mass destruction and on conscription are introduced into the *Yomiuri* draft. Both sets of proposals seek to distinguish the functions of the two houses of Parliament from each other, thus in effect enhancing the role of the House of Councillors. The *Yomiuri* suggestion that there should be a special constitutional court, and that the judicial review powers of the Supreme Court should be ceded to that court, may be seen perhaps as a step in the direction of administrative courts, and, while not removing the power of judicial review, removing it from the purview of the mainstream judicial system. On the other hand, the *Yomiuri* draft suggests hardly any change in the area of local government, and, except in so far as the introduction of a new article on the environment is seen as a strengthening of public and collective rights, it can hardly be seen to disadvantage private and individual rights. Indeed the additional emphasis on the 'right of privacy' and 'freedom to conduct business' would seem to shift the balance of rights somewhat in the direction of the rights of the individual.

Perhaps, however, the biggest gap in virtually all the constitutional revision proposals that have emerged in Japan since the 1950s is a failure to tackle – or to tackle adequately – the problems created by the unusual degree of power exercised by unelected government bureaucratic agencies, over which inadequate political control is exercised. Even though, by attempting to strengthen the power of the prime minister and Cabinet, the *Yomiuri* proposals go some way to addressing this problem, what is proposed seems unlikely to be a sufficient remedy. Given that, in the view of most knowledgeable observers, Cabinet exercises little decision-making power in practice, the prime minister's position is hedged around with obstacles, semi-independent ministries spend much time and effort fighting over 'turf', bureaucrats expand their reach by 'descending from heaven', while policy communities consisting of government officials, *zoku* politicians and interest group representatives in effect determine (or veto) policy initiatives, some effort to redefine the role of government ministries and agencies would seem to require action at a fundamental constitutional level. The problem is, however, that hitherto those wishing for revision to the Constitution have had a quite different agenda from this, while those defending the present Constitution have largely been concerned with the peace clause. It could be argued that reform in this area is a political task not requiring a revision of the Constitution. Maybe so, and maybe constitutions are decorative aspects of political systems which do not need to reflect political reality too closely. In the case of Japan, however, the 1946 Constitution should be regarded historically as an absolutely crucial instrument of democratic change and renewal. More than half a century after its coming into force, however, there is room for a further exercise in rather radical constitutional renovation. The *Yomiuri* proposal goes some way in this direction by increasing and highlighting the emphasis on popular sovereignty, and emphasizing the powers of prime minister and Cabinet. Much more, however, is needed, in order to enable the people's representatives responsibly to direct and control what are largely unaccountable agglomerations of unchecked bureaucratic power.

11

Domestic Political Issues

In Japan the average person is more concerned with 'bread and butter' issues liable to be affected by domestic economic policy than the broad constitutional, environmental or personal liberty issues that tend to interest intellectuals. Even, for instance, in such a sensitive political area as the siting of nuclear power stations, it tends to be locally affected fishing and farming groups that are most vigorous in protest, rather than nationally based organizations which do not have to sell a product in a volatile market.

In this, there is little evidence that the Japanese are much different from electorates in other parts of the world. If we are adequately to understand the ways in which politics actually works in Japan, it is essential that we grasp the basic pragmatism with which most people react to issues having a political content. The Japanese electorate has, by international standards, a conspicuously high level and broad spread of education, and is not lacking the means to understand where its interests lie. That is not to say, however, that it is possible to arrive at an accurate and balanced understanding of Japanese domestic politics without a much broader perception of political dynamics than is pro- vided by this simple observation about the individual's primary concern with his or her interests. Interests are in fact channelled in ways conditioned by predominant social structures and norms, habits of political interaction and patterns of power distribution, and such things as the traumatic legacies of history, and ideas about the nature of nationality.

In this chapter domestic political issues will be grouped under nine headings, given below. Before introducing these categories, however, three caveats are needed. The first is that under the heading 'political issues' two rather different sorts of phenomena will be combined: on the one hand, issues which are the stuff of political conflict and debate, such as taxation policy or policy towards minorities; and, on the other hand, issues which concern one's understanding of how the system works, such as the reasons for bureaucratic power or the roots of gender inequality. All these, however, are 'issues' in the sense that an understanding of Japanese politics requires analysis both at the obvious level of how particular issues have been handled and at the deeper level of the forces that motivate those concerned.

The second caveat is that a number of the issues to be examined have more than one aspect in terms of the categories. Thus for instance agriculture has been an important political issue, but it touches on questions of economic distribution, power distribution, public welfare and even nationality. It is placed, however, under economic distribution since that appears to have been the most fundamental aspect involved.

Thirdly, the selection of issues obviously cannot be comprehensive, but issues have been chosen issues with a view, so far as possible, to painting an accurate and balanced picture.

The following are our nine categories:

1. Socio-economic structure
2. Economic distribution
3. Economic management
4. Power distribution
5. Accountability
6. Public welfare
7. Legacies of history
8. Nationality and minorities
9. Communication and expression

1. Socio-economic Structure

It is often argued that Japan is not a class society, and the apparent finding that some 90 per cent of the Japanese population identifies itself as 'middle class' is routinely cited in justification of this belief. Even though the view of a 'classless Japan' has been strongly attacked from the left,[1] it seems difficult to make a convincing case for the view that social class differences – as normally under-stood at least in Europe – are strongly or widely felt in Japan. Social class as a basis for political party formation has been a minority phenomenon, and one that in the 1990s seems to have largely atrophied.

Two reasons stand out as explanations for this. The first is the system of 'vertical loyalties', which has in recent times bound an employee to his place of employment rather than to his fellow workers in the same occupation or craft but in other establishments. The role of the labour union has thus been primarily to secure the interests of the employees of the company to which the labour union is confined, and for the most part the union will refrain from doing anything that would put the firm at a serious disadvantage in relation to its rivals. Although most labour unions belong to union federations, they are jealous of their own rights when it comes to day-to-day bargaining with employers. Overall wage-fixing agreements affecting large segments of industry are thus highly unusual, although, through the device of the 'Spring Struggle' (*shuntō*), the campaigns of individual unions have been well co-ordinated.

Union consciousness is strongest in declining industries and among government employees, and union membership has declined from over 40 per cent of the workforce in the 1970s to less than 25 per cent of the workforce in the 1990s. Such decline, however, parallels what has happened in the mature economies of western Europe and elsewhere, since in 'new' high-tech industries unionism typically does not flourish.

This is not to argue that Japan has a particularly docile workforce, or one that is slow in the pursuit of its own interests.[2] In high growth periods workers have achieved impressive wage increases, but during the period of low economic growth for most of the 1990s wage increases have been restrained. Employees bargain for improvements in their wages and conditions almost entirely within individual firms, in whose profitability they have a direct and continuing interest. Employers seek to maintain, and where possible expand, their firm's share of the market, and the workforce is given every incentive by their situation and treatment to contribute to the atmosphere of acute competitiveness with other similar firms to which this leads. It should not be assumed that such a system would have been voluntarily agreed to by workers if they had really had a choice. The disadvantages suffered by a worker leaving one place of employment to seek work elsewhere are so serious that from necessity workers under permanent employment contracts simply accept the normality of the permanent employment system. Indeed, it has been cogently argued that the system originated from oligopolistic co-operation between large employers faced with an acute shortage of skilled labour, which, had employers not agreed to act in concert, could have exploited its scarcity through craft or industrial unions to extract disproportionately high wages.[3] Reinforced by a group-centred tradition from which employers could draw examples, and by the experience of pre-war and wartime mobilization, the system survived and was strengthened during the high economic growth period from the 1950s.

From the above it should not be assumed that the whole – or even the bulk – of the workforce benefits from permanent employment arrangements or long-term security of tenure with the same firm. Indeed, such an assumption seems to be widely believed outside Japan and should be regarded as one of the most persistent fallacies about the Japanese business and employment structure. The system is in fact far more complicated than this, with permanent employment contracts at one end of a spectrum that runs through limited-term contracts of varying lengths in large firms, relatively long-term employment but with insecure tenure in economically vulnerable small firms, a vast range of casual and part-time jobs down to the employment of day labourers resident in the *doya-gai* which are to be found in most big cities.[4] It has been estimated that the proportion of the total workforce enjoying permanent contracts of employment is somewhat less than one third. Their position, however, has been strategic, for a number of reasons. Firstly, they have represented a work situation to which others aspire, an ideal which not all can attain but which it seems right to aim at, or to use different language, a 'labour aristocracy'. Those employed under such happy conditions have enjoyed a predictable system of promotion through seniority (*shūshin koyōsei*), munificent pay and generous fringe benefits and bonuses, but are expected to become multi-skilled generalists, work long hours on exacting tasks and to allow their lives and those of their families to become encapsulated by the interests of their firm to an extent that would astonish workers in most Western companies.[5]

We have preferred the perfect to the present tense in the previous paragraph, because during the 1990s much publicity has been given to what is regarded as the erosion of the permanent employment system under the impact of difficult economic conditions persisting over several years. This has forced many firms to qualify the conditions offered to its 'permanent' workforce in the direction of a rather freer labour market. Thus, for instance, instead of offering its core workers security of tenure and seniority increments up to retirement age, some firms have taken to cutting these off after age 40 or 45, above which employees are given preference according to demonstrated merit. Even so, the balance of the evidence suggests that these are adjustments to a system which in essence remains intact, rather than indicating a trend towards the abandonment of the system as a whole and the substitution of free market-based hiring and firing.

That this should be so may strike foreign observers as surprising. To retain 'surplus' labour in depressed economic conditions when operating in a competitive market might appear irrational from the standpoint of free-market economics, especially when the conditions of employment of such labour mean that it becomes ever more expensive with age. Two factors in particular, however, go far to explain the persistence of this institution. One is that in a society where a high value is accorded to loyalty, the ability to harness a core of 'shock troops' exhibiting an exceptional level of loyalty to the organization may outweigh considerations of overmanning or an expensive payroll. Another is that, as we have seen, it is quite possible to use market-based hiring and firing practices in respect of those on less permanent employment contracts in the same firm. And thirdly, large firms are able quite easily to put additional pressure on those firms to which they subcontract work in such a way as to cushion themselves against adverse economic conditions.[6]

The system outlined above has the obvious political implication that it seriously inhibits *conscious* social class formation. Where the primary interests of much of the workforce lie in identification with the organizations by which it is employed, solidarity between similarly placed workers in different organizations (firms) is difficult to sustain. Indeed, when we look back at the bitter disputes that took place between the late 1940s and the 1970s between advocates of class-based confrontational unionism and advocates of unionism which should promote co-operative relations between capital and labour, it seems reasonable to argue that one important motivation for the promotion by employers and managers of intense company loyalty was fear of the disruptive potential of Marxist-influenced unions that became powerful after the war. Many famous companies in the late 1940s and 1950s fought battles royal with left-wing unions for control of company destinies – a fact that seems difficult to comprehend when one surveys the industrial scene of the 1990s.[7] It is important not to jump too easily to the conclusion that the structure of labour–management relations in Japan is simply a natural outgrowth of indigenous social norms and values, since conscious institution-building was an important part of the picture in an earlier period. Taking a long perspective it seems possible to argue that the formation of a single, generally moderate, labour union federation at the beginning of the 1990s (*Rengō*), and the gradual decoupling of labour unions from left-of-centre parties which has been occurring during the 1990s, represents the eventual outcome of struggles for control of the union movement that were at their height three or four decades previously.

The system of labour–management relations has had a crucial impact on the employment position of women, and here the career aspirations of increasing numbers of women (particularly those with high levels of education) come increasingly into conflict with the established norms of an employment system which has conspicuously relegated women to jobs of inferior quality, pay and tenure to those on offer to men. Speaking broadly, the expectations of women until relatively recently have been to occupy casual, or short-tenure positions before marriage, and then to return to somewhat similar types of employment after raising a family. Moreover, the expectations of women's behaviour in the workplace laid a heavy responsibility on them to subordinate their personal interests to those of their male workplace colleagues.[8] In this context the expectations placed on women in the home intersected with what was expected of them at work. Under the pre-war Emperor-ideology the ideal woman was portrayed as *ryōsai kenbo* (good wife and wise mother): in other words she was expected to devote herself to home duties with a notoriously low status within the family (at least until her children were raised and married). That was a period in which not only the social, but also the legal, status of women was greatly inferior to that of men in matters of property, divorce, right to vote (it was lacking) and other rights. The post-war reforms to the legal code place women on a level of virtual equality with men but, not surprisingly, social norms were slow to catch up with women's enhanced legal status, particularly in a society where resort to the courts was avoided wherever possible and tended to carry a social stigma.

Here again, in the post-war period, social factors combined with institutional factors to preserve and even reinforce an unequal outcome. Some well-meaning legislation during the post-war period placed restrictions on the conditions of women's labour, such as banning night work. This, however, often had the result that employers in hiring labour would prefer men to women because they could be deployed more flexibly, not being subject to the legal restrictions which affected to the employment of women. Women were, of course, cheaper to employ, but for many types of work, flexibility was seen as more valuable an asset than cheapness. On the other hand, in many small firms in which casual workers predominated, the proportion of women tended to be high.

In 1985, legislation was introduced reinforcing requirements for equality of employment opportunities between men and women. Although this put pressure on employers to pay equal wages and accord similar conditions to their female and male employees, the reality of treatment was slow to catch up with what the law prescribed. Nevertheless, the law at least provided a standard by which treatment could be judged, and was thereby useful for those working for greater equality. Perhaps just as important, however, was the changing nature of the economy – and thus of employment opportunities – in the 1980s and 1990s. The advance of high-tech industries, and the increasing weight within the economy of the service sector, opened up greater opportunities for highly qualified women, who constituted a huge pool of talent which could not sensibly be ignored. Particularly in the big cities, the number of companies either run by women, or having a policy of active recruitment of women for responsible positions, was growing. At lower levels of qualification, however, the slow growth of the economy in the 1990s served to reduce female employment opportunities. Meanwhile, in the realm of politics, Doi Takako's 'madonna boom' of 1989–90 made the idea of women parliamentarians less exotic than it had previously been, and there was at least one woman cabinet minister in most cabinets from the first Kaifu Cabinet (formed 1989) onwards.[9]

Among many specific issues relating to women's equality was one which came before Parliament in 1997. According to the Civil Law, a husband and wife on marriage 'shall assume the surname of the husband or wife in accordance with the agreement made at the time of marriage'.[10] In practice, in some 98 per cent of cases, the couple takes the surname of the husband, although the possibility of them taking the surname of the wife was originally to allow for *yōshi* adoptions, where in order to permit the continuation of a family name where there were no male offspring, that family 'adopts in' a male heir, who as an adult marries a daughter of the family and adopts her surname. Early in 1997 the *Minshutō* sponsored a bill, which went to the Legal Affairs Committee of the House of Representatives, to permit couples to register separate names on their *koseki* (family register), as well as on driving licenses, passports etc. The LDP, many of whose members were strongly opposed to permitting couples to register separate surnames, on the grounds that this might weaken family ties and cause associated social problems, eventually presented a compromise bill, which would require the couple to choose a single name so far as the family register was concerned, but would permit separate surnames on other official documents, including passports.[11] The issue split the parties broadly along right–left lines, with the LDP and *Shinshintō* expressing caution and warning of the danger of tampering with the tradition of the Japanese family,[12] but most of the other parties favouring change, in the interests of personal freedom, and in particular considering the wishes of many couples pursuing separate careers.

To understand the background of the movement of opinion that brought this issue to Parliament in 1997, we need to consider two factors. The first is the traditional overtones of the system of family registers, seen by increasing numbers of younger people as perpetuating a patriarchal system imposing disproportionate responsibility for care of family members upon the wife and mother, and discriminating against various forms of 'irregular' relationship and their offspring.[13] The second is the effect of affluence, which has enabled large and increasing numbers of women to attain financial independence and high career status. On the other hand we should not neglect the presence of widespread conservative sentiment upset by the growing phenomenon of 'houses with two separate nameplates outside'.[14]

2. Economic Distribution

In any political system, issues of economic distribution are likely to be at the centre of political negotiation and debate. Such issues, however, are likely to be more acute where the economic surplus being created is static or declining than when it is growing. We should expect a zero-sum distribution to be accompanied by more acute political conflict than a positive-sum distribution. In Japan between about 1958 and 1973 economic growth averaged over 10 per cent per annum, which meant that the surplus for distribution through wage increases and the use of tax revenues was continually increasing without the need to increase tax rates. In those years, since rapid economic development was concentrated in big cities along the Pacific coastline, the government took seriously the task of *regional* redistribution. In 1971 Kobayashi Takeji, a minister in the Cabinet of Satō Eisaku, got into trouble and was eventually dropped from the Cabinet for declaring in a speech that the opposition parties were irrelevant to the task of budget making. What he said is instructive:

> Democracy, in plain language, is a kind of levelling movement. It is the central Government that must of necessity divert tax revenue from rich areas to poor areas. Therefore every prefecture, town and village must count on the central Government. This cannot be helped. It follows that the Government run by us, the Liberal Democratic Party, will be willing to accommodate the wishes of mayors and governors if they are affiliated to our party.[15]

What Kobayashi was talking about was specifically *regional* redistribution. A decade and a half of the fastest rate of sustained economic growth that the world had ever seen at that time had brought about distributional distortions expressed in the phrase *kaso kamitsu* (depopulation and over-concentration of population). A massive exodus from the countryside had left many rural areas (especially in the mountains) suffering from population decline, while in the cities basic services had not been able to keep up with the influx of population. Tanaka's plan for the 'Reconstruction of the Japanese Archipelago', launched some 18 months after Kobayashi's speech, was designed to tackle this problem by opening up some of the remoter areas to industrial and commercial activity, but it had only limited success. More effective were the kinds of government activity referred to by Kobayashi, namely redistributing tax revenues by various schemes benefiting the poorer rural prefectures.

Since, however, such redistribution was the result of decisions by government ministries, often with little concern for market efficiency, a result which came to be much deplored in later years was the fostering of a wide variety of vested interests, able to lobby effectively for the continuation of subsidies and handouts. Until the 1990s it was extremely difficult to attack this system because it was bolstered by the gross malapportionment of parliamentary constituencies in favour of rural, and to the disadvantage of big city, areas. The *raison d'être* of many parliamentarians representing constituencies in remoter parts of the countryside had become that of ensuring the delivery of government 'pork' to their constituents. An unfortunate long-term effect of this was to reduce the incentive for local industries (especially agriculture) to improve their productivity fast enough to compete in a globalizing market and, by the same token, to create intense pressures against the opening up of internal markets to external competition.

Following the first oil crisis of 1973–4, the Japanese economy entered a period of much slower growth, and even though growth rates increased again later in the decade, the greatly increased commitments entered into by the Tanaka Government of 1972–4 in respect of social welfare spending (among other purposes) had given much more of a zero-sum character to distributional issues by the beginning of the 1980s. Even though the politico-economic structure based on the compensating of powerful interests had not substantially changed,[16] the Suzuki and Nakasone Governments of the early and middle 1980s were successful in challenging such interests to the extent that the principle of 'zero-ceiling' budgeting was established for a number of years (with defence, pensions and foreign aid partially exempted), with the aim of eliminating deficit financing by government. What is interesting about this is that it was achieved without conspicuous social disruption.

In the 1990s, by contrast, the failure of the economy to grow has been accompanied by a profound and at times radical questioning of the ways in which redistribution is carried out. The combination of an egalitarian 'fair shares' principle with the protection of myriad vested interests by politico-bureaucratic structures has come under sustained attack from those who would allow the market free rein in determining distribution. On the other hand, there is a not inconsiderable backlash from those who fear a potentially dangerous erosion of the relatively equal distribution of income, wealth and opportunity that they see as one of the great strengths of Japan in the half century from 1945. There is already some evidence of widening income disparities, even though Japan remains reasonably equal by most international comparisons. Much of the debate about educational reform since the 1980s revolves around the question of 'equality with uniformity' against 'inequality and choice', and much the same can be said about debates concerning the health service and social welfare. In distributional questions of this kind, Japan faces much the same kind of dilemma as most other mature societies.

3. Economic Management

Issues of economic management in Japan go to the heart of our understanding of the Japanese political economy. They are, moreover, much more complex than is commonly realized, and could well be the subject of a number of new books.

Here we shall confine ourselves to a brief examination of some of the principal points of controversy. These include the efficacy or otherwise of what is often called 'industrial policy', the development of taxation policy, the oversight of the economy by the Ministry of Finance (MOF) and the Bank of Japan (BOJ), and budget making.

A great deal has been written about the industrial policy of Japan, particularly as it operated over the first three post-war decades. Chalmers Johnson's study of how industrial policy was put into practice by the Ministry of International Trade and Industry (MITI) is arguably the most significant book written in English about the Japanese system.[17] In it, Johnson argues that Japan is a 'Developmental State', in which government plays a major market-conforming role, through industrial policy, in promoting economic development. In this enterprise, MITI plays a central role, in conjunction with the *zaikai* and other key players.

Although, as we have argued in chapter 7 and elsewhere, ministries and agencies of central government still exercise a great deal of influence over decision making, more recent studies than that of Johnson suggest that exercises in industrial policy were notably less successful in the 1980s than in the period up to 1975. For instance, Scott Callon argues that even though MITI in the 1980s was far more insulated from political pressures in developing projects than would be the case in the United States, it was nevertheless misguided and unsuccessful in its promotion of key high-tech projects, notably fifth generation computers, supercomputers, artificial intelligence and so on, at a time when a new computer industry was being developed based on microprocessors and computerized software.[18] Robert Wade, in contrast, argues that in other ways the role of government bureaucracy has made a great deal of difference to the way the Japanese economy has developed, and that this influence has, on the whole, been positive. He emphasizes, for instance, the role of government in 'closing the domestic market to imports in the case of industries to be encouraged'.[19]

As we have already seen in earlier chapters, the most politically contentious issue in taxation policy has been the attempt to shift some of the burden of taxation away from direct towards indirect taxes. This movement, which began at least as early as the late 1970s, was advanced on a variety of grounds, but was stimulated by constraints on tax revenue that appeared as a result of economic slowdown following the first oil crisis. The desire to provide the financial resources to deal with problems created by Japan's rapidly aging society was widely cited in its favour, while the regressive nature of taxes on consumption compared with the progressive character of contemporary income tax scales was the most important reason why it was so fiercely opposed during the 1980s. The introduction of a 3 per cent consumption tax (*shōhizei*) on 1 April 1989 was one of the main reasons for the LDP defeat in the upper house elections of July 1989. Early in 1994, accepting strongly asserted advice from the MOF, Prime Minister Hosokawa proposed raising the level of this tax from 3 per cent to 7 per cent, and found himself at loggerheads with his Finance Minister as a result. Later, Prime Minister Murayama brokered a scheme for a delayed and moderated increase, and on 1 April 1997 consumption tax was increased to 5 per cent.[20]

Oversight of the economy by the MOF and the BOJ has come under intense criticism during the 1990s, as a result of policies that allowed economic overheating to occur in the late 1980s, failed to curb a speculative land price boom, and, following the collapse of the 'bubble economy' in 1991, sought to protect a number of financial institutions, including the *jūsen*, facing bankruptcy because of collossal quantities of non-performing loans. More fundamentally, perhaps, the MOF in particular found itself under attack for 'financial socialism', for pursuing a 'convoy formula' which carried weaker institutions along with the stronger,[21] and because of the slow pace at which liberalization of the financial markets was taking place. The 'Big Bang' in financial markets announced in 1997 for a four year period up to 2001 was an attempt both to meet these criticisms and to restructure the system. Whether the restructuring would really overcome preferences given to protected interests – the ultimate core of the problem – remained to be seen.

Preparation for the annual budget was a matter that involved set budgetary shares under the control of the various ministries, and thus lent itself to incrementalist budget making. A political input was permitted during the passage of the budget through Parliament, but this was generally restricted to a small percentage of the whole. The Fiscal Investment and Loan Programme (FILP) permitted greater flexibility, but it was essentially a mechanism for channelling funds from the post office savings system into capital works programmes. In budget making, as in other aspects of macroeconomic management, politico-bureaucratic empires working together with vested interests remained entrenched.

4. Power Distribution

Inherent in some of the points that have been made above are issues relating to the distribution of power within the politico-economic system and how far this distribution has been changing. One change that is plainly visible is the far greater capacity on the part of Japanese corporate firms to exercise power within the system as a whole than was the case in the 1950s and 1960s, when their financial resources were much weaker, and they were more hemmed in by government regulations and dependent upon government-controlled sources of capital. The development of the Japan-based multinational corporation is an important development which has shifted the power balance within Japan itself in favour of the corporate sector. It is hardly surprising, therefore, to find that the clamour for deregulation and a 'small State' is more vociferous in the 1990s from corporate ranks than in was in earlier periods. There is a certain shifting of the ground away from cosy relationships between Government and Business towards a more critical corporate appraisal of bureaucratic control. This point should not be exaggerated, because close interaction between them and a sense of mutual advantage is still not unusual, but behind the tendency of some business spokesmen to denigrate certain ministries for corruption or incompetent management lies an enhanced self-confidence based on wealth and economic power.

An aspect of corporate attitudes and corporate influence is provided by the controversial issue of antimonopoly policy. During the Occupation an antimonopoly law was introduced and a body called the Fair Trade Commission (*kōsei torihiki iinkai*) set up to administer it. By common consent both the antimonopoly law and the FTC had little opportunity to exercise much influence during the high-growth period, but their degree of effectiveness following the first oil crisis is more controversial. There is a tendency among many commentators outside (and to some extent inside) Japan to dismiss both the law and the Commission as window dressing, but recent careful analysis shows that the situation has been much more complicated than this: even though by American standards Japan does not enjoy an extremely vigorous antitrust regime, the FTC has at times been able to act with some effectiveness against some forms of cartel and collusive activity.[22]

One of the most intriguing features of power relationships in Japan in the post-war period has been the weakness of consumer interest groups and the marked imbalance between them and the far more powerful producer groups. Instances of pricing policy where the interests of consumers are virtually ignored in favour of those of producers abound, including the readiness of some consumer groups to back highly protectionist policies apparently against their best interests *as consumers*. Indeed, it seems strange to hear consumer groups citing 'food security' and 'food safety' as reasons for supporting agricultural protection, despite the high prices that such policies entail.

Finally, centre–local relations provide a spectacle of pushes and pulls, co-operation and conflict. The structure of local government is complex and has evolved over the past half century. Formally speaking, it is based upon articles 92–5 of the Constitution, from which stem a number of laws, notably the Local Autonomy Law, the Local Public Service Law, the Local Taxation Law and the Public Offices Election Law.

The system consists of two levels, the prefectural and the municipal. The first level is that of the prefecture, which is roughly equivalent in geographical area to an English county or a French *département*. Prefectures were set up, replacing the system of *han*, after the *Meiji ishin* and still reflect the population geography of that period. There are now 47 prefectures which are known collectively as *to-dō-fu-ken* (Tokyo is referred to as *to*, Hokkaidō as *dō*, Osaka and Kyoto both as *fu* and the rest as *ken*, but there is no practical difference of meaning between the different designations).

At the municipal level the local unit of administration may be a city (*shi*), town (*chō* or *machi*) or village (*son* or *mura*), being so designated according to population and degree of urbanization, while in Tokyo, wards (*ku*) have a special administrative status.[23] Some functions which are prefectural in areas where the municipal authority is a town or village are performed by city administrations in areas under their jurisdiction. There are, moreover, a number of large 'designated cities', whose administrations have wider functions than those of ordinary cities.[24] In such cases, the powers of the prefecture over the region covered by the city area are correspondingly reduced. So far as towns and villages are concerned, they all have identical functions, at least in principle. Since the end of the Occupation there has been widespread amalgamation of existing areas of administration into larger and presumably more effective ones, often reflecting, however, bureaucratic convenience rather than actual communities. This has been a particular problem at the level of the village. Contemporary Japanese villages are often quite large administrative units, incorporating several traditional *buraku* (hamlets) which are natural communities. Using the device of the 'property ward', an area of forest (say) which previously belonged to one of the village's constituent *buraku* can remain in effect the property of that *buraku*. In some parts of Japan the *buraku* remains the most indigenous unit of local association, which because of its use before and during the war as a local instrument of government control, became a target of Occupation hostility.[25]

Power relations between central government and local authorities are characterized by unequal distribution of funding (and thus power) in favour of the former. Despite the introduction of local self-government after the war, with a dual system of elections for chief executives (governors of prefectures and mayors of cities, towns and villages), and for local assemblies, replacing the pre-war system of administrative dominance, the influence of the national bureaucracy over local authorities is extensive. A potent method of central control is what is known as 'agency delegation', whereby central government may require local governors and mayors to undertake certain tasks on behalf of central government. Such tasks fall under many different categories and have proliferated since the post-war period. In addition, the process whereby local authorities apply to central government ministries for various forms of financial grant to perform activities of their own devising is such as to entangle local chief executives in the preferences and procedures of central ministries to a great extent. Moreover, prefectures and provincial cities typically become arenas for competition between different ministries, each promoting their own administrative programmes.[26]

It is possible that co-ordinated activity by regions incorporating a number of prefectures could have redressed the balance to some extent in favour of the localities against the centre. This has only occurred, however, to a limited extent, since prefectures in the same region are typically in competition with each other for funds.[27] Despite the restrictions on local self-government, and the weakness of local assemblies in a two-tier local electoral system, local politics is often lively and contentious, with local citizens' groups playing an active part in competition with more conservative elements.[28] In the second half of 1997 legislation was being prepared to increase substantially the powers of local authorities and correspondingly reduce the powers of central ministries over local government.

5. Accountability

The political philosopher Maruyama Masao proposed that Japanese politics was characterized by 'collective irresponsibility'. Although his analysis was directed at the politics of the prewar period,[29] a similar argument has been advanced by Karel van Wolferen, writing principally about the 1980s. According to van Wolferen, in Japan:

> [n]oone is ultimately in charge. These semi-autonomous components, each endowed with discretionary powers that undermine the authority of the state, are not represented by any central body that rules the roost. ... There is, to be sure, a hierarchy or, rather, a complex of overlapping hierarchies. But it has no peak; it is a truncated pyramid. There is no supreme institution with ultimate policy-making jurisdiction. Hence there is no place where, as Harry Truman would have said, the buck stops. In Japan, the buck keeps circulating.[30]

Leaving aside the tricky question of whether the final resting place of the buck can readily be identified in many other political systems (including the American), this approach has the merit of alerting us to a problem of accountability in the Japanese system. The basic issue is this. While Japan has democratic forms and many of the actual practices of a democratic state, it has considerable areas of activity that do not seem either properly accountable to the electorate or subject to legal scrutiny. Personal linkages and networks, often cemented by large amounts of money, create irresponsible zones where power and its maximization are the principal motivator.[31]

The most visible manifestation of this phenomenon is corruption, or 'money politics', which takes a variety of forms. A notorious example is the granting by local authorities of contracts without open tendering procedures, through a process of collusion known as *dangō*, whereby bids are rigged to ensured that the contract goes to the firm that is favoured, for whatever combination of reasons. Corruption in election campaigns, and attempts to control it, have been discussed earlier in this book. A less well-known manifestation of what should be regarded as 'corrupt' behaviour is where ultra-rightist groups, members of religious cults or of groups representing minorities have issued threats or otherwise put pressure on writers or publishers of works they regard as critical of them, with a view to suppressing publication or punishing those involved with issuing a published work. The ineffectiveness of the courts in most of these cases is compounded by the reluctance of some publishers to face up to such pressure.[32]

6. Public Welfare

Issues relating to public welfare include, in Japan as elsewhere, a huge list of problems closely affecting people's lives. These include medical questions, most prominently health-care provision and the financing of it, but also the vexed question of organ transplants and the definition of the point of death, policy towards the spread of HIV and AIDS, contraception and abortion, *karōshi* (death from work-related stress and similar causes), tobacco, alcohol and drugs, and regulation of the sex industry. A closely related area is that of social welfare, including pensions, unemployment payments, workers' compensation and other benefits and the gamut of policy issues which is frequently lumped together under the heading 'the aging society'.

Education contains a set of policy issues at least as momentous as the above, in that they are subject to similar levels of public concern. The education system is widely seen as ripe for reform, and in various ways encapsulates a number of the key ideological issues of Japanese politics since the Occupation.

Policies towards the environment have been debated since at least the late 1960s, and have occasioned a number of important government initiatives over the years. Worries about the safety of nuclear power stations are often discussed in the media. Although it is more a 'quality of life' than an environmental issue, Parliament has also been active during the 1990s drafting legislation on product liability.

Finally, although Japan is widely seen as a society enjoying a relatively low level of violent crime, issues relating to crime prevention and punishment, juvenile delinquency, gun control, police behaviour and procedures, terrorism and political crime, *yakuza* and *bōryokudan* gangs, the problem of *sōkaiya* (gangsters who disrupt shareholders' meetings), white collar fraud, and how to handle hijackings and kidnappings, excite lively concern and controversy.

We lack the space to discuss all of these issues in depth, but we shall refer to salient points about them.

Japan enjoys a sophisticated system of health insurance in which large-scale public financing (*kokumin hoken*, national insurance) is combined with wide-spread private provision, including company schemes for their employees. A system of health-care provision based on large public hospitals, smaller private hospitals and individual doctors' surgeries is complex and impossible to describe in a short space. Policy making centrally involves the Ministry of Health and Welfare, interested politicians (including a small number of parliamentarians having a medical background), pressure groups such as the Japan Medical Association, the insurance industry, the pharmaceutical industry, and last but not least the Ministry of Finance. A central reason why the MOF has been so concerned since the 1970s to establish and then increase the kind of indirect taxation provided by the consumption tax was to prepare for the conditions anticipated in the early decades of the twenty-first century, when Japan was expected to have a higher proportion of its population over the age of 65 than any other comparable country. Even more so, this consideration affected future provision for pensions. But in the case of medical care, the rapid advances in medical treatment experienced during the last decades of the twentieth century was creating – in Japan as elsewhere – tremendous pressure on costs, and in turn creating a dilemma involving an inevitable trade off between quality and choice, on the one hand, and equality, on the other.[33]

If health-care provision issues showed much similarity with such issues elsewhere, the long-running controversy over organ transplants had features peculiar to Japan. After the first Japanese doctor to perform a heart transplant, in the late 1960s, was pursued through courts for alleged malfeasance, organ transplants more or less came to a halt, in the face of the fact that following Buddhist tradition it was difficult to accept brain death as the true death of the body. After many years of debate, in 1997 a bill passed through Parliament which, in effect, broke through this inhibition, so that organ transplants could proceed without fear of doctors being prosecuted. It is interesting to note, however, that whereas the bulk of Liberal Democrat and many *Shinshintō* members, who had been heavily lobbied by the Japan Medical Association, voted in favour, numbers of parliamentarians from left-of-centre parties voted against, in part because of a concern that the medical profession might not always scrupulously respect the donor's rights. The bill contained a clause requiring the prior permission of the donor before his or her organs could be extracted for a transplant.[34] It also did not attempt a definition of the point of death.

The education system was a target for drastic reform during the Occupation, and subsequently remained an arena of ideological conflict. Indeed, during at least the first three decades after the war, it would scarcely have been possible to find an area in which Japanese were more thoroughly polarized than that of education. The Occupation reformers had sought to reform the content, democratize the structure and expand the scope of the pre-war education system. In place of nationalistic history textbooks, officially sanctioned *tennō*-worship and government-designed courses on 'ethics', the content of instruction was liberalized and modernized. Instead of a monolithic structure of control enforcing uniform practice in schools which had a hierarchy of levels between them, much decision-making power was placed in the hands of local 'boards of education' administering schools whose structure was essentially uniform. Finally, to make education available to all, the number of state schools and universities was greatly expanded.

During the 1950s the second category of reform in particular was subjected the conservative politics of the 'Reverse Course'. The Ministry of Education (*Monbushō*) resumed control from local boards, and refused to negotiate or communicate with the left-wing Japan Teachers Union (*Nikkyōso*), whose influence had been strong on the Boards of Education. Since the bulk of teachers at that period were affiliated with *Nikkyōso*, the map of educational politics took on the character of 'camp conflict'.[35]

By the 1990s the educational scene had changed substantially in various ways. The influence and membership of the union had been gradually declining, and in 1990 it split between the mainstream *Nikkyōso* which had moved to a much more conservative and co-operative position, and a minority group called *Zenkyō*, which retained left-wing confrontational attitudes towards the educational bureaucracy. Meanwhile, a national debate of considerable intensity had developed about the alleged uniformity and stultifying character of state education, which force-fed facts into pupils, was excessively examination-oriented and obsessed by petty regulation of behaviour. School violence, including violence by teachers against pupils, was a matter of popular concern.[36] A further issue, causing much controversy inside and outside Japan, was Ministry control of school textbooks and alleged rewriting of history to play down the nastier aspects of Japanese behaviour in Asia and the Pacific between 1937 and 1945.[37]

In the late 1960s, and again in the 1980s, serious attempts were made to effect educational reform. The exercise in the latter case was strongly backed from the very top, by Nakasone as Prime Minister, who sought to replace uniformity of educational provision by the introduction of a substantial measure of choice. Rather than adhesion to the principle of equality as the supreme value in educating the nation's children, he envisaged a system in which a variety of types of school – and types of educational approach with the same school – would become possible, thus encouraging creativity and experimentation. In part, Nakasone's design was inspired by a dislike of the Occupation's educational legacy, and was an aspect of his somewhat nationalistic attempt to 'settle accounts with the post-war period'. But it also resonated with much current thinking about the need for drastic reform of the system of education.

In the short term at least, the efforts of the Ad Hoc Council on Education (*Rinkyōshin*) ended in failure, largely because the day-to-day running of it fell into the hands of the Ministry of Education, which was desperately anxious to maintain control of education and run it in the way it knew best. Ironically, the Japan Teachers Union found itself in a position analogous to that of the Ministry, of defending a system which constituted its power base and opposing reforms which would have weakened that base.[38] This may be linked with the partial rapprochement between the Ministry and the Union which occurred in the 1990s, and to the split in the latter, mentioned above.

If, however, the Nakasone reforms were in the main unsuccessful, this was not the end of the story. Although it would be premature to say that the system of education has been decisively changed away from central control, uniform provision and the principle of equality, pressure for reform has been building up in the 1990s. Apart from other factors, this pressure has been the inevitable consequence of the partial privatization of education (particularly at the secondary level) brought about by the extensive use of cram schools (*juku*) to prepare pupils for university entrance examinations, and the increased popularity of academically oriented senior high schools outside the public sector.[39] At tertiary level, of course, the largest number of universities have long been essentially private foundations, even though the role of the Ministry of Education throughout tertiary education remains extensive. We do not have space to discuss tertiary education here, except to say that it is also subject to widespread criticism in the 1990s, and that certain reforms are under way.[40]

In any case, even though there have been many problems with education since the post-war reforms, it has succeeded in delivering high levels of literacy and numeracy to the vast majority of the school-age population. The argument that the system's purpose has been to provide 'cannon-fodder for industry' rather than people trained to think for themselves, is not entirely without validity, but the problems seen elsewhere of allowing an essentially illiterate and non-numerate sub-class of the population to develop appear to be problems of a more serious order. The genuine and valid cricitisms now being made need to be seen against the backdrop of this basic fact that the broad mass of the population has a good level of competence in the essential skills needed for living in an advanced society.

Under the heading of public welfare we should also briefly consider the issue of environmental protection. In the post-war period Japan was slow to recognize the importance of the environment, which was largely ignored in a headlong rush for economic growth. A number of appalling tragedies resulted, of which the best known was the appearance of 'Minamata disease', a type of mercury poisoning affecting the nervous system, from the 1950s. A company producing nitrogenous fertilizer, at the fishing port of Minamata, in Kyūshū, was over a long period discharging mercury effluent into the bay, where it entered the food chain and disastrously affected many hundreds of people.[41]

The environmental situation had become so bad by the late 1960s that the LDP came to perceive it as an issue that could lead it to lose governmental office. The consequent changes in policy are an interesting example of governmental responsiveness to the pressure of an electorate that held the ruling party's fate in its hands. During the 1970s, environmental regulations were tightened up, particularly in relation to control of air and water pollution. The air in big cities became noticeably more bearable as polluting factories were forced out, and car exhausts emitted smaller quantities of toxic fumes. The Government succeeded in what was perhaps its principal purpose, namely to reduce the political impact of the environment as an issue. Nevertheless, important problems remained. Although a tightening of regulations made it unlikely that disasters on the scale of Minamata would recur, individual victims of such disasters still found the task of gaining compensation through the cumbersome court system a time-consuming and exhausting business. Highly polluting factories forced to relocate outside big cities often moved offshore, typically to parts of Southeast Asia having less stringent environmental regulations, giving rise to accusations abroad that Japan was 'exporting its pollution'. By the 1980s Japan had developed an unenviable reputation overseas for predatory action in relation to the natural environment, and found herself in the spotlight in relation to whaling, the stripping of tropical timber from Borneo and elsewhere, the issue of importing ivory from Africa and a range of other concerns. The politics of the Japanese response to such criticism is complex and involves a combination of foreign and domestic pressure.[42] Finally, within Japan itself, even though much has been done to improve the quality of air and water, and to ensure the safety of consumer products, problems of what may be called 'visual pollution' remain severe. Whether it is in the cities or in the countryside, functional but highly unaesthetic concrete buildings provide an unappealing foreground to what is often spectacular natural scenery. Similarly, many rivers are encased in concrete, nearly all are dammed, and concrete has invaded long stretches of formerly natural coastline. These are not life-threatening or health-threatening issues in the sense that other pollution issues have been, nor is Japan alone in blighting its landscape, but train journeys in many parts of Japan can be a depressing experience to anyone brought up to expect zoning regulations, preservation of green belts and prevention of 'ribbon development'.[43] Gavan McCormack has coined the term 'Construction State', to describe these phenomena, and argues that the economic and political power of the cement lobby, and more broadly of the notoriously corrupt construction industry, makes it difficult to resist pressures for often mindless development for development's sake.[44]

An environmental issue which has attracted particular attention is that of nuclear power stations. For a country as resource-poor as Japan it is not surprising that the production of electricity from nuclear power should have been seen as an attractive option. The government conducted a concerted campaign of persuasion in the late 1970s and early 1980s to convince people that nuclear power for Japan was an attractive and safe option, producing much less pollution than conventional power stations. A number of well-publicized problems at nuclear power stations over the years has, however, from time to time cast doubt on the competence of management in the industry, with particular concern being expressed about cover-ups.[45]

The broad area of policy towards crime contains a range of contentious policy issues. With good reason, Japan is often praised as a nation where the level of crime – particularly violent crime – is at a low level by international standards. A key reason normally cited in explanation is the extremely tight gun laws, which make personal ownership of most types of gun virtually impossible, though some guns are in the hands of *yakuza* gangs. Another is efficient control and prevention of drugs entering the country. The ways in which the police handle crime are also widely regarded as crucial to the understanding of the low crime rate. The police were anxious to live down their unenviable reputation for arrogance in the pre-war period and during the war. Their approach has been based essentially on community policing, with the institution of the local police box (*kōban*) being the symbol of their closeness to local communities. This means that the police generally have more, and more detailed, knowledge about the comings and goings of people in their area than would be normal – or acceptable – in most Western nations, but this intrusiveness has been a price felt worth paying for a crime-free environment.[46] So far as hardened criminals are concerned, the police are used to being tough, and the regime in prisons is by all accounts, harsh. Capital punishment remains on the statute books, and a small number of executions are carried out (though there have been periods without executions), with minimum publicity and little media interest.[47]

The relations between the police and *yakuza* gangs remain controversial, and stories abound of semi-co-operative relationships between the two. This is no doubt explicable in terms of a police preference for having criminals in an organized environment where surveillance is easier than in the case of random crime by individuals, though accusations of police corruption in this sphere sometimes surface. In any case, the law relating to *yakuza* gangs was tightened up in the 1980s, forcing some such groups to organize as semi-legal businesses. The role of *sōkaiya* (criminals who extract payment from companies against a promise not to disrupt shareholders' meetings, or alternatively are employed by companies to keep shareholders' meetings in order) became highly controversial in the late 1990s, with some company directors facing disgrace for having paid off *sōkaiya* – a practice previously regarded as inevitable and acceptable. So far as political crime is concerned, it is to be noted that the police, no doubt acting under political instructions, have been far tougher on ideological violence conducted by the far left than on similar activities by the far right. Governments, on the other hand, have a history of caving in to terrorist demands in hijackings and kidnappings, though this may have changed in the 1990s, on the evidence of the notably tougher attitude of the Hashimoto Government in the early months of 1997 towards the handling by the Peruvian Government of the seige by Tupac Amaru gunmen of many hostages in the Japanese Ambassador's residence in Lima.

7. The Legacy of History

Even though the fiftieth anniversary of the end of the war was passed on 15 August 1995, the legacy of the 1930s and the first half of the 1940s continues to haunt Japan. By a strange quirk of history, the first half century from the defeat was completed under a Socialist Prime Minister, Murayama Tomiichi. Murayama, as we saw in chapter 6, invested a great deal of effort in persuading Parliament to pass a resolution apologizing for Japanese actions during the war. In the event, the resolution was much less forthright and unqualified than the Prime Minister would have wished, and many parliamentarians abstained. Nevertheless, Parliament went on record as deploring what had happened in the years up to 1945. Prime Ministers Hosokawa and Murayama had made personal statements of regret for the war which went substantially beyond what any of their predecessors had said, though by the exacting standards of some critics even they stopped short of a full apology.

   The fact was that among conservative politicians and their backers there was no consensus in favour of apologizing for the war, and the issue was profoundly divisive politically. A succession of government ministers over the years had made public statements favourable to some, at least, of what Japan had done during the war, often citing the impetus created by Japanese military campaigns in Asia towards ridding Asia of European colonial rule. In many cases such ministers had paid the price of making this kind of statement – which tended to cause an outraged reaction in China, South Korea and elsewhere – by being forced to resign their ministerial positions.[48] Even so, what is remarkable is that such incidents continued to occur with some regularity. Visits by the

Prime Minister and cabinet ministers to the Yasukuni Shrine in Tokyo are similarly controversial because the souls of a number of condemned war criminals have been 'enshrined' there. When Nakasone in 1985 made a visit to the Yasukuni Shrine *in his official capacity*, he was met with strong protests from China and South Korea, as well as from within Japan itself. Indeed, there is evidence that neither the administration of the Yasukuni Shrine, nor some members of ex-service organizations, were happy with the political use of the Shrine being made by Nakasone at that time.[49]

Another highly divisive issue which has come into the open in the 1990s is how far Japan should apologize to (and compensate) those non-Japanese women forced into prostitution in brothels organized by the Imperial Armed Forces throughout Asia during the war. Most of these women were Asian, the largest number Korean, but also many from the Philippines and elsewhere. A series of not wholly satisfactory compromises was entered into by the Japanese governments of the mid-1990s, apologies of a kind were made, and some compensation was organized from private rather than State funds to the now elderly women who had been recruited as 'sex slaves'.

It is easy to cite such episodes as evidence that the peace-loving spirit embodied in the Constitution is skin-deep, and that a more aggressive – conceivably militaristic – Japanese State is in the making. In reality, the situation is more complicated than this. The Liberal Democrats (and more broadly in the 1990s, the conservative camp) have been deeply divided about the Constitution, how the years 1931 to 1945 ought to be evaluated, and Japan's international role. There has been an uneasy *modus vivendi* between politicians with contrasting ideas on these issues, and in consequence what may be described as 'immobilist' politics. Some conservative politicians expressing revisionist views about the war are particularly dependent for political support on ex-service organizations that tend to equate apologizing for the war with lack of reverence for the souls of Japanese servicemen who perished on active service up to 1945. Somewhat similarly, in debates over the bowdlerization of reference to Japanese war atrocities in school textbooks, the view is expressed that to denigrate the actions of previous generations in war would risk breaking down that respect for ancestors which is at the heart of the family and societal system. Whether reverence for departed souls or respect for ancestors is more important than concern for and reflection on an accurate understanding of history, is a question that troubles many in contemporary Japan.

Finally, perhaps the most perplexing legacy of history, so far as contemporary politics is concerned, is how to handle the role of, and symbolism associated with, the *tennō*. We have touched on this issue in earlier chapters. What needs to be emphasized here is that the death of the Shōwa *Tennō* (Hirohito) in 1989 greatly reduced, even if it did not entirely remove, the taboos which had been widely observed about the *tennō* system so long as the old *tennō* was alive. Much more documentary information was published about the vexed issue of the Shōwa *Tennō*'s role during the war, including the diaries of various of his chamberlains, after his death. Even though the new *tennō* had to go through ancient and arcane ceremonies – possibly some reinvention of tradition was involved – at the time of his accession, and though the Palace bureaucracy remained a byword for conservatism, it was possible to detect a new and slightly more open atmosphere in relation to the institution of royalty than used to prevail.

8. Nationality and Minorities

The area of nationality involves a range of issues of increasing importance in the 1990s, which we do not, however, have space to treat in detail here.

Japanese citizenship, in law, is transmitted in principle through patriality, not through place of birth. This has acted as a mechanism whereby the vast bulk of Japanese citizens are of ethnic Japanese origin, and in turn perpetuated the concept of Japanese as a homogeneous ethnic group all sharing the same citizenship. Much the largest group of Japanese residents, most of whom lack Japanese citizenship, are Koreans. These now include many third generation Japanese residents, with little or no knowledge of the Korean language. At its height, the number of Koreans in Japan was some eight hundred thousand, and most of them were excluded from public service positions (including teaching) because they were not Japanese citizens. The feeling of being excluded from mainstream Japanese society set up numerous frictions between ethnic Koreans and Japanese, and this was further exacerbated by the fact that the Koreans in Japan were divided in their loyalties between North and South Korea. A symbolic issue for many Koreans and others was the fingerprinting requirement for the issue of visas. This requirement was relaxed (but not entirely abolished) in the early 1990s.

Another large group which has suffered some discrimination is the Okinawans, who tended to be regarded as inferior by mainland Japanese before the war, suffered horrendous losses during the battle for Okinawa in 1945, and were directly administered by the United States between 1945 and 1972. The rape by American servicemen of an Okinawan schoolgirl in September 1995 brought the Okinawan issue back into the headlines, and though the matters in dispute largely related to US military bases, an underlying theme was Okinawan resentment at being treated in certain senses as second-class citizens. A much smaller group is the Ainu in the northern island of Hokkaidō. Most of them intermarried with ethnic Japanese, from whom, nevertheless, they are physically distinguishable. Ainu identity was a live issue, particularly in the 1980s and 1990s, with an official tendency to treat Ainu culture in the manner of a theme park being a source of some resentment.

The largest minority group, however, was not an ethnic minority at all, but rather a separate caste (at least in its origins), namely the *hi-sabetsu burakumin* or 'village people subject to discrimination', to give them their politically correct contemporary title. Descendents of various outcast groups from the Tokugawa period, the *hi-sabetsu burakumin*, whose numbers were estimated at somewhere between a million and a half and three million people, were concentrated in western Japan, from the Kansai to Kyūshū. Subject to widespread discrimination in the job market and in respect of marriage, they were politically well organized and forceful in defence of their own interests. Tension, however, between those who sought to 'pass' as mainstream Japanese and those who were assertive of their own identity, was high in the 1980s and 1990s.

All the groups briefly mentioned above are long-standing minorities within Japanese society. From the late 1980s, however, a new phenomenon arose, namely the arrival of large numbers of immigrants from other Asian countries and from Latin America (largely Brazil where there is a substantial population of Japanese ethnic origin), to fulfil the need for labour in the booming industries of Japan's 'bubble economy'. A major social problem was created by the fact that many Asians working on building sites and in other, mainly low-status, occupations, were visa overstayers and in Japan illegally. In June 1990 the immigration laws were tightened in an attempt to control the flow of illegal immigrants, but considerable numbers remained and continued to enter Japan. Many instances of exploitation were reported and efforts were being made by some local authorities to cater to the much neglected needs of this new wave of Asian immigrants.

The issue of Japanese nationality and of minorities presents much material supportive of a rather exclusive approach to national identity, but in the changing world of the 1990s there were some signs of a more relaxed – though still highly cautious – official approach. Meanwhile, the influx of new foreign residents was taken lightly, for the most part, by the mainstream population.

9. Communication and Expression

Once again, the issues here can only be briefly touched upon. Japan, formally speaking under the 1946 Constitution, prides itself on strong guarantees of freedom of communication and expression. In practice, as in other advanced states, expression of opinions is curbed in various ways, though more by various forms of social pressure than by law. Social sanctions against too vigorous forms of individual protest have been one factor (another is legal delay) inhibiting litigious behaviour by citizens. As elsewhere, freedom of expression in the mass media is limited to some extent by concentration of ownership, with the four main newspapers, *Yomiuri, Asahi, Mainichi* and *Nihon Keizai*, having circulations of many millions and dominating political and other reporting. The big four newspapers have a notably serious approach to news and tend to avoid the more sensational items, but many of the weekly magazines (*shūkanshi*) are prepared to report less well-authenticated and more risky items of news, often in a sensational fashion. It is arguable that the *shūkanshi* are the functional equivalent of the British tabloid press.

There have been some well-authenticated instances of the press as a whole failing to take up important stories that would be embarrassing to particular public figures, until forced to do so by attention given in the foreign press to these same stories.[50] There were also accusations in the 1970s that some newspapers were reporting on China favourably to the Chinese regime as the result of deals with the Chinese Government. What these stories have in common is a certain tendency of the media to become too close to certain of its sources of information. Journalists are typically attached to particular politicians or other public figures, and the temptation to become at least psychologically part of that person's organization is strong. Newspapers are aware of the problem and typically will report a particular political issue with the aid of considerable numbers of journalists each of whom has a different attachment. Television stations in their reporting of news tend to be either cautious and dull, as in the case of the State-supported *Nippon Hōsō Kyōkai* (NHK), or superficial, silly and mainly concerned with sound-bites, as with most of the commercial stations.[51]

It is difficult to summarize our conclusions in respect of the plethora of domestic issues outlined above. We venture, however, the following generalization. Japan in the 1990s is in a state of transition from a decision-making process based on long-standing power relationships and established practices to a much more fluid and dynamic system, where both the nature of issues and the best ways of handling them contain much uncharted ground. As the transition proceeds, we may expect to find some surprising and unexpected policy outcomes but also the gradual development of a more open and accountable system.

12

Issues of Foreign Policy and Defence

It is often said that Japanese foreign policy in the 1990s is in a state of transition from one governed by considerations of the Cold War and Japan's overwhelmingly important relationship with the United States, to something more appropriate for the post-Cold War world. On the other hand, the changes that had taken place by 1997 were hardly spectacular. In 1981 the present writer expressed the following opinion about the prospects for Japanese foreign policy:

> ... [E]ven from the perspective of the early 1980s it is difficult to argue that Japan has already emerged on the world scene with a clearly definable and positive role.
> ... Even though since the late 1970s there has been a perceptible shift in the climate of official opinion in favour of a more positive defence policy, it is still too early to say that there has been a 'breakthrough' or a conclusive departure from past attitudes and practices.[1]

Seen from the late 1990s there is a certain sense of *déja vu* about this statement. Japanese security is still closely dependent on American guarantees through the Security Treaty, the integrity of which was reiterated by President Clinton and the Japanese Prime Minister, Hashimoto, early in 1997. Although some observers perceive a greater regional emphasis than hitherto in Japanese foreign policy, it is hardly an enormous shift, and the economy of Japan remains global, rather than regional, in its reach and orientation. At the same time there is little sense of any breakthrough in the Government's willingness to chance its arm in international affairs, and despite of much talk of forging a disinctive identity in international affairs, it remains unclear what this is supposed to be. Although Japan has put in a bid for permanent membership of the United Nations Security

Council, the issue does not seem likely to be resolved quickly. With the collapse of Soviet power, the Russian threat has apparently been removed, but this has hardly freed up the Self-Defence Forces for coping with alternative, clearly defined, threats.

Indeed, if we consider developments in Northeast and Southeast Asia generally since the ending of the Cold War at the beginning of the 1990s, it becomes evident that much less has changed in certain important respects that has changed in other regions of the world, notably Europe and the former Soviet Union. China, much the largest and potentially most powerful state in the region, remains under the commanding rule of a self-styled Communist Party. Although Hong Kong reverted to China on 1 July 1997 under the principle of 'one country, two systems', there is little sign of a resolution of the dispute over the status of Taiwan, so that the 'two China' problem is still alive. The Korean peninsula remains divided between two highly antagonistic states, tension remains extremely high, and despite attempts by the United States to broker a dialogue, little progress is made towards a settlement.

Between Japan and Russia, no substantive progress has been made towards resolving the territorial dispute between them about the 'Northern Territories' (or 'Southern Kuriles'), which continues to inhibit the development of normal economic and other relations between them. Minor territorial disputes between Japan and South Korea, over Takeshima (Dokto), and between Japan and China, over the Senkaku islands (Taioyutai), which have been simmering for years, still flare up from time to time, and are far from solution. As previously mentioned, the Japan–United States Mutual Security Treaty, despite calls from some quarters for it to be scrapped, rethought or rewritten, remains in force. The economic relationship between the United States and Japan, though it was placed under a great deal of strain by the Japanese economic boom of the late 1980s, and still suffers from serious imbalances in bilateral trade, has survived and continues to create one of the largest trade flows in the world. In Southeast Asia the biggest change, perhaps, is the progressive liberalization of the economy of Vietnam, and the entry of that State into ASEAN, consequent upon the withdrawal of Soviet troops and advisers. Apart from that, however, the political shape of the region has not radically shifted.

Let us compare this picture with the enormous political transformations that have taken place in Europe and Russia, with the unification of Germany, breakup of the former Soviet Union into 15 successor states, civil war in the former Yugoslavia and its disintegration into several ethnic mini-states, massive political transition in many former Communist states of Eastern Europe and the prospective entry of some of them both into NATO and the European Union, extreme political instability and economic collapse in Russia and some other successor states, accompanied by a shaky and painful transition to a market economy. By this standard of comparison, what has been going on in East Asia during the 1990s presents us with much greater sense of continuity with the past than of discontinuity.

Having said all this, we need to take into account a range of less spectacular, but nevertheless significant, processes of evolutionary change that have been taking place since the early 1980s in the environment within which Japanese foreign policy is made.

The first of these, which seems likely to have incalculable long-term effects upon the region, is the rapid growth of the economy of at least the coastal regions of the People's Republic of China since the coming to power of Deng Xiaoping at the end of the 1970s. Deng's policies, which involved releasing the entrepreneurial and commercial abilities of the Chinese people without relinquishing central control by the Chinese Communist Party, have taken China a long way towards the goal of becoming a modern economic superpower. The process is far from complete, however, and if it proceeds along the present path may well take a further two or three decades to complete. Needless to say, the political consequences of this, not only for the region, but also for the political shape of China itself, are impossible to predict. The reversion of Hong Kong to China was greatly assisted by Chinese economic reforms which created a substantial degree of convergence between the free-wheeling market economy of Hong Kong and the liberalizing economy of southern coastal China, but it seems less certain that the same calculation can be made in relation to Taiwan.

For Japan, a principal concern about the rapid economic development of the PRC has emerged in the field of defence. A programme of modernizing China's armed forces during the 1990s, in part with purchases of military equipment from the successor states of the former USSR, some assertive actions by China in relation to her claim to the Senkakus and the Spratly islands further south, and, perhaps most significantly, PRC missile firings in the Taiwan Strait in the early months of 1995 to warn Taiwan against moving towards independence, have suggested to defence policy makers in Japan that China, if not an actual military threat at present, certainly needs to be watched.

A second area of concern for Japan where change is important is the Korean situation. The death of Kim Il Sung, the durable North Korean Stalinist dictator, in 1995, and uncertainty about the character of the successor regime under his son, Kim Jong Il, created anxiety in turn compounded by the knowledge that the North Korean economy was in a truly catastrophic state, and that the regime could no longer effectively feed its people. The suspicion that the North Korean regime was developing its own nuclear weapons early in 1994 led after some weeks of acute international tension to an American-brokered settlement over nuclear power stations. Japanese concern was exacerbated by the belief that the North Koreans possessed rockets capable of being fired as far as the outer suburbs of Tokyo.

A third significant change has already been discussed in chapter 6, namely the passage in 1992 of the Peace Keeping Operations (PKO) bill through Parliament, as a delayed consequence of the failure of Japan to provide a contingent for the Expeditionary Force in the Gulf War in 1991. As we have seen, this was an important psychological breakthrough towards a more participatory stance by Japan towards international peacekeeping, and although the results, in terms of actual participation in UN peacekeeping missions, have hardly been spectacular, the Gulf War and its aftermath apparently produced a long-term effect on public opinion in favour of greater international participation by Japan.

A fourth development were the 'Guidelines' drawn up by the Clinton and Hashimoto administrations in June 1997 to put more substance into operations under the Mutual Security Treaty. In particular, Japan agreed to assist US forces in time of conflict in certain ways that had not been agreed previously. For instance, if US naval vessels were damaged in combat, Japan agreed that they could be repaired at Japanese ports, and if US civilians needed to be evacuated from a crisis zone, the Japanese Self-Defence Forces would co-operate and injured personnel could be treated in Japan.[2]

A fifth development, again dating from the early northern hemisphere summer of 1997, was an agreement between Japanese and Russian officials to allow a somewhat more co-operative relationship, especially in economic matters, in the absence of an agreement over the Northern Territories.[3] The Japanese Foreign Ministry in particular had a traditional policy of inhibiting substantive links between the two countries until and unless a satisfactory territorial settlement was reached. Japanese–Russian relations had been largely in the doldrums since the collapse of the Soviet Union, partly because of the failure of a territorial settlement to emerge, but also, no doubt, because in the chaotic state of the post-Soviet Russian economy Japanese businesses were hardly attracted by the prospect of doing business in Russia. With signs, however, of a dynamic Russian economy emerging on the ruins of the old Soviet one, it made more sense to seek some withdrawal of political barriers erected by the Japanese foreign affairs bureaucracy.

Two further developments having a longer term character also need to be pointed out. The first is that, despite continued inhibitions on military activity, defence spending throughout the 1980s increased steadily at a rate of about 7 per cent per annum. Such levels of spending were characteristic of the Nakasone years and had the cumulative effect by the end of the decade of enabling the Self-Defence Forces to become a modernized high-tech force. Even though spending increases were cut back during the 1990s, the final decade of the Cold War saw a considerable transformation of Japanese defence capacity, always remembering, of course, the close linkage between the Self-Defence Forces and American forces stationed in Japan under the terms of the Security Treaty.

The second development to occur during the 1980s was an impressive increase in the quantity – and also, though to a lesser extent, in the quality – of Japan's overseas development aid. Apparently as the result of decisions taken at the beginning of the 1980s, the aid budget was exempted (like defence spending) from the general restrictions created by the principle of 'zero budgeting', so that by the end of the decade Japan had become the largest provider of overseas aid, slightly ahead of the United States.[4] Even though Japanese aid was heavily concentrated in the Southeast Asian region, and had always contained within it an element of commercial promotion on behalf of Japanese enterprises, the net result of increased aid spending was to raise Japan's international profile throughout the region and beyond.

In the 1990s, therefore, Japan was already not only the world's largest economic power after the United States, but also had laid much of the basis for 'normal power' status in terms of defence capacity and the projection of international influence through such avenues as overseas aid. Whether and to what extent Japan would in future act as a 'normal power' depended on political developments at home and abroad. Considerable inhibitions still remained.

Japan–US Relations: Background

By far the most salient factor in Japan's foreign policy since the Occupation has been her relationship with the United States. As the Japanese economy grew and the war receded into the background, the nature of that relationship changed from a tutelary one in the 1950s, through many painful adjustments and antagonisms, to one based on complex, though largely co-operative, interactions between two major powers.

The American decision from the latter part of the Occupation to treat Japan as a major Cold War ally had profound repercussions on the relationship between the two States. Through the Security Pact of 1951, revised in 1960 as the Mutual Security Treaty, Japan received guarantees of protection in case of attack at fairly low cost in terms of her own defence expenditure. The continued occupation of Okinawa not only provided the United States with its most important strategic base in the Western Pacific, but gave the Americans a hostage to Japanese good intentions, which they did not give up until May 1972. Japan also benefited from considerable quantities of American aid (including military aid), profited greatly from the 'Korea boom' in special procurement orders for the UN forces fighting in Korea, also did well economically out of the Vietnam war, and developed a massive trade with the United States.

One crucial aspect of the Japan–US relationship after the Occupation was that it entailed a radical restructuring of foreign relations away from the pattern than had developed starting in the Meiji period. Up to 1945, Japan had been largely an Asian power, with an extensive overseas empire which included Korea and Taiwan, and with ever-growing interests in China. In the 1930s Manchuria became a Japanese puppet state, and from 1937 Japan began to occupy large areas of China proper. For many years she was in close and largely hostile contact with Russian (later Soviet) interests in Northeast Asia. Finally, for a brief period beginning in 1941, Japan held in her possession a huge colonial empire in East and Southeast Asia and the Western Pacific.

With defeat, Occupation and the onset of the Cold War, all this suddenly changed. Japan was now a weak and defeated nation co-opted as a not very significant American ally in the fight against 'international communism'. For many years her interaction with her principal neighbours on the continent of Asia was minimal. Diplomatic relations were not established with the USSR until 1956, and even then the two states could not agree on a peace treaty or on the disposition of the 'Northern Territories'. Formal relations with the Republic of Korea (South Korea) were not entered into until 1965; with the Democratic People's Republic of Korea (North Korea) they are still to be established; and with the PRC, despite enormous pressure from within Japan itself, they were not established until 1972. Relations with Southeast Asian countries at this period were conducted largely on the economic level, with little political content.

Japan–US relations were briefly shaken by the Security Treaty revision crisis in 1960, but it was not until the early 1970s that a new and more problematic phase in their relationship was inaugurated. In July 1971 President Nixon took a dramatic new initiative, without prior consultation with Tokyo, by announcing his coming visit to Beijing. The following month he announced that the floating of the dollar in terms of gold and a 10 per cent surcharge on imports enter-ing the United States, with the primary and successful aim of forcing a revalu-ation of the yen. Japanese diplomatic recognition of the PRC and the return of Okinawa to Japan from American administration took place the following year, but all these events were dwarfed by the impact of the first 'oil shock' of 1973–4.

The oil shock brought to an end the 15 year period of ultra-rapid economic growth, and forced Japan to restructure its economy and reconsider many of its priorities. From about this period also, the American view of the Japanese economy was becoming much more hard-headed, regarding it as potentially threatening to US interests. Such threat perceptions attained their apogee in the late 1980s, at a time when the Japanese trade surplus had ballooned out and when a speculative boom in Japan was prompting many Japanese firms to make daring and in some cases provocative investments in the United States. This in turn led to severe trade frictions between the two countries, a series of top-level negotiations – most having little effect – aimed at keeping the relationship afloat, and the emergence of widely read 'revisionist' literature designed to show that the Japanese system was different and threatening.

Over this whole period, however, the cement holding the Japan–US structure together was the common threat perception engendered by the Cold War. It is hardly surprising, therefore, that the ending of the Cold War should have given rise to fears that the structure – with the threat suddenly removed – might fall apart. The fact that by the late 1990s it still remained intact may in part be attributed to the slow economic growth in Japan at this period, but also to the fact, alluded to above, that key aspects of the old international order were still in evidence in East Asia.

The keystone of Japan–US relations since the 1950s has been the Mutual Security Treaty, and it is to a more detailed analysis of this that we now turn. As we have noted earlier in the book, Yoshida's policy of resisting American demands for a massive Japanese military commitment had considerable success, although under the 1951 Security Treaty and the Mutual Security Assistance (MSA) Agreement of 1954 Japan found her freedom of action in the sphere of defence and foreign policy quite severely restricted by the American presence. Negotiations for revision of the Security Treaty between 1958 and 1960 were motivated on the Japanese side largely by the search for greater equality within the framework of continuing security guarantees. Although it was obscured at the time by the domestic political discord which the whole issue aroused, it was Kishi's achievement to have obtained, through tough bargaining with the Americans, a number of quite significant concessions which in effect placed Japan in a more equal and favourable position than she enjoyed under the old Treaty.

The first concession, which had a considerable symbolic significance, was that the Americans agreed to renegotiate the Treaty at all. Thus the stigma that attached to the old Treaty, of having been entered into by Japan when she was technically an occupied power and thus not fully a free agent, was removed. Two specific restrictions on Japanese freedom of action (however academic they may seem in retrospect) were also allowed to lapse. One was the 'internal dis-turbance clause' in article I of the 1951 Treaty. This had provided that American forces stationed 'in and about Japan' might 'be utilised to contribute to the maintenance of international peace and security in the Far East and to the security of Japan against armed attack from without, including assistance given at the express request of the Japanese Government to put down large-scale riots and disturbances in Japan, caused through instigation or intervention by an outside power or powers'. The other was the provision of article II that Japan would not grant, 'without the prior consent of the United States of America, any bases or any rights, powers or authority whatsoever, in or relating to bases or the right of garrison or of maneuver, or transit of ground, air or naval forces to any third power'.

On the positive side, the most important achievement from Japan's point of view was the inclusion of article IV of the new Treaty, the 'prior consultation' clause. This read as follows:

> The parties will consult together from time to time regarding the implementation of this Treaty, and, at the request of either Party, whenever the security of Japan or international peace and security in the Far East is threatened.

What this article was supposed to mean in practice was spelled out in the important exchange of notes between Kishi and Secretary of State Herter of 19 January 1960 (the date on which the revised Treaty was signed):

> Major changes in the deployment into Japan of United States armed forces, major changes in their equipment, and the use of facilities and areas in Japan as bases for military combat operations to be undertaken from Japan other than those conducted under Article V of the said Treaty, shall be the subjects of prior consultation with the Government of Japan.

The exact interpretation of this understanding, as well as its propriety, were subjects of recurring dispute between the Government and the Opposition parties. One of the main reasons which the Socialists put forward in 1960 for opposing the revised Treaty was that the 'prior consultation' clause did not provide the Japanese Government with a veto over potentially dangerous military activities by the American forces stationed in and around Japan.

The prior consultation clause was at issue in a recurring controversy during the 1970s and 1980s concerning the 'introduction' of nuclear weapons into Japanese ports on US naval vessels. Since the Satō administrations of the late 1960s, official policy was to ban the 'manufacture, stockpiling and introduction' of nuclear weapons in Japan. The problem, however, was what was meant by 'introduction' (*mochikomi*). Successive Japanese governments maintained that the 'introduction' of nuclear weapons was subject to the prior consultation clause. Apparently, however, the American side interpreted the word to exclude the berthing at Japanese ports of US naval vessels carrying nuclear weapons, whereas the official Japanese view was that 'introduction' included just such an event. Since the established American policy was never to comment when asked whether its vessels were loaded with nuclear weapons, the Japanese Government could still argue that, in a legal sense, it was complying with the prior consultation clause, and also adhering to the three non-nuclear principles inherited from the Satō Government. The credibility of such statements, however, was not high, and the issue periodically caused embarrassment.

A further indication of the greater equality which Japan achieved – a least on paper – in the new Treaty was the fact that she assumed greater obligations to contribute to a mutual defence effort. Article III of the 1960 Treaty in effect committed Japan to a continuing programme of rearmament, though the phrase 'subject to their constitutional provisions' was a ritual obeisance by the Americans to the peace clause of the Japanese Constitution. There was a similar provision in article V, which sanctioned joint action by the two states in the event of 'an armed attack against either party in the territories under the administration of Japan'. As mentioned above, the Self-Defence Forces in the 1990s constitute a high-quality, high-tech military force, and systems facilitating joint action in conceivable circumstances are – three decades later – being put in place.

The 1960 Treaty contained three separate references (in the preamble, and in articles 4 and 6) to the 'peace and security of the Far East'. This was the subject of a lengthy debate in Parliament during the early months of 1960 about the precise geographical definition of the term 'Far East'. Government spokesmen at the time came out with differing answers to the question, but it seemed to be accepted that it included not only the Japanese islands themselves, but also South Korea and Taiwan, at the minimum. As the Government subsequently interpreted the Treaty, however, there was no question of Japanese forces being sent overseas in joint operations with the United States to defend the 'peace and security of the Far East'. In the 1990s the beginnings are visible of a breach with this principle, in the shape of the PKO bill of 1992. Nevertheless, much of the inhibition remained in place as of 1998.

It need not be supposed that the Japanese Government was acting here out of a scrupulous regard for the Constitution as such. But a combination of domestic political pressures, suspicion of Japanese intentions on the part of neighbouring states and a preference not to be too closely identified with American policies in Asia all contributed to an official interpretation of the Security Treaty which virtually confined the Japanese contribution to a role in the defence of Japanese territory, while providing facilities for American operations elsewhere. Even though US congressmen and government officials would complain from time to time that Japan was not pulling her weight in collective security (a concept not officially admissible in Japan), and would accuse Japan of 'taking a ride on the Security Treaty', in practice the arrangements worked out over many years under the Treaty suited the United States quite adequately. Japan occupied a strategic location off the coast of Northeast Asia, so that it was advantageous to maintain bases there, and by the 1990s Japan was bearing the great majority of the costs of maintaining the bases.[5] The great advantage from the American point of view was the possession of a forward base area in a country that was politically fairly stable, and whose semi-pacifist aspirations in practice ensured passive, if hardly active, co-operation, with US military strategic aims. Occasional murmurings emanating from the US military that the real purpose of the Security Treaty was to forestall irresponsible activity by Japan were of course never repeated in any official statement.

The most difficult issue in administering the Security Treaty has always been the question of Okinawa. The Satō governments of the latter half of the 1960s laboured hard and long to secure the reversion of Okinawa (and surrounding islands) from American administration to Japanese sovereignty. This constituted the biggest irredentist movement in Japan's history, compounded by the strategic position of the American bases on Okinawa in the waging of the Vietnam war. The presence of nuclear weapons on the Okinawan bases (never, of course, formally acknowledged), created a crucial problem from Satō's point of view, since if the islands became re-incorporated in Japan as Okinawa Prefecture with the nuclear weapons still there, the second of the three non-nuclear principles, referred to above, would be breached. In the event, Satō achieved a settlement in his talks with President Nixon in November 1969, whereby Okinawa would revert to Japan in 1972 with the nuclear weapons removed, but as has recently been revealed with the publication of his diaries, there was also a secret protocol to the agreement, providing that in case of a war emergency, nuclear devices could be brought back in.[6]

Okinawa once more, as we have seen, became international news in September 1995, when three American servicemen raped a local schoolgirl. The outrage provoked by this incident reverberated through local and national politics, prompting a tenacious campaign by the popular prefectural Governor to have American bases reduced in size and scope, and eventually removed altogether. The fact that a number of base land leases were due for renewal by the summer of 1997 prompted a refusal by the Governor to sanction renewal. This faced the Prime Minister with the difficult decision of whether to override the Governor's veto, and after consultation with President Clinton, he ultimately decided so to act. What is particularly significant about this episode is that despite the ending of the Cold War, the chief executives of Japan and the United States should decide that their mutual interest in the preservation of their Mutual Security Treaty was sufficiently strong to override provincial objections in an aggrieved region on the Japanese periphery.

Relations between Japan and the Soviet Union/Russia

Japan and her northern neighbour[7] have rarely enjoyed cordial relations in their modern history. From 1956, when diplomatic relations were entered into but no peace treaty was signed because of the northern islands dispute,[8] until the collapse of the Soviet Union at the end of 1991, the two countries regarded each other coolly. Memories of the way Stalin unilaterally broke the Neutrality Pact in August 1945 and of the treatment of Japanese prisoners after the war did not entirely disappear, and the two countries had little in common either culturally or politically. Relations between Japan and the new Russia have been a little better, but the territorial dispute seems no closer to solution and until very recently the catastrophic state of economic activity and public order in Russia gave little incentive to Japanese businesses to become involved in trading or investment activities there.[9]

The Japanese Foreign Ministry (*Gaimushō*) has over a long period taken an extremely hard line over Japan's claim for return of the Northern Territories, maintaining that substantive economic relations should not be pursued until the claim is settled to Japan's satisfaction. The reasons for this position have varied.

At the height of the Cold War the Foreign Ministry was concerned above all with the integrity of the security relationship with the United States, and determined to inhibit so far as possible the receptiveness of Japanese businessmen to tempting business opportunities in the Soviet Union which might upset the Americans.[10] With the collapse of the Soviet regime the concern was rather more with the territorial claim itself, since economic collapse might have tempted the Russian leaders to trade territory for economic support. This calculation, however, proved illusory, since neither Gorbachev, who visited Japan early in 1991, nor Yeltsin, who came later, were politically strong enough to be able to override nationalist opposition to territorial concessions. A third motivation, in all probability, is fear of nationalist reaction in Japan itself should a deal be done on the northern islands which involves less than full reversion of the territories to Japan. Some elements on the far right of the political spectrum regard the northern islands as sacred Japanese lands. Mainstream political institutions in Japan have a history of submission to ultranationalist demands under implied or explicit threats of violence. A recent slight softening, however, of the long-standing inflexibility of approach over the islands has already been noted.

Relations between Japan and the People's Republic of China

The China issue fundamentally divided political opinion in Japan throughout the years from the end of the Occupation to the recognition of the Beijing regime in 1972, and even to some extent until the Peace and Friendship Treaty of 1978. How to deal with China was central to the debate between supporters of the alliance with the United States and advocates of some form of non-aligned or, broadly, more independent foreign policy. It also touched upon a cultural complex which is formed out of a Japanese sense of indebtedness to China for the origins of its culture. A sense – sometimes greatly exaggerated – of the potential importance to Japan of the China market was a key factor in the enthusiasm of sections of the business world for trade with the PRC. On the other hand, the right wing of the LDP and associated business interests, which were able to make their views prevail throughout the Satō period (1964–72), were extremely reluctant to prejudice relations with Taiwan or with the US for the sake of what they regarded as dangerous political entanglements with the mainland.

Until President Nixon's unexpected announcement of July 1971, many Japanese regarded relations with the PRC as the reverse side of the coin of relations with the US. Shortly after the San Francisco Peace Treaty came into force in 1952, the Yoshida Government, under pressure from the US, signed a separate peace treaty with Taiwan acting in the name of 'China'. This ended the state of war with 'China', but was of course regarded as evidence of hostile intent by the regime in Beijing. A long and complicated period of political manoeuvring between Beijing and Tokyo followed, with the PRC making good use of the extensive pro-PRC sentiment in Japan. Four successive 'unofficial' trade agreements during the 1950s were the framework for a certain amount of trade, but in 1958 the Chinese cut off trade completely following an alleged slight to their national flag at a trade fair in Nagasaki. Trade gradually revived again in the 1960s, and reached somewhat higher levels than in the 1950s.[11]

The official line of the Japanese Government at this time was that 'politics should be separated from economics' (*seikei bunri*), in other words that trade on an unofficial basis was acceptable provided that nothing was done to imply political recognition of the Beijing regime. The Chinese responded by treating trade as a political instrument. On several occasions Japanese trade negotiators were effectively forced to sign communiqués highly critical of the Japanese Government, as the price of continuing trade. In 1970, Chou En-lai enunciated a set of principles which made it difficult for firms with interests in South Korea or Taiwan to conduct trade with the PRC. During the final two years of Satō's prime ministership his position was progressively weakened by his unsympathetic attitudes towards the PRC, and his position was ultimately undermined by the shift of influential opinion towards normalizing relations with that country.

Considering the strained condition of Japan–PRC relations in the Satō years, the rapidity and smoothness with which Tanaka's new approach was accepted in Beijing is remarkable. In the 1972 agreement for restoration of diplomatic relations, Japan apologized for the damage she had caused China up to 1945, and the Chinese agreed to waive reparations. Japan 'fully understood and respected' the Chinese position on Taiwan, and a reference to article 8 of the Postdam Declaration (which restricts Japanese sovereignty to the main Japanese islands and 'such minor islands as we shall determine') signified the renunciation of any Japanese claim to Taiwan. There was no reference to the Japan–Republic of China Treaty of 1952, and no new peace treaty was entered into between Tokyo and Beijing, although there was a reference to 'the termination of the state of war'. Japan was not required to sever *de facto* relations with Taiwan, nor was the Japan–US Security Treaty or the contentious 1969 Nixon-Satō communiqué referred to. These were quite lenient conditions from the Japanese point of view.

It was to be six years before the problems inherent in the new relationship were satisfactorily ironed out. Although the problem of who owned the Senkaku (Taioyutai) islets, which reverted to Japan along with the reversion of Okinawa, was easily – if temporarily – disposed of, Japan's continuing *de facto* connections with Taiwan were more difficult to reconcile with the Beijing relationship. When Ōhira Masayoshi, as Foreign Minister in the Tanaka Government, signed an airlines agreement with Beijing, Taipei responded by cancelling Japan Airlines' landing rights in Taiwan for an indefinite period. Eventually a face-saving formula was found which permitted air services to be operated between Japan and both the PRC and Taiwan.

It took much longer to bring about a satisfactory solution of the issue of 'hegemony'. At an early stage in the negotiations for a peace and friendship treaty, the Chinese side indicated that it wanted the treaty to contain a clause stating that both sides opposed 'hegemony' (*haken* in Japanese) in international affairs. Since this was Chinese shorthand for the international policies of the Soviet Union, the Japanese Government refused to accede to this requirement. Ultimately, during the tenure of the Fukuda Government in 1978, a formula was agreed in which 'hegemony' was mentioned in one clause, but its exclusive applicability to the USSR denied in another.[12] The Japan–China trade agreement signed earlier the same year provided the formal basis for a substantial expansion of trade between the two countries.

These treaties more or less coincided with the start of the new economic policies of Deng Xiaoping. There followed a major increase throughout the 1980s of economic intercourse between Japan and China, though the process was not without its problems. At times the Chinese authorities, faced with an overheating economy, would engage in large-scale cancellation of contracts with Japanese companies, and at other times there would be complaints from the Chinese side of a reluctance on the part of Japanese firms to transfer advanced technology. Japan was faced with a serious policy dilemma after the massacre of protesting students on Tiananmen Square in Beijing in 1989. With other states, Japan responded with a suspension of aid, but was the earliest of the major states to resume full economic intercourse with the PRC once the furore over the massacre had begun to die down. During the 1990s, Japan has become well entrenched in the rapidly advancing Chinese economy, but faces perennial problems of lack of trust from the Chinese side.

Relations between Japan and the two Koreas

Japan's relations with Korea also have a difficult and stormy history. The legacy of harsh colonial rule over Korea by Japan between 1910 and 1945 created long-standing resentments on the part of the Koreans, while Japanese have at times tended to look down upon Koreans. During the Korean war, Japan was a staging post for American forces engaged in the UN operation against North Korea. President Rhee Syngman of South Korea was so anti-Japanese that no progress was possible towards normalization of Japan–South Korea relations until after his overthrow in 1960. Park Chung-Hee, his successor after a brief interregnum, was prepared to deal with Japan, and diplomatic relations were with difficulty established between the two states in 1965. The rapid growth of the South Korean economy from the 1960s provided plenty of opportunities for Japanese businesses, but relations at most levels remained cool. The kidnapping of the opposition leader, Kim Dae-Jung, from Japan in 1973 by agents of the South Korean regime, and subsequent events, caused great friction between the two governments, although the Nakasone administration in the 1980s exerted itself to mend fences with the government in Seoul. Relations gradually improved as South Korea from the late 1980s gradually transformed itself from a dictatorship into a form of democracy. Perhaps, however, the most potent force for improvement of relations came from the Korean emergence into the ranks of advanced industrial economies, which had been achieved by the early 1990s.

Japan has never entered into diplomatic relations with North Korea, and trading links between them remain minimal. Talks between representatives of the Japanese and North Korean governments have been held from time to time, usually in order to solve contingent crises, such as the North Korean detention of Japanese fishermen.[13] The principal concern of the Japanese Foreign Ministry has been with the possibility that friction between the two Koreas might trigger general instability in the region. The crisis over the North Korean nuclear programme in 1994, referred to above, caused acute anxiety in Tokyo, as has the North Korean food crisis of 1996–7, with reports of widespread malnutrition and even starvation in some areas. Indeed, the prospect of a sudden collapse of the now largely isolated regime in the north could create military conflict with unpredictable consequences on the peninsula and beyond. The Seoul Government has come to regard sudden collapse with horror, because of the enormous cost of rehabilitating the North.[14] At the same time the prospects of promoting peaceful change towards a more responsible, effective and less dangerous regime in the North do not seem bright. For Japan, therefore, the Korean peninsula remains a pressing concern of its foreign policy, as it has been for more than 40 years.

Broad Considerations about Japanese Foreign Policy

As we suggested early in this Chapter, less appears to have changed in the parameters of Japanese foreign policy in the 1990s than might have been expected given the radical transformation of the international system since the ending of the Cold War and the breaking up of the Soviet Union. We suggested one reason for this, namely the persistence of important elements characteristic of the Cold War world in Asia when they had disappeared from Europe and from Russia. There are, in addition, three further possible reasons – none of them new – which have been advocated to explain the conservative and relatively unchanging nature of Japanese foreign policy.

One is that Japan, having known the bitter taste of defeat and the horrors of atomic attack, and possessing a 'Peace Constitution' which commands widespread respect among the electorate, cannot aspire to more positive, nationalistic or adventurous foreign and defence policies because that would not be acceptable to public opinion. A second explanation is that politics in Japan is seriously fragmented, with the politics of factional and sectional advantage inhibiting clear and sustained policy initiatives, since all that can be expected to emerge from discussion between opposed groups is a weak and watered-down consensus. Foreign policy making, in other words, is a function of an immobilist political system. A third explanation is that, by concentrating over a long period on economic development, developing a strong position in international trade and by concentrating on the projection of 'soft power'[15] in its various aspects, Japan has maximized national advantage at minimal cost, and continues with the same lines of policy because they are tried and tested, and are seen to work.

All these three explanations contain a considerable element of truth, but they need to be looked at critically, and also tested against Japan's domestic and external situation of the late 1990s.

The antiwar sentiment based on the Constitution has not disappeared, but by comparison with earlier decades it seems to be taken for granted by the electorate rather than actively promoted. Article 9 of the Constitution has not prevented the formation and development of a significant body specialized in the arts of war, equipped with the latest high-tech devices and known euphemistically as the 'Self-Defence Forces'. During the 1980s more money than ever before was spent on it, resulting in a notable upgrading of its capacities. Since 1992, it has been able to participate in UN peacekeeping missions, though with certain restrictions on its activities. All public opinion polls now reveal overwhelming support for the existence of the Self-Defence Forces, but a cautious attitude towards further expansion of their activities in an overtly military direction. For the first time in the 1990s many polls show a majority in favour of constitutional revision, although what kind of revision might be favoured by the electorate is less certain.[16] Most significantly on the face of it, the JSP (now SDP) has virtually collapsed, and with it the ancient core of last-ditch support for the Peace Constitution. Even so, we should not read too much into the collapse of the Socialists, since the ethos of the 1946 Constitution has penetrated more deeply into the body politic than its opponents sometimes realize.

Sectionalism (including factionalism) and consensus politics have also tended to make it hazardous for governments to pursue obviously innovative policies in sensitive areas of foreign policy and defence. The most famous examples of crises so engendered are the Security Treaty revision crisis of 1960, and the crisis over contributing to the American-led Expeditionary Force in 1991 following the Iraqi invasion of Kuwait. In the first case the Prime Minister was forced out of office and in the second all that could be put together was an (admittedly substantial) financial package. Nevertheless, it is worth noting that in 1960 the revised Security Treaty did pass through Parliament, and the debate over the Gulf Crisis did lead, a year and a half later, to the passage of the PKO bill. In other words, immobilist politics does not, in the Japanese case, mean a total inability to effect political change, rather that a cumbersome process of consensus-building and of exhausting all possibilities has to be gone through for change to eventuate. The politics of the late 1990s provide a further example of this generalization, since while much of the reforming impetus of the Hosokawa Government and its immediate successors ran into the sand, a very similar agenda was being implemented after the October 1996 elections by the Hashimoto Government, which had been expected to oppose it.

This leads on to the third explanation, that the successes hitherto of a foreign policy emphasizing economic development and the projection of 'soft power' have been sufficient to convince generations of decision-makers that it is worth while. Even though economic growth in the 1990s is at a low level when compared to previous decades, the sheer size of the Japanese economy, second only to the United States in the world and overwhelmingly dominant in Asia, places Japan in a position where certain things can be achieved without a great deal of overt pushing. Despite, or perhaps because of, apparently unassertive policies in her myriad interactions with the international system, Japan manages to have considerable success in promoting her national interests.

On the whole, this third explanation appears to be the most convincing, although the other two should certainly not be discounted. The three are of course connected, in the sense that the line of least resistance – of avoiding controversial political decisions because of the domestic complications they involve and the resistance of public opinion – has through a combination of luck and astute judgement been made to work in such a way that it has paid off.

What needs to concern us, however, is whether it will continue to pay off in the system of international relations that has been emerging in aftermath of the Cold War. We have already given reasons for expecting that change will be slow rather than precipitate. Nevertheless, a series of developments in the domestic economy since the late 1980s – in particular, failures of financial oversight and a crisis of the banking system – have after considerable delay started to precipitate measures of reform. The pressures of a globalizing financial system make it increasingly difficult for Japan to continue to operate a financial system with tight bureaucratic controls. It may be expected, therefore, that the Japanese financial (and more broadly, economic) system will progress further in the direction of openness, more in order to ensure economic survival than from any desire to conform to American norms. In the words of one observer, the Japanese bureaucratic and business world 'has been going through a gigantic exercise in soul-searching. What used to work no longer works.'[17]

It would be unwise, however, to assume that adaptation of her financial system to globalizing pressures means that the Japanese 'system' faces defeat. As McRae argues: 'Japan is simply applying good foreign practice to its own institutions',[18] something of which there have been many instances in her modern history. What Drifte calls Japan's *soft power* 'derives from its economic, financial and technological power'.[19] Japan's economic power derives essentially from the sheer size of its economy, which enables it, for instance, to influence the shape of international regimes regulating trading relationships. Drifte quotes the then LDP President, Kōno Yōhei, writing in 1995, to the effect that with the ending of the Cold War Japan was no longer so constrained by loyalty to the Western cause as before, and could work towards the establishment of international regimes that reflected her own interest.[20] Examples of such a tendency are Japanese policy towards the Uruguay round of tariff reductions, concluded at the end of 1993, foreign investment as a means of shaping trade relationships and spreading the appeal of Japanese management and working practices, ODA for infrastructure development in such a way as to benefit Japanese commercial interests, but also to promote political ends such as democracy and human rights, inducing other Asian countries to take Japan as an economic model, and what is termed 'techno-nationalism' (the exercise of control over technology etc. in such a way as to insulate Japanese business from international interdependence).[21]

When we turn from 'soft power' to matters of security and defence, the prospects of major change in the security regime of which Japan is a part seem slight in the short to medium term. This proposition would of course be subject to revision if there were an outbreak of hostilities, or large-scale breakdown in social order, on the Korean peninsula, or if the PRC were to turn belligerent, for instance in an attempt to reunify Taiwan with the mainland. Even so, situations of extreme tension combined with remarkable stability have been characteristic of relations between the two Koreas and between the two Chinas for more than four decades. Perhaps we should recall Gibbon's dictum about the Roman Empire in its decline, that 'this intolerable situation lasted for more than three hundred years'.

Although Japan has been accused of being a 'free rider' in security matters, the Clinton–Hashimoto agreements, referred to above, strongly suggest a common interest between the US and Japan in the continuation of current security arrangements, albeit with some fine tuning. It is sometimes argued that Japan's own security has suffered from inadequate spending on defence and from the various constitutional restraints which have been maintained upon military-related activity. The question is difficult to answer. Perhaps one way of resolving it would be to ask what Japan would look like in the late 1990s if since the war, without constitutional inhibition, she had been spending a similar proportion of her GNP on defence (including possibly nuclear weapons) to that of the United States, the major European states or the two Koreas. Quite apart from the domestic impact of such a policy, one needs to ask whether, had it been pursued, China and the USSR at the time of the Sino–Soviet dispute might not have developed strategies of Asian defence directed primarily against Japan rather than primarily against each other. Had that been the case, Japan would presumably have been forced into still greater military efforts, and one wonders how this would have affected the domestic economy, political stability and the security of the East Asian region.

In 1981 the present writer wrote:

> While the foreign policy and defence policy problems of Japan in the 1980s may well be complex and difficult to resolve, the caution and restraint which have been characteristic of Japanese policy for several years have put down deep roots, and are unlikely to be abandoned lightly.[22]

It may be some measure of political stability and continuity that there seems rather little need to vary that assessment from the perspective of 1998. We should remember, however, that Japan, despite having a bigger economy than in 1981, is facing serious economic difficulties, is no longer locked into a Cold War situation, and is grappling with foreign pressures to conform to global regimes in finance and other areas of international interaction. Bearing these factors in mind, the outlook for Japanese foreign policy need not be quite so stable and predictable as it appeared in 1981.

13

Conclusions: The Analytical Challenge of Japanese Politics

The most fundamental analytical challenge of Japanese politics is that Japan is the first, and arguably the most important, nation-state outside the Western, Judaeo-Christian tradition, to adopt democratic forms of government. To an extent arguably greater, therefore, than between states sharing that tradition, it should be possible – in principle at least – to test how far factors of cultural difference affect the working in practice of democratic forms of government.

Japan, moreover, is a mature industrialized state with a consciousness of its own history and national identity going back for many centuries. That history, it is true, included a long period of virtual seclusion from the outside world, from the early seventeenth to the mid-nineteenth centuries, during which time Japan missed out on most of the dramatic modernizing changes that occurred in Europe and elsewhere. Japan, however, pursued its own idiosyncratic path of development during that period. So far as government and politics is concerned, the experience of operating political and governmental institutions under a formal written constitution goes back to 1889, and even though that constitution was not – and was not intended to be – democratic, (though it included limited democratic elements) politics and political conflict occurred during its period of validity in an at least partially structured framework. In 1946 the Constitution of 1889 was replaced by the still current Constitution, which was intended to structure politics and government along democratic lines.

The evolution of Japanese politics under the 1946 Constitution of course reflects many contingent factors including the massive psychological and structural impact of defeat in war and foreign occupation. At the same time, political phenomena such as elections, parliamentary debates and legislative activity, government ministries and interest groups operated in a regular fashion and could be studied. On the face of it, it ought to be a straightforward matter to make comparisons between the ways in which politics is conducted in Japan and the ways in which it is conducted elsewhere.

Unfortunately such a direct approach has been confronted by a body of literature in Japan (reflected occasionally in writings outside Japan by non-Japanese), whose main premise is that simple comparison is bound to be misleading, since Japan in a fundamental sense is different, Japan is unique. The dubious nature of much of this *nihonjinron* literature has been exposed by a number of writers, cited in chapter 3. Some of it seems to have had a political purpose, to provide a justification for self-serving action by Japan in terms of international trading regimes and similar structures. More seriously, much of its intellectual underpinnings were fragile, to say the least. As Peter Dale has shown, the literature fed upon itself, ever recycling facile dichotomies between Japan and the West.[1]

Despite its dreadful faults, however, this literature may perhaps be said to have performed a purpose in warning us of the dangers of a too facile equation between Japanese institutions and practices and those to be found elsewhere. It has long been recognized among political scientists that the business of comparing different systems is not as simple as it might seem at first sight.[2] Where cultural tradition and historical experience are as divergent as between Japan and say, Britain or France, we need to take especial care to be sure that in making comparisons we are comparing like with like. It is easy to assume that political parties (let us say) behave in Japan much as they do in Britain or elsewhere, maintaining nationwide organizations promoting explicit policy programmes and contesting elections whose outcomes are uncertain on a party basis rather than on the basis of local candidates and their connections. When we find that in Japan the main parties typically fight highly predictable elections around candidates who are local notabilities, that the party platform can be quite insubstantial and party organization subordinate to local organizations run by candidates who in turn are members of intra-party *habatsu*, we realize that comparison may be a delicate matter.[3]

Approaches to the study of Japanese politics and government since the war have passed through a succession of phases. In the decade and a half from 1945 a democracy paradigm predominated, focusing on the Occupation's democratic experiment and seeking the causes of authoritarian rule in the 1930s and early 1940s. In the 1960s, however, a very different paradigm took over, prompted by the already obvious successes of the economy, so that many observers came to concentrate their analysis on development and modernization. This included the notion of 'political development', which meant essentially the formation of complex and sophisticated political structures. The modernization paradigm, in turn, was overtaken by New Left criticism from the end of the 1960s. New Left writers directed their fire at the costs of development in terms of human exploitation, and although much of what they wrote about was pre-war history, they also uncovered exploitative relationships existing within contemporary industry, between large firms and the small firms to which went the subcontracted work, and between privileged, permanently employed workers and those casually employed on much lower take-home pay. This in turn gave way to a 'Japan as Number One' paradigm late in the 1970s. Ezra Vogel, in *Japan as Number One*,[4] developed arguments having much in common with the modernization paradigm, but in addition he maintained that Japan had created a model from which positive lessons could be learnt by Western countries, including the United States. Ironically, the book sold many more copies in Japan than in the US.

During the 1980s a different kind of challenge emerged to established approaches to the study of Japan. This was the revisionist paradigm, referred to earlier in the book. Sharing with Vogel the belief that Japan had a different 'system' from the United States, the revisionists, however, did not regard Japan as a model, but rather as a threat. The influence of the revisionist paradigm on American thinking concerning Japan during the latter half of the 1980s, when Japan was in the middle of her 'bubble economy' and US–Japan trade frictions were at their height, was profound. Revisionists, most prominently Chalmers Johnson, maintained in essence that what drove the Japanese economy was not market economics but bureaucratic control, that the system as it had developed got ahead by exploiting other economies through a closed domestic market, rigged tendering for contracts and predatory export drives, corruption being endemic, not peripheral, and democratic politics being essentially window-dressing.[5]

The 1990s has witnessed furious controversy between some exponents of the revisionist paradigm and those favouring a contrasting paradigm more recently applied to Japan, that of 'rational choice theory'. So far as Japanese politics is concerned, the most widely noted product of the rational choice paradigm is a book entitled *Japan's Political Marketplace* by Ramseyer and Rosenbluth.[6] Inspired by the principle that politicians will act so as to maximize their interests within the rules of the political game that exist, the authors arrived at the counter-intuitive conclusion that Japanese politicians essentially control bureaucrats, seen by the authors as politicians' agents, rather than the other way round. The book, which was polemically written, attracted fierce attack from revisionists, especially Johnson.[7]

Rather than entering into the detail of a rather sterile controversy between revisionists and rational choice specialists, we wish to single out one particular aspect which seems of significance. Ramseyer and Rosenbluth make a particular point of excluding from serious consideration cultural factors, which other writers have brought into play to explain aspects of Japanese politics.[8] The argument, therefore, essentially boils down to one of rational individuals making calculations of advantage within structures of given rules. Others, not adhering to a rational choice paradigm, have in the past to good effect castigated excessive resort to cultural stereotypes to 'explain' Japan. At its most extreme the use of culturally specific models leads to the kind of 'East is East and West is West' thinking that inspires the *nihonjinron*. Nevertheless, we need to ask whether we really want to exclude cultural considerations from our understanding of Japanese politics altogether. The view of this writer is that we should not. If by 'culture' we mean those aspects of current practice which are influenced by relatively long-standing patterns of social interaction and by expectations about the behaviour of others conditioned by the norms and values of the society in which individuals operate, then to exclude 'culture' is to risk missing absolutely vital clues about the ways in which politics functions in practice.[9]

In seeking an understanding of the dynamics of Japanese politics, it is crucial to step back from established theories of politics (though it may be useful to know about them) and adopt an approach which is sensitive both to the formal and informal rules of the system and also to the cultural nuances of political behaviour. A particularly useful set of clues for understanding recent Japanese politics is provided by Muramatsu and Krauss, with their use of the concept 'patterned pluralism'. They explain that this is not a classical concept of pluralism 'in which policy was merely the outcome of open-ended, competitive lobbying by pressure groups on a relatively weak government'.[10] Rather:

> The government and its bureaucracy are strong, but the boundaries between state and society are blurred by the integration of social interest groups with the government and by the intermediation of political parties between social interest groups and the government. The government is not weak, but it is *penetrated* by interest groups and political parties.[11]

In the decade since Muramatsu and Krauss wrote the above, The single-party dominance and government–opposition ideological confrontation on which their approach was in part premised has given way to a more fluid and less predictable interaction between parties, different parts of the government bureaucracy and an even wider variety of interest groups. Labour, for instance, has come to be part of the system to a greater extent than was the case before 1990.[12] Moreover, the mood is favourable to political change, which adds a further dimension of fluidity. It is arguable that the pluralist element in Japanese politics is thereby further enhanced, but it would be unwise to assume that the 'patterning' has thereby been greatly reduced.

In somewhat similar vein, Inoguchi writes of 'bureaucracy-led, mass inclusionary pluralism'.[13] The important word here is 'inclusive'. It is possible to detect a tendency since the end of the Occupation for more and more groups to be *in*cluded in decision making and fewer and fewer groups to be *ex*cluded.

The point, however, that we wish in conclusion to emphasize is Japan, which by any set of criteria is a *major* economy, also has what should be described as *divided* politics. It is no longer so much divided as it used to be in terms of ideological camp conflict on Marxist/anti-Marxist lines. That was always an unequal struggle with the anti-Marxist LDP-dominated forces of the Establishment dictating most of the policy but the Marxist (or semi-Marxist and pacifist) Opposition exercising a certain amount of veto power. In the 1990s, the divisions are of a different kind. Powerful sectional coalitions, combining political, bureaucratic, commercial, industrial and even religious interests confront other sectional coalitions made up of different combinations of similar elements. Policy making has to take into account the power relationships between these combinations and, in consequence, it is a complicated matter to change policy, let alone to develop and implement coherent government strategy across the gamut of issues. There is an intractable problem of corruption which continues to bedevil the politics of Japan, and, worryingly, this has come to affect the bureaucracy as well as politics and business. Nevertheless, though governments have to step carefully, they are not entirely without power. Sectional conflicts are not a recipe for total stalemate. Accommodations eventually emerge, and when the national mood alters decisively in a given direction – though it may take a long time – policy is likely to move in that direction too. The system is imperfectly democratic (as are many other so-called 'democracies'), but the very fact that Japan enjoys divided politics ensures that it does not develop some of the less pleasant characteristics of some plainly non-democratic nation states.

Notes

Chapter 1

1   For a detailed analysis of this general election to the House of Representatives, see chapter 6, and for discussion of the various election systems that have existed in Japan, see chapter 8. International press reaction to the October 1996 election results reflected disappointment, mixed with some puzzlement. Philippe Pons, writing in *Le Monde*, 22 October 1996, emphasized 'les batailles de clocher' (battles over the church steeple) which the new system had reinforced. Andrew Pollack in the *International Herald Tribune*, 22 October 1996, wrote: '[a]s Japan has wallowed through the last few years of economic stagnation and turmoil, corporate executives have been looking to their government for two things: stable and strong leadership, and economic deregulation that would lay the groundwork for Japan Inc. to roar again in the 21st century'. But, he concluded: '[t]the result of Sunday's national elections will most likely produce none of those things completely'. According to William Dawkins, writing in the *Financial Times* (London), 21 October 1996: '[y]esterday's Japanese general election puts the conservative Liberal Democratic party back in the driving seat after three years of muddled coalition governments, but leaves it in charge of a vehicle loaded with dissatisfied passengers.'

2   The SDP (JSP) decline in the 1990s was indeed sharp. In the successive House of Representatives elections of 1990, 1993 and 1996 it won, respectively, 136, 70 and 15 seats. The 1996 result no doubt related to the fact that it had entered into a coalition government with the Liberal Democrats and a minor party in 1994, being forced in the process to jettison much of its traditional platform, but a more immediate reason was that it had split, with many of its members joining the *Minshutō* (Democratic Party), formed in September 1996.

3   Discussion, 12 October 1996.

4   For further discussion, see chapter 3. See Peter Dale, *The Myth of Japanese Uniqueness*, London, Routledge, 1986 and subsequent editions; Kosaku Yoshino, *Cultural Nationalism in Contemporary Japan*. London and New York, Routledge, 1992; Joy Hendry, *Understanding Japanese Society*. London, Routledge, 2nd edn,

1995. Ann Waswo, *Japanese Society*, Oxford, Oxford University Press, 1996, pp. 99–103.

5   Discussion with Maurice Wright, Japan Politics Group Colloquium, University of Sheffield, September 1994. The discussion was in the context of the comparative study of budget-making.

6   See chapter 2.

7   See chapter 3.

8   J. A. A. Stockwin, *Japan: Divided Politics in a Growth Economy*. London, Weidenfeld and Nicolson, 1975, 1982.

9   Ibid., p. xii.

10   Herman Kahn, *The Emerging Japanese Superstate: Challenge and Response*. Englewood Cliffs, NJ, Prentice Hall, 1970.

11   The honour of being the first should perhaps go to Norman McRae of the *Economist*. See The Economist, *Consider Japan*. London, Duckworth, 1963.

12   Ruth Benedict, *The Chrysanthemum and the Sword: Patterns of Japanese Culture*. Boston, Houghton Mifflin, 1946, pp. 114–44.

13   Kahn, ibid., pp. 186–213.

14   Bernard Crick, *In Defence of Politics*. London, Penguin, 2nd edn, 1982.

15   For instance: 'This general homogeneity of Japanese society contributes naturally to the consensual nature of decision making in the country, and to the ease of implementing decisions once they are reached.' T. J. Pempel, *Policy and Politics in Japan: Creative Conservatism*. Philadelphia, PA, Temple University Press, 1982, p. 25. Pempel, it is true, later qualifies this statement by writing that: '... the relatively undifferentiated homogeneity of the Japanese populace is complicated by many lines of organizational and social cleavage'. Ibid., p. 26.

16   See J. A. A. Stockwin, 'Japan's Political Crisis of 1980', *Australian Outlook*, vol. 35, no. 1 (April 1981), pp. 19–32.

17   See for instance Gavan McCormack, *The Emptiness of Japanese Affluence*, Armonk, NY and London, M.E. Sharpe, 1996.

18   Zbigniew Brzezinski, *The Fragile Blossom: Crisis and Change in Japan*. New York and London, Harper and Row, 1972.

19   Nagai Yōnosuke, *Jūkōzō shakai to bōryoku* (The Flexible Frame Society and Violence). Tokyo, Chūō kōronsha, 1971.

20   On financial deregulation see James Horne, *Japan's Financial Markets: Conflict and Consensus in Policymaking*. Sydney, London and Boston, George Allen and Unwin, 1985. Gary D. Allinson and Yasunori Sone (eds), *Political Dynamics in Contemporary Japan*. Ithaca and London, Cornell University Press, 1993, pp. 105–54.

21   The one political party staying consistently outside any such coalition or process of incorporation in the 1980s and 1990s was the Japan Communist Party (JCP). Interestingly enough it increased its lower house representation at the general elections of October 1996 from 15 to 26 seats and its percentage of the total vote from 7.7 to 12.6 per cent (13.1 per cent in the proportional representation constituencies), no doubt owing to the fact that it was perceived as the only party prepared to take on a genuinely oppositional or 'outsider' role.

22   For advocacy somewhat along these lines by a Japanese politician who is perhaps the most high profile of the 1990s reformers, see Ichiro Ozawa, *Blueprint for a New Japan: the Rethinking of a Nation*. Tokyo, New York and London, Kodansha International, 1994.

23   Francis Fukuyama, *The End of History and the Last Man*. London, Hamish Hamilton, 1992.

24   David Williams, *Japan: Beyond the End of History*. London and New York, Routledge, 1994.

Chapter 2

1 The same may well apply in the case of analysts from non-Western countries, including those elsewhere in Asia, even though the actual assumptions made may be radically different from Western ones. For instance, contemporary Chinese assumptions about the politics of Japan incline to emphasize the danger of a resurgent Japanese militarism for reasons that plainly reflect Chinese – not Western – historical experience in relation to Japan.

2 In Japan this includes, at a popular level, television *samurai* dramas and historical episodes portrayed in widely read *manga* (cartoon story) magazines and books.

3 The political interpretation of Japanese behaviour during the Second World War in Asia by some Japanese leaders has led from time to time to serious international controversy between the Japanese government and the governments of the People's Republic of China (PRC) and the Republic of Korea (ROK).

4 William Coaldrake, *Architecture and Authority in Japan*. London, Routledge, 1996, p. 12.

5 W. G. Beasley, *The Meiji Restoration*. Stanford, CA, Stanford University Press, 1972, pp. 38–9.

6 I. J. McMullen, 'Rulers or Fathers? A Casuistical Problem in Early Modern Japanese Thought', *Past and Present*, no. 16 (August 1987), pp. 56–97.

7 Charles Boxer, *The Christian Century in Japan, 1549–1650*. Berkeley and Los Angeles, University of California Press, 1967.

8 Ronald Dore, *British Factory, Japanese Factory*. London, George Allen and Unwin, 1973.

9 Inoguchi, following Brown and Kasaya, argues that the feudal lords Oda Nobunaga and his successor Toyotomi Hideyoshi, in the late sixteenth century, both aimed in vain to create an absolutist state, and though Hideyoshi finally succeeded in unifying the country, he did so only by entering into extensive compromises with other centres of power. The ultimate founder of the Tokugawa peace, Tokugawa Ieyasu, was relatively weak in terms of his own political power, but through his shrewdness was able to establish a political system that lasted two and a half centuries. Inoguchi Takashi, 'The Programmatic Development of Japanese Democratic Politics', in Michèle Schmiegelow (ed.), *Democracy in Asia*, Frankfurt, Campus-Verlag, 1997. Philip Brown, *Central Authority and Local Autonomy in Early Modern Japan*. Stanford, Stanford University Press, 1993. Kasaya Kazuhiko, *Shi no shisō* (The Idea of being a Warrior), Nihon Shuppan, 1993.

10 The main exception to this was the Dutch trading post at Deshima, an island in Nagasaki harbour. Some contact was also maintained with China, and a little with Korea. Through these 'windows on the world' some external developments became known to well-placed intellectuals. For instance the invention of smallpox vaccine was known about in Japan by the 1840s.

11 For instance the *sankin kōtai* system required that feudal lords should travel to Edo every other year with their retinue, and in the intervening years should leave close relatives in Edo as hostages to their good behaviour.

12 Below the merchants, however, were to be found various categories of 'outcast' or 'non-people' (*hinin*), who are basically the ancestors of the low status category known in contemporary Japan as *burakumin* ('village people').

13 Ronald Dore, *Education in Tokugawa Japan*. London, Routledge and Kegan Paul, 1965 (London, Athlone, 1984).

14 Inoguchi, in Schmiegelow, ibid.

15 For a readable account of the events leading up to the Meiji Restoration, see W. G. Beasley, *The Rise of Modern Japan*, London, Weidenfeld and Nicolson, 1990

(revised version of *The Modern History of Japan*. London, Weidenfeld and Nicolson, 1963 and later editions). See also Marius B. Jansen, 'The Meiji Restoration', in Marius B. Jansen (ed.), *The Cambridge History of Japan*, vol. 5, 'The Nineteenth Century'. Cambridge, Cambridge University Press, 1989, pp. 308–66.

16 See Jansen, ibid., pp. 313–14.

17 With the overthrow of the *bakufu*, the Emperor's court was moved from Kyoto to Edo (where the *shōgun* had previously resided) and the name Edo was changed to Tokyo or 'Eastern Capital'.

18 It may be noted that two post-war prime ministers, Kishi Nobusuke and Satō Eisaku, (who despite having different surnames, were brothers) came from Yamaguchi prefecture, the area of the former Chōshu *han*.

19 Stephen Vlastos, 'Opposition Movements in Early Meiji, 1868–1885', in Jansen (ed.), ibid., pp. 367–431.

20 George Akita, *Foundations of Constitutional Government in Modern Japan, 1868–1900*. Cambridge, MA, Harvard University Press, 1967.

21 Article 38: 'Both Houses shall vote upon projects of law submitted to it by the Government, and may respectively initiate projects of law.'

22 Article 39: 'A Bill, which has been rejected by either the one or the other of the two Houses, shall not be again brought in during the same session.'

23 It is possible to find occasions where a *tennō* took some kind of personal initiative, and controversy continues about how far the Shōwa *tennō* (Hirohito) influenced political decisions between 1926 and 1945. For a definitive and up-to-date account of this controversy, see Stephen Large, *Emperor Hirohito and Shōwa Japan*. London, Routledge, 1992.

24 Ito Hirobumi, *Commentaries on the Constitution of the Empire of Japan*. Translated by Ito Miyoji. 2nd edn, Tokyo, 1906.

25 Akita, ibid., pp. 76–89.

26 Banno Junji, *Meiji kenpō taisei no kakuritsu* (The Establishment of the Meiji Constitutional System). Tokyo, Tokyo University Press, 1971. Translated into English (J. A. A. Stockwin translator) as *The Establishment of the Japanese Constitutional System*. London, Routledge, 1992.

27 For a detailed examination of the ambiguities inherent in the Meiji Constitution, and the political consequences of these, see Taichiro Mitani (Peter Duus translator), 'The Establishment of Party Cabinets, 1898–1932', in Peter Duus (ed.), *The Cambridge History of Japan*, vol. 6, 'The Twentieth Century'. Cambridge, Cambridge University Press, 1988, pp. 55–96.

28 John K. Fairbank, Edwin O. Reischauer and Albert M. Craig, *East Asia, The Modern Transformation*. Cambridge, MA, Harvard University Press, 1965, pp. 554–63.

29 Roger F. Hackett, 'Political Modernisation and the Meiji Genro', in Robert E. Ward (ed.), *Political Development in Modern Japan*. Princeton, NJ, Princeton University Press, 1968, pp. 65–97.

30 Mitani, ibid., pp. 76–96.

31 Sadako N. Ogata, *Defiance in Manchuria: the Making of Japanese Foreign Policy, 1931–1932*. Berkeley and Los Angeles, University of California Press, 1964.

32 Richard Storry, *The Double Patriots*. London, Chatto and Windus, 1957.

33 Indeed, fanatical loyalty to the emperor sometimes went along with advocacy of his replacement by somebody more favourable to the national chauvinist cause. Large identifies this threat as a factor which inhibited the Shōwa Emperor from taking a more active line against extremism. Large, ibid., pp. 56–75.

34 Gordon M. Berger, *Parties out of Power in Japan 1931–1941*. Princeton, NJ, Princeton University Press, 1977.

35 See Ben-Ami Shillony, *Politics and Culture in Wartime Japan*. Oxford, Clarendon Press, 1981.
36 Gary D. Allinson, *Japanese Urbanism: Industry and Politics in Kariya, 1872–1972*. Berkeley, Los Angeles and London, University of California Press, 1975.

Chapter 3

1 Some details have been changed, to preserve confidentiality.
2 J. A. A. Stockwin, *The Japanese Socialist Party and Neutralism*. Melbourne, Melbourne University Press, 1968, p. 75.
3 The compromise did not last. After four years the party split once again.
4 For a negative view by an overworked participant, see Satoshi Kamata, (with introduction by Ronald Dore), *Japan in the Passing Lane: an Insider's Account of Life in a Japanese Auto Factory*. Boston, London and Sydney, George Allen and Unwin, 1983.
5 See chapter 8.
6 Emiko Ohnuki-Tierney, *Illness and Culture in Contemporary Japan: an Anthropological View*. Cambridge, Cambridge University Press, 1984, pp. 39–46. Joy Hendry, *Understanding Japanese Society*. London, Routledge, 2nd edn, 1995, pp. 43–5.
7 For instance, 'do you see it?' turns into *sore, miru no* (to a child); *sore wa, mimasu ka* (to a friend); *sore wa, goran ni narimasu ka* (to a hierarchical superior, or being super-polite for whatever reason). We should note English is not wholly free from such distinctions. For instance, 'got it?' (to a child); 'do you understand?' (to a friend); 'has your Grace taken the point?' (to an archbishop). In both languages, in principle, the more polite an expression, the longer it is.
8 Ruth Benedict was the first to emphasize the importance of mutual obligation, in *The Chrysanthemum and the Sword*. Boston, Houghton Mifflin, 1946.
9 See 'vignette 10' above. The pre-scripted debate in the prefectural assembly avoided the kind of unpredictability that might expose individuals to public criticism.
10 In such cases of adult adoption, the bridegroom would take the surname of the *ie* into which he was marrying. This practice is much less common today than it was before the war and in the early post-war period, when the problem of keeping intact an agricultural inheritance was widespread.
11 Chie Nakane, *Kinship and Economic Organisation in Rural Japan*, London School of Economics Monograph on Social Anthropology, No. 32. London, Athlone Press, 1967, p. 172. See also her widely read book *Japanese Society*. London, Weidenfeld and Nicolson, 1970.
12 Nakane, *Kinship*, ibid., p. 21.
13 For instance Yoshio Sugimoto, 'The Manipulative Bases of "consensus" in Japan', in Gavan McCormack and Yoshio Sugimoto (eds), *Democracy in Contemporary Japan*. Sydney, Hale and Iremonger, 1986, pp. 65–89.
14 See chapter 9.
15 See chapter 9.
16 Takeo Doi, *The Anatomy of Dependence*. Tokyo, Kodansha International, 1973, 1981.
17 Kazuko Tsurumi, *Social Change and the Individual: Japan Before and After Defeat in World War II*. Princeton, NJ, Princeton University Press, 1970, pp. 91–2. This usage is derived from the work of Maruyama Masao.
18 *Kojinshugi*, which is the direct translation of 'individualism', normally has a pejorative connotation in Japan, suggesting selfishness. There is another word,

however, *kosei*, connoting 'individuality of character' which is regarded far more positively.

19 Defining corruption is always difficult. The most widely used definition in Japan assumes that corrupt activity must contravene the law.

20 Chalmers Johnson, 'Tanaka Kakuei, Structural Corruption, and the Advent of Machine Politics in Japan', *Journal of Japanese Studies*, vol. 12, no. 1 (winter 1986), pp. 1–28.

21 See especially chapter 6.

22 An early exponent of a connection between collectivism and achievement in the Japanese case was Ezra Vogel. See Ezra F. Vogel, *Japan's New Middle Class: The Salary Man and his Family in a Tokyo Suburb*. Berkeley and Los Angeles, University of California Press, 1963.

23 See for instance the Imperial Rescript on Education, which was read out regularly, and reverentially, in schools after it was issued in 1890. Text in Arthur Tiedemann, *Modern Japan: a Brief History*. New York, D. Van Nostrand, 1962, pp. 113–14.

24 John W. Bennett and Iwao Ishino, *Paternalism in the Japanese Economy: Anthropological Studies of Oyabun-Kobun Patterns*. Minneapolis, University of Minnesota Press, 1963.

25 See chapter 9.

26 The classic study on *zaibatsu* and the Occupation's attempt to break them up is: Eleanor M. Hadley, *Antitrust in Japan*. Princeton, NJ, Princeton University Press, 1970.

27 Murakami Yasusuke, 'The Age of New Middle Mass Politics: The Case of Japan', *Journal of Japanese Studies*, vol. 8, no. 1, (winter 1982), pp. 29–72. See also the controversy which the article aroused, as recorded in later issues of the same journal.

28 See for instance Rob Steven, *Classes in Contemporary Japan*. Cambridge, Cambridge University Press, 1983.

29 Ross Mouer and Yoshio Sugimoto, *Images of Japanese Society: A Study in the Structure of Social Reality*. London, New York, Sydney and Henley, KPI, 1986. Peter Dale, *The Myth of Japanese Uniqueness*. London, Routledge, 1986 (and later editions). See also Kosaku Yoshino, *Cultural Nationalism in Contemporary Japan*. London, Routledge, 1992.

30 Dale was able to point out fascinating linkages between some of the *nihonjinron* literature and certain pre-war German writers. Dale, ibid., pp. 77–99, and passim.

31 Mouer and Sugimoto, ibid., pp. 64–83.

32 Chalmers Johnson, *MITI and the Japanese Miracle*. Stanford, CA, Stanford University Press, 1982.

33 Karel van Wolferen, *The Enigma of Japanese Power*. London, Macmillan, 1989.

34 For a critical review of the van Wolferen book by the present author, which generated a subsequent correspondence, see *Times Literary Supplement*, 28 April–4 May, 12–18 May, 19–25 May, 26 May–1 June and 2–8 June 1989.

35 David Williams, *Japan: Beyond the End of History*. London and New York, Routledge, 1994. David Williams, *Japan and the Enemies of Open Political Science*. London and New York, Routledge, 1996.

Chapter 4

1 The appalling destruction of Hiroshima and Nagasaki is rightly the subject of international concern, but it should not be forgotten that in the fire raids on Tokyo conducted by the US airforce in May 1945, more people died (excluding subsequent deaths from radiation sickness) than in the atomic bombing of Hiroshima.

2   For instance Herman Kahn, *The Emerging Japanese Superstate*. Harmondsworth, Penguin, 1970.

3   MacArthur is alleged to have said on a public occasion: 'The Occupation of Japan is an unprecedented revolution in the social history of the world.'

4   The other was demilitarization. One aspect of this, demobilization of the armed forces, was achieved with remarkable speed. Another was an attempt to reduce the likelihood of Japan rearming by introducing a 'no-war' clause into the Constitution. See especially chapter 10.

5   In practice, the way executive power is exerted by the Japanese Cabinet differs from the case of the British Cabinet in the sense that Japanese Government ministries have a greater degree of independence in the exercise of their functions than do departments of the British Government. See chapter 7.

6   'National Parliament' is preferred to the common translation 'National Diet', which has an old-fashioned ring.

7   A *kami* (god) in Shinto had a status much closer to that of a man than is the case of the God–man distinction in Christianity.

8   The most authoritative source of Occupation policy up to 1948 commented: '[t]he Emperor is now no more than the crowning pinnacle of the structure, bearing no functional relation to the frame itself.' Supreme Commander for the Allied Powers, *Political Reorientation of Japan, September 1945 to September 1948*, 2 vols., Westport, CT, Greenwood Press, 1970 (reprint of original, published by US Government Printing Office, 1949), vol. 1, p. 114. For popular attitudes to the *tennō*, see Watanabe Osamu, *Nihonkoku kenpō 'kaisei' shi* (A History of 'Revising' the Japanese Constitution), Tokyo, Nihon Hyōronsha, 1987. Stephen Large, *Emperor Hirohito and Shōwa Japan*. London and New York, Routledge, 1992. David A. Titus, *Palace and Politics in Prewar Japan*. New York, Columbia University Press, 1974.

9   The *tennō* does not even enjoy the power attributed by some authorities to the British monarch, of choosing the prime minister in circumstances where there is no clear party majority in Parliament. In the Japanese case, Parliament votes on who shall become prime minister.

10   The term generally used for the occupying authority.

11   See chapters 6 and 8.

12   See chapters 10 and 12.

13   This was interpreted to mean 'civilians at the present time', and therefore not excluding those who had served in the armed forces during or before the war.

14   Unions in the pre-war period had frequently been subjected to police harassment and surveillance, as well as closure by the authorities. Solomon B. Levine, *Industrial Relations in Postwar Japan*. Urbana, University of Illinois Press, 1958. Stephen S. Large, *Organized Workers and Socialist Politics in Interwar Japan*. Cambridge, Cambridge University Press, 1981.

15   Hans H. Baerwald, *The Purge of Japanese Leaders under the Occupation*. Berkeley, University of California Press, 1959.

16   Thomas A. Bisson, *Zaibatsu Dissolution in Japan*. Berkeley, University of California Press, 1954; Eleanor M. Hadley, *Antitrust in Japan*. Princeton, NJ, Princeton University Press, 1970. Michael Beeman, 'Public Policy and Economic Competition in Japan: The Rise of Antimonopoly Policy, 1973–1995'. D.Phil. Thesis, University of Oxford, 1997.

17   The ceiling in Hokkaidō was 12 *chō*.

18   The classic work on the land reform is R. P. Dore, *Land Reform in Japan*. London, Oxford University Press, 1959.

19   Kurt Steiner, *Local Government in Japan*. Stanford, NJ, Stanford University Press, 1965.

20   For instance Herbert Passin, *The Legacy of the Occupation of Japan* (Occasional Papers of the East Asian Institute, Columbia University), New York, Columbia University Press, 1968.

21   A further related reform, which has remained something of a curiosity, was the provision for periodic popular referenda on the suitability of Supreme Court judges. The referenda coincide with general elections. In practice they have always resulted in heavy votes of approval for the Supreme Court judges.

22   The Occupation did not help its own cause by changing its policies in mid-stream. This aspect will be discussed on pp. 47–8.

23   The Meiji period slogan *fukoku kyōhei* was achieved at least in terms of its first element, the creation of a 'prosperous country'.

24   Passin, ibid., p. 27.

25   See chapter 11.

26   SCAP's *The Political Reorientation of Japan*, ibid., glosses over the differences between the two systems. See the following comment: 'The device of parliamentary responsibility procures the answerability of the executive branch of government to the people through their duly elected representatives. In the United States this responsibility is enforced through direct election of the President and Vice President. In England and the European democracies, the pattern is similar to that of Japan. In either case, the result is the same. The executive branch of government has no legal authority, excuse or justification for acting in defiance of the mandate of the people. Every public officer, every public employee is the agent and servant of the people' (pp. 115–16).

27   Some Occupation officials do not seem entirely to have appreciated the implications of the reforms they were introducing. Thus some of them seem to have expected Parliament to act more independently of Cabinet than a familiarity with British or British Commonwealth patterns would have led them to expect. They thought, for instance, that Parliament and not Cabinet would have the final say on when Parliament would be dissolved, whereas practice (and an ambiguity in the Constitution) dictated the opposite. D. C. S. Sissons, 'Dissolution of the Japanese Lower House', in D. C. S. Sissons (ed.), *Papers on Modern Japan 1968*. Canberra, Australian National University, 1968, pp. 91–137.

28   See for instance Richard J. Samuels, *The Business of the Japanese State; Energy Markets in Comparative and Historical Perspective*. Ithaca and London, Cornell University Press, 1987.

29   Sheldon Garon, *The State and Labor in Modern Japan*. Berkeley, Los Angeles and London, University of California Press, 1987.

30   William M. Tsutsui, *Banking Policy in Japan; American Efforts at Reform During the Occupation*. London and New York, Routledge, 1988.

31   The Prime Minister was Prince Higashikuni Naruhiko, a general and cousin of the Emperor.

32   J. W. Dower, *Empire and Aftermath: Yoshida Shigeru and the Japanese Experience, 1878–1954*. Cambridge, MA, and London, Harvard University Press, 1979 . Ōtake Hideo, *Adenauer to Yoshida Shigeru* (Adenauer and Yoshida Shigeru). Tokyo, Chūō Kōronsha, 1986.

33   About 15 per cent of conservative members of Parliament in the 1949 elections. Later, the percentage was to stabilize at about 25 per cent. See Haruhiro Fukui, *Party in Power: The Japanese Liberal-Democrats and Policy-Making*, Canberra, Australian National University Press, 1970, pp. 40–1.

34   See chapter 8.

35 Nishio Suehiro, a leading figure on the right wing of the JSP, was arrested on suspicion of breaking the law on campaign contributions.
36 The plan was drawn up by Joseph Dodge, a Detroit banker.
37 The Soviet Union, Poland, Czechoslovakia, India, Burma and Yugoslavia did not sign, though the last three signed peace treaties with Japan later. Neither the People's Republic of China nor the Republic of China (Taiwan) were invited to the peace conference, but Japan shortly afterwards signed a separate peace treaty with the latter.
38 Security Treaty between the United States and Japan, 8 September 1951, Preamble. The Peace Treaty also reaffirmed Japan's right of defence.
39 Kishi had been a member of General Tōjō's war cabinet, and was designated as a Class A war criminal by the Occupation, though later released. He was an intelligent an innovative politician, but the boldness of his approach, combined with his background, alienated much articulate opinion.
40 D. C. S. Sissons, 'The Dispute over Japan's Police Law', *Pacific Affairs*, vol. 31, no. 1 (March 1959), pp. 34–45.
41 For details of the revisions to the Security Treaty and the issues involved, see chapter 12. For a detailed investigation of the Security Treaty crisis, see George Packard III, *Protest in Tokyo: The Security Treaty Revision Crisis of 1960*. Princeton, NJ, Princeton University Press, 1966. For shorter discussions see Robert A. Scalapino and Junnosuke Masumi, *Parties and Politics in Contemporary Japan*. Berkeley and Los Angeles, University of California Press, 1962, pp. 125–53, and F. C. Langdon, *Japan's Foreign Policy*. Vancouver, University of British Columbia Press, 1973, pp. 7–21.
42 See chapter 10.
43 A US spy plane was shot down over the Soviet Union and the pilot detained.
44 This required action by the House of Representatives steering committee, and an affirmative vote in the plenary session, both opportunities for further Socialist obstruction.
45 A proposal to involve elements of the Self-Defence Forces was apparently vetoed by the Minister in charge of the Defence Agency, Akagi Munenori. Had the SDF been brought in, the crisis might have been much worse than it turned out to be.
46 The second vote was taken just after midnight, when the new session had just started, some 15 minutes after the old one had terminated.
47 One powerful faction leader, Kōno Ichirō, seems to have come close to pulling his faction out of the party. Interestingly, it was his son, Kōno Yōhei, who in 1976 led a defection from the LDP over the Lockheed scandal (see chapter 5).

Chapter 5

1 In June 1960 the Socialist leader Kawakami Jōtarō, and in July Kishi himself, were injured by stabbing, in both cases by ultra-rightist indivividuals. In October 1960 the JSP Chairman, Asanuma Inejirō, was assassinated in front of television cameras by a 17-year-old youth influenced by ultra-rightist groups. In February 1961, an ultra-rightist intending to kill the editor of *Chūō Kōron*, a leading intellectual journal, wounded the editor's wife and killed a maidservant. Later the same year an amateurish plot to assassinate the whole Cabinet was discovered in time.
2 For a perceptive analysis of the 'structural reform' movement and the reasons for its failure, see Stephen Johnson, 'Strategies for Realignment: Japanese Opposition Politics Under a One Party Dominant Regime 1955–1993', D.Phil. Thesis, University

of Oxford, 1995, pp. 38–89. Johnson argues that organizational, rather than ideological, factors were the more salient in explaining Opposition party failures in the period of LDP dominance.

3　In March 1959 the JSP Secretary-General, Asanuma Inejirō, remarked in Beijing that 'American imperialism is the common enemy of Japan and China'.

4　The DSP until it merged with other parties to form the *Shinshintō* in 1995 usually polled between 6 and 8 per cent of the vote and ranged between 17 and 35 seats.

5　The standard work on Sōka Gakkai in English is James W. White, *Sōkagakkai and Mass Society*, Stanford, Stanford University Press, 1970.

6　The difference in surname was occasioned by one having been adopted into another family.

7　Okinawa and the surrounding Ryūkyū (Loochoo in Chinese) islands, which had been semi-independent up to the Meiji period, then became a Japanese prefecture, and were the scene of one of the bloodiest battles of the Asia-Pacific war. With Japan's defeat, they came under American jurisdiction, though Japan was said to have 'residual sovereignty' over them. Their use as a key US base in pursuance of the Vietnam war, and in particular the presence of nuclear weapons there, became a major source of political conflict in Japan during the Vietnam war period. Reversion of a 'nuclear-free' Okinawa to Japan in 1972 marked a signal victory for Satō's diplomacy, though the islands remained a potential source of controversy after returning to Japan, and the issue duly flared up again in September 1995. See chapters 6 and 12.

8　In the 1970s and early 1980s the third of these principles, 'introduction' (*mochikomi*) became controversial when it became clear that nuclear weapons were coming into Japanese ports on board US naval vessels.

9　In the summer of 1995 the yen touched a value of around 80 yen to one US dollar.

10　Articles in the press outside Japan often repeat the statement that Tanaka resigned as a result of the Lockheed scandal (see below). This is wholly incorrect, since the Lockheed issue first came to light in February 1976, 15 months after his resignation.

11　Michael Beeman, 'Public Policy and Economic Competition in Japan: the Rise of Antimonopoly Policy, 1973–1995', D.Phil thesis, University of Oxford, 1997.

12　As the media entertained the public with ever more lurid details of Lockheed's alleged subversion of Japanese decision-makers all too willing to be subverted, the outlines of the story became well established. Lockheed, it was alleged, had used three main avenues for the channelling of money into Japan: the Marubeni Corporation, All Nippon Airways and an ultra-rightist activist called Kodama Yoshio. The unsavoury nature of Kodama's past record, and the allegation that his contacts with LDP politicians were sufficiently intimate to make him a worthwhile intermediary for Lockheed, added to the morbid fascination which the affair held for the Japanese public. It also drew public attention to the problem of *kōzō oshoku* (structural corruption) – the fact that the cost of running political campaigns was so great that politicians found it hard to avoid becoming tainted with corruption.

13　See table 9.8 for vote percentages at successive elections.

14　The allocation of committee memberships to parties is proportional to party representation in the House. This means that in a situation of near parity between Government and Opposition parties, the LDP would lose control of those committees to which it was required to provide the (non-voting) chairman.

15　The JCP, resurgent in the late 1960s and early 1970s, became the subject of an investigation of an alleged 1930s spy-lynching case, and began to lose support, while the Chairman of the *Kōmeitō* resigned in unexplained circumstances.

16　For instance Governor Minobe of Tokyo, the best known 'progressive governor', had initiated great improvements in the safety of pedestrians throughout the city.

17 Had the Opposition parties chosen to do so, they could have easily determined the choice of Prime Minister by voting for one or other LDP candidate, but instead they each voted for their own party leader.

18 Chief Cabinet Secretary in the Ōhira Government.

19 The Opposition parties taken together did not lose votes, but a 6.5 per cent increase in the turnout of electors over the 1979 House of Representatives elections was accompanied by an increase in votes for the LDP. For a fuller analysis of the 1980 crisis, see J. A. A. Stockwin, 'Japan's Political Crisis of 1980', *Australian Outlook*, vol. 35, no. 1 (April 1981), pp. 19–32.

20 This raises the interesting point that several 'outsiders' have become prime minister during the LDP's tenure of office.

21 The label of 'incompetent' attached itself to Suzuki in particular in the aftermath of his visit to the US in 1981, when on his return he disassociated himself with the phrase 'alliance relationship' (between Japan and the US) appearing in the joint communiqué issued during the visit. This led to the resignation of his Foreign Minister, Itō Masayoshi. In mitigation it may be argued that he was merely reiterating a standard (if legalistic) line of argument that the Japan–US security relationship did not as such constitute an alliance.

22 For a perceptive account of the *Rinchō*, see Daiichi Ito, 'Policy Implications of Administrative Reform', in J. A. A. Stockwin et al., *Dynamic and Immobilist Politics in Japan*. London, Macmillan, 1988, pp. 77–105.

23 For the argument that LDP governments have tended to buy themselves out of political trouble by compensating aggrieved groups, see Kent E. Calder, *Crisis and Compentasion: Public Policy and Political Stability in Japan, 1949–1986*. Princeton, NJ, Princeton University Press, 1988. The *Rinchō* may be regarded as a strategy to overcome the sorts of dilemma that such an approach inevitably creates.

24 Chalmers Johnson, 'Tanaka Kakuei, Structural Corruption, and the Advent of Machine Politics in Japan', *Journal of Japanese Studies*, vol. 12, no. 1 (Winter 1986), pp. 1–28. Hayashi Shigeru and Tsuji Kiyoaki (eds), *Nihon naikaku shi roku*. (6), Tokyo, Daiichi Shuppan, 1981, pp. 218–19.

25 For a eulogistic account of Tanaka, see Hayasaka Shigezō, *Tanaka Kakuei kaisōroku*. Tokyo, Shōgakkan, 1987. See *Asahi Shinbun* (*gogai*), 12 October 1983, for an extremely critical account of Tanaka. The *Asahi* may be said to have spearheaded the campaign against him in the media.

26 Mike Mochizuki, 'Public Sector Labor and Privatization', in Gary D. Allinson and Yasunori Sone, *Political Dynamics in Contemporary Japan*. Ithaca and London, Cornell University Press, 1993, pp. 181–99.

27 Mochizuki, ibid.

28 See chapter 12.

29 Aurelia George, 'Japan and the United States: Dependent Ally or Equal Partner?', in J. A. A. Stockwin et al., *Dynamic and Immobilist Politics in Japan*, ibid., pp. 237–96, at p. 237.

30 His first attempt to do this was thwarted by factions opposed to him in the LDP, but he succeeded on the second attempt, at the end of 1986.

31 Hiromitsu Ishi, *The Japanese Tax System*. Oxford, Clarendon Press, 1993, pp. 310–42.

32 Leonard Schoppa, *Education Reform in Japan; a Case of Immobilist Politics*. London and New York, Routledge, 1991. A recent study argues against Schoppa's conclusions, suggesting that the long-term effects of the *Rinkyōshin* were more radical than appeared initially to be the case. Christopher Hood, 'Nakasone; Understanding the Conflicts and his Involvement in Education Reform', Paper to Japan Politics Group Colloquium, University of Stirling, September 1996.

33   Whether double elections specifically favour the LDP is a matter of some controversy.
34   The Japanese market for rice was entirely closed to imports until the final stage of the Uruguay Round at the end of 1993.
35   See Nakasone Yasuhiro, *Seiji to jinsei; Nakasone Yasuhiro Kaikoroku* (Politics and Life; the Memoirs of Nakasone Yasuhiro). Tokyo, Kōdansha, 1992.
36   Ishi, ibid., pp. 322–4
37   In the prefectural constituencies the JSP won 26.4 per cent of the vote against 30.7 per cent for the LDP, but in the proportional representation constituency the percentages were 35.1 for the JSP against 27.3 for the LDP.
38   Almost all other constituencies in both houses, in the electoral arrangements then operating, elected more than one member, again by the first-past-the-post principle, except for the proportional representation (national) constituency of the House of Councillors. See chapter 8.

Chapter 6

1   Eric Hobsbawm, *The Age of Extremes: The Short Twentieth Century*. London, Michael Joseph, 1994.
2   Customs relating to the naming of Japanese emperors often cause confusion among non-Japanese. Even though the former *tennō* bore the name 'Hirohito' and the current *tennō* bears the name 'Akihito', these names are seldom used (or even known of) in Japan. The normal way of referring to a current *tennō* is *tennō heika* (roughly translatable as 'His Majesty the Emperor'), though *Kinjō heika* ('the current Emperor') may also be used. Attached to the reign of each *tennō* is an 'era name' (*gengo*), and the counting of years according to era name became official in 1978 following a referendum. Thus 1985 was 'Shōwa 60', since the previous *tennō* ascended the throne in 1926 and his reign was given the era name 'Shōwa' (Enlightened peace). And 1995 was 'Heisei 7', since the current *tennō* came to the throne in 1989 on the death of his father. Interestingly, the first week of 1989 was 'Shōwa 64' and the rest of the year was 'Heisei 1' (*Heisei gannen*), since the former *tennō* died on 7 January. It is said that in choosing a new era name, any name beginning with 'S' had to be avoided, because many computers coded 1985, for instance, as 'S60'.
3   Stephen Large, *Emperor Hirohito and Shōwa Japan; A Political Biography*. London and New York, Routledge, 1992.
4   For fascinating interpretations of what happened see Large, ibid., pp. 198–203; Watanabe Osamu, *Sengo seiji no naka no tennōsei* (The Emperor System in Post-War Politics), Tokyo, Aoki Shoten, 1992; David Williams, 'Reporting the Death of the Japanese Emperor', Nissan Institute Occasional Paper Series No. 14 (1990); Thomas Crump, *The Death of an Emperor: Japan at the Crossroads*, Oxford and New York, Oxford University Press, 1991; Norma Field, *In the Realm of the Dying Emperor*, New York, Pantheon Books, 1991.
5   Williams, ibid., pp. 15–16.
6   Muramatsu Michio, private conversation.
7   Following the 1989 House of Councillors elections 23 out of 232 upper house members were women.
8   *Asahi Shinbun*, 1 November 1990.
9   The former Prime Minister, Nakasone, netted 74 and the former professional wrestler-turned-politician, Antonio Inoki, bagged 39.
10   Another objection proved less serious for the Government. Opposition speakers objected on constitutional grounds to the possibility that the $9 billion would be

used to buy armaments for the Multinational Force. President Bush obligingly came to the rescue by giving an opinion that the funds would not be used for this purpose.

11 The practice whereby a ruling party or group, frustrated by the obstruction of opposition parties, seeks to 'subvert' or 'incorporate' them through negotiations in which they are offered both policy benefits and some part in the ruling order, has a long history in Japan. An early example was the formation by the *genro* Itō Hirobumi of the *Seiyūkai* party, incorporating previously obstructive 'popular party' elements, in 1900. Another more recent example is the formation at the end of the 1980s of the *Rengō* labour union federation. A most important aspect of the process leading to its formation was the continuing efforts of management and government to wean the more radical elements in the union movement away from confrontational unionism on to a unionism that would be essentially co-operative with management.

12 After the Gulf War was over, the Government of Kuwait publicly thanked the states that had contributed to the military operation that had successfully ended the Iraqi occupation of Kuwait. Japan was pointedly omitted from the list of states that were thanked.

13 A reformist group of members of the House of Representatives first elected in February 1990, known as the New Wave Society, became seriously disillusioned with the Doi leadership, which they came to see as ignoring the need for much overdue reforms of party structure and policies. See J. A. A. Stockwin, 'From JSP to SDPJ: The New Wave Society and the "New" *Nihon Shakaitō*', *Japan Forum*, vol. 3, no. 2 (October 1991), pp. 287–300.

14 One is reminded of the 1850s and 1860s, when the Shogunate accorded an advisory role to certain *Daimyō* (*han* lords), only to find its own authority eroded by this decision to consult.

15 *Asahi Nenkan*, 1993, p. 205.

16 This did not, however, restore the LDP majority because the JSP still retained the large number of seats won in the previous upper house elections in 1989.

17 Takeshita had been embarrassed by the activities of an ultra-right-wing mini-party, the *Kōmintō* (Emperor People Party), which was publicly singing his praises – a practice known as *homegoroshi* ('killing by praising'). In November 1992 Kanemaru (who was related to Takeshita through the marriage of their children) admitted to having contacted the head of the Inagawakai, a gangster organization, to ask his good offices in order to have the *Kōmintō* call off its campaign.

18 The name has nothing to do with the religion *Shintō*, which is written with quite different characters meaning 'way of the gods'.

19 *Asahi Nenkan*, 1994, p. 108.

20 The LDP actually increased by one seat the total it held immediately prior to the election, lending credence to the view that it was the split in its ranks which brought about its downfall, rather than its desertion by the electorate. Given the strength of local political machines, many voters seem to have continued to vote for the same candidates, whether they had remained within the LDP, or had affiliated with the *Sakigake* or *Shinseitō*.

21 *Shinseitō* members obtained the posts of Foreign Minister, Finance Minister, Minister of Agriculture, Forestry and Fisheries, Minister of International Trade and Industry, and Defence Agency Director. *Asahi Shinbun*, 10 August 1993.

22 *Asahi Shinbun*, 8 September 1993. Hosokawa's support had fallen to 60 per cent by December, but this was still close to a record high level for a prime minister. *Asahi Shinbun*, 22 December 1993.

23 Ichiro Ozawa, *Blueprint for a New Japan*. Tokyo, New York and London, Kodansha International, 1994.

24　In a foretaste of what was to happen later in the upper house, five JSP members voted against and one abstained, but this was neutralized by the 13 LDP votes in favour and seven LDP abstentions.

25　Ironically, by helping to defeat the earlier bill in the upper house, the Socialist defectors had ensured that an even less favourable bill – from their perspective – went on to the statute books.

26　Interview, 27 September 1995.

27　Corruption allegations from a much earlier period were cited in explanation, but the full story is not clear.

28　This episode added further gloss to Ozawa's reputation for hatching bold political stratagems which led to unwanted consequences. His disastrous attempt to manipulate the Tokyo city governorship election in 1991 has already been mentioned.

29　The reverse process may be observed following the general elections of October 1996 and in the early months of 1997, when opposition parties were having difficulty stopping their members defecting to a revived LDP, and indeed some of the smaller opposition parties were tempted to move right into the LDP's orbit. See *Asahi Shinbun*, 8 February 1997.

30　For instance, the former Prime Minister, Takeshita Noboru, is quoted as saying: 'We have swallowed the Socialists and we have them in our stomach. All that remains is for the gastric juices to digest them.' *Tokyo Insideline*, no. 30, 30 July 1994, p. 1.

31　In the new Cabinet, the LDP had 13 positions, the JSP five and the *Sakigake* two. This more or less reflected the balance of strength between the three parties.

32　There were also similarities between the JSP and *Sakigake* in respect of their basic policy attitudes at this juncture, even though a plan to unite the two parties into a single organization was later to prove elusive.

33　For instance a bill to assist surviving victims of the atomic bombings of Hiroshima and Nagasaki became law in December 1994, reflecting elements of the JSP agenda.

34　The flag and anthem issues were controversial because of the association of both with pre-1945 nationalism and the Emperor system, as well as being symbolic of attempts by the Ministry of Education allied with right wing LDP parliamentarians to suppress 'progressive' tendencies in education. The *kimi* in *Kimigayo* is commonly understood to refer to the *tennō*, and the anthem as a whole to involve an invocation of the Emperor.

35　An accurate English translation would be 'New Progress Party', but 'New Frontier Party' was chosen after President Kennedy's New Frontier. For several months before its launch the embryo party was known as the 'New, New Party'. In Japanese this was also *Shinshintō*, since it happens that the character for 'new' and the character for 'progress' are both pronounced *shin* though they are written differently.

36　Before merging into the *Shinshintō*, the *Kōmeitō* decided to split its organization, so that its local branches and some of its upper house members would remain independent, while lower house parliamentarians would enter the new party. This decision reflected the complex relationship existing between the *Kōmeitō* and the *Sōka Gakkai* religion.

37　Speech by Kubo Wataru, *Asahi Shinbun*, 23 October 1994.

38　*Hanshin* means 'Osaka-Kobe', using alternative pronunciations of the *saka* of Osaka and the *Kō* of Kōbe

39　For a critical account in Engilsh, see Gavan McCormack, *The Emptiness of Japanese Affluence*. Armonk, NY and London, M. E. Sharpe, 1996. McCormack uses the Kōbe earthquake as a metaphor for what is wrong with Japanese government.

40　*Aum* is a Tibetan word having mystical significance. The Japanese pronunciation is *ōmu*.

41 The *Aum* headquarters at Kamikuishiki village on the slopes of Mount Fuji was found to contain sophisticated chemical plant, at which it was alleged that the sarin gas was manufactured.

42 *Asahi Shinbun*, 1 February 1997.

43 The *Shinshintō* received nearly one and a half million more votes than the LDP.

44 For instance, in April 1995 Aoshima Yukio was elected Governor of Tokyo and Yokoyama Knock was elected Governor of Osaka, defeating the well-financed candidates of the main political parties. Both were independent members of the upper house but were known to the public as television comedians.

45 It seems that Ozawa's links with the *Kōmeitō*, which went back at least to the Tokyo governorship election campaign of 1991, were forged in the full understanding of the electoral potential that lay in this factor.

46 The text of the June resolution is given in *Asahi Shinbun*, 10 June 1995. The text of the Prime Minister's 15 August speech is given in *Asahi Shinbun*, 15 August 1995 (evening edition).

47 *Asahi Shinbun*, 9 September 1997.

48 See chapter 9 for details of the parties formed after the collapse of the *Shinshintō*.

49 For a pessimistic account of the prospects for the Japanese economy as it approaches the millennium, see David Asher and Andrew Smithers, 'Japan's Key Challenges for the 21st Century: Debt, Deflation, Default, Demography and Deregulation', *SAIS Policy Forum Series*, Washington DC, Johns Hopkins University, March 1998.

50 Ibid. pp. 30–6.

Chapter 7

1 Francis Fukuyama, 'The End of History', *The National Interest*, summer 1989, pp. 3–18.

2 This is different from van Wolferen's use of the term 'system' (a word deliberately avoided here) in relation to the Japanese political structure and process. Our usage presupposes evolution and a considerable degree of open-endedness, whereas van Wolferen seems to import into 'system' a strong element of closure. Karel van Wolferen, *The Enigma of Japanese Power*. London, Macmillan, 1989.

3 The maximum term for the House of Representatives is four years, but only one government since the war, that of Miki in 1976, has gone to full term.

4 A very minor exception is the period from 1983 to 1986, when the LDP was in coalition with the tiny New Liberal Club. But strictly speaking the LDP did not need a coalition partner at that time, since it had a small parliamentary majority in its own right. The immediate purpose of the coalition was to enable the LDP to control all lower house committees, but the underlying purpose was to attract the NLC defectors back into the LDP, which duly took place in 1986.

5 A rare example of this is the defeat of the Ōhira Government in a no-confidence motion in May 1980. In June 1994 the minority Hata Government anticipated defeat in a no-confidence motion by resigning.

6 Haruhiro Fukui, *Party in Power: The Liberal Democratic Party Policy Making*. Canberra, Australian National University Press, 1970, pp. 224 and 272–3.

7 Between Attlee in 1945 and Blair in 1998 Britain had 11 prime ministers. Over the same period, between Shidehara and Obuchi, Japan had 25!

8 The *Jimu jikan kaigi* (Conference of Administrative Vice-Ministers) normally takes decisions for confirmation by cabinet, leaving only those on which it cannot agree to be hammered out in cabinet. The *jimu jikan* are the permanent heads of ministries, and thus government officials, not politicians.

9   There were of course *habatsu* in other parties as well, but, during the period of LDP dominance, LDP *habatsu* had certain unique characteristics. See chapter 9.

10   For a more detailed treatment, see chapter 8.

11   At certain times, notably when Kishi and Nakasone were prime minister, significant inroads were made into structures and practices derived from the Occupation, but their success was limited.

12   Inoguchi Takashi, *Gendai Nihon seiji keizai no kōzu*. Tōyō Keizai Shinpōsha, 1983, pp. 3–29.

13   *Asahi Shinbun*, 22 January 1997.

14   For instance, in February 1997, a former official of the Ministry of Transport was accused of having taken kickbacks from a businessman in exchange for allotting him a contract relating to the servicing of the newly built Kansai International Airport. *Asahi Shinbun*, 28 February 1997.

15   This is one aspect of the broader practice whereby political and business deals are cemented in private rooms at expensive restaurants.

16   *Asahi Shinbun*, 16 April 1997.

17   For details, see J. A. A. Stockwin et al., *Dynamic and Immobilist Politics in Japan*. London, Macmillan, 1988, table on p. 41.

18   A famous example is the YKK group, consisting of Yamazaki Taku, Katō Kōichi and Koizumi Junichirō. The three members of this group all occupied prominent positions in the Hashimoto Cabinet in the first half of 1997.

19   *Bōeichō setchi hō* (Law no. 164 of 9 June 1954, as amended), article 62.

20   This was noted as long ago as the late 1960s. See Okabe Shirō, *Gyōsei kanri* (Administrative Control). Tokyo, Yūhikaku, 1967, pp. 100–1.

21   Chalmers Johnson, *MITI and the Japanese Miracle; The Growth of Industrial Policy, 1925–1975*. Stanford, CA, Stanford University Press, 1982.

22   James Abegglen (ed.) and the Boston Consulting Group, *Business Strategies for Japan*. Tokyo, Sophia University in cooperation with TBS Britannica Co. Ltd, 1970.

23   Daniel I. Okimoto, *Between MITI and the Market*. Stanford, CA, Stanford University Press, 1989, pp. 3–8 and passim.

24   Scott Callon, *Divided Sun: MITI and the Breakdown of Japanese High-Tech Industrial Policy, 1975–1993*. Stanford, CA, Stanford University Press, 1995, p. 204ff.

25   George C. Eads and Kozo Yamamura, 'The Future of Industrial Policy', in Kozo Yamamura and Yasukichi Yasuba (eds), *The Political Economy of Japan: Volume 1, The Domestic Transformation*. Stanford, CA, Stanford University Press, 1987.

26   Brian Woodall, *Japan under Construction: Corruption, Politics and Public Works*. Berkeley, Los Angeles and Oxford, University of California Press, 1996.

27   Bradley Richardson, *Japanese Democracy: Power, Coordination and Performance*. New Haven and London, Yale University Press, 1997, chapter 9.

28   Principally the *Kokka kōmuin hō* (National Public Service Law): Law No. 120 of 21 October 1947.

29   I am grateful to Professor Yabuno Yūzō for this example.

30   For a post-war expression of this view, see Tsuji Kiyoaki, *Kanryō kikō no onson to kyōka* (The Preservation and Strengthening of Bureaucratic Organs), in Oka Yoshitake (ed.), *Gendai Nihon no seiji katei* (The Political Process of Modern Japan). Iwanami, 1958, pp. 109–25.

31   The term *amakudari* is confined to the phenomenon of civil servants moving on retirement to the boards of companies or other organizations, and is not used in relation to their becoming parliamentarians.

32   *Japan Times*, 29 March 1997.

33   The six *jimu jikan* (Administrative Vice-Ministers), who retired from the MOF between 1988 and 1993, subsequently assumed the top positions in, respectively,

the Japan Development Bank, The Overseas Economic Co-operation Fund, the Yokohama Bank, the Fair Trade Commission, the Japan Export–Import Bank and the People's Finance Corporation. Tsutsumi Kazuma, with an afterword by Yamaguchi Jirō, *Kanryō amakudari hakusho* (White Paper on the Descent from Heaven of Bureaucrats). Tokyo, Iwanami Booklet No. 425, 1996, p. i. This source is a mine of fascinating information about *amakudari*.

34 J. Mark Ramseyer and Frances McCall Rosenbluth, *Japan's Political Marketplace*. Cambridge, MA, and London, 1993, pp. 115–19.

35 This involves a variety of informal (not legally sanctioned but not necessarily illegal) techniques whereby public officials put pressure on companies and other organizations to follow policies desired by their ministries.

36 Even though the most widely quoted examples of nonsensical regulations, citing the special properties of Japanese snow, or the unusual length of Japanese intestines (to exclude certain imports of skis and medicines respectively), may well be apocryphal or exaggerated, the following example, cited by Mark Tilton, has the ring of authenticity about it. A Japanese company which set up an indoor ski run was required by the Ministry of Transport to install a wind gauge, because regulations said that all ski runs had to be fitted with a wind gauge. Mark Tilton, 'Regulatory Reform, Market Opening, and Japan's Security', Paper given at the Institute of Social Science, University of Tokyo, 28 February 1997, p. 3.

37 Kent E. Calder, *Strategic Capitalism: Private Business and Public Purpose in Japanese Industrial Finance*. Princeton, NJ, Princeton University Press, p. 69. See also p. 15 and p. 271.

38 J. A. A. Stockwin et al., *Dynamic and Immobilist Politics in Japan*. Ibid.

39 Edward J. Lincoln, *Japan's Unequal Trade*. Washington, D.C., Brookings Institution, 1990, p. 2. See also Keizai Koho Center, *Japan [various years]: An International Comparison*. Tokyo, Keizai Koho Center [various years].

Chapter 8

1 *Nihonkoku kenpō* (The Constitution of Japan), article 42. Henceforth 'Constitution'.

2 Constitution, article 43. See also article 44.

3 Constitution, article 45.

4 Constitution, article 46.

5 Constitution, article 48.

6 See Kuroda Satoru, *Kokkaihō* (The Parliamentary Law). Hōritsu Gakkai Zenshū (Collected Works of the Legal Academy), no. 5. Yūhikaku, 1968. Asano Ichirō (ed.), *Kokkai jiten: yōgo ni yoru kokkaihō kaisetsu* (Parliamentary Dictionary; Guide to Parliamentary Law through Terminology). Yūhikaku, 3rd edn, 1997.

7 Constitution, article 55.

8 Constitution, article 57.

9 Constitution, article 58.

10 Constitution, article 58.

11 Constitution, article 16. This article gives a general right of petition, without actually specifying Parliament as its receiver.

12 Constitution, article 62.

13 Constitution, article 50. On 4 April 1997 the House of Councillors unprecedentedly voted by an overwhelming majority to strip Tomobe Tatsuo, accused of fraud in relation to a pensions scheme, of his membership of the house, and thus of his parliamentary immunity. *Asahi Shinbun*, 4 April 1997 (evening).

14 Constitution, article 51.

15   Constitution, article 96. To revise the Constitution a two-thirds majority of the *members* (not just those present at the vote) of both houses is required, followed by a simple majority in a national referendum.

16   Constitution, article 69. It was established early in the history of the Constitution that Parliament can be dissolved simply by application of article 7, and does not require a vote of no-confidence to be passed. In recent years two governments have been forced to dissolve the House of Representatives after failing to win the confidence of the house: the Ōhira Government in May 1980 and the Miyazawa Government in June 1993. In June 1994 the minority Hata Government resigned without facing a no-confidence motion, which it knew it could not win. See chapters 5 and 6 for details of these cases.

17   Constitution, article 54. The double elections of June 1980 and of July 1986 were only possible because the House of Councillors had come to the end of its term.

18   Constitution, article 54. This has not happened since the Yoshida Government convoked emergency sessions of the upper house, in each case immediately after the close of a lower house session, in August 1952 and in March 1953. The first lasted one day and the second three days. In both cases the object was to finish off business from the previous session, rather than because of anything that could reasonably be called a 'national emergency'. Kuroda, ibid., pp. 74–5. Asano, ibid., pp. 47–8.

19   Constitution, article 59, para. 2. A majority of two-thirds of the members present is a less onerous requirement than the two-thirds of *members*, required to amend the Constitution. No doubt reflecting on the difficulties posed by this clause for the LDP governments after 1989, the *Yomiuri* constitutional revision proposals (to be discussed in chapter 10) included a proposal to change 'two-thirds' to 'three-fifths'. 'Nihonkoku kenpō o kangaeru toki ga kita' (The Time has come to Think about the Japanese Constitution), *This is Yomiuri*, December 1994, pp. 40–121, at p. 85.

20   Constitution, article 59, para. 3. On the other hand, where a bill originates in the House of Councillors and strikes trouble in the House of Representatives, the latter is not obliged to agree to a joint committee of both houses, although the former may request this. *Kokkaihō* (Law No. 79, of 30 April 1947, as amended), article 84, para. 2. [Henceforth cited as 'Parliamentary Law'.] See Kuroda, ibid., p. 175. Asano, ibid., p. 29.

21   Constitution, article 59, para. 4.

22   Constitution, article 60, para. 1.

23   Constitution, article 60, para. 2.

24   Kuroda, ibid., p. 178. See also Asano, ibid., pp. 28–9, 138–41, 219–21.

25   Constitution, article 61.

26   Langdon quotes the coal debate of 1962 as an instance where the Opposition was able to use delaying tactics in the House of Councillors to talk out a piece of legislation, which therefore lapsed at the end of the session and had to be revived in the next regular session. This would normally be impossible in the case of the budget – or of a treaty, although even here the rigidity of session timetables can cause difficulties for governments. See Frank Langdon, *Politics in Japan*. Boston and Toronto, Little, Brown and Co., 1967, p. 160.

27   Constitution, article 67.

28   Ishikawa Masumi and Hirose Michisada, *Jimintō – chōki shihai no kōzō* (The LDP – the Structure of its Long-term Control). Iwanami Shoten, 1989, pp. 35–60.

29   Constitution, article 52.

30   Parliamentary Law, articles 2 and 10.

31   Parliamentary Law, article 12, para. 2. Before 1955 as many as five extensions of one ordinary session were known.

32 Constitution, article 53.
33 Constitution, article 54, para. 1. Parliamentary Law, article 1, para. 3.
34 Parliamentary Law, article 12, para. 2.
35 Parliamentary Law, article 13.
36 Parliamentary Law, article 68. The concept of 'non-continuity of sessions' is based on the principle that Parliament has existence only when it is in session and that there is no 'continuity of will' from one session to the next. This is one area where Meiji constitutional practice itself derived from nineteenth-century German models, has influenced current practice. Kuroda, ibid., pp. 65–67. Asano, ibid., pp. 37–9.
37 Constitution, article 62.
38 Parliamentary Law, article 56, para. 3.
39 Parliamentary Law, article 42. If they do not, their parties are given compensating weighting in the allocation of members on committees.
40 Parliamentary Law, article 46.
41 Parliamentary Law, article 25.
42 Kuroda, ibid., p. 100. The principle here is 'winner take all'. There are, however, a number of 'directors' (*riji*) appointed in each committee, and the Opposition parties obtain some of these positions even when they do not have the numbers to secure committee chairmanships.
43 Parliamentary Law, article 45.
44 *Asahi Nenkan*, 1996, p. 243.
45 *Asahi Nenkan*, 1981, p. 215; 1996, pp. 242–3.
46 Parliamentary Law, article 51.
47 See Kuroda, ibid., pp. 110–11. Langdon, ibid., pp. 166–7. Asano, ibid., pp. 196–202.
48 See Ichiro Ozawa, *Blueprint for a New Japan*. Tokyo, New York and London, Kodansha International, 1994, pp. 54–61. Ozawa also complains that the LDP, as ruling party, submits 'requests' to 'the government'. Ibid., p. 55.
49 'A Japanese scholar compares many laws passed in the Diet to contracts signed before being read.' Karel van Wolferen, *The Enigma of Japanese Power*. London, Macmillan, 1989, p. 210.
50 Nagata-chō is the area of Tokyo in which the Parliament building stands, and is often used in the press to refer to the centre of the political world.
51 In this context it may be significant that the majority of non-Japanese analysts of Japanese politics are American. It seems possible that some of them subconsciously use their own Congress as a frame of reference when evaluating the Japanese Parliament, even when they are well aware of the systemic differences.
52 For instance, through extensive powers of delegated legislation granted to ministries (as in Britain), through the 'extra-legal' practice of administrative guidance, through *amakudari*, and, in some sectors, in official tolerance of clearly illegal or semi-legal behaviour, such as the formation of various forms of industrial and commercial cartel. See Mark Tilton, *Restrained Trade: Cartels in Japan's Basic Materials Industries*. Ithaca and London, Cornell University Press, 1996.
53 The general election of 1946 was held using a different system.
54 The island of Amami Ōshima, for historical reasons, was a separate constituency electing only one member, until the early 1990s, when it was absorbed into Kagoshima Prefecture.
55 The number of seats was 512 for the 1986 and 1990 elections.
56 By 1993 the unique single-member constituency of Amami Ōshima had been absorbed into Kagoshima No. 1 constituency. Two seats were taken away from Hokkaidō and one each from Hyōgo and Fukuoka, while one each was added to Miyagi, Saitama, Kanagawa and Gifu.

57 The Public Offices Election Law is Law No. 100 of 15 April 1950, as revised: henceforth 'Election Law'.

58 Election Law, articles 9–11.

59 See Gerald Curtis, *Election Campaigning Japanese Style*. New York and London, Columbia University Press, 1971, pp. 38ff. for a pioneering analysis of the 'hard vote'.

60 The question is nevertheless important to raise because the LDP's way of optimizing its vote given SNTV in MMCs is not the only possible way, even for a large party. It would be perfectly possible for the party to take firm charge of the campaign in each constituency, which it would divide into segments, urging or instructing the voters to vote for one of its candidates in one segment and another in another segment. Indeed, this was precisely the strategy adopted by the *Kōmeitō* in the former 'first fifty past the post' national constituency of the House of Councillors, with astonishing success. The fact that the LDP has not done this, but has relied on a decentralized strategy of personal candidate-centred campaigns based on candidates' *kōenkai*, suggests that it has been heavily influenced by the patterns of social interaction in rural Japan where a deep rooted sense of mutual obligation makes pork-barrel methods secure the ever-reliable 'hard vote'.

61 The four basic electoral reform bills became law under the Hosokawa Government on 4 March 1994. On 21 November 1994, under the Murayama Government, a bill establishing the new boundaries of the lower house single-member constituencies became law, as did a bill strengthening parliamentarians' liability by association (*renzasei*), and a bill on the status of political associations. For a useful summary of this legislation, see *Asahi Nenkan*, 1995, p. 263.

62 Political Funding Control Law, section 5.

63 Ibid.

64 In the course of debates within the Hosokawa coalition Government in 1993–4, the Socialists and others had argued for still tighter limits.

65 Ibid., section 6.

66 Ibid.

67 Ibid.

68 In the case of candidates who under the new system were elected both in a single member constituency and in a regional proportional representation constituency, a conviction for election law violations relating to the former would result in the invalidation of his election in both the former *and the latter*. Ibid.

69 The figure originally proposed by the Hosokawa Government in 1993 was ¥500.

70 314,114 electors were on the roll in Chiba No. 4 as against 81,096 in Hyōgo No. 5.

71 See 'Kanao et al. vs. Hiroshima Prefecture Election Commission', judgment translated in Lawrence W. Beer and Hiroshi Itoh, *The Constitutional Case Law of Japan, 1970 through 1990*. University of Washington Press, 1996, pp. 394–405.

72 'Shimizu et al. vs. Osaka Prefecture Election Commission et al. (1983)', in Beer and Itoh, ibid., pp. 375–94.

73 I am grateful to Mark Rebick for first pointing out to me the significance of this aspect.

Chapter 9

1 For instance van Wolferen, writing in 1989, did not rule out altogether a scenario in which the LDP might lose power, but implied that it was exceedingly unlikely barring a revolutionary change in the 'system'. Karel van Wolferen, *The Enigma of Japanese Power*. London, Macmillan, 1989, passim. Ramseyer and Rosenbluth

suspected that if electoral reform were ever achieved, some things might change, but they seem not to have seriously considered the idea of the LDP losing power. Their book was actually published shortly *after* the LDP lost office to the Hosokawa coalition government. J. Mark Ramseyer and Frances McCall Rosenbluth, *Japan's Political Marketplace*. Cambridge, MA, and London, Harvard University Press, 1993, esp. pp. 182–201.

2   The nearest approach to a two-party system was between 1955 and 1959, when the LDP and JSP between them had a near-monopoly of seats in the lower house, but, as we shall see, not only did this not last, it also was rather illusory, even at the time.

3   It is interesting to note that in the interwar period Japan had something approaching a two-party alternating system, though parties as a whole had a most fragile grip on power.

4   This assumes a negative correlation between high rates of economic growth and LDP support, which seems to be supported by electoral statistics since the 1950s.

5   The figures in table 9.3 ignore those who stood as Independents, but affiliated themselves with the LDP after being elected.

6   This contrasts with the situation in Great Britain, where local loyalties are a less vital – though not totally absent – part of electoral calculations, and where it is relatively common for a member defeated in, say, Bristol, to be subsequently elected for a constituency in, say, Yorkshire.

7   See J. A. A. Stockwin, *Japan: Divided Politics in a Growth Economy*. London, Weidenfeld, 2nd edn, 1982, tables on pages 120 and 187–92.

8   Ibid., p. 189.

9   It can be seen from table 9.5 that five out of the 155 *Shinshintō* members graduated from *Sōka* University, which derives from the *Sōka Gakkai* religion. But the data indicate that most of the *Sōka Gakkai* element within the *Shinshintō* had attended standard mainstream universities.

10   See T. J. Pempel, *Policy and Politics in Japan; Creative Conservatism*. Philadelphia, PA, Temple University Press, 1982. T. J. Pempel (ed.), *Uncommon Democracies; The One-Party Dominant Regimes*. Ithaca and London, Cornell University Press, 1990.

11   For an early description of *jiban* in electoral campaigns, see Nobutaka Ike, *Japanese Politics: an Introductory Survey*. New York, Knopf, 1957.

12   A classic analysis of *kōenkai* is Gerald Curtis, *Election Campaigning Japanese Style*. New York and London, Columbia University Press, 1971.

13   At each election, however, a small number of 'Independents', who had applied for but been refused LDP endorsement, nevertheless contested the seat and had sufficient local support, typically through their *kōenkai*, to be elected. In most cases they were then readily admitted into the party and became officially LDP members of Parliament.

14   Percentages for the *Shinshintō* were 12.5 per cent, for the *Minshutō* 15.4 per cent, but 0 per cent for the JCP and SDP. *Asahi senkyo taikan*, Asahi Shinbunsha, 1997, p. 121.

15   See the figures for 'secretary to MP' in table 9.6.

16   It is instructive to pay a visit to a parliamentarian's office in one of the office blocks opposite the Parliament building in Tokyo. From this author's observation many MPs are visited by an almost unending stream of visitors (often groups of people) from their constituency. See chapter 3, vignette no. 3.

17   Great care should, however, be taken in the matter of comparison, since phenomena analogous to *habatsu* may be found in a number of political systems, including some in Europe, particularly that of Italy.

18   Shinobu Tomohito, *Kantei no kenryoku* (Power in the Prime Minister's Office). Chikuma Shinsho, 1996, p. 49. Shinobu quotes the former Prime Minister Ōhira Masayoshi as saying: 'Where there are three politicians, two factions will emerge'. Ibid.

19   The JSP in its earlier years also had enough support to promote multiple candidacies in many constituencies, but JSP *habatsu* were much more concerned with ideological differences between them than were the *habatsu* of the LDP. With the exception of the JCP in Kyoto, no other party up to 1993 was ever strong enough to run more than one candidate in any constituency.

20   This phrase needs qualification since LDP *habatsu* do not run candidates in national or local elections under their own label, nor are many voters necessarily aware of which faction an LDP candidate belongs to. In other ways, however, they have the attributes of parties: often sophisticated organization, central offices in Tokyo, staff, publications (mainly in-house), networks of supporters and a large budget. For a detailed study of one LDP *habatsu* up to the late 1980s, see David Morris, *A Historical and Contemporary Account of the Miki/Komoto Faction of the LDP*. Unpublished D.Phil. thesis, University of Oxford, 1990.

21   One source gives precise figures for the membership of 'former' LDP *habatsu* at the end of 1996, as follows (identified by the names of their leaders or former – in one case deceased – leaders):

    Obuchi   88 (lower house 50; upper house 38)
    Mitsuzuka   86 (lower house 61; upper house 25)
    Miyazawa   73 (lower house 57; upper house 16)
    Watanabe   68 (lower house 52; upper house 16)
    Kōmoto   21 (lower house 17; upper house 4)

Asahi Nenkan, 1997, p. 200. It should be noted that the largest 'former' faction was in direct line of succession from the Tanaka/Takeshita faction which had dominated the LDP during the 1980s.

22   Shinobu, ibid., pp. 43–7, argues that Kishi was responsible for institutionalizing frequent cabinet reshuffles as a means of satisfying the various *habatsu*, but he also regards Yoshida, and indeed the American Occupation, as to blame for creating a seriously weakened cabinet.

23   Cabinets under single-party dominance were reshuffled at least once a year, but there was a tendency for the tenure of ministers in key portfolios to stay in post longer. For data on this, see J. A. A. Stockwin et al., *Dynamic and Immobilist Politics in Japan*. London, Macmillan, 1988, pp. 42–6.

24   The classic account of *zoku* is Inoguchi Takashi and Iwai Tomoaki, *Zoku giin no kenkyū*. Tokyo, Nihon Keizai Hyōronsha, 1987.

25   For a fuller account, see J. A. A. Stockwin, 'The Social Democratic Party (formerly Japan Socialist Party): A Turbulent Odyssey', in Ronald Hrebenar (ed.), *The Japanese Party System*. Boulder, CO, Westview, 3rd edn, forthcoming, 1999.

26   Watanabe Osamu, lecture, Bunkyōkumin Kaikan, Tokyo, 2 March 1997, emphasized the crucial and long-term consequences of this decision.

27   In April 1997 a much weakened SDP became the only party apart from the Communists to oppose the Hashimoto Government's legislation to extend leases in Okinawa for American base facilities, thus overriding the rights of landlords. *Asahi Shinbun*, 12 April 1997. Murayama abstained from voting.

28   For instance, in the pre-1980s national constituency of the House of Councillors, which was elected on the principle of 'first fifty past the post', the *Sōka Gakkai/ Kōmeitō* would calculate with great accuracy its likely total vote, work out how many candidates could be elected safely if the vote were evenly divided between them, divide Japan into regions, and instruct voters in region A to vote for candidate A,

in region B to vote for candidate B, and so on. The success of this policy was astonishing.

29 These were the *Shinseitō, Kōmeitō, Nihon Shintō*, DSP, as well as various splinter groups recently defected from the LDP. *Asahi Nenkan*, 1995, p. 260.

30 Ozawa polled 1,120,012 votes and his rival Hata Tsutomu 566,998 votes. *Asahi Nenkan*, 1996, p. 262.

31 Nishihira Shigeki, 'Hajimete heiritsusei senkyo wa dō okonawareta ka' (How was the First Mixed System Election Conducted?), in Yoron kagaku kyōkai, *Shijō chōsa*, no. 233 (October 1997), pp. 4–19, at pp. 16–17.

32 *Asahi Shinbun*, 31 December 1997, 5 January 1998.

33 Short for *Minshu yūai taiyō kokumin rengō* (Democratic Amity Sun People's League)! *Asahi Shinbun*, 8 January 1998.

34 A group linked with the *Rengō* union federation in the upper house.

35 A mini-party formed by Hosokawa when he left the *Shinshintō* in June 1997. The name used by the party was in English.

Chapter 10

1 Yomiuri Shinbunsha (ed.), *Kenpō: 21 seiki ni mukete* (The Constitution: Facing the 21st Century). Yomiuri Shinbunsha, 1994.

2 Lawrence W. Beer and Hiroshi Itoh, *The Constitutional Case Law of Japan, 1970 through 1990*. Seattle and London, University of Washington Press, 1996, p. 4.

3 An example from the late 1990s is an editorial in *Yomiuri Shinbun*, 25 March 1997. According to the editorial: 'It goes without saying that the current Constitution was written by a foreigner. No matter how elegant the preamble sounds, it is still a translation of what was written by a US Navy commander. This makes Japan's Constitution unique in the world.' By contrast Beer and Itoh argue that the views of the Occupation officials and 'those of the 1946 House of Representatives were not far apart and were more representative of Japan's constitutional consciousness since the Second World War than those of the "lame duck" government (late 1945–early 1946) and later revisionists. Moreover, origins are less critical to the legitimacy of a constitution than its enduring support by a nation's adult populace, as in "autonomous" Japan since 1952.' Beer and Itoh, ibid, p. 13.

4 For a classic account see Robert E. Ward, 'The Commission on the Constitution and Prospects for Constitutional Change in Japan', *Journal of Asian Studies*, vol. xxiv, no. 3 (May 1965), pp. 401–29 (henceforth cited as Ward, 'Commission'). For a survey of the published documents of the Commission, which run to some 40,000 pages of text, see John M. Maki, 'The Documents of Japan's Commission on the Constitution', ibid., pp. 475–89. See also Watanabe Osamu, *Nihonkoku kenpō 'kaisei' shi* (A History of 'Revising' the Japanese Constitution). Tokyo, Nihon Hyōronsha, 1987.

5 This was also a theme of the 'United States Initial Post-Surrender Policy for Japan', issued as a presidential directive to General MacArthur on 6 September 1945. The issue was also complicated by an ambiguity in the Potsdam Declaration between coercive and voluntarist principles. See Robert E. Ward, 'The Origins of the Present Japanese Constitution', *American Political Science Review*, vol. 50, no. 4 (December 1956), pp. 980–1010, at p. 983 (henceforth cited as Ward, 'Origins').

6 Prince Konoe also busied himself with proposals for constitutional reform, but his efforts were repudiated by MacArthur.

7 Theodore McNelly, 'The Japanese Constitution, Child of the Cold War', *Political Science Quarterly*, vol. 74, no. 2 (June 1959), pp. 176–95.

8   Supreme Commander for the Allied Powers, *Political Reorientation of Japan, September 1945 to September 1948.* 2 vols, Westport, Connecticut, Greenwood Press, 1970 (Reprint of original, published by US Government Printing Office, 1949), vol. 1, p. 102.

9   Ward acidly comments: 'This awesome display of speed and "efficiency" without a doubt represents the world's record time for the devising and acceptance of a constitution for a major modern state.' Ward, 'Origins', p. 995. Yoshida, in his Memoirs, after pointing to the impending general election as a probable reason for haste, concludes: 'The fact remains, however, that there was a good deal of the American spirit of enterprise in the undertaking of such a fundamental piece of reform as the revision of the Constitution within two months of Japan's defeat; as for wishing to see that reform realised in so short a period as half a year or a year, one can only put it down to that impulsiveness common to military people of all countries.' Shigeru Yoshida, *The Yoshida Memoirs: The Story of Japan in Crisis.* Translated by Kenichi Yoshida, London, Heinemann, 1961, p. 136.

10 Quoted in *Political Reorientation of Japan*, vol. 2, p. 421.

11 McNelly, ibid., p. 184.

12 This account is that of Satō Tatsuo, who was a leading official of the Cabinet Bureau of Legislation, and closely involved with the constitutional drafting process, for part of the time as assistant to Matsumoto. See also Koseki Shōichi, *The Birth of Japan's Post-war Constitution.* Boulder, Colorado, Westview, 1997. Koseki's book is an excellent recent account of the origins of the Constitution.

13 McNelly, ibid., p. 187.

14 Whitney, on the other hand, has an account in which he boasts of telling the Cabinet members that he and his aides had been 'enjoying your atomic sunshine'. Major-General Courtney Whitney, *MacArthur, his Rendezvous with History.* New York, Knopf, 1956, pp. 250–2.

15 Kenzo Takayanagi, 'Some Reminiscences of Japan's Commission on the Constitution', in Dan F. Henderson (ed.), *The Constitution of Japan: its First Twenty Years, 1947–67*, Seattle and London, University of Washington Press, 1969, pp. 71–88, at pp. 77–8. See especially footnote 13.

16 *Political Reorientation of Japan*, vol. 1, p. 105.

17 Ward, 'Origins', p. 996.

18 Ibid., p. 999.

19 Ibid., p. 1002.

20 Beer and Itoh, ibid., p. 13.

21 Kazuo Kawai, *Japan's American Interlude.* Chicago, Chicago University Press, p. 52.

22 Beer and Itoh, ibid., p. 13.

23 D. C. S. Sissons, 'The Pacifist Clause of the Japanese Constitution: Legal and Political Problems of Rearmament', *International Affairs*, vol. 37, no. 1 (January 1961), pp. 45–59, at p. 45. McNelly also quotes instructions received from Secretary of State Byrnes in October 1945, which left open the possibility of future armed forces for Japan. McNelly, ibid., pp. 179–80.

24 At one point the Cabinet attempted to have the clause relegated to the Preamble, but this was not acceptable to SCAP.

25 *Military Situation in the Far East* (Hearings before the Committee on Armed Service and the Committee on Foreign Relations, United States Senate, Eighty-second Congress, first Session ... Part 1), Washington, US Senate, 1951, p. 223. The relevant section is quoted in Sissons, ibid., p. 45.

26 Shidehara Kijurō, *Gaikō gojūnen* (Fifty Years in Diplomacy), Tokyo, Yomiuri Shinbunsha, 1951, pp. 211–13. Shidehara in effect claims responsibility for the peace clause, without specifically mentioning a meeting with MacArthur. He relates

an encounter with a young man on a tram, who was emotionally haranguing his fellow-passengers on the despair and destruction that the war had brought upon Japan. Shidehara contrasts this with the enthusiastic support which the people gave the Government in the Russo-Japanese War, and says this brought home to him how utterly people's attitudes to war had changed. He therefore decided, as Prime Minister, but unknown to others, that war and armaments should be banned in perpetuity. So far as he was concerned, the Constitution was not imposed by the Americans against the will of the Japanese.

27 Takayanagi, ibid., pp. 86–8.
28 Sissons, ibid., p. 46. For instance Yoshida, who was a cabinet minister at the time, and later succeeded Shidehara as Prime Minister, thought it more likely that that MacArthur suggested the peace clause to Shidehara, who may then have 'replied with enthusiasm'. *The Yoshida Memoirs*, ibid., vol. 1, p. 102.
29 Quoted in *Political Reorientation of Japan*, vol. 1, p. 102.
30 Sissons, ibid., p. 47.
31 Ibid., p. 48.
32 For an analysis of public opinion polls on the Constitution up to the 1980s, see J. A. A. Stockwin, 'Japanese Public Opinion and Policies on Security and Defence', in Ronald Dore and Radha Sinha, with assistance from Mari Sako, *Japan and World Depression, then and now: Essays in Memory of E.F. Penrose*. London, Macmillan, 1987, pp. 111–34.
33 In favour 13%; against 81% (*Asahi Shinbun*, 1 January 1991). In favour 2.9% (out of five possible suggested opinions relating to the peace clause) (*Yomiuri Shinbun*, 2 May 1991). In favour 5.1% of those expressing a revisionist view (*Yomiuri Shinbun*, 31 March 1994).
34 51.0%, ahead of 28.1% for environmental issues (*Yomiuri Shinbun*, 2 May 1991). 69%, ahead of 29% each for the *tennō* as 'symbol', and human rights (This poll asked what the main contributions of the Constitution were, rather than which aspects interested the respondents) (*Mainichi Shinbun*, 27 April 1993). 32.8%, ahead of 26.4% for environmental issues (*Yomiuri Shinbun*, 31 March 1994). 45.7%, ahead of 28.0% for environmental issues (*Yomiuri Shinbun*, 6 April 1995). 34.3%, ahead of 25.4% for environmental issues (*Yomiuri Shinbun*, 5 April 1996).
35 Good Constitution? Good 61%, Not good 24% (*Asahi Shinbun*, 1 January 1991). Constitution broadly good or bad? Good 82.6%, Bad 7.4% (*Yomiuri Shinbun*, 2 May 1991). Constitution broadly a positive or negative influence in Japan since the war? Positive 80.4%, Negative 12.5% (*Yomiuri Shinbun*, 31 March 1994). (Same question as in previous poll) Positive 74.5%, Negative 17.8% (*Yomiuri Shinbun*, 6 April 1995).
36 Pro-revision 33.3%, Anti-revision 51.1% (*Yomiuri Shinbun*, 2 May 1991). Pro-revision 44%, Anti-revision 25% (*Mainichi Shinbun*, 27 April 1993). Pro-revision 44.2%, Anti-revision 40.0% (*Yomiuri Shinbun*, 31 March 1994). Pro-revision 50.4%, Anti-revision 30.9% (*Yomiuri Shinbun*, 6 April 1995). Pro-revision 46.7%, Anti-revision 36.4% (*Yomiuri Shinbun*, 5 April 1996).
37 Difficulty (because of the peace clause) of making an international contribution 62.0% (*Yomiuri Shinbun*, 31 March 1994). (Same reason as in previous poll) 56.9% (*Yomiuri Shinbun*, 6 April 1995). (Same reason as in previous poll) 53.7% (*Yomiuri Shinbun*, 5 April 1996).
38 The proposal may be found both in the newspaper's monthly magazine and in a specially published book: 'Tokushū: Nihonkoku kenpō o kangaeru toki ga kita' (The Time has Come to Think about the Japanese Constitution), *This is Yomiuri*, December 1994, pp. 40–121. Yomiuri Shinbunsha (ed.) (Nishi Osamu, compiler),

Kenpō, 21 seiki ni mukete (The Constitution, Aiming at the 21st Century), Yomiuri Shinbunsha, 1994. (Henceforth, *Kenpō*). An English language version of the proposals was published as: The Yomiuri Shimbun: *A Proposal for the Revision of the Text of the Constitution of Japan*. The Yomiuri Shimbun, 3 November 1994 (Henceforth: *A Proposal*). Textual quotations are from this last source.

39   *mitomenai*. The original is *hōki suru* (renounce).

40   Strictly speaking, this should be translated: 'the Japanese people'. The Japanese version is *Nihon kokumin*, just as it is in the first paragraph. The problem is, however, that both could also be translated 'the Japanese nation'. In the proposed article 11, para. 1, 'Japan' is a translation of *Nihonkoku*, literally 'the country Japan'.

41   *Jiei*. This is a word which has acquired softer connotations from *bōei* (defence), and is the key element is in the current *jieitai* (Self-Defence Forces).

42   *Kenpō*, pp. 46–7. *A Proposal*, p. 17.

43   *gunji taikokuka e no hadome*.

44   *Kenpō*, p. 48.

45   These are defined in the commentary as nuclear, biological and chemical weapons. Ibid., p. 49.

46   Ibid., p. 51.

47   Ibid., pp. 53–6.

48   A translation of the judgment is given in John M. Maki, with translations by Ikeda Masaaki, David C. S. Sissons, and Kurt Steiner, *Court and Constitution in Japan: Selected Supreme Court Decisions, 1948–60*, Seattle, University of Washington Press, 1964, pp. 362–5.

49   Ibid., p. 48.

50   *Kenpō*, pp. 114–6. *A Proposal*, pp. 43–4.

51   For a translation of the judgment, supplementary opinions and opinions of the various Supreme Court judges in the Sunakawa case, see John M. Maki, *Court and Constitution in Japan: Selected Supreme Court Decisions, 1948–60*, Seattle, University of Washington Press, 1964, pp. 298–361.

52   Maki, *Court and Constitution in Japan*, pp. 305–6.

53   For details of these cases, see Beer and Itoh, ibid., pp. 30–32 and 83–141.

54   Ibid., p. 111.

55   Ibid., p. 32.

56   See Lawrence W. Beer, *Freedom of Expression in Japan*. Tokyo and New York, Kodansha International, 1984.

57   See Lawrence W. Beer, 'The Public Welfare Standard and Freedom of Expression in Japan', in Dan F. Henderson (ed.), *The Constitution of Japan: its First Twenty Years, 1947–1967*. Seattle and London, University of Washington Press, 1969, pp. 205–38; Maki, *Court and Constitution in Japan*; D. C. S. Sissons, 'Human Rights under the Japanese Constitution', in D.C.S. Sissons (ed.), *Papers on Modern Japan, 1965*. Canberra, Australian National University, 1965, pp. 50–69.

58   Beer and Itoh, ibid., pp. 29–30.

59   Ibid., pp. 32–3 and 143–81.

60   Ibid., pp. 34–6 and 183–221.

61   Ibid., pp. 38–41 and 355–421.

62   Ibid., pp. 41–4 and 423–48.

63   Ibid., p. 44.

64   Constitution, article 20, paragraph 3.

65   Beer and Itoh, ibid., pp. 478–91, at p. 483.

66   *Kenpō*, pp. 57–81.

67   *Kenpō*, pp. 82–98.

68   *Kenpō*, p. 99.

69   *Kenpō*, p. 102.

70 In the 1946 Constitution these powers rest with the *tennō*, 'with the advice and approval of the Cabinet'. See *Kenpō*, pp. 37–8 and 103–4.
71 *Kenpō*, p. 31.
72 *Kenpō*, p. 37.
73 The issue is examined in Watanabe Osamu, *Sengo seijishi no naka no tennōsei* (The Emperor System in Postwar Political History). Tokyo, Aoki shoten, 1992, passim, but especially pp. 369–410.
74 *Kenpō*, pp. 145–50.
75 Ronald Dore, *Japan, Internationalism and the UN*. London, Routledge, 1997, pp. xxvi–xxviii.
76 Robert E. Ward, 'The Commission on the Constitution and Prospects for Constitutional Change in Japan', *Journal of Asian Studies*, vol. xxiv, no. 3 (May 1965), pp. 401–29, at p. 416.
77 In the British parliamentary system a strong prime minister and cabinet is consistent with a strong *majority* party, whereas the ability of *opposition* parties to affect events is rather slight, though their turn may come at the next general election. Parliament, meanwhile, is the *arena* of debate and politicking, rather than powerful in its own right.

Chapter 11

1 Rob Steven, *Classes in Contemporary Japan*. Cambridge, Cambridge University Press, 1983. Steven, writing from a Marxist perspective, marshalls a great deal of evidence for his claim that the distinction between the permanently employed and the casually (or less-permanently) employed workforce is in Marxist terms a class distinction. For a deconstruction of the argument that nearly all the population in fact regards itself as middle class, see Earl Kinmonth, paper presented at the annual conference of the British Association of Japanese Studies, University of Manchester, April 1993.
2 Ronald Dore even argues that Japanese industry had a social democratic revolution after the war which in some respects left Japanese labour unions in a more advantageous legal position than British unions had achieved after decades of slow pressure. Ronald Dore, *British Factory–Japanese Factory: The Origins of National Diversity in Industrial Relations*. London, George Allen and Unwin, 1973, pp. 115–19. See also Ikuo Kume, *Disparaged Success: Labor Politics in Postwar Japan*. Ithaca and London, Cornell University Press, 1998.
3 E.S. Crawcour and Hiromi Hata, 'Japanese Labour Relations', in Peter Drysdale and Hironobu Kitaoji (eds), *Japan and Australia: Two Societies and their Interaction*. Canberra, Australian National University Press, 1981, pp. 236–53.
4 *Doya* is *yado* (inn) reversed and means 'doss-house'. Thus *doya-gai* means 'doss-house street' or 'doss-house area', and describes places such as Sanya in Tokyo (whose name has been expunged from contemporary maps), Kamagasaki in Osaka and Kotobukichō in Yokohama, where day labourers congregate and obtain sporadic work on a daily hiring basis. Characterized by high levels of alcoholism, illegal gambling, absent families and a shortened expectation of life, they are also home to some of the most rugged and original individualists to be found in Japanese society. See Tom Gill, 'Sanya Street Life under the Heisei Recession', *Japan Quarterly*, vol. XLI, no. 3 (July–September 1994), pp. 270–86. Carolyn S. Stevens, *On the Margins of Japanese Society: Volunteers and the Welfare of the Urban Underclass*. London and New York, Routledge, 1997.
5 Kamata Satoshi, *Japan in the Passing Lane: An Insider's Account of Life in a Japanese Auto Factory*. Boston, London and Sydney, George Allen and Unwin, 1983.
6 See Norma Chalmers, *Industrial Relations in Japan: The Peripheral Workforce*. London and New York, Routledge, 1990.

7   See for instance Rodney Clark, *The Japanese Company*. New Haven, Yale University Press, 1979.

8   Thomas Rohlen, *For Harmony and Strength. Japanese White Collar Organization in Anthropological Perspective*. Berkeley, University of California Press, 1974. Susan J. Pharr, *Losing Face: Status Politics in Japan*. Berkeley, Los Angeles and Oxford, University of California Press, 1990; pp. 59–73: 'Gender-Based Conflict: the Revolt of the Tea Pourers'. Dorinne Kondo, *Crafting Selves: Power, Gender and Discourse of Identity in a Japanese Workplace*. Chicago, University of Chicago Press, 1990. Takie Sugiyama Lebra, *Japanese Patterns of Behavior*. Honolulu, University of Hawaii Press, 1984.

9   In the House of Representatives elections of October 1996, 23 out of 500 parliamentarians elected were women, or 4.6%. The breakdown according to party was: LDP 4 (1.6%); *Shinshintō* 8 (5.1%); *Minshutō* 3 (5.8%); JCP 4 (15.4%); SDP 3 (20%). Women's chances appeared to have been assisted by the introduction of proportional representation for 200 seats. Sixteen women were elected for the proportional representation seats as against seven for the single-member seats. The figures for women elected in previous lower house elections were: 1946, 39; 1947, 15; 1949, 12; 1952, 9; 1953, 9; 1955, 8; 1958, 11; 1960, 7; 1963, 7; 1967, 7; 1969, 8; 1972, 7; 1976, 6; 1979, 11; 1980, 9; 1983, 8; 1986, 7; 1990, 12; and 1993, 14. The total number of seats varied between 466 and 512. *Asahi Nenkan*, 1994, table on p. 131. Ibid., 1997, p. 193, p. 208.

10   *Minpō*, article 750.

11   *Japan Times*, 5 March 1997, 6 March 1997. *Asahi Shinbun*, 9 March 1997.

12   Thus for instance the Finance Minister, Mitsuzuka Hiroshi (LDP) was quoted as saying: 'Good traditions of Japan have been built within the family. There is also the word "lineage" [*sujō*]. This aspect of our culture seems to be approaching a critical juncture.' *Asahi Shinbun*, 14 March 1997.

13   Family registers are also often criticized for allegedly making it easier to discriminate against minority groups in employment or marriage.

14   It is worth noting that the insistence that married couples assume a single surname is not general in East Asia. Both Chinese and Korean women on marriage normally retain their original surname.

15   *Japan Times*, 12 February 1971.

16   Kent Calder, *Crisis and Compensation: Public Policy and Political Stability in Japan, 1949–1986*. Princeton, NJ, Princeton University Press, 1988.

17   Chalmers Johnson, *MITI and the Japanese Miracle. The Growth of Industrial Policy, 1925–1975*. Stanford, CA, Stanford University Press, 1982.

18   Scott Callon, *Divided Sun: MITI and the Breakdown of High Tech Industrial Policy, 1975–1993*, pp. 182–207.

19   Robert Wade, *Governing the Market: Economic Theory and the Role of Government in East Asian Industrialization*. Princeton, NJ, Princeton University Press, 1990, p. 330. See also Ronald Dore, *Flexible Rigidities: Industrial Policy and Structural Adjustment in the Japanese Economy 1970–1980*. Stanford, CA, Stanford University Press, 1986.

20   For a detailed exposition of the issues involved, see Hiromitsu Ishi, *The Japanese Tax System*. Oxford, Clarendon Press, 2nd edn, 1993. For a fine analysis by a political scientist, see Junko Kato, *The Problem of Bureaucratic Rationality: Tax Politics in Japan*. Princeton, NJ, Princeton University Press, 1994.

21   See editorial in the *Nikkei Weekly*, 24 June 1996.

22   See chapter 5, note 11. See also Mark Tilton, 'Regulatory Reform, Market Opening, and Japan's Security', Paper given at the Institute of Social Science, University of Tokyo, 28 February 1997.

23 For a municipality to designated a city, population must be over 50,000, it must provide facilities 'suitable to a city', and the number of inhabitants engaging in 'industrial, commercial and other employment of an urban nature' must not be less than 60 per cent of the total population. Some exceptions can be made down to a population of 30,000.

24 There were 13 designated cities in 1994.

25 See Local Autonomy Law, articles 294–7. The urban equivalent of the *buraku* was the *tonarigumi* (neighbourhood association), but for the most part this has proved a less tenacious institution than the *buraku*.

26 For further detail, see Hitoshi Abe, Muneyuki Shindō and Sadafumi Kawato (James W. White, translator), *The Government and Politics of Japan*. Tokyo, University of Tokyo Press, 1994, pp. 55–79.

27 An example of a regional initiative of this kind is the Intelligent Cosmos Project in the Tōhoku region, which brings together seven prefectures in various joint development schemes.

28 See Richard J. Samuels, *The Politics of Regional Policy in Japan: Localities Incorporated?* Princeton, NJ, Princeton University Press, 1983. Purnendra Jain, *Local Politics and Policymaking in Japan*. New Delhi, Commonwealth Publishers, 1989.

29 Masao Maruyama (Ivan Morris, translator), 'Thought and Behaviour Patterns of Japan's Wartime Leaders', in Masao Maruyama (Ivan Morris, ed.), *Thought and Behaviour in Modern Japanese Politics*. London, Oxford University Press, 1963, pp. 84–134.

30 Karel van Wolferen, *The Enigma of Japanese Power*. London, Macmillan, 1989, p. 5.

31 See Ibid., p. 433. The present writer differs to some extent from van Wolferen in being critical of parts of the system rather than the system in its totality, and in seeing it as to an extent open-ended rather than closed and circular.

32 A 1997 example is that of the Korean-Japanese woman writer Yu Mi I (Yu Mi Ri), winner of an important literary prize for her novel *Family Cinema*. A book signing ceremony in a department store was cancelled by the publisher after threats were received from an ultranationalist, complaining that the novel was 'anti-Japanese'. The author subsequently complained to the press that her rights were being infringed by the cancellation.

33 See John C. Campbell, *How Policies Change: the Japanese Government and the Aging Society*. Princeton, NJ, Princeton University Press, 1992. Kwansei Gakuin University Policy Studies Association, *Journal of Policy Studies*, no. 2 (September 1996): Special Symposium Issue on Health Care Policy in the United Kingdom and Japan, passim.

34 *Asahi Shinbun*, 25 April 1997.

35 T. J. Pempel, *Patterns of Japanese Policymaking: Experiences from Higher Education*. Boulder, CO, Westview, 1978, pp. 185–96.

36 In June 1997 the nation was shocked by the confession of a 14-year-old junior high school student to the grisly murder of a younger pupil, and to other acts of violence and cruelty. He had written messages railing against the system of compulsory education. Although it seems likely that this was an isolated case of a psychopathic personality, the media were quick to make a connection between his acts and a repressive system of education.

37 The dispute over textbook control between Japan and the PRC is carefully researched in Caroline Rose, *Interpreting History in Sino-Japanese Relations: A Case Study in Political Decision-Making*. London, Routledge, 1998.

38 The best account of the attempts to reform the education system is Leonard Schoppa, *Education Reform in Japan: A Case of Immobilist Politics*. London and New York, Routledge, 1991.

39   Christopher Hood, 'Nakasone; Understanding the Conflicts and his Involvement in Education Reform', paper presented to the fourth annual Colloquium of the Japan Politics Group, University of Stirling, September 1996.

40   Among the principal targets of reform are the modification of university entrance examinations, scrapping faculties of 'general education' in the first two years of undergraduate education, improving and increasing postgraduate education, and making the system more 'international'.

41   A moving photographic account of the Minamata tragedy is W. Eugene Smith and Aileen M. Smith, *Minamata.* London, Chatto and Windus, 1975.

42   Miranda A. Schreurs, 'Domestic Institutions and International Environmental Agendas in Japan and Germany', in Miranda A. Schreurs and Elizabeth Economy (eds), *The Internationalization of Environmental Protection*, Cambridge University Press, 1997, pp. 134–61.

43   The siting of a huge power station, immediately adjacent to Matsushima, near Sendai in Miyagi Prefecture – one of Japan's most famed beauty spots – is a shocking example of 'visual pollution'. Cultural explanations explaining this kind of thing in terms of a 'Japanese appreciation of beauty but capacity to ignore ugliness' seem, to this writer, to miss the point. Explanations in terms of the power of economic and political interests appear more pertinent. There was, for instance, much visual pollution in Britain before governments were able to develop the will, and the capacity, to tackle the problem.

44   Gavan McCormack, *The Emptiness of Japanese Affluence*, New York, M. E. Sharpe, Inc., 1996, pp. 25–77.

45   For instance an explosion at the nuclear power plant at Tōkai mura, north of Tokyo, led to the decision by the Hashimoto Government, in April 1997, to dissolve *Dōnen*, the organization responsible for running it.

46   It is also worth noting that schoolteachers are also involved in community policing to the extent that they often act to keep their charges out of pleasure arcades and the like.

47   Noel Williams, *The Right to Life in Japan.* London, Routledge, 1997, pp. 41–50.

48   Thus, for instance, in August 1994, Sakurai Shin resigned as Director of the Environment Agency after saying that Japan did not intend to wage a war of aggression earlier in the century, and in November 1995 Etō Takami resigned as Economic Planning Agency Minister having said in a leaked, off-the-record statement that Japan did some good things as a colonial power in Korea between 1910 and 1945. The Etō statement prompted a joint protest from the leaders of South Korea (listing some 30 such statements from Japanese politicians) and China, and led to a 'heartfelt apology' to these leaders from Prime Minister Murayama. *Nikkei Weekly*, 20 November 1995.

49   David Forfar, private communication.

50   The classic instance of this is the failure of the daily press to report on the alleged financial dealings of Prime Minister Tanaka in 1974 – even though these had been itemized in a weekly magazine – until the foreign press took up the issue.

51   For a full discussion of the range of issues concerning freedom of expression, see Lawrence Beer, *Freedom of Expression in Japan.* Tokyo and New York, Kodansha International, 1984. See also a forthcoming work by Ellis Krauss, *NHK: Broadcasting Politics in Japan*, forthcoming, 1999.

Chapter 12

1   J. A. A. Stockwin, *Japan: Divided Politics in a Growth Economy.* London, Weidenfeld and Nicolson, 2nd edn, 1982, p. 245.

2   *Asahi Shinbun*, 9 June 1997.

3   In November 1997 Yeltsin and Hashimoto, meeting in Moscow, came to an agreement to sign a peace treaty by 2000, presumably entailing a negotiation of the territorial issue beforehand. *Asahi Shinbun*, 3 November 1997.

4   Alan Rix, *Japan's Foreign Aid Challenge: Policy Reform and Aid Leadership*. London and New York, Routledge, 1993.

5   The 1960 Treaty was to run for ten years, after which either side could give one year's notice of termination. In 1970 the two governments agreed that it should continue indefinitely, and since then no revisions to the text have been made.

6   *Asahi Shinbun*, 5 October 1997.

7   It is sometimes imagined that Russia is all located to the north and west of Japan, but a glance at a regional map shows that Russian territory actually stretches for as much as two time zones further *east* than Japan.

8   Japan claims the two southernmost islands of the Kurile chain (known in Japanese as Chishima: a thousand islands), which stretches from the tip of the Kamchatka Peninsula to the north-east, to near the Nemuro Peninsula in eastern Hokkaidō. These islands are called Iturup and Kunashir in Russian, Etorofu and Kunashiri in Japanese. Japan also claims the island of Shikotan and the Habomai archipelago, which are close to the coast of Hokkaidō, of which they formed an administrative part up to 1945. Soviet leaders at times expressed a willingness to return Shikotan and Habomai on concluding a peace treaty, but Japan has held out for Iturup (Etorofu) and Kunashir(i) as well. For a detailed analysis, see Kimie Hara, *Japanese–Soviet/Russian Relations since 1945: a Difficult Peace*. London and New York, Routledge, forthcoming, 1998.

9   As an eminent Japanese banker said to the author in the early 1990s: 'putting money into Russia is like pouring water into a bucket with holes in it'.

10 At one point a Japanese firm sold submarine propellers to the Soviet authorities, making it possible for submarines to move more quietly, thus becoming harder to detect. The Americans, understandably, were less than thrilled by this example of 'economistic' foreign policy making.

11 For a detailed analysis of the interrelationships between Japan–Soviet and Japan–China relations in this period, see Christopher Braddick, *Japan and the Sino–Soviet Rift, 1950–1964*. University of Oxford, D.Phil. thesis, 1997.

12 Chae-Jin Lee, 'The Making of the Sino-Japanese Peace and Friendship Treaty', *Pacific Affairs*, vol. 52, no. 3 (Fall 1979), pp. 420–45.

13 For instance, the visit to Pyongyang in September 1990 by Kanemaru Shin of the LDP and Tanabe Makoto of the JSP had this as its primary purpose.

14 The reunification of Germany was intensively studied in Seoul, and most Koreans involved in such studies concluded that the cost of reunifying Korea in similar circumstances to those of Germany in 1989–90 would be completely unaffordable.

15 For the concept of 'soft power', see Reinhard Drifte, *Japan's Foreign Policy in the 1990s*. Basingstoke and London, Macmillan, 1996, pp. 87–143.

16 See chapter 10.

17 Hamish McRae in *The Independent*, London, 22nd July 1997.

18 Ibid.

19 Drifte, ibid., p. 87.

20 Drifte, loc. cit.

21 Drifte, ibid., pp. 87–143.

22 J. A. A. Stockwin, *Japan: Divided Politics in a Growth Economy*. London, Weidenfeld and Nicolson, 1982, p. 271.

Chapter 13

1   Peter Dale, *The Myth of Japanese Uniqueness*. London, Routledge, 1986 and later editions.

2   To take an obvious example, the US Congress and the British Parliament are both representative assemblies within democracies, but, because the two systems of government and politics are different, what they actually do is markedly discrepant.

3   This is not to say that there is no experience of such kinds of party and party organization in Western countries. But in recent times the centralized party has tended to predominate.

4   Ezra Vogel, *Japan as Number One; Lessons for America*. Cambridge, MA, Harvard University Press, 1979. Tokyo, Tuttle, 1980.

5   A variant of the revisionist paradigm was the view of van Wolferen, which may be caricatured as saying that the system had 'no pilot and no brakes', but that this rudderless ship was nevertheless a menace on the high seas. See Karel van Wolferen, *The Enigma of Japanese Power*. London, Macmillan, 1989.

6   J. Mark Ramseyer and Frances McCall Rosenbluth, *Japan's Political Marketplace*. Cambridge, MA, and London, Harvard University Press, 1993.

7   Chalmers Johnson and E. B. Keehn, 'A Disaster in the Making: Rational Choice and Asian Studies', *The National Interest*, summer 1994, pp. 14–22. Christopher Pokarier, 'Rational Actor Theory and the Interpretation of Japanese Politics', paper presented to the 10th Biennial Conference of the Japanese Studies Association of Australia, Melbourne, 9 July 1997. Stephen Johnson, 'Opposition Party Fragmentation under the 1955 System: an organizational Imperative or rational choice?', *Japan Forum*, vol. 9, no. 1 (1997), pp. 39–41.

8   Ramseyer and Rosenbluth, ibid., pp. 2–3.

9   For instance, 'rational choice' expectations about the October 1996 lower house elections did not fit well with the actual behaviour of politicians in those elections, nor with the results. See chapters 1 and 8.

10 Michio Muramatsu and Ellis S. Krauss, 'The Conservative Policy Line and the Development of Patterned Pluralism', in Kozo Yamamura and Ysukichi Yasuba (eds), *The Political Economy of Japan: Volume 1: The Domestic Transformation*. Stanford, CA, Stanford University Press, 1987, pp. 516–54, at p. 537.

11 Loc. cit.

12 The Pempel and Tsunekawa notion of 'corporatism without labour' implied that labour was excluded from an essentially 'corporatist' system. Whether or not the system was ever corporatist, it is no longer entirely 'without labour'. T. J. Pempel and Keiichi Tsunekawa, 'Corporatism without Labor: The Japanese Anomaly', in Philippe C. Schmitter and Gerhard Lehmbruch (eds), *Trends towards Corporatist Intermediation*. Beverly Hills, CA, Sage, 1979.

13 Inoguchi Takashi and Iwai Tomoaki, 'Zoku giin no kenkyū; jimintō seiken o gyūjiru shuyakutachi' (A Study of 'Tribal' Parliamentarians; the Leading Actors Driving the LDP Regime). Tokyo, Nihon Keizai Shinbunsha, 1987, pp. 5–7.

Further Reading

General Reading on Japan and Japanese Politics

For useful reference about various aspects of Japan, see Richard Bowring and Peter Kornicki (eds) *The Cambridge Encyclopedia of Japan* (Cambridge University Press, 1993); and *Japan: An Illustrated Encyclopedia* (2 vols, Kodansha, 1993). Worthwhile texts on politics include: Hitoshi Abe, Muneyuki Shindō and Sadafumi Kawato (translated and with an introduction by, James W. White) *The Government and Politics of Japan* (University of Tokyo Press, 1994); Bradley Richardson, *Japanese Democracy* (Yale University Press, 1997); Gary D. Allinson and Yasunori Sone (eds), *Political Dynamics in Contemporary Japan* (Cornell University Press, 1993); J. A. A. Stockwin, Alan Rix, Aurelia George, James Horne, Daiichi Itō and Martin Collick, *Dynamic and Immobilist Politics in Japan* (Macmillan, 1988); Jun-ichi Kyogoku (translated by Nobutaka Ike), *The Political Dynamics of Japan* (University of Tokyo Press, 1987); Kozo Yamamura and Yasukichi Yasuba (eds), *The Political Economy of Japan; Volume 1, The Domestic Transformation* (Stanford University Press, 1987); Purnendra Jain and Takashi Inoguchi, *Japanese Politics Today: Beyond Karaoke Democracy?* (Macmillan Education Australia, 1997).

Historical Background

The most comprehensive recent history of Japan in English is *The Cambridge History of Japan* (Cambridge University Press, various years), in six volumes. For modern history, see vol. 5 (The Nineteenth Century), edited by Marius Jansen, 1989; and vol. 6 (The Twentieth Century), edited by Peter Duus, 1988. One single-volume history that has stood the test of time is Richard Storry, *A History of Modern Japan* (Penguin, 1960 and later editions). Another is

W. G. Beasley, *The Modern History of Japan* (Weidenfeld and Nicolson, 1963 and later editions). An excellent recent history focusing on social aspects is Ann Waswo, *Japanese Society, 1868–1994* (Oxford University Press, 1996). On the *tennō* system, see David A. Titus, *Palace and Politics in Prewar Japan* (Columbia University Press, 1974); and Stephen S. Large, *Emperor Hirohito and Showa Japan* (Routledge, 1992). On the last of the *genrō*, who played a crucial advisory role in the 1920s and 1930s, see Lesley Connors, *The Emperor's Adviser: Saionji Kinmochi and Pre-war Japanese Politics* (Routledge, 1987). For detailed accounts of the formative period of the Meiji Constitution (broadly the 1890s), see Junji Banno, *The Establishment of the Japanese Constitutional System* (translated by J. A. A. Stockwin, Routledge, 1992); and Andrew Fraser, R. H. P. Mason and Philip Mitchell, *Japan's Early Parliaments, 1890–1905* (Routledge, 1995).

Japanese Society

A most useful introductory text on Japanese society is Joy Hendry, *Understanding Japanese Society* (Routledge, 2nd edn, 1995). Other useful books are: Tadashi Fukutake, *The Japanese Social Structure* (University of Tokyo Press, 1982); Robert Smith, *Japanese Society* (Cambridge University Press, 1983); Susan Pharr, *Losing Face: Status Politics in Japan* (University of California Press, 1990); Roger Goodman and Kirsten Refsing (eds), *Ideology and Practice in Modern Japan* (Routledge, 1992); Hiroshi Ishida, *Social Mobility in Contemporary Japan* (Macmillan, 1993); Yoshio Sugimoto, *An Introduction to Japanese Society* (Cambridge University Press, 1997); Sheldon Garon, *Molding Japanese Minds: The State in Everyday Life* (Princeton University Press, 1997); Carolyn Stevens, *On the Margins of Japanese Society* (Routledge, 1997).

The American Occupation and Political History since 1945

The best synoptic view of the Occupation is: Robert E. Ward and Yoshikazu Sakamoto, *Democratizing Japan: the Allied Occupation* (Hawaii University Press, 1987), while for a contemporary 'official' account, see Supreme Commander for the Allied Powers, *Political Reorientation of Japan* (2 vols, Greenwood Press reprint of original 1949 edition). Good political histories of Japan since the war are few and far between, but the following are recommended: Masumi Junnosuke (Lonny E. Carlile translator), *Postwar Politics in Japan, 1945–1955* (Institute of East Asian Studies, University of California, Berkeley: Japan Research Monograph No. 6, 1985); Masumi Junnosuke, *Contemporary Politics in Japan* (University of California Press, 1995); Ann Waswo, *Modern Japanese Society, 1868–1994* (Oxford University Press, 1996). Andrew Gordon (ed.), *Postwar Japan as History* (University of California Press, 1993).

The Government Bureaucracy

Contrasting views of the nature, role and effectiveness of the government bureaucracy are to be found in the following books: Chalmers Johnson, *MITI and the Japanese Miracle: The Growth of Industrial Policy, 1925–1975* (Stanford University Press, 1982); Daniel Okimoto, *Between MITI and the Market: Japanese Industrial Policy for High Technology* (Stanford University Press, 1989); Scott Callon, *Divided Sun: MITI and the Breakdown of Japanese High-Tech Industrial Policy* (Stanford University Press, 1995); Brian Woodall, *Japan Under Construction: Corruption, Politics and Public Works* (University of California Press, 1996); B. C. Koh, *Japan's Administrative Elite* (University of California Press, 1989); Paul S. Kim, *Japan's Civil Service System: Its Structure, Personnel and Politics* (Greenwood Press, 1988).

Decision Making, Public Policy and Interest Groups

There is now a fairly extensive literature on public policy and decision making in Japan. The following is a selection: Minoru Nakano, *The Policy Making Process in Contemporary Japan* (Macmillan, 1997); Kent E. Calder, *Crisis and Compensation: Public Policy and Political Stability in Japan, 1949–1986* (Princeton University Press, 1988). John C. Campbell, *How Policies Change: The Japanese Government and the Aging Society* (Princeton University Press, 1992); Kenji Hayao, *The Japanese Prime Minister and Public Policy* (University of Pittsburgh Press); Leon Hollerman, *Japan, Disincorporated* (Stanford University Press, 1988); Junko Katō, *The Problem of Bureaucratic Rationality: Tax Politics in Japan* (Princeton University Press, 1995); Frances M. Rosenbluth, *Financial Politics in Contemporary Japan* (Cornell University Press, 1989). On interest groups, see in particular: Aurelia George, 'Japanese Interest Group Behaviour: an Institutional Approach', in J. A. A. Stockwin et al., *Dynamic and Immobilist Politics in Japan* (Macmillan, 1988); Ulrike Schaede, 'The "Old Boy" Network and Government-Business Relationships in Japan', *Journal of Japanese Studies,* vol. 21, no. 2 (summer 1995); Malcolm V. Brock, *Biotechnology in Japan* (Routledge, 1990).

The Electoral System and Voting Behaviour

The workings of the House of Representatives electoral system which operated until 1994 are described in greater or lesser detail in most general books on Japanese politics. The post-1994 system is discussed in Purnendra Jain and Takashi Inoguchi, *Japanese Politics Today: Beyond Karaoke Democracy* (Macmillan Education Australia, 1997). On voting behaviour, the classic work is Scott C. Flanagan, Shinsaku Kohei, Ichiro Miyake, Bradley M. Richardson and Joji Watanuki, *The Japanese Voter* (Yale University Press, 1991).

Party Politics

There are a number of good books on party politics in Japan, though some writers have tended to extract the LDP from the arena of party politics and treat it virtually as part of the government. The following contain useful information and analysis: Ronald J. Hrebenar, *Japan's Postwar Party Politics* (Westview, 3rd edn, forthcoming, 1999); Gerald L. Curtis, *The Japanese Way of Politics* (Columbia University Press, 1988); Masaru Kohno, *Japan's Postwar Party Politics* (Princeton University Press), 1997. Haruhiro Fukui (ed.), *Political Parties of Asia and the Pacific* (Greenwood, 1985, vol. 1, section on Japan).

The Constitution

Accounts of the 1946 Constitution, the case law to which it has given rise and the controversies which surround it, are given in the following books: John M. Maki, *Court and Constitution in Japan: Selected Supreme Court Decisions, 1948–1960* (University of Washington Press, 1964); Hiroshi Itoh and Lawrence W. Beer, *The Constitutional Case Law of Japan: Selected Supreme Court Decisions, 1961–1970* (University of Washington Press, 1978); Lawrence W. Beer and Hiroshi Itoh, *The Constitutional Case Law of Japan, 1970 through 1990* (University of Washington Press, 1996). The huge volume of relevant information about constitutional issues unearthed by the *Kenpō Chōsakai* (Commission on the Constitution) in the late 1950s and early 1960s is introduced and analysed in John M. Maki (translator and editor), *Japan's Commission on the Constitution: The Final Report* (University of Washington Press, 1980) and in a seminal article by Robert E. Ward, 'The Commission on the Constitution and Prospects for Constitutional Change in Japan', *Journal of Asian Studies*, vol. XXIV, no. 3 (May 1965). For a recent analysis of the Constitution's origins, see Koseki Shūichi (edited and translated by Ray A. Moore), *The Birth of Japan's Postwar Constitution*. Boulder, Colorado, Westview, 1997.

Local Politics and Government

The classic text on local politics and government is Kurt Steiner, *Local Government in Japan* (Stanford University Press, 1965). Most general books have a relevant section, but the following are more specialist works: Richard J. Samuels, *The Politics of Regional Policy in Japan: Localities Incorporated?* (Princeton University Press, 1983); Purnendra Jain, *Local Politics and Policy-making in Japan* (New Delhi, Commonwealth Publishers, 1989); Michio Muramatsu, *Local Power in the Japanese State* (University of California Press, 1997).

The Politics of Labour

The politics of labour has been a somewhat neglected field in the 1980s and 1990s, which is surprising because extremely interesting developments have taken place, especially with the formation of the *Rengō* Federation. The following may be recommended: Hirosuke Kawanishi, *Enterprise Unionism in Japan* (Kegan Paul International, 1992): Gary D. Allinson and Yasunori Sone, *Political Dynamics in Contemporary Japan* (Cornell University Press, 1993), part 3: Purnendra Jain and Takashi Inoguchi, *Japanese Politics Today* (Macmillan Education Australia, 1997), chapter 10 (by Toru Shinoda). See especially Ikuo Kume, *Disparaged Success: Labor Problems in Postwar Japan.* Ithaca and London, Cornell University Press, 1998.

Women in Politics

The classic work on this topic, though now dated, is Susan Pharr, *Political Women in Japan* (University of California Press, 1981). For more recent works, see: Dorinne Kondo, *Crafting Selves: Power, Gender and Discourses of Identity in a Japanese Workplace* (Chicago University Press, 1990); and Tomoaki Iwai, 'The "Madonna Boom": Women in the Japanese Diet', *Journal of Japanese Studies,* vol. 19, no. 1 (winter 1993).

The Politics of Agriculture

With the opening of the rice market from 1994, change has been afoot in Japanese agricultural politics. This and many other issues are assessed in a major new work by Aurelia George Mulgan, forthcoming 1999.

The Politics of Education

Much good research has been done on the politics of education in Japan. See especially: William K. Cummings, *Education and Equality in Japan* (Princeton University Press, 1980); Leonard J. Schoppa, *Education Reform in Japan: A Case of Immobilist Politics* (Routledge, 1991); Mike Howarth, *Britain's Educational Reform: A Comparison with Japan* (Routledge, 1991); Roger Goodman, *Japan's 'International Youth': The Emergence of a New Class of Schoolchildren* (Clarendon Press, 1990).

Foreign and Defence Policy

There is a very extensive literature in this area. The following books cover various areas of the field: Reinhard Drifte, *Japan's Foreign Policy in the 1990s* (Macmillan, 1996); Leonard J. Schoppa, *Bargaining with Japan* (Columbia University Press, 1997); Takashi Inoguchi, *Japan's Foreign Policy in an Era of Global Change* (Pinter, 1993); Alan Rix, *Japan's Foreign Aid Challenge: Policy Reform and Aid Leadership* (Routledge, 1993); Caroline Rose, *Interpreting History in Sino–Japanese Relations: A Case Study in Political Decision-Making* (Routledge, 1998).

Democracy in Japan

This subject tends to excite radically different responses, as can be seen if one compares the following two books: Gavan McCormack and Yoshio Sugimoto (eds),

Democracy in Contemporary Japan (Hale and Iremonger, 1986); and Takeshi Ishida and Ellis S. Krauss (eds), *Democracy in Japan* (University of Pittsburgh Press, 1989).

Controversial Approaches

In a sense, all books worth their salt are likely to be controversial, but it seems worth while, finally, to pick out a small number of volumes which for a variety of reasons have excited particular controversy and debate. They will be listed without comment at this point, and in random order: Gavan McCormack, *The Emptiness of Japanese Affluence* (M. E. Sharpe, 1996); David Williams, *Beyond the End of History* (Routledge, 1994); Chalmers Johnson, *Japan: Who Governs? The Rise of the Developmental State* (W. W. Norton, 1995); J. Mark Ramseyer and Frances McCall Rosenbluth, *Japan's Political Marketplace* (Harvard University Press, 1993); Peter N. Dale, *The Myth of Japanese Uniqueness* (Routledge, 1986 and later editions); Karel van Wolferen, *The Enigma of Japanese Power: People and Politics in a Stateless Nation* (Macmillan, 1989); Jon Woronoff, *Politics The Japanese Way* (Lotus Press, 1986) – and several other books by the same author; W. Eugene Smith and Aileen M. Smith, *Minamata* (Chatto and Windus, 1975); Ezra Vogel, *Japan as Number One: Lessons for America* (Harvard University Press, 1979); Robert Wade, *Governing the Market: Economic Theory and the Role of Government in East Asian Industrialization* (Princeton University Press, 1990).

Index

Abegglen, James, 104
accountability, 42, 191–2, 201
Ad Hoc Council on Education, 65–6,
    194–5
Administrative Management Agency, 102
adoption, 185
Agricultural Co-operative Association,
    see Nōkyō
agriculture, 6, 67, 97, 181, 186, 190
    beef and citrus, 6, 67, 68, 71
    rice, 6, 84, 105
Allied Occupation of Japan, 37–48, 96,
    99, 133
    'reverse course', 44, 53
Anti-Monopoly Law, 57, 97, 189
armed forces, 20–2, 38–9, 96
Asahara Shōkō, 87
Ashida Hitoshi, 47, 115, 167–8
    Ashida Government, 47, 55
Asian economic crisis (1997–), 91–2
Aum Shinrikyō, 87–8
Automobile Industry Association, 110

bakufu, 12–13, 15
Bank of Japan, 100, 188
banking, 45
    banking debt crisis, 92, 215
Benedict, Ruth, 3, 27–8
'Big Bang', see deregulation
Brzezinski, Zbigniew, 5
Buddhism, 11, 193
budget, 18–19, 39, 91, 100, 115, 117,
    188–9
    FILP, 189

buraku, 190
bureaucracy, 8, 14, 20, 42–3, 90, 91,
    96–7, 99–100, 101–9, 112, 216, 220,
    222
    administrative guidance, 108, 110
    advisory committees, 110
    amakudari, 43, 45, 53, 96, 107–9, 110,
        112
    'bureaucracy-led, mass-inclusionary
        pluralism', 221
    entry of ex-bureaucrats into parties, 43,
        45, 46, 53, 96, 101, 109, 112, 120,
        178–9, 190
    and Hosokawa Government, 84
    interministerial rivalries, 25–6, 96
    officials speaking in Parliament, 120
Bush, George, 75

Cabinet, 19, 20, 44, 95, 101, 102–4, 149,
    176, 178–9
    'responsible', 18, 20, 39, 44
    'transcendental', 18, 20, 39, 44
Cabinet Legislative Bureau, 103
Cabinet Secretariat, 103
Callon, Scott, 188
Central Association of National
    Medium and Small Industry
    Groups, 110
Charter Oath, 42
Chief Cabinet Secretary, 103, 104
Christianity, 11–12, 38, 175, 219
citizens and residents movements, 111,
    141
Clinton, William, 202, 204–5, 210, 216

Cold War, 99, 202, 205, 207, 214, 215, 217
collectivism, *see* group orientation
'comfort women' issue, 89, 198
Conference of Parliamentary Vice-Ministers, 104
Conference of Permanent Vice-Ministers, 104
'conflict' model, 34
Confucianism, 11–12, 14, 32, 173
'consensus' model, 3–4, 28, 34, 117, 214
Constitution of 1889, 17–19, 38–9, 42, 102, 218
Constitution of 1946, 9, 49, 50–1, 99, 102, 114, 123, 152, 162–79, 198, 209, 214–15, 218
  article 9 (peace clause), 38–9, 46, 75, 152, 163, 166–72
  Ashida amendment, 167–8
  and bureaucracy, 178–9
  and central government structures, 175–7
  GHQ draft, 163–5, 167
  Kenpō Chōsakai, 51, 152, 162, 163, 177
  origins, 163–6
  and patricide cases, 173
  and public opinion, 168, 168n, 169, 169n
  revision clause, 166, 177
  revisionism, 166
  rights and freedoms, 172–5
  separation of state and religion, 175
  and Supreme Court, 170–2, 173–4
  Yomiuri revision draft, 162, 169–70, 175–9
construction industry, 92, 196
consumer groups, 111, 189–90
corruption, 31, 83, 98–9, 101, 110, 124, 126–7, 192, 221
Crick, Bernard, 4
crime, 192, 196–7
  capital punishment, 196
  gun control, 196
  prisons, 196
  terrorism, 197
crises of the polity, 8–9
'cultural downgrading' approaches, 33–4, 220

Dale, Peter, 34, 219
Daybreak Club, 157
decentralization, 41, 43–4, 56, 82

defence, 49, 50, 53, 62, 153, 216
  'interoperability', 64
  Nakasone reforms, 64, 205
  1 per cent of GNP budget limit, 64
  sea lane protection, 64
  see also Defence Agency; Self-Defence Forces
Defence Agency, 102, 103, 105
democracy, 38, 52, 219, 222
Democratic Liberal Party, 47
Democratic Party (1996–), 2, 90, 91, 92, 130, 138, 139, 141, 144, 151, 153, 154, 155, 156, 157, 185
Democratic Party (post-war), 47, 49
Democratic Socialist Party, 55, 73, 76, 77, 78, 82, 86, 151–3
Deng Xiaoping, 213
deregulation, 1, 7, 82, 84, 93, 107, 108, 189
  of financial markets, 91, 92, 109, 188
'designated cities', 190
'divided politics', 3–4, 221
Dodge Line, 48
Doi Takako, 68, 77, 82, 83, 90, 115, 125, 152, 185
Doi Takeo, 30–1
Doko Toshio, 61
Dōmei, 50, 152, 153
dominance and cohesion of governments and oppositions, 132–7
Dore, Ronald, 12, 177
doya-gai, 182, 182n
dual government, 22, 44
Dulles, John Foster, 48

economy, 92, 100, 215
  collapse of 'bubble', 80
  economic distribution, 185–7
  economic management, 187–9
  as principal policy focus, 53
Eda Saburo, 55, 58
Eda Satsuki, 154
education, 16, 41, 43–4, 49, 50, 62, 65, 112, 192, 193–5
  cram schools (*juku*), 194
  'ethics' courses, 50, 193
  teachers' efficiency rating system, 50
  textbook approval issue, 50, 105, 194, 198
  Universities Control Bill, 56
  see also Ad Hoc Council on Education
Eisenhower, Dwight, 52, 115

election campaigning, 126
elections for House of Councillors
1974, 57, 118
1980, 66, 118
1986, 66, 67, 68, 118
1989, 66, 69, 71, 72, 76, 115, 118–9, 135, 151, 152, 188
1992, 79
1995, 88
1998, 92, 157
elections for House of Representatives
1946, 47
1947, 47
1949, 49
1958, 151
1960, 55
1963, 55
1969, 60, 133
1976, 58, 118
1979, 59
1980, 4, 60, 61, 66, 118
1983, 66, 118
1986, 66, 67, 68, 118
1990, 71–2, 152
1993, 81
1996, 1–2, 129–31, 151, 152, 155
women candidates, 68, 185n
electoral system reform, 77–8, 80, 82–4, 123, 126–9
public funding of elections, 127
see also malapportionment
electoral systems in House of Representatives
single, non-transferable votes (SNTVs) in multi-member constituencies (MMCs), 98, 122, 123, 124–9, 147
1994 system, 122, 123
electoral systems in House of Councillors, 122–3, 129
Electrical Manufacturing Federation, 110
Emperor, *see tennō*
employment, 182–5
of women, 184–5
environment, 56, 59, 61, 106, 192, 195–6
'export of pollution', 195
'Minamata disease, 195
'visual pollution', 196, 196n

factions and factionalism, 33, 52, 97–8, 101, 110, 135–7, 147–50, 215
and electoral systems, 148
Fair Trade Commission, 57, 102, 189

Fallows, James, 34–5, 66
family registers (*koseki*), 185
Far Eastern Commission, 164, 166, 167, 168
February 1936 Incident, 20, 22
Federation of Economic Organizations, *see Keidanren*
foreign pressure, 5, 7, 56, 64–5, 66–7, 78
From Five, 157
fukoku kyōhei, 16, 19, 21
Fukuda Takeo, 4, 56, 58, 59–61, 137, 149
Fukuda Government, 58, 212
Fukuyama, Francis, 8, 94
fusion of powers, 44, 95

gaiatsu, see foreign pressure
gakubatsu, 33
genrō, 17, 20, 39
Gensuikyō, 50
globalization, 94, 186, 216, 217
Great Hanshin-Awaji earthquake, 87
group orientation, 27, 31–2
core and periphery, 30
'growth economy', 4–5
Gulf Crisis of 1990–1, 72–7, 115, 152, 168–9, 215
despatch of minesweepers, 75
financial contributions by Japan, 73, 74–5
hostages issue, 74
and Saddam Hussein, 74–5
transport of refugees, 75
see also Peace Keeping Operations (PKO) Bill; United Nations Peace Force Co-operation Bill
gunbatsu, 33

habatsu, see factions and factionalism
hakai kōdō bōshi hō, see Subversive Activities Prevention Law
hakuchū jidai, 58, 137
han, 13–14, 15, 16
hanbatsu, 33
Hashimoto Ryūtarō, 89–92, 135, 149, 150, 202, 210
Hashimoto Government, 89–92, 100, 101, 102, 117, 154, 156, 197, 204–5, 215
Hata Tsutomu, 79, 80, 81, 84–5, 89, 90, 155, 156
Hata Government, 84–5, 86, 117, 152

Hatoyama Ichiro, 47, 48, 49, 90, 123,
    135
  Hatoyama Government, 50, 162
Hatoyama Kunio, 90, 156
Hatoyama Yukio, 90, 156
Heiseikai, 120
hierarchy, 27
HIV-contaminated blood issue, 90, 107
Hokkaidō, 141, 146
Hokkaidō and Okinawa Development
    Agency, 102
homegoroshi, 79n
Hong Kong, 203, 204
Hosokawa Morihiro, 79, 81–4, 91, 126,
    155, 157, 188, 197
  Hosokawa Government, 82–4, 85, 115,
    117, 127, 145, 152, 153, 154, 155,
    215
  reform programme, 82, 91, 215

ianfu, see 'comfort women'
ie, 28–30, 32–3
Ikeda Daisaku, 88
Ikeda Hayato, 53, 54–5, 78, 135, 137
Imperial Household Agency, 102
Imperial Household Ministry, 20, 39
industrial policy, 187–8
industrial relations, 45
Inoguchi Takashi, 100
interest groups, 100, 109–12
Ishibashi Masashi, 68
Ishibashi Tanzan, 49
Itō Hirobumi, 18, 19, 47
Itō Masayoshi, 60, 60n

Japan as a model, 94
Japan–China (mainland) relations, 11–12,
    14, 56–7, 58, 135, 197, 198, 203,
    207, 211–13, 216, 217
  and Chinese economic development,
    204
  and Chou En-lai principles, 212
  and 'hegemony', 58, 212
  Japan–China trade agreement, 212
  Nagasaki flag incident, 211
  and *seikei bunri*, 212
  Senkaku (Tiaoyutai) issue, 203, 204,
    212
  Sino–Japanese Treaty of Peace and
    Friendship, 58, 211, 212
  Spratly islands issue, 204
  and Tiananmen massacre, 213

Japan–China (Taiwan) relations, 56–7,
    204, 209, 211, 216
  and airlines agreement, 212
  Japan–Republic of China Treaty, 212
Japan Communist Party, 25, 40, 49, 50,
    51, 55, 81, 90, 92, 124–5, 126, 130,
    139, 141, 145, 153–4, 157, 165
Japan–Iraqi relations, *see* Gulf Crisis
Japan–Korea (Pyongyang) relations, 204,
    206, 213–14, 216
  and food crisis, 213
  nuclear weapons, 204, 213
Japan–Korea (Seoul) relations, 56, 197,
    198, 203, 209, 213–14, 216
  1965 Treaty, 56, 206
  and Kim Dae-Jung kidnapping, 213
  and President Park Chung Hee, 213
  and President Rhee Syngman, 213
  Takeshima (Dokdo) issue, 203
Japan Medical Association, 111, 193
Japan National Railways, 63
Japan New Party, 79, 81, 83, 86, 126,
    154–5
Japan Renewal Party, 81, 82, 84, 86, 126,
    130, 155
Japan Socialist Party, 2, 24, 26, 40, 47,
    48–9, 51, 53, 55, 68, 69, 74, 80,
    81–3, 85–7, 90, 91, 119–20, 124–5,
    130, 141, 144, 150, 151–2, 156, 208,
    215
  and 1946 Constitution, 152
  and 1989 upper house elections, 69,
    71–2
  and Gulf Crisis, 76–7
  'structural reform', 55
  and Tokyo governorship elections, 77
  'unarmed neutralism', 50
Japan–Southeast Asian relations, 206
Japan Steel League, 110
Japan Teachers Union, 50, 105, 194
Japan–US Mutual Security Treaty, 6, 24,
    26, 46, 48, 49, 50, 64, 86, 203, 206,
    207–10, 216
  1960 Security Treaty crisis, 49, 51–3,
    115, 152, 206, 207, 215
  1970 extension, 56
  1997 'Guidelines', 204–5
  and the Far East, 209
  'prior consultation' clause, 208
Japan–US relations, 206–10
  economic issues, 58, 64–5, 66–7,
    109–10, 203, 207

Japan–USSR/Russia relations, 58, 64, 80, 203, 205, 206, 210–11, 217
and Gorbachev, 211
territorial issue, 204, 206, 210, 210n
and Yeltsin, 211
jiban, 145
jieitai, see Self-Defence Forces
Jiyū Kaikaku Rengō, 86
Jiyuminshutō, see Liberal Democratic Party
Jiyūtō, see Liberal Party
Johnson, Chalmers, 34, 66, 104, 187, 220
judiciary, 20, 41
and elections, 128
jūsen housing loan companies, 89–90, 107, 117, 155, 188
jūshin, 39

Kades, Charles, 163
Kahn, Herman, 3, 5
Kaifu Toshiki, 69, 71–8, 86, 115, 123, 156
Kaifu Government, 71–8, 115, 185
Kaikaku kurabu, see Reform Club
Kaishin, see Renovation
Kajiyama Seiroku, 92, 149
Kan Naoto, 90, 91, 92, 154, 156, 157
Kanemaru Shin, 79
Kano Michihiko, 157
karōshi, 192
kaso kamitsu, 186
Katayama Tetsu, 47, 85
Katayama Government, 47, 55
Kato, Koichi, 149
Keidanren, 61, 110, 111
keigo, see respect language
keiretsu, 33, 97, 100, 108
Keizai Dōyūkai, 111
Khrushchev, Nikita, 52
Kishi Nobusuke, 3, 49, 50, 52, 115, 135, 208
Kishi Government, 49–52, 162
Kobayashi, Takeji, 186
kōenkai, 98, 131, 138, 141, 145–8
inheritance of, 147
Koizumi Junichiro, 89, 92
Kokumin no koe, see Voice of the People
Kokurō, 63
Kōmeitō, 55, 73, 75, 76, 77, 78, 80, 86, 88, 124, 126, 153, 156, 157
Kōmoto Toshio, 71
Komoto faction, 71

Kōno Ichirō, 135
Kōno Yōhei, 58, 66, 83, 89, 150, 154, 216
Konoe Fumimaro, 22, 79, 163n
Korean war, 48, 206

labour unions, 6, 32, 39–40, 45, 48, 49–50, 80, 141, 151, 181–2, 221
banning of general strike, 48
spring struggle, 181–2
see also Kokurō; Rengō; Zendentsū
land price issue, 66, 68
land reform, 40–1, 43
Large Stores Law, 110–11
Liberal Democratic Party, 1, 3, 4, 7, 8, 45, 49, 52, 53, 71–2, 80–1, 83, 85, 90–2, 96–8, 99–100, 110, 118–20, 121, 125–6, 129–30, 132–51, 157, 185, 193, 198, 211
candidate endorsement, 147
'directorate', 149–50
factionalism in, 61–2, 147–50
primary elections for party presidency, 59, 149
promotion system in, 101, 149
Liberal Party (1997–), 91, 157
Liberal Party (post-war), 47, 49, 133
local government, 190–2
'agency delegation', 191
dango, 192
see also decentralization
Lockheed scandal, 57, 57n, 58, 61, 62, 66, 68

MacArthur, Douglas, 37, 46, 48, 163, 166–7
Maekawa Report, 65
malapportionment ('negative gerrymander'), 41, 105, 124, 127–9, 174, 186
Manchurian Incident, 20
marxism, 26, 50, 58, 151–2, 181n, 183, 221
Matsumoto Jōji, 163–5
Matsushita School of Politics and Economics, 154
Meiji Constitution, *see* Constitution of 1889
Meiji ishin, 14–15, 42
Miki Takeo, 57–8
Ministry of Agriculture, Forestry and Fisheries, 102, 105, 111

Ministry of Construction, 102, 105, 107
Ministry of Education, 50, 66, 102, 105, 107, 194, 195
Ministry of Finance, 84, 100, 102, 104, 107, 188, 193
Ministry of Foreign Affairs, 102, 105, 210
Ministry of Health and Welfare, 102, 105, 193
Ministry of Home Affairs, *see* Ministry of Local Autonomy
Ministry of International Trade and Industry, 102, 104–5, 107, 187
Ministry of Justice, 102, 105
Ministry of Labour, 102, 105
Ministry of Local Autonomy, 41, 102, 105
Ministry of Posts and Telecommunications, 102, 105
Ministry of Transport, 102, 105, 107
Minkairen, 157
Minobe Tatsukichi, 20, 21
minorities, 192, 199–200
  Ainu, 199
  Brazilian *nikkeijin*, 200
  hi-sabetsu *burakumin*, 199
  Koreans, 199
  Okinawans, 199
Minseitō (1998), 157
Minshatō, *see* Democratic Socialist Party
Minshujiyūtō, *see* Democratic Liberal Party
Minshutō, *see* Democratic Party
Minyūren, 157
Miyazawa Kiichi, 78–81, 92, 123
  Miyazawa Government, 78, 80–1
modernization, 219–20
Mori Yoshirō, 149
Mouer, Ross E., 34
multinational corporations, 94, 189
Murakami Yasusuke, 34
Murayama Tomiichi, 83, 85–9, 188, 197
  Murayama Government, 85–9, 152, 155
mutual obligation, 27–8
Mutual Security Assistance Agreement, 50, 207

Nagai Yōnosuke, 5
Naganuma and Hyakuri base cases, 172
Nakane Chie, 29–30, 34

Nakasone Yasuhiro, 6, 59, 60, 61, 62–7, 68, 71, 118, 133, 135, 213
  and presidential government, 62
  and Yasukuni Shrine, 64, 198
national anthem and flag issue, 86
National Defence Council, 103
National Land Agency, 102
National Personnel Authority, 103–4, 107
National Police Reserve, 48
National Public Safety Commission, 102
nationalism, 46, 211
nationality, 199–200
New Frontier Party, 1, 86–7, 88, 89–91, 100, 101, 117, 118–19, 129–30, 135, 138, 139, 141, 144, 145, 153, 155–6, 157, 185, 193
New Liberal Club, 58, 66, 118, 154
New Party Amity, 153, 157
New Party Harbinger, 80–1, 83–4, 85, 90, 91, 150, 155, 156
New Party Peace, 153, 157
New Wave Society, 77n
newspapers, 200–1
  and reporting on China, 200
Nihon Kyōsantō, *see* Japan Communist Party
Nihon Shakaitō, *see* Japan Socialist Party
Nihon Shintō, *see* Japan New Party
nihonjinron, 2, 7, 34, 219, 220
  21 seiki, *see* Twenty First Century
Nikkeiren, 111
Nikkyōso, *see* Japan Teachers Union
Nippon Telephone and Telegraph (NTT), 63
Nishio Suehiro, 55, 152
Nisshō, 111
Nixon, Richard, 56, 163
  'Nixon shocks', 56, 135, 206–7
Nōkyō, 71, 111
'normal state', 1, 7, 82, 205
nuclear issues, 192, 196
  Bikini atoll test, 50
  and Okinawa, 210
  three non-nuclear principles, 56, 208
  see also Nuclear Non-Proliferation Treaty
Nuclear Non-Proliferation Treaty, 57

Obuchi Keizō, 79, 92
Occupation, *see* Allied Occupation of Japan
OECD, Japan's entry into, 54–5

Ōhira Masayoshi, 4, 59–60, 67, 78, 149, 212
  death, 4, 60
  forty day crisis, 59–60
  no-confidence motion, 60
  Ōhira Government, 59–60
oil crisis of 1973–4, 4, 57, 61, 186, 207
oil crisis of 1979–80, 59
oil stockpiles, 72
Ōkinawa, 206, 209–10
  reversion to Japan, 56, 56n, 113, 122, 123, 207, 210, 212
Ōno Banboku, 135
opposition parties, role of, 99, 100
organ transplants, 193
overseas development aid, 205, 213, 216
oyabun-kobun, 32–3
Ozawa Ichirō, 73, 76, 78, 79, 80, 81, 82, 83–4, 85, 89, 90, 91, 155–6, 157
Ozawa Tatsuo, 157

Parliament under 1889 Constitution, 17
  House of Peers, 38, 113, 165
  House of Representatives, 165
Parliament under 1946 Constitution, 38, 39, 54, 60, 89, 113–21, 178
  committee system, 40, 114, 117–21
  contrast with US Congress, 120, 121
  dissolution power, 114
  filibustering, 79, 116–17
  House of Councillors, 52, 73, 75, 86, 91, 96, 113, 114, 115, 174, 175–6
  House of Representatives, 52, 80, 86, 91, 95, 96, 113, 114, 115, 128, 165, 174, 175–6
  Management Committee, 116, 117
  private members' bills, 117
  types of session, 116
  women members, 68, 71–2
Parliamentary Law, 118
participation in politics, 39–42
Passin, Herbert, 44
'patterned pluralism', 221
Peace Keeping Operations (PKO) Bill, 78–9, 117, 168, 204, 214–15
  mission to Cambodia, 78
peerage, 38
Plaza Accords, 65
police, 41, 42, 43–4, 49
Police Duties Amendment Bill, 49
Political Contributions Control Law, 79, 127

political innovation from 1952, 45–6
political parties, 19–20, 110, 132–61
  absence of two party system, 132–3
  absence of 'winner take all' principle, 133
  age profile of members, 136–8
  educational background of members, 139–40, 142–3
  local origin of members, 139
  professional background of members, 140–1, 144
  regional distribution of support, 141, 146
popular rights movement, 16–17
post office savings system, 189
Prestowitz, Clyde, 34–5, 66
prime minister, 44, 97, 98, 103, 176, 178–9
  designation by Parliament, 115
privatization, 62, 63
Privy Council, 18, 20, 39, 165
product liability, 192
Provisional Council on Administrative Reform, 60–1
Public Offices Election Law, 123, 127, 190
public opinion, 73–4, 76–7, 78, 82, 168–9, 214–15
'public servant', 106
purge, 40, 43, 47, 49

quality of life issues, 56, 59, 61, 106, 192

rational choice theory, 220
Reagan, Ronald, 64
recent history, influence of, 44–5
Recruit scandal, 68, 71, 101
Reform Club, 157
Reform Forum 21, 79
Reimei kurabu, see Daybreak Club
Religious Corporate Body Law, 88
Rengō, 69, 79, 82, 86, 153, 183–4
Renovation, 85
respect language, 27
'revisionism', 94, 207, 220
Rinchō, see Provisional Commission on Administrative Reform
Rinkyōshin, see Ad Hoc Council on Education

Sagawa Kyubin scandal, 79
Saigo Takamori, 16

Sakigake, see New Party Harbinger
samurai, 15, 16
San Francisco Peace Treaty, 47
Satō Eisaku, 3, 53, 55–6, 61, 133, 135,
    210, 211, 212
    awarded Nobel Peace Prize, 56
    Satō Government, 55–6, 186, 209–10
Science and Technology Agency, 102
Seiyūkai, 19, 47, 76n
Self-Defence Forces, 38–9, 48, 50, 72–3,
    86, 168, 178, 205, 209, 214–15
    Maritime Self-Defence Forces, 64, 75,
    168
    see also defence
separation of powers, 44, 95
Shakai minshutō, see Japan Socialist Party
Shakaiminshurengō, see Social Democratic
    League
Shaminren, see Social Democratic League
Shidehara Kijurō, 46, 167
    Shidehara Government, 46, 163
Shinjiyū kurabu, see New Liberal Club
Shinseitō, see Japan Renewal Party
Shinshintō, see New Frontier Party
Shintō heiwa, see New Party Peace
Shintō religion, 11, 175
Shintō Sakigake, see New Party Harbinger
Shintō yūai, see New Party Amity
Shōwa Denkō scandal, 47
shūshin koyōsei, 182–3
Sirius, 79
situational ethics, 30
small and medium-sized industry, 97, 108,
    110–11
'small state', 7, 189
social class, 181, 183
Social Democratic League, 58, 79, 152,
    154
Social Democratic Party, *see* Japan
    Socialist Party
social welfare, 56, 59, 61, 153, 186, 192–3
    ageing society, 192–3
    health care, 192–3
'soft power', 214, 215
Sōhyō, 50, 51, 55, 152
Sōka Gakkai, 55, 88, 90, 91, 124, 153,
    156, 157
sōkaiya, 192, 197
sovereignty, location of, 37–9, 42
standard of living, 9, 34
Subversive Activities Prevention Law, 49,
    88

suffrage, 42, 113
    female, 39
    male, 20
Sugimoto, Yoshio, 34
Suharto of Indonesia, 92
Sun Party, 90, 156, 157
Supreme Court, 41
    power of judicial review, 41
surnames and marriage, 185
Suzuki Shunichi, 76
Suzuki Zenkō, 60–2, 78, 133

Taisei yokusankai, 22
Taiyōtō, see Sun Party
Takayanagi Kenzō, 165
Takemura Masayoshi, 80–1, 83–4,
    85, 155
Takeshita Noboru, 65, 67–9, 71, 135
    Takeshita faction, 67, 77, 79, 92,
    133, 135, 155
Tanaka Kakuei, 3, 4, 56–8, 59, 61–2,
    66, 123, 135, 137, 145, 153, 186–7,
    212
    arrested, 57
    and bureaucrats, 62
    stroke, 67
    Tanaka faction, 61–2, 66, 133
taxation, 16, 59, 62, 65, 67, 75, 92, 100,
    188
    consumption tax, 67–8, 84, 188, 193
'techno-nationalism', 216
television, 201
tennō, 14, 17–18, 19–20, 21, 28, 32, 38,
    42, 70, 70n, 71, 79, 96, 105, 177,
    193, 198–9
    death of *Shōwa Tennō*, 70–1
    surrender broadcast, 46
    as 'symbol', 38
tobacco industry, 97, 150
Tokugawa Shogunate, 11, 12–14, 42
Tomobe Tatsuo, 156
trade unions, *see* labour unions
traditions, influence of, 42–4
treaties, 115
Tsurumi Kazuko, 31
Twenty First Century, 90, 157

U2 Incident, 52
ultra-rightist groups, 192
'uniqueness of Japan' argument, 2, 24, 219
United Nations Peace Force Co-operation
    Bill, 73

United Nations Security Council, 202–3
Uno Sōsuke, 69, 71
Uruguay Round of the GATT, 67, 84, 105, 216

van Wolferen, Karel, 34–5, 66, 191
Vietnam war, 56
Vogel, Ezra, 220
Voice of the People, 157
voting behaviour, 8–9, 78, 91, 92, 98, 100–1, 107, 157

Wade, Robert, 188
war apology issue, 89, 197–8
Watanabe Michio, 72
weekly magazines, 200
Whitney, Courtney, 163–5
Williams, David, 8, 34–5

yakuza, 192, 197
Yamagata Aritomo, 21
Yamagishi Akira, 63, 82
Yamahana Sadao, 82, 83, 87, 156
Yamasaki Taku, 149
yen currency value, 56, 65, 88, 92, 207
Yokomichi Takahiro, 156
Yoshida Shigeru, 40, 47, 48, 54, 55, 115, 135, 168, 207
  Yoshida doctrine, 53
  Yoshida Government, 47, 96, 133
yuchaku, 91

zaibatsu, 33, 40, 45, 110
Zendentsū, 63
Zengakuren, 51
Zenkyō, 194
zoku, 96–7, 99, 108, 121, 150